SCHOLASTIC

LITERACY PLACE

IT ...AND KIDS LIKE IT!

SCHOLASTIC LITERACY PLACE

IT... ...AND KIDS LIKE IT!

Manageable Instructional Plans

Literacy Place follows a clear, consistent pattern of

instruction and provides support for all learners. The

Teacher's Edition includes explicit skills instruction and

integrates the language arts.

The Strongest System for Beginning Readers

Literacy Place provides direct instruction in phonics and

phonological awareness and fully reflects current and

confirmed research.

Assessment Tools to Monitor and Modify Instruction

Literacy Place features focused assessment that informs

instruction and measures progress. The program offers

strategies targeting students who need skills intervention,

language-development support, and enrichment.

Power and Confidence for the Information Age

Literacy Place uses technology as an integral part

of learning while connecting the classroom to the

real world.

3

The Matrix

Look for the Unit-by-Unit Extensions in the Literacy Place area.

PERSONAL LITERACY

Creative Expression

People express themselves in many creative ways.

INTELLECTUAL LITERACY

Managing Information

Finding and using information helps us live in our world.

SOCIAL LITERACY

Community Involvement

Communities are built on the contributions of the people who live there.

Express Yourself

Big Idea We express ourselves through songs, sounds, stories, dance, and art.
Mentor Author: *Pat Mora*
Place Author's Studio
Project Storybook

I Spy!

Big Idea Information is all around us.
Mentor Farmer: *Steven Powell*
Place Gardening Center
Project Garden Journal

Join In!

Big Idea We help our community.
Mentor Singer/Songwriter: *Tom Chapin*
Place Performance Stage
Project Community Sing

Imagine That!

Big Idea Imagination lets us look at things in new ways.
Mentor Muralist: *William Walsh*
Place Artist's Studio
Project Story Mural

Information Finders

Big Idea Information comes from many sources.
Mentor Marine Biologist: *Laela Sayigh*
Place Aquarium
Project Big Book of Information

Home Towns

Big Idea We are all members of a community.
Mentor Mayor: *Steve Yamashiro*
Place Mayor's Office
Project Visitor's Map

Story Studio

Big Idea People express themselves through stories and pictures.
Mentor Author & Artist: *Tomie dePaola*
Place Author's Studio
Project Picture Book

Animal World

Big Idea We use information to understand the interdependence of people and animals.
Mentor Zoo Curator: *Lisa Stevens*
Place Zoo
Project Zoo Brochure

Lend a Hand

Big Idea People can make a difference in their communities.
Mentor Police Officer: *Nadine Jojola*
Place Police Station
Project Community Expo

Hit Series

Big Idea A creative idea can grow into a series.
Mentor Author & Illustrator: *Joanna Cole & Bruce Degen*
Place Publishing Company
Project New Episode

Time Detectives

Big Idea Finding information in stories and artifacts brings the past to life.
Mentor Archaeologist: *Dr. Ruben Mendoza*
Place Archaeological Site
Project Time Capsule

Community Quilt

Big Idea In a community, some things continue and some things change.
Mentor Community Garden Director: *Lorka Muñoz*
Place Community Garden
Project Community Quilt

The Funny Side

Big Idea Sometimes humor is the best way to communicate.
Mentor Cartoonist: *Robb Armstrong*
Place Cartoonist's Studio
Project Comic Strip

Nature Guides

Big Idea Gathering and using information help us understand and describe the natural world.
Mentor Park Ranger: *Veronica Gonzales-Vest*
Place National Park Headquarters
Project Field Guide

It Takes a Leader

Big Idea In every community there are people who inspire others to take action.
Mentor Editor: *Suki Cheong*
Place Newspaper Office
Project Op-Ed Page

In the Spotlight

Big Idea We use our creativity to reach an audience.
Mentor Drama Coach: *José García*
Place Actor's Workshop
Project Stage Presentation

America's Journal

Big Idea Considering different points of view gives us a fuller understanding of history.
Mentor Historian/Author: *Russell Freedman*
Place Historical Museum
Project Historical Account

Cityscapes

Big Idea Cities depend on the strengths and skills of the people who live and work there.
Mentor Urban Planner: *Karen Heit*
Place Urban Planner's Office
Project Action Plan

Components

Pupil's Editions & Teacher's Editions

Literacy Place Kindergarten

provides a rich learning environment including Big Books, Read Alouds, Sentence Strips, Audiocassettes, Phonics Manipulatives, Workbooks, Teacher Editions, and much more.

K

Grades 1-5

▶ Literacy Place brings you what you would expect from Scholastic—authentic, award-winning children's literature.

▶ Our Teacher's Editions are easy to use, and provide explicit skills instruction.

▶ You'll also find a management CD-ROM to help you customize instruction to state and district standards.

scholastic.com
Check it out! You'll find a wealth of professional support resources, plus a lot of great stuff for kids and parents.

1

2

3

4

5

Pupil's Editions   **Teacher's Editions**

Support Materials

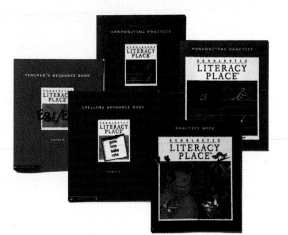

Practice
Literacy Place includes comprehensive practice resources.

- ✔ My Reading Workbook (1)
- ✔ Workshop and Project Cards (K-2)
- ✔ Practice Books (1-5)
- ✔ Spelling Resource Book (1-5)
- ✔ Grammar Resource Book (1-5)
- ✔ Handwriting Practice Book (K-3)
- ✔ ESL/ELD Resource Book (K-5)
- ✔ Skills Overhead Transparencies (2-5)
- ✔ Vocabulary Overhead Transparencies (2-5)
- ✔ Place Cards (3-5)

Assessment
Literacy Place provides a wide range of assessment and evaluation options. (K-5)

- ✔ Placement Tests
- ✔ Assessment Handbook
- ✔ Classroom Management Forms
- ✔ Selection Tests (for every story!)
- ✔ Unit Tests (Forms A and B)
- ✔ Oral Reading Assessment
- ✔ Scholastic Reading Inventory
- ✔ TAAS Preparation and Practice Book
- ✔ Assessment System CD-ROM

Technology
We set the industry standard.

- ✔ Phonics Practice CD-ROM (K-2)
- ✔ WiggleWorks Plus CD-ROM (K-2)
- ✔ Smart Place CD-ROM (3-5)
- ✔ Scholastic Management Suite (K-5)
- ✔ Staff Development Videos (K-5)
- ✔ Meet the Mentor Videos (K-5)
- ✔ Scholastic Network (K-5)
- ✔ Selection Audiocassettes (1-5)
- ✔ Classroom Resources CD-ROM (K-5)

Scholastic Solutions
Only Scholastic can offer you the diverse range of materials you need for your classroom. Please call 1-800-Scholastic for a catalog. Ask about these exciting products:

- ✔ High-Frequency Readers (K-1)
- ✔ Sound and Letter Books (K-1)
- ✔ Big Books/Little Books (K-2)
- ✔ Phonemic Awareness Kit (K-2)
- ✔ Phonics Readers (K-3)
- ✔ Phonics Chapter Books (1-3)
- ✔ Phonics Workbooks (K-2)

- ✔ Guided Reading Program (K-5)
- ✔ Bilingual Support (K-5)
- ✔ Solares (K-5)
- ✔ Transition Program (3-6)
- ✔ Sprint Plus Intervention (3-6)
- ✔ READ 180 (4-8)
- ✔ Reading Counts! (K-8)

Advisors

Program Consultants

SKILLS, STRATEGIES, INSTRUCTION
James Bauman
Professor, University of Georgia,
Athens, Georgia

PHONICS AND EARLY READING
Wiley Blevins
Consultant and Educational Writer
New York, New York

ESL/ELD
Jacqueline Kiraithe-Cordova
Professor, California State, California

STAFF DEVELOPMENT
Nancy Cummings
Western Director of Implementation
Success For All School Restructuring
Phoenix, Arizona

BILINGUAL EDUCATION
James Cummins
Professor, Ontario Institute for
Studies in Education
Ontario, Canada

EARLY LITERACY DEVELOPMENT
Nell K. Duke
Michigan State University

ASSESSMENT/WRITING
Adele Fiderer
Consultant and Educational Writer
Scarsdale, New York

HANDWRITING
Steve Graham
Professor, University of Maryland
College Park, Maryland

WRITING
Shelley Harwayne
Director of Manhattan New School
New York, New York

SPELLING
Richard E. Hodges
Professor, University of Puget Sound
Tacoma, Washington

SPELLING
Louisa Moats
County Office of Education
Sacramento, California

VOCABULARY
William E. Nagy
Assistant Professor, University of Illinois
Champaign-Urbana, Illinois

FLEXIBLE GROUPING
Michael Opitz
Professor, University of Colorado
Boulder, Colorado

ESL/ELD
Robert Parker
Consultant, Brown University
Providence, Rhode Island

ESL/ELD
Cao Anh Quan
ESOL Program Specialist
Tallahassee, Florida

ESL/ELD
Kim Quan Nguyen-Lam
California State University
Long Beach, California

WRITING
Michael Strickland
Author, Consultant
Orange, New Jersey

Teacher Reviewers

Kim Andrews
Fourth Grade Reviewer
Baltimore, Maryland

Shirley Beard
Fourth Grade Reviewer
El Paso, Texas

Barbara Bloom
Fifth Grade Reviewer
Wall Lake, Iowa

Sherry Brown
Third Grade Reviewer
Georgetown, Texas

Lisa Buchholz
First Grade Reviewer
Wheaton, Illinois

Kathy Burdick
Fifth Grade Reviewer
Austin, Texas

Marianne Chorba
Fourth Grade Reviewer
Baltimore, Maryland

Peggy Colley
Third Grade Reviewer
Rocky Face, Georgia

Carol Curry
Third Grade Reviewer
Tallahassee, Florida

Claire Dale
First Grade Reviewer
National City, California

Mildred DeStefano
First Grade Reviewer
Brooklyn, New York

Doris Dillan
Grade Two Reviewer
San Jose, California

Oneaster Drummer
First Grade Reviewer
Cincinnati, Ohio

Ethel Durham
Third Grade Reviewer
Grand Rapids, Michigan

Patty Ernst
Second Grade Reviewer
Naples, New York

Alzada Fowler
First Grade Reviewer
Lake Helen, Florida

Jane Ginn
First Grade Reviewer
Rohnert Park, California

Amy Gordon
Third Grade Reviewer
New City, New York

Janet Gray
Fourth Grade Reviewer
Lake Helen, Florida

Velma Gunn
Fourth Grade Reviewer
New Rochelle, New York

Annie Ruth Harris
Third Grade Reviewer
Decatur, Alabama

Barbara Ann Hawkins
Second Grade Reviewer
Hamer, South Carolina

Amy Hom
Second Grade Reviewer
New York, New York

Min Hong
First Grade Reviewer
Brooklyn, New York

Susan Howe
Third Grade Reviewer
Ellicott City, Maryland

Barbara Jansz
First Grade Reviewer
Naperville, Illinois

Michele Jessen
First Grade Reviewer
El Paso, Texas

Ellen W. Johnson
Second Grade Reviewer
Chalfont, Pennsylvania

Vera Johnson
First Grade Reviewer
Uniondale, New York

Carol Kaiser
Third Grade Reviewer
Los Angeles, California

Karen Kolsky
Third Grade Reviewer
Philadelphia, Pennsylvania

Judy Keyak
Second Grade Reviewer
St. Petersburg, Florida

Jacqueline Krass
Second Grade Reviewer
Gulfport, Mississippi

Warren Livesley
Fourth Grade Reviewer
New York, New York

Libby Lesley
First Grade Reviewer
San Angelo, Texas

Dora I. Magana
Fourth Grade Reviewer
El Paso, Texas

Tim Mason
Second Grade Reviewer
Willington Florida

Carol Mercer
Fourth Grade Reviewer
National City, California

Betty Milburn
Third Grade Reviewer
Grand Prairie, Texas

Jane Moore
Third Grade Reviewer
Dallas, Texas

Sandy Nolan
Third Grade Reviewer
Salem, Wisconsin

Carol Ochs
Fifth Grade Reviewer
Noble, Oklahoma

Lynn Olson
Fifth Grade Reviewer
Omaha, Nebraska

Cynthia Orange
Second Grade Reviewer
Bronx, New York

Sue Panek
Fourth Grade Reviewer
Hawthorne, New Jersey

Deborah Peale
Fourth Grade Reviewer
Miami, Florida

Arturo Perez
Second Grade Reviewer
Ventura, California

Jeanette Reber
First Grade Reviewer
Rock Hill, South Carolina

Charlene Richardson
Fourth Grade Reviewer
Everett, Washington

Daria Rigney
Fifth Grade Reviewer
Brooklyn, New York

Andrea Ruff
First Grade Reviewer
Brooklyn, New York

Carol Shirmang
First Grade Reviewer
Palatine, Illinois

Wendy Smiley
Fourth Grade Reviewer
Syracuse, New York

Barbara Solomon
Second Grade Reviewer
Hempstead, New York

Alicia Sparkman
First Grade Reviewer
Plant City, Florida

Elaine Steinberg
Third Grade Reviewer
Fresh Meadows, New York

Bobby Stern
Third Grade Reviewer
Winston-Salem, North Carolina

Laura Stewart
First Grade Reviewer

Kate Taylor
Fifth Grade Reviewer
Baltimore, Maryland

Vasilika Terss
Second Grade Reviewer
St. Louis, Missouri

Linda Thorn
Fifth Grade Reviewer
Cranford, New Jersey

Gayle Thurn
Second Grade Reviewer
Piedmont, South Carolina

Jerry Trotter
Fifth Grade Reviewer
Chicago, Illinois

Julia Tucker
First Grade Reviewer
Hampton, Virginia

Patricia Viales
First Grade Reviewer
Salinas, California

Janielle Wagstaff
Second Grade Reviewer
Salt Lake City, Utah

Gail Weber
Fourth Grade Reviewer
Sherman Oaks, California

Elizabeth White
First Grade Reviewer
Bronx, New York

Karla Hawkins-Windeline
Second Grade Reviewer
Hickman, Nebraska

National Advisory Council

Barbara R. Foorman, Ph. D.
Professor of Pediatrics
Director of the Center for
Academic and Reading Skills
Houston, TX

Dr. Wilmer Cody
Commissioner of Education
Kentucky State Department
of Education
Frankfort, KY

Ms. Judy Mountjoy
Vice President
The National PTA
Chicago, IL

Ms. Anne Bryant
Executive Director
National School Boards
Association
Alexandria, VA

Dr. Anthony Alvarado
Chancellor for Instruction
San Diego City Schools
San Diego, CA

TEACHER'S EDITION

SCHOLASTIC
LITERACY
PLACE®

UNIT 1

What's New?

LITERACY PLACE AUTHORS

CATHY COLLINS BLOCK
Professor, Curriculum and Instruction, Texas Christian University

LINDA B. GAMBRELL
Professor, Education, University of Maryland at College Park

VIRGINIA HAMILTON
Children's Author; Winner of the Newbery Medal, the Coretta Scott King Award and the Laura Ingalls Wilder Lifetime Achievement Award

DOUGLAS K. HARTMAN
Associate Professor of Language and Literacy, University of Pittsburgh

TED S. HASSELBRING
Co-Director of the Learning Technology Center and Professor in the Department of Special Education at Peabody College, Vanderbilt University

ADRIA KLEIN
Professor, Reading and Teacher Education, California State University at San Bernardino

HILDA MEDRANO
Dean, College of Education, University of Texas-Pan American

GAY SU PINNELL
Professor, School of Teaching and Learning, College of Education, Ohio State University

D. RAY REUTZEL
Provost/Academic Vice President, Southern Utah University

DAVID ROSE
Founder and Executive Director of the Center for Applied Special Technology (CAST); Lecturer, Harvard University Graduate School of Education

ALFREDO SCHIFINI
Professor, School of Education, Division of Curriculum Instruction, California State University, Los Angeles

DELORES STUBBLEFIELD SEAMSTER
Principal, N.W. Harllee Elementary, Dallas, Texas; Consultant on Effective Programs for Urban Inner City Schools

QUALITY QUINN SHARP
Author and Teacher-Educator, Austin, Texas

JOHN SHEFELBINE
Professor, Language and Literacy Education, California State University at Sacramento

GWENDOLYN Y. TURNER
Associate Professor of Literacy Education, University of Missouri at St. Louis

Acknowledgments and credits appear on pages R93-R94, which constitute an extension of this copyright page.

Copyright © 2000 by Scholastic Inc.   All rights reserved.   Published by Scholastic Inc.   Printed in the U.S.A.

ISBN 0-439-07895-4 (National)

SCHOLASTIC, SCHOLASTIC LITERACY PLACE, and associated logos and designs are trademarks and/or registered trademarks of Scholastic Inc.

3 4 5 6 7 8 9 10   14   07 06 05 04 03 02 01 00

TABLE OF CONTENTS

What's New?

THEME
We learn about our world through new experiences.

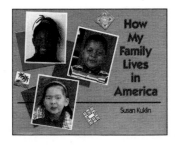

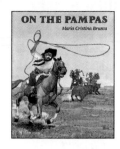

Trade Book Library

UNIT 1

UNIT AT A GLANCE

READ

LITERATURE	PHONICS	COMPREHENSION	VOCABULARY	LISTENING/ SPEAKING/ VIEWING
WEEK 1 *Gila Monsters Meet You at the Airport* pp. T17–T54	☑ HOMOPHONES, p. T20	☑ COMPARE/CONTRAST, p. T38 ☑ FACT/OPINION, p. T40	☑ SELECTION WORDS: ✔ *buffaloes, chaps, spurs,* Gila monsters, horned toads, ✔ *stampedes,* p. T18	• MAKE A POETRY BOOK, p. T53 • NONFICTION ARTICLE, p. T53 • CREATE A RADIO SHOW, p. T54 • TELL ABOUT A TRIP, p. T54
WEEK 2 *Ramona Forever* pp. T55–T98	☑ VOWEL /i/i, igh, y, i-e, ie, p. T64	☑ LITERARY ELEMENT: Character, p. T84	☑ SELECTION WORDS: ✔ *contagious, chickenpox,* ✔ *stethoscope,* ✔ *inflammation, wheelchair, prescription,* p. T62	• WRITE A PERSUASIVE SPEECH, p. T97 • DESCRIBED MIXED EMOTIONS, p. T97 • DIAGRAM THE STORY SETTINGS, p. T98 • REENACT STORY SCENES, p. T98
WEEK 3 *How My Family Lives in America* pp. T105–T144	☑ WORDS WITH /ə/, p. T114	☑ EVALUATE AUTHOR'S PURPOSE, p. T130	☑ SELECTION WORDS: ✔ *orchid,* ✔ *calligraphy, sesame noodles, chopsticks, soy sauce,* ✔ *scallion,* p. T112	• INTERVIEW A CHARACTER, p. T143 • MAKE A BOOK OF TRADITIONS, p. T143 • BOOK REVIEW, p. T144 • MAKE A PICTURE COOKBOOK, p. T144
WEEK 4 *On the Pampas* pp. T145–T149	☑ ONE-, TWO-, THREE-SYLLABLE WORDS, p. T154	☑ LITERARY ELEMENT: Setting, p. T180	☑ SELECTION WORDS: *pampas,* ✔ *grazing, gauchos, manes, lasso,* ✔ *corral,* ✔ *bridles,* p. T152	• PERSONAL NARRATIVE, p. T193 • CREATE AN ADVENTURE STORY, p. T193 • MAP STORY LOCALES, p. T194 • GIVE A PERSUASIVE TALK, p. T194
WEEK 5 *How the World Got Wisdom* pp. T201–T240	☑ VOWEL /ô/a, au, aw, p. T210	☑ CAUSE/EFFECT, p. T226	☑ SELECTION WORDS: *wisdom, sense, thought,* ✔ *idea,* ✔ *wise,* ✔ *knowledge, skills,* p. T208	• INTERVIEW SPIDER AND KUMA, p. T239 • PERSUASIVE LETTER, p. T239 • WRITING SLOGANS, p. T240 • COMPARE FOLK TALES, p. T240
WEEK 6 *Unit Wrap-Up* pp. T241–T263	**TRADE BOOK LIBRARY** • *Uncle Jed's Barbershop* by Margaree King Mitchell • *Muggie Maggie* by Beverly Cleary • *Hannah* by Gloria Whelan • *The Chalk Box Kid* by Clyde Robert Bulla			

WRITE

EXTEND SKILLS

SPELLING/ GRAMMAR, USAGE, MECHANICS	WRITING	INTEGRATED CURRICULUM	REAL WORLD SKILLS/ STUDY SKILLS	LEVELED RESOURCES
Ⓢ **SPELLING:** Homophones, ✔ pp. R4–R5 Ⓢ **GRAMMAR, USAGE, MECHANICS:** Statements and Questions, pp. R6–R7	Ⓢ **WRITING WORKSHOP:** Humorous Story, p. T44 • **WRITER'S CRAFT:** Descriptive Details, p. T45 • **JOURNAL,** p. T22	• **MATH:** How Far West?, p. R8 • **SCIENCE:** Make a Western Desert, p. R8 • **SOCIAL STUDIES:** The Old West, p. R9 • **THE ARTS:** Make a Gila Monster Mask, p. R9	• **MEET THE MENTOR VIDEO,** p. T9 • **STUDY SKILLS:** Parts of a Book, p. T48 • **TECHNOLOGY:** pp. T27, T31, T37, T45, T49, T54	• **UNIT TRADE BOOKS** • **GUIDED READING PROGRAM**
Ⓢ **SPELLING:** Words With Long *i*, ✔ pp. R12–R13 Ⓢ **GRAMMAR, USAGE, MECHANICS:** Exclamations and Commands, pp. R14–R15	Ⓢ **WRITING WORKSHOP:** Realistic Description, p. T88 • **WRITER'S CRAFT:** Vivid Verbs, p. T89 • **JOURNAL,** p. T66	• **MATH:** Graph Growth, p. R16 • **SCIENCE:** A Growing List of Skills, p. R16 • **SOCIAL STUDIES:** Old Enough, p. R17 • **THE ARTS:** Life Collage, p. R17	• **WORKSHOP 1:** How to Make a Milestone Chart, p. T99 • **STUDY SKILLS:** Getting Ready to Take a Test, p. T92 • **TECHNOLOGY:** pp. T71, T77, T83, T89, T93, T97	• **PHONICS CHAPTER BOOK:** *Kids Care* • **UNIT TRADE BOOKS** • **GUIDED READING PROGRAM**
Ⓢ **SPELLING:** Words With *a-* and *be-*, ✔ pp. R20–R21 Ⓢ **GRAMMAR, USAGE, MECHANICS:** Common and Proper Nouns, pp. R22–R23	Ⓢ **WRITING WORKSHOP:** Nonfiction Description, p. T134 • **WRITER'S CRAFT:** Logical Order, p. T135 • **JOURNAL,** p. T116	• **MATH:** A Chinese Puzzle, p. R24 • **SCIENCE:** Classify a Chinese Recipe, p. R24 • **SOCIAL STUDIES:** Find a Route to China, p. R25 • **THE ARTS:** Chinese Writing, p. R25	Ⓢ **STUDY SKILLS:** Alphabetical Order, p. T138 • **TECHNOLOGY:** pp. T121, T125, T129, T135, T139, T143	• **PHONICS CHAPTER BOOK:** *The Internet* • **UNIT TRADE BOOKS** • **GUIDED READING PROGRAM**
Ⓢ **SPELLING:** Words With *ng* and *nk*, pp. R28–R29 ✔ Ⓢ **GRAMMAR, USAGE, MECHANICS:** Singular and Plural Nouns, pp. R30–R31	Ⓢ **WRITING WORKSHOP:** Brochure, p. T184 • **WRITER'S CRAFT:** Opinion and Supporting Facts, p. T185 • **JOURNAL,** p. T156	• **MATH:** How Big Is Argentina?, p. R32 • **SCIENCE:** Stars in Argentina, p. R32 • **SOCIAL STUDIES:** Find Other Pampas, p. R33 • **THE ARTS:** Dance the Zamba, p. R33	• **WORKSHOP 2:** How to Write a Friendly Letter, p. T195 Ⓢ **STUDY SKILLS:** Using a Dictionary, p. T188 • **TECHNOLOGY:** pp. T161, T167, T179, T185, T189, T193	• **PHONICS CHAPTER BOOK:** *History Mystery* • **UNIT TRADE BOOKS** • **GUIDED READING PROGRAM**
Ⓢ **SPELLING:** Words With the Vowel Sound in *saw*, ✔ pp. R36–R37 Ⓢ **GRAMMAR, USAGE, MECHANICS:** Singular and Plural Pronouns, pp. R38–R39	Ⓢ **WRITING WORKSHOP:** Character Sketch for a Folk Tale, p. T230 • **WRITER'S CRAFT:** Precise Adjectives, p. T231 • **JOURNAL,** p. T212	• **MATH:** Graph Folk Tales, p. R40 • **SCIENCE:** Compare Characters, p. R40 • **SOCIAL STUDIES:** Jobs That Spread Wisdom, p. R41 • **THE ARTS:** Spider Design, p. R41	• **ORAL LANGUAGE:** Tell a Story to Entertain, p. T234 • **TECHNOLOGY:** pp. T215, T219, T225, T235, T239	• **PHONICS CHAPTER BOOK:** *The Great Time Travel Ride* • **UNIT TRADE BOOKS** • **GUIDED READING PROGRAM**

WRITING PROCESS: Write a Folk Tale

WRITER'S CRAFT: Natural Dialogue

PROJECT: Write an Anecdote

PRESENTATION SKILL: Speak to Entertain

TECHNOLOGY: Smart Place

UNIT 1

LAUNCH THE UNIT

UNIT TRADE BOOK LIBRARY

Uncle Jed's Barbershop by Margaree King Mitchell

Lexile Level: 680

Hannah by Gloria Whelan

Lexile Level: 740

Muggie Maggie by Beverly Cleary

Lexile Level: 730

The Chalk Box Kid by Clyde Robert Bulla

Lexile Level: 270

KEY

- ■ Cultural Connections
- ★ Social Studies
- ▲ Kid Picks
- ◆ Math
- ☀ Science
- ✚ The Arts

BOOKS FOR INDEPENDENT READING

EASY/AVERAGE

The Best Bug to Be
by Delores Johnson
Scholastic, 1992 ✚ ★
Kelly can't wait to be in the class play—until she finds out that she's the bumblebee.

Daniel's Duck
by Clyde Robert Bulla
Illustrated by Joan Sandin
HarperCollins, 1979 ✚ ▲
Daniel learns about giving to others when he makes a wood carving.

My Buddy
by Audrey Osofsky
Illustrated by Ted Rand
Holt, 1993 ★ ☀ ■
A dog named Buddy helps a boy who cannot walk.

Nate the Great and the Missing Key
by Marjorie Weinman Sharmat
Putnam, 1987 ▲ ◆
Once again Nate can't resist a mystery—and soon Nate and Sludge are hot on the trail of a missing key.

What Kind of Baby-sitter Is This?
by Delores Johnson
Macmillan, 1991 ▲
Much to Kevin's surprise, his new baby-sitter shares his love of baseball.

Willie's Not the Hugging Kind
by Joyce Durham Barrett
Illustrated by Pat Cummings
HarperCollins, 1989 ★ ■
In this story, an African-American boy stops hugging his family because his friend thinks it's silly.

Charlie's House
by Clyde Robert Bulla
Illustrated by Arthur Dorros
HarperCollins, 1983 ★ ■
A poor English boy comes to America as an indentured servant in the early 1700s and is befriended by a slave.

Class Clown
by Johanna Hurwitz
Scholastic, 1992 ★ ▲
Lucas tries to be the perfect student in third grade.

The Courage of Sarah Noble
by Alice Dalgliesh
Scholastic, 1986 ★ ■
Sarah and her father go West and form a lifelong friendship with the neighboring Native Americans.

Dumpling Soup
by Jama Kim Rattigan
Illustrated by Lillian Hsu-Flanders
Little Brown, 1993 ★ ■
For the first time, Marisa makes the dumplings for her family's celebration of the Chinese New Year.

I'm New Here!
by Bud Howlett
Houghton Mifflin, 1993 ★ ■
In this photo essay, Jazmin describes her move from El Salvador to the US.

AVERAGE/CHALLENGE

Konnichiwa! I Am a Japanese-American Girl
by Tricia Brown
Photos by Kazuyoshi Arai
Holt, 1995 ★ ■
A girl and her family celebrate San Francisco's Cherry Blossom Festival.

My Mama's Little Ranch on the Pampas
by María Cristina Brusca
Holt, 1994 ☀ ■
In this prequel to *On the Pampas*, Cristina and her brother live on their mother's ranch in Argentina.

Thinking Big
by Susan Kuklin
Lothrop, 1986 ★ ☀ ■
This appealing photo essay about a girl who is a dwarf won an IRA Children's Choice Award.

Eskimo Boy
by Russell Kendall
Scholastic, 1992 ★ ■
With beautiful photos and a simple text, Russell Kendall explores the life of a Native-American boy living in Alaska.

Maggie Marmelstein for President
by Marjorie Weinman Sharmat
HarperCollins, 1975 ★ ▲
In this funny novel, Maggie faces stiff competition when she runs for class president.

Seminole Diary: Remembrances of a Slave
by Delores Johnson
Macmillan, 1994 ★ ■
This book is based on the actual experiences of African Americans who joined the Seminoles and became members of their communities.

The Shoeshine Girl
by Clyde Robert Bulla
Illustrated by Leigh Grant
Crowell, 1975 ★ ▲ ◆
Ten-year-old Sarah Ida becomes less self-centered and more self-reliant after a summer job at her aunt's.

Wind in the Long Grass: A Collection of Haiku
edited by William Higginson
Simon & Schuster, 1992 ✚ ■
This IRA Children's Choice Book encourages children to write their own poems.

Books in Other Languages

SPANISH

La calle es libre
by Curusa
Ekaré, 1995 ★ ■
In a barrio in Caracas, Venezuela, a group of children find a way to build a playground.

Canciones y poemas para niños
by Federico Garcia Lorca
Lectorum, 1995 ✚ ■
The poems in this book express Lorca's curiosity about the world and his love of surprises.

El coraje de Sarah Noble
by Alice Dalgliesh
Lectorum, 1991 ★ ■
Sarah and her father go West and form a lifelong friendship with the neighboring Native Americans.

Mis primeras lecturas poéticas
selected by Angelina Gatell
Lectorum, 1983 ✚ ■
This anthology introduces readers to the finest poets from the Spanish-speaking world.

Ramona y su padre
by Beverly Cleary
Lectorum, 1987 ★ ▲
In this book, Ramona helps her father cope with losing his job.

¡Viva Ramona!
by Beverly Cleary
Lectorum, 1990 ▲
Ramona's world is turned upside down by her aunt's wedding, her father's new job, and the arrival of her new baby sister.

La Peineta colorada
by Fernando Picó
Lectorum, 1995 ★ ■
In Puerto Rico during the mid-1800s, Vitita and her grandmother help a runaway slave.

CHINESE

Blooming Waterlilies
edited by Chao Kuo-chong
Shen's Books and Supplies, 1994 ✚ ■
Traditional Chinese rhymes are presented in two colorful volumes and audiocassettes.

Children's Songs
by Zhao Lin
Shen's Books and Supplies, 1994 ✚ ■
This five-volume collection of children's songs and verses in Chinese spans the history of China.

Ramona Quimby, Age 8
by Beverly Cleary
Shen's Books and Supplies, 1994 ★ ▲
This is a lively Chinese translation of the popular book.

Technology

You'll find this Scholastic technology referenced in the Literacy Place Teacher's Editions.

AUDIO

Literacy Place Listening Library
Selections from the student anthology as well as every Big Book in grades K–2 are available on audiocassette.

VIDEO

Literacy Place Meet the Mentor
One Meet-the-Mentor video per unit gives children an opportunity to meet a real-life professional who models ways in which literacy is used in his or her career.

SOFTWARE

Smart Place
Scholastic (Win/Mac)
This CD-ROM component for Grades 3–6 of Literacy Place is designed to support students' reading, writing, and problem-solving development.

Scholastic Reading Counts!
Formerly known as The Electronic Bookshelf, this interactive reading motivation and management program is for students at all reading levels.

Spelling Studio
Scholastic (Win/Mac)
An innovative CD-ROM program for Grades 3–6 that engages students in spelling and proofreading activities.

I Spy
Scholastic (Win/Mac)
These scavenger-hunt games build reading, math, problem-solving, and logic skills.

Usborne's Animated First Thousand Words
Usborne/Scholastic (Win/Mac)
This fun-to-use vocabulary tool introduces pre- and beginning readers to 1,000 common English and Spanish words.

INTERNET

www.scholasticnetwork.com
This comprehensive online curriculum service for grades K–8 features unit-by-unit extensions for Literacy Place.

www.scholastic.com
Scholastic's corporate web site includes Literacy Place resources and unit-related Internet links.

Other Sites
The Internet is growing and changing every day, so be sure to preview all sites before your students visit them.

For more information about Scholastic's technology, please call 1-800-SCHOLASTIC.

The Baseline Assessment activity helps you determine the conceptual level at which each student starts the unit. Repeat the task at the end of the unit.

Have students write a paragraph of three sentences describing a recent new experience they've had, such as learning or doing something new. They should tell if and how the experience changed their thinking, or how they now feel about the experience or things related to it. Save these paragraphs to use for comparison at the end of the unit.

K-W-H-L

Start a K-W-H-L chart for *What's New* that you will return to at the end of the unit. Ask students the following questions:

- How do you feel about having new experiences or experiences that you didn't expect? Are they fun or scary, or both?

- What do all new experiences have in common?

What do we know?	What do we want to know?	How do we find out?	What did we learn?

Use Practice Book 1, pages 7–8.

SET UP THE PLACE: WILDERNESS SCHOOL

The idea of surviving in the wilderness can ignite a young person's imagination. A wilderness school provides a context in which your students can explore their personal responses to meeting challenges and identify ways they grow through experience. Transform a corner of your classroom into a workplace model of a wilderness school. The learning center also provides a focus for self-directed and cooperative activities.

Idea File: Wilderness School

- Invite students to write an interesting fact about nature or wilderness activities, such as hiking or camping, on an index card and add it to a file. As the collection of cards grows, encourage students to categorize the facts for easier reference.

- Include firsthand narratives of wilderness adventures along with novels and field guides in the Wilderness School library. Have students add their own stories and reports to the collection.

- Write to the National Park Service for pamphlets about wilderness areas, and combine them with maps and articles to create an archive.

- Invent a name for your Wilderness School and use **Smart Place** PlaceMaker to make banners, calendars, and posters.

- Post the Literacy Place Cards, and encourage students to develop their communication skills by following step-by-step directions for independent activities.

- Prompt independent activities with challenging suggestions, such as "If you were hiking and met a bear, what would you do? Read about bears in the library, and then write a list of tips for hikers."

"Learn everything you can about what you're going to do. Ask questions."

—KEITH JARDINE

MEET THE MENTOR: KEITH JARDINE

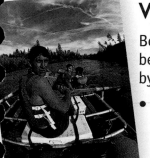

View the Video

Before viewing the mentor video, tell students that they'll be watching a video about a challenging experience shared by a group of people—white water river rafting.

- Ask students to look for ways that Wilderness Guide Keith Jardine and other rafters deal with new experiences.

Think About the Video

After viewing, give students time to discuss their thoughts and opinions about the video. Use questions such as:

> **How did these young people feel as they were getting ready to go rafting? What kinds of things did they say?**

> **What kinds of things did they say after the trip?**

> **How do you think this experience changed them?**

Ask students to imagine rafting down the river with Keith Jardine. Discuss how going through an experience like this might help them in another situation.

Encourage students to create an "Adventure Chart," and to write their initials next to the adventures they would like to experience.

VIEWING AS A LEARNING TOOL

TEACH/MODEL Explain that setting a purpose for viewing means having a clear idea of what you want to learn from the video you are about to watch. This purpose helps you focus your attention and remember more.

THINK ALOUD *I know this video is about a group of young people who go white water rafting with Keith Jardine. I will watch to find out how they deal with the experience and what they learn about themselves.*

PRACTICE/APPLY Invite students to set their own purposes for viewing. After viewing, discuss whether the video provided the information they wanted to learn and what else they discovered about the river rafters' experiences.

REAL-WORLD SKILLS

- Reflect on the past to note progress and make predictions.
- Understand the value of new experiences and learning new things.
- Develop a positive approach to meeting new challenges.
- Express oneself in a written anecdote.

PREVIEW OF WORKSHOPS AND PROJECT

The Workshops and Project will give students an opportunity to apply to hands-on activities what they have learned about the mentor and place.

WORKSHOP 1
How to Make a Milestone Chart
(T99–T104)
Students will recall important events in their lives and create a milestone chart.

WORKSHOP 2
How to Write a Friendly Letter
(T195–T200)
Students will write a friendly letter in which they tell about a recent achievement.

PROJECT
How to Write an Anecdote
(T248–T253)
Students will write personal anecdotes about an interesting or funny event that happened to them, and then tell the anecdote to the class.

FAMILY LITERACY NIGHT

Involve families every step of the way and close the unit with a Family Literacy Night. See page T256 for details.

HOME INVOLVEMENT

TAKE HOME

Families who are informed are more likely to become involved. Distribute the following items for students to take home and read with their families:

- *Family Letter* in the **Literacy-at-Home Kit**
- *Family Literacy Newsletter* on pages T5–T6 of the Practice Book
- *Family Newsletter* on page T206 of the **Literacy Place Spelling Teacher's Resource Book**
- **Take-Home Practice Readers**

Family Literacy Tips

TEACHER'S EDITION

In the Teacher's Edition you'll find these valuable tips at point of use.

- **FAMILY LITERACY RESOURCES** Family members want to help their children learn to read. See the tip on page T75.
- **TEACHER/FAMILY COMMUNICATION** The technology tip on page T93 involves parents and students in preparing for upcoming tests.
- **TIME MANAGEMENT** Setting up routines and schedules at home can help students achieve success at school. See the 1-minute tip on page T119.
- **HELP WITH HOMEWORK** The 1-minute activity on page T177 can help families play a direct role in improving their children's homework performance.
- **FAMILY LITERACY** Family members can enrich the literacy experiences of all students. See the literacy tip on page 223.

Internet

Suggest that parents visit the Scholastic web site at **www.scholastic.com** for links to valuable resources. Parents can learn all about their children's favorite books, authors, and characters.

Gila Monsters
Meet You at the Airport

Main Selection
Genre: Humorous Fiction
Award: Irma Simonton Black Honor Book

Paired Selection
Genre: Humorous Poetry
Award: ALA Notable
Children's Book

Selection Summary

A young boy doesn't want to move "out West" along with his family. He believes that everyone there wears cowboy hats, that nobody plays baseball, and that Gila monsters are everywhere—they even meet you at the airport! When he finally arrives "out West," the boy discovers that he was wrong about western life.

CONNECTING TO POETRY These fanciful poems focus on two kinds of animals that appear in the story: alligators and Gila monsters.

Author

MARJORIE WEINMAN SHARMAT prepared to write *Gila Monsters Meet You at the Airport* by getting input from her children and from personal experience. She incorporated comments by children about how they pictured the "other side" of the country.

Weekly Organizer

Visit Our WebSite
www.scholastic.com

Gila Monsters Meet You at the Airport

	DAY 1	DAY 2
READ and Introduce Skills • VOCABULARY • PHONICS • COMPREHENSION • LITERARY ELEMENT	**BUILD BACKGROUND, ▲,** p. T17 ☑ **VOCABULARY, ▲ ■,** p. T18 Transparency 1 Practice Book 1, p. 9 ☑ **DAILY PHONICS: ▲ ■** Homophones, p. T20 Practice Book 1, p. 10 **PREVIEW AND PREDICT,** p. T22 **READ: ▲ ✳ ■ ●** *Gila Monsters Meet You at the Airport,* pp. T22–T27 Genre: Humorous Fiction, p. T23 ☑ **COMPREHENSION SKILL:** Compare/Contrast, p. T25	**READ: ▲ ✳ ■** *Gila Monsters Meet You at the Airport,* pp. T28–T31 "Gila Monster March," pp. T32–T33 "Alligator Stomp," pp. T34–T35 **COMPREHENSION:** Fact/Opinion, p. T29 ☑ **DAILY PHONICS:** Homophones, p. T31 **GENRE:** Humorous Poetry, p. T33
WRITE and Respond • GRAMMAR • USAGE • MECHANICS • SPELLING • WRITING	**WRITING WORKSHOP:** Introduce, p. T17 **JOURNAL:** Make Predictions, p. T22 ☑ **SPELLING:** Pretest: Homophones, p. R4 Spelling Resource Book, p. 9 ☑ **GRAMMAR, USAGE, MECHANICS:** Teach/Model: Statements and Questions, p. R6 **ORAL LANGUAGE,** p. T27	**WRITING WORKSHOP:** Prewrite, T35 Practice Book 1, p. 11 ☑ **SPELLING:** Practice Vocabulary, p. R4 Spelling Resource Book, pp. 10–12 ☑ **GRAMMAR, USAGE, MECHANICS:** Practice, p. R6 **ORAL LANGUAGE,** p. T35
EXTEND SKILLS and Apply to Literature • INTEGRATED LANGUAGE ARTS • LISTENING/SPEAKING/VIEWING • INTEGRATED CURRICULUM • GUIDED READING • INDEPENDENT READING	**READ ALOUD,** p. T27 **GUIDED READING,** pp. R2–R3 **INTEGRATED CURRICULUM:** Social Studies, p. R9 Science, p. R8 **TRADE BOOKS** • *Hannah* • *The Chalk Box Kid*	**READ ALOUD,** p. T35 **GUIDED READING,** pp. R2–R3 **INTEGRATED CURRICULUM:** The Arts, p. R9 Math, p. R8 **TRADE BOOKS** • *Uncle Jed's Barbershop* • *Muggie Maggie*
TECHNOLOGY and **REAL-WORLD SKILLS**	**CD-ROM ENCYCLOPEDIA** Matching Technology to Task, T27	**SMART PLACE CD-ROM** Find the Facts, T31 **WORKSHOP 1,** pp. T99–T104

Support for flexible groups

MODIFY INSTRUCTION	
● INTERVENTION ▲ ESL/ELD ■ EXTRA HELP	
✹ GIFTED AND TALENTED ☑ = TESTED SKILL	

DAY 3

REREAD:
Gila Monsters Meet You at the Airport

COMPREHENSION: ▲ ■
Compare/Contrast pp. T38–T39
Transparency 2
Practice Book 1, pp. 14–16
Fact/Opinion, pp. T40–T41
Transparency 3
Practice Book 1, pp. 15, 17–18

INTERVENTION: ● p. T42
Daily Phonics: Homophones
Conprehension: Compare/Contrast
Fluency: Reading Aloud

RESPOND: ▲
Think About Reading, p. T36
Write a Postcard, p. 37
Practice Book 1, p. 12

SPELLING:
Write/Proofread, p. R5
Spelling Resource Book, p. 13

GRAMMAR, USAGE, MECHANICS:
Practice, p. R7

ORAL LANGUAGE, p. T37

RESPOND: Literature Circle, p. T37

READ ALOUD, p. T43

GUIDED READING, pp. R2–R3

OPTIONAL MATERIALS, ● p. T43
Wiggleworks Stage C:
Look-Alike Animals
Gila Monsters Meet You at the Airport
audiocassette

DAY 4

LITERATURE CONNECTION:
Gila Monsters Meet You at the Airport,
p. T44

☑ **REVIEW VOCABULARY,** p. T46

☑ **DAILY PHONICS: ▲ ✹**
Homophones, p. T47

Skills practice every day

WRITING WORKSHOP:
Humorous Story, p. T44
Writer's Craft: Descriptive Details, p. T45
Transparency 4
Practice Book 1, p. 11

SPELLING:
Study/Review, p. R5
Spelling Resource Book, p. 200

GRAMMAR, USAGE, MECHANICS:
Apply, p. R7

ORAL LANGUAGE, p. T45

READ ALOUD, p. T49

GUIDED READING, pp. R2–R3

EXPAND VOCABULARY:
Synonyms, p. T46

☑ **STUDY SKILLS:**
Parts of a Book, pp. T48–T49
Practice Book 1, p. 20

DAY 5

READING ASSESSMENT: Selection
Test, p. T50

MODIFYING ASSESSMENT, p. T50
ESL/ELD: Vocabulary
Extra Help: Comprehension

PERFORMANCE-BASED ASSESSMENT:
1-Minute Fluency, p. T51
Conference, p. T51

☑ **DAILY PHONICS:** Dictation, P. T51

WRITING ASSESSMENT, p. T52
Student Model
Students' Writing Rubric

☑ **SPELLING:**
Posttest, p. R5
Spelling Resource Book, p. 202

☑ **GRAMMAR, USAGE, MECHANICS:**
Assess, p. R7

ORAL LANGUAGE, p. T52

READ ALOUD, p. T54

GUIDED READING, pp. R2–R3

INTEGRATED LANGUAGE ARTS:
Make a Poetry Book, p. T53
Nonfiction Article, p. T53
Create a Radio Show, p. T54
Tell About A Trip, p. T54

SMART PLACE CD-ROM
Language Development, T37

WORKSHOP 1, pp. T99–T104

SMART PLACE CD-ROM
Study Skills, T49

WORKSHOP 1, pp. T99–T104

AUDIOCASSETTE
Speaking Skills, T54

WORKSHOP 1, pp. T99–T104

ASSESSMENT PLANNING

USE THIS CHART TO PLAN YOUR ASSESSMENT OF THE WEEKLY READING OBJECTIVES.

- Informal Assessment is ongoing and should be used before, during and after reading.
- Formal assessment occurs at the end of the week on the selection test.
- Note that intervention activities occur throughout the lesson to support students who need extra help with skills.

ASSESSMENT HANDBOOK

YOU MAY CHOOSE AMONG THE FOLLOWING PAGES IN THE ASSESSMENT HANDBOOK.

- Informal Assessment
- Anecdotal Record
- Portfolio Checklist and Evaluation Forms
- Self-Assessment
- Second-Language Learners
- Using Technology to Assess
- Test Preparation

SKILLS AND STRATEGIES

> Every story focuses on a key comprehension strategy

	Informal Assessment
COMPREHENSION Compare/Contrast 🔑	**OBSERVATION p. T25** • Did students identify comparisons and contrasts that the author directly states in the text? **QUICKCHECK p. T38** • Can students identify comparisons and contrasts that are implied or directly stated in the text? **CHECK PRACTICE BOOK 1, p. 14** **CONFERENCE p. T51**
COMPREHENSION Fact/Opinion	**OBSERVATION p. T29** • Did students distinguish between a fact and an opinion? **QUICKCHECK p. T40** • Can students distinguish between facts and opinions? **CHECK PRACTICE BOOK 1, p. 17** **CONFERENCE p. T51**
PHONICS/DAILY Homophones	**OBSERVATION p. T31** • Did students recognize homophones? **CHECK PRACTICE BOOK 1, p. 10** **DICTATION p. T51**
VOCABULARY Selection Words ✔buffaloes ✔spurs horned toads chaps Gila monsters ✔stampedes	**OBSERVATION p. T24** • Did students use picture clues to figure out the words? **CHECK PRACTICE BOOK 1, p. 9**

Formal Assessment	INTERVENTION and Instructional Alternatives	Planning Notes
SELECTION TEST • Questions 1–3 check students' mastery of the key strategy, compare/contrast. **UNIT TEST**	If students need help with compare/contrast, then go to: • **Instructional Alternatives, p. T39** • **Intervention, p. T42**	
SELECTION TEST • Questions 4-6 check students' mastery of the comprehension skill fact/opinion. **UNIT TEST**	If students need help with fact/opinion, then go to: • **Instructional Alternatives, p. T41**	
SELECTION TEST • Questions 7–9 check students' ability to identify homophones. **UNIT TEST**	If students need help identifying homophones, then go to: • **Intervention, p. T42** • **Review, p. R43** • **Reteach, R52**	
SELECTION TEST • Questions 10–12 check students' understanding of the selection vocabulary.	If students need additional practice with the vocabulary words, then go to: • **Vocabulary Review, p. T46**	

A test for every story including phonics and vocabulary

Technology

Use CD-ROM for more activities that support the story

SMART PLACE

EXPLORING THE SMART PLACE SELECTION

Your students can interact with an electronic version of the literature selection in this lesson. Use this activity to direct your students as they explore the Smart Place CD-ROM.

STEP 1 Explore a Smart Spot	Invite students to read *Gila Monsters Meet You at the Airport* on the **Smart Place** CD-ROM. Have students click the Smart Spot on screen 11 to hear what summer, spring, winter, and fall are like in the eastern United States. Encourage students to talk about what the seasons are like where they live.
STEP 2 Plan a Warm Welcome	Imagine that a new student has just moved to your town after growing up in a part of the country where the climate is the opposite of yours. Perhaps this person has never seen snow before or has never walked in sand. What will your students do to help this newcomer adjust to life in your part of the country? Work together to brainstorm some ideas.
STEP 3 Share Seasonal Activities	Have students use PlaceMaker to create a card showing how kids in your town have fun throughout the year. Students can show one season on each of the four sides of the card. Have them describe their favorite thing to do during each season and then illustrate their work.
STEP 4 Publish a Guidebook	Use a hole-punch and yarn to bind the cards together into an activity guidebook for students. Create a cover for the book and encourage all the authors to sign their names. Then, add the book to your classroom library to be borrowed by anyone who needs an idea for a fun activity throughout the year.

Gila monsters meet you at the airport

by Marjorie Weinman Sherman   pictures by Byron Barton

Smart Place CD-ROM

Sure, the weather Back East snows and blows in the winter. But it also blooms in the spring, shimmers in the summer, and explodes in crackling colors in the fall.

Click the pictures to find out what kids like about the eastern seasons.

Eastern Seasons

Smart Place CD-ROM

SUMMER

I love to go fishing in July and August. There are a lot of trout in this area. I usually let them go after I catch them. That way I can catch them again next summer.

WINTER

While people in some parts of the country are building sand castles, I am building snow castles. I use shoe boxes to make blocks of snow. Then I pile the blocks to make a castle wall.

Smart Place CD-ROM

Build Background

Facing a challenge can change the way you think about yourself. What happens when you're moving across the country and everything in your life is about to change?

Activate Prior Knowledge

SHARE INFORMATION

Explain to students that this selection is about a boy who is moving to the Southwest. Help students locate this region on a map or a globe. If possible, display pictures of the Southwest and discuss them. Have volunteers tell what they know about this region.

DISCUSS MOVING

If any students have moved encourage them to share their experiences.

> **How did you feel about moving?**

> **What was the hardest thing to get used to about your new home?**

> **Did anything funny happen? What was it?**

WRITING WORKSHOP *Humorous Writing*

INTRODUCE Build background for humorous writing. Have students write two or three sentences describing a funny thing that has happened to them.

DAY 1 OBJECTIVES

Daily pacing suggestions

STUDENTS WILL:

READ 45 MINUTES

- **Build Background**
- **Vocabulary**
- **Daily Phonics: Homophones**
- *Gila Monsters Meet You at the Airport*, pp. 12–17
- **Key Comprehension Skill: Compare/Contrast**
- **Comprehension Skill: Fact/Opinion**

WRITE 25 MINUTES

- **Writing Workshop: Introduce Humorous Writing**
- **Quickwrite: Predict**
- **Spelling: Homophones**
- **Grammar, Usage, Mechanics: Statements and Questions**
- **Oral Language**

EXTEND SKILLS 20 MINUTES

- **Integrated Curriculum**
- **Read Aloud**
- **Guided Reading**

RESOURCES

- **Vocabulary Transparency 1**
- **Transparency 1**
- **Practice Book 1, pp. 9, 10**
- **Spelling Resource Book, p. 9**

MODIFY Instruction

ESL/ELD

▲ Have students tell what countries they come from. Label their home countries on a world map. Ask volunteers to talk about how they felt before, during, and after the move. Be sensitive to the fact that not only English language learners may want to share their experiences. **(MAKE CONNECTIONS)**

Continuous practice and review

VOCABULARY TRACE

Build Background for
Vocabulary Words . . . . . p. T18
Categorize Words . . . . . . p. T18
ESL/ELD . . . . p. T18
Predict-o-Gram . . . . p. T19
Bonanza Word . . . . p. T25
Decoding . . . . p. T24
Context Clues . . . . p. T34
Extend Vocabulary . . . . . p. T46

PHONICS AND SPELLING LINKS

Phonics See selection words that are homophones on page T20.

Spelling See selection words that are homophones on page R4.

Vocabulary

Ⓐ TEACH WORD MEANINGS

INTRODUCE CONCEPT

Explain that *Gila Monsters Meet You at the Airport* has many words about the Southwest, including names of animals, plants, clothing, and events that take place there.

PRESENT VOCABULARY

List the words and their definitions on the chalkboard. Encourage students to discuss what each word means.

✔ = Tested	VOCABULARY WORDS
✔ buffaloes	wild oxen of North America that have large, shaggy heads (p. 13)
chaps	leather coverings worn over pants to protect legs (p. 14)
✔ spurs	pointed metal pieces worn on the heels of boots and used to drive horses onward (p. 14)
Gila monsters	large, poisonous lizards that live in the southwestern part of the United States and in Mexico (p. 17)
horned toads	small reptiles with short tails and spines on the head (p. 17)
✔ stampedes	sudden wild movement of herds of animals (p. 20)

Ⓑ BUILD ON PRIOR KNOWLEDGE

CATEGORIZE WORDS

Draw the chart below. Have students use their prior knowledge about the Arctic and the Southwest and the vocabulary words to complete it.

	Arctic		Southwest	
Animals	polar bears	seals	Gila monsters	stampedes
Clothing	parkas	snow boots	horned toads	buffaloes
Events	ice fishing	Iditarod	chaps	spurs

MODIFY Instruction

ESL/ELD

▲ Reinforce key vocabulary words by creating a Reptile Web on the chalkboard. Show students the display materials and have them page through the story looking for pictures of reptiles to place on the web. Help them discover and name one common feature of all the reptiles (*no hair or fur*). **(GRAPHIC DEVICE)**

EXTRA HELP

■ Using books and pictures of the Southwest that you may have on display, have volunteers point to images that correspond to the vocabulary words as you name them. The visual display will reinforce the meaning of the concept words and provide background for the setting. **(USE VISUALS)**

Name _____

VOCABULARY

OUT WEST!
Read the words and their definitions. Use the words to label the drawing.

buffaloes: wild oxen of North America that have large, shaggy heads
Gila monsters: large, poisonous lizards that live in the southwestern part of the United States and Mexico
chaps: leather leg coverings worn over pants to protect a cowhand's legs
spurs: pointed metal pieces worn on boot heels and used to drive horses onward
horned toads: small reptiles with short tails and spines that look like horns
stampedes: sudden rushes of herds of animals

stampedes
chaps
spurs
buffaloes
horned toads
Gila monsters

You are a cowhand. Write about yourself. Use at least three words from the box.

Unit 1 • What's New? • *Gila Monsters Meet You at the Airport* **9**

PRACTICE BOOK 1, p. 9

C APPLY THROUGH MEANINGFUL SENTENCES

MODEL MEANINGFUL SENTENCES

Write or say the following sentences. Ask volunteers to underline or name the context clues that help define the vocabulary word.

1. Stay away from <u>poisonous lizards</u> like **Gila monsters**.
2. Those <u>large, shaggy animals</u> are **buffaloes**.
3. Cowhands <u>wear</u> **chaps** to <u>protect their legs</u>.
4. The cowgirl used her **spurs** to make her <u>horse run faster</u>.
5. **Horned toads** have <u>hornlike spines</u> on their heads.
6. <u>Herds of cattle run wild</u> during **stampedes**.

Sentences on Vocabulary Transparency 1

WRITE MEANINGFUL SENTENCES

Suggest that students ask themselves questions about each word to help them write meaningful sentences, such as: *What is it? What does it look like?*

USE TRANS-PARENCY 1

Have students complete the Predict-o-Gram. Discuss how words under the same heading are related.

SUPPORT WORDS

> **howdy** hello or hi (p. 14)*
>
> **sandwiches** food that has a filling between two slices of bread (p. 15)
>
> **chili** a spicy dish of beans, peppers, and usually meat (p. 15)*
>
> **kin** family or relatives (p. 25)*
>
> * Vocabulary instruction is presented where words appear in the selection.

Strategy: Overview

Get Word Wise*

▶Tell students that there are several steps they can take to figure out a word they don't know. Copy the steps on the How-To chart. Then use the Think Aloud to demonstrate each step. Write:

• *My best friend is Seymour, and we like to eat salami <u>sandwiches</u> together.*

THINK ALOUD *When I see a word I don't know, I try to sound it out. If the word I pronounce isn't a word I recognize, I look for familiar word parts. I see* **sand***, so I say* **sand-wiches.** *Since the sentence is about eating, the word* **sandwiches** *makes sense. If none of these steps helps me figure out the word, I look it up in a dictionary.*

* The goal of Get Word Wise is to help students become flexible in their use of word identification strategies listed in "How to Figure Out a New Word." Therefore, subsequent lessons will focus on only one or two strategies at a time.

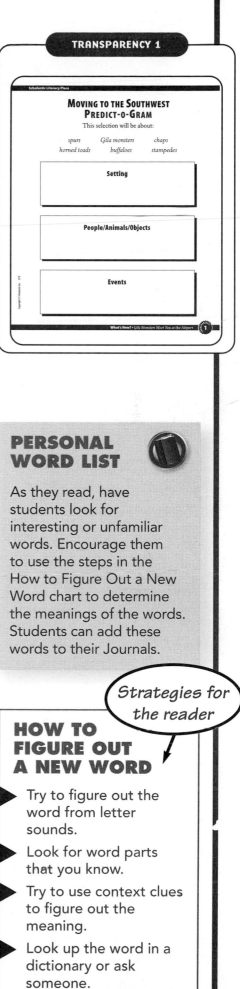

TRANSPARENCY 1

Scholastic Literacy Place

MOVING TO THE SOUTHWEST PREDICT-O-GRAM
This selection will be about:

spurs   Gila monsters   chaps
horned toads   buffaloes   stampedes

Setting

People/Animals/Objects

Events

What's New? • Gila Monsters Meet You at the Airport ①

PERSONAL WORD LIST

As they read, have students look for interesting or unfamiliar words. Encourage them to use the steps in the How to Figure Out a New Word chart to determine the meanings of the words. Students can add these words to their Journals.

Strategies for the reader

HOW TO FIGURE OUT A NEW WORD

▶ Try to figure out the word from letter sounds.

▶ Look for word parts that you know.

▶ Try to use context clues to figure out the meaning.

▶ Look up the word in a dictionary or ask someone.

SELECTION WORDS
That Are Homophones

to	too
know	no
right	write
new	knew
see	sea
they're	their
	there

Continuous practice and review

SKILLS TRACE

HOMOPHONES [TESTED]

Introduce . . . . . pp. T20–T21
Practice .pp. T31, T42, T47, T51
Review . . . . .p. R43
Reteach . . . . .p. R52

Preteach the phonics skills

DAILY PHONICS

Homophones

Ⓐ TEACH/MODEL

INTRODUCE HOMOPHONES Write the words **here** and **hear** on the chalkboard and read them aloud. Then ask students to use each word in a sentence.

> I hear that there are Gila monsters here.

- Help students recognize that **here** and **hear** are homophones, words that sound alike but have different meanings and spellings.

- Tell students that when they see homophones in their reading, they should first look carefully at how the word is spelled. Then they can use other words in the sentence to help them figure out what the word means.

THINK ALOUD *When I see a homophone in a sentence, I can look at the words around it to check its meaning. For example, when I read the words "I can hear the radio in my room," I can tell that* hear *means "to sense sound through your ears." The other homophone,* here, *doesn't make sense in this sentence.*

- On the chalkboard, begin a chart of homophones and their meanings. Use the Selection Words that are homophones.

Homophone	What It Means
there	in that place
their	belonging to them
they're	they are

Ask students to use each word in a sentence and then spell the homophone.

MODIFY
Instruction

too busy

time to go

you know

no problem

ESL/ELD

▲ Create "phrase cards" that use common homophones in context. Include the phrases too *busy*, *time* to *go*, no *problem*, you *know*, *out* there, *and out of* their *way.* Hold up a card. Ask students to say the phrase aloud and spell the homophone. **(USE WORD CARDS)**

EXTRA HELP

■ Write homophones on index cards and their meanings on the back. Shuffle them and give one to each student. Have students find partners with matching homophones. Have them read aloud the homophones and definitions. **(WORK IN PAIRS)**

B PRACTICE/APPLY

MAKE A HOMOPHONE LIST Write the following list of words on the chalkboard:

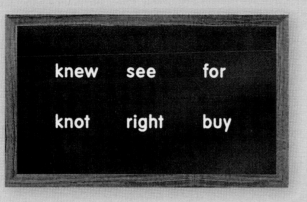

knew	see	for
knot	right	buy

- Ask pairs of students to write a homophone for each word in the list and then use each new homophone in a sentence. Have volunteers add the new words to the Homophone list.

- Encourage partners to add other examples of homophone pairs to the chart.

CREATE HOMOPHONE SENTENCES Challenge pairs of students to write sentences that include two or more homophones. Offer this example: *I can't believe I ate eight apples!*

Have students exchange sentences with other partners and underline the homophones in each other's sentences.

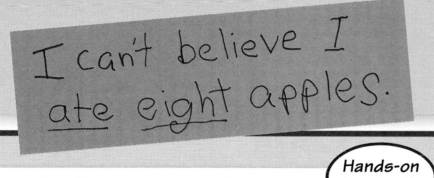

I can't believe I ate eight apples.

Hands-on practice

WORKING WITH WORD PARTS

Write the following sets of syllables on the chalkboard. Have students read each aloud. Point out the following:

- If a syllable ends in a vowel, the vowel usually has a long sound. (open syllable)
- If a syllable ends with a consonant, the vowel usually has a short sound. (closed syllable)

em	nap	de	ba	ab	rab
re	ref	ef	jo	bit	on
li	lim	im	fi	kin	im
bit	ta	af	ug	sug	su

PRACTICE BOOK 1, p.10

PROFESSIONAL DEVELOPMENT

JOHN SHEFELBINE

How Can "Working With Word Parts" Help?

Recognizing common syllables is important to fluent reading. The Working With Word Parts activities help students read, recognize, and use common syllables. The syllables shown are open and closed syllables. A closed syllable ends in a consonant. The vowel sound is generally short. Examples of words with two closed syllables include rab bit *and* nap kin. *Open syllables end in a vowel. The vowel sound is generally long. Examples of open syllables include the first syllable in the words* table *and* lion.

COMPREHENSION

▶ Preview and Predict

Read the title to students. Point out that they are about to read a funny story that could happen to them. Encourage students to preview the first few pages of the selection.

> **From what you have seen, who is the main character in this story?**

> **Where do you think the story might take place?**

Help students make predictions before they read by asking a question. Then have them read silently page 13.

> **What do you think will happen at the airport?**

JOURNAL

Make Predictions

Ask students to write their ideas and predictions about the story in their Journals. Suggest that they record what they want to find out when they read *Gila Monsters Meet You at the Airport.*

▶ Set a Purpose

Guide students to set a purpose for reading. They may want to compare the main character's ideas about life in the West with what he actually finds when he arrives there.

HUMOROUS FICTION

Gila monsters meet you at the airport

AWARD WINNER

165

by Marjorie Weinman Sharmat
illustrated by Byron Barton

12

CLASSROOM Management

WHOLE CLASS

On-Level Use the questions, Think Alouds, and Skills and Strategies to guide students through the story. Point out changes of setting signaled by chapter numbers.

Below-Level Have students listen to the story on audiocassette to familiarize themselves with the story sequence and vocabulary.

INDEPENDENT

Above-Level Students can read independently or with a partner while you do a guided reading with the rest of the class. Have these students join the group for the story discussion.

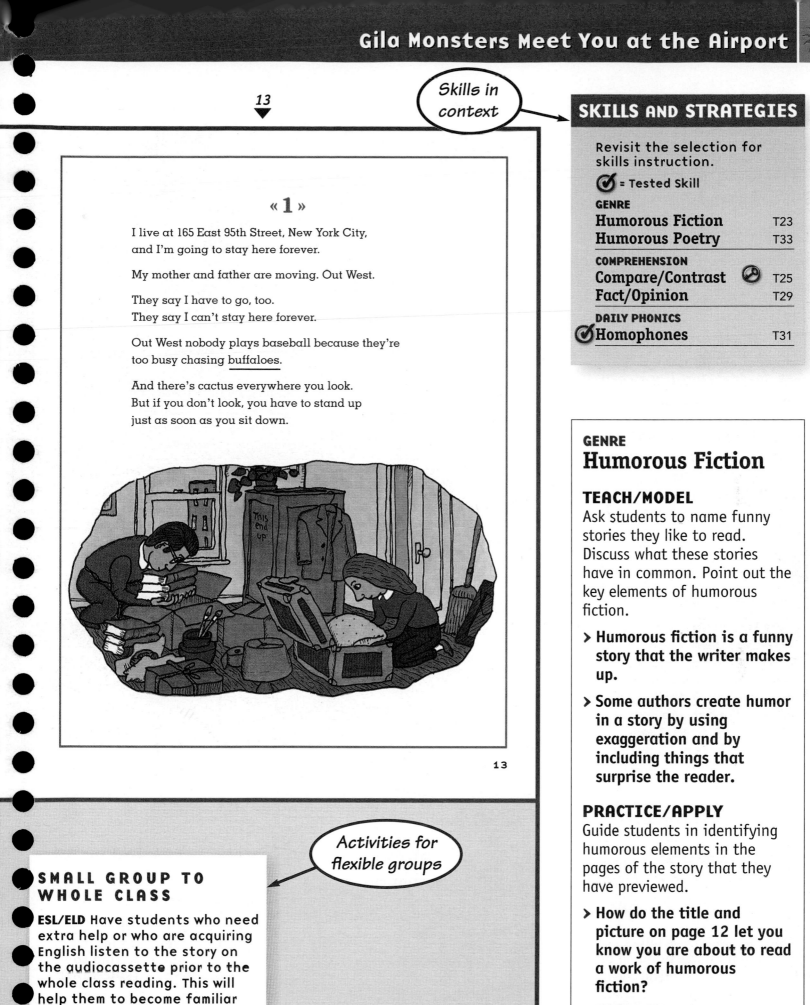

Skills in context

13 ▼

« 1 »

I live at 165 East 95th Street, New York City,
and I'm going to stay here forever.

My mother and father are moving. Out West.

They say I have to go, too.
They say I can't stay here forever.

Out West nobody plays baseball because they're
too busy chasing buffaloes.

And there's cactus everywhere you look.
But if you don't look, you have to stand up
just as soon as you sit down.

13

SKILLS AND STRATEGIES

Revisit the selection for
skills instruction.

✓ = Tested Skill

GENRE
Humorous Fiction   T23
Humorous Poetry   T33

COMPREHENSION
Compare/Contrast   T25
Fact/Opinion   T29

DAILY PHONICS
✓Homophones   T31

GENRE
Humorous Fiction

TEACH/MODEL
Ask students to name funny
stories they like to read.
Discuss what these stories
have in common. Point out the
key elements of humorous
fiction.

> Humorous fiction is a funny
story that the writer makes
up.

> Some authors create humor
in a story by using
exaggeration and by
including things that
surprise the reader.

PRACTICE/APPLY
Guide students in identifying
humorous elements in the
pages of the story that they
have previewed.

> How do the title and
picture on page 12 let you
know you are about to read
a work of humorous
fiction?

> Do you think the pictures
on page 14 use
exaggeration? Why or
why not?

Activities for flexible groups

SMALL GROUP TO WHOLE CLASS

ESL/ELD Have students who need
extra help or who are acquiring
English listen to the story on
the audiocassette prior to the
whole class reading. This will
help them to become familiar
with the story sequence and
vocabulary. Make sure that
students pay attention to the
pre- and post-listening
activities. **(AUDIO CLUES)**

COMPREHENSION

1 **AUTHOR'S CRAFT: DIALOGUE**

> **How would the boy say "Howdy, Pardner"? How do you know?** *(Possible answer: The boy would draw out the syllables. The author put hyphens between each letter and repeated some letters.)*

2 **COMPARE/CONTRAST**

> **The boy imagines what he will wear out West. How will his western clothes be different from the clothes he wears in New York City?** *(Possible answer: He imagines he'll wear chaps, spurs, a bandanna, and a huge hat instead of his jacket and cap.)*

SELF-MONITORING STRATEGY

Decoding

THINK ALOUD *How can I figure out what the word c-h-i-l-i is. I know ch together stands for the sound /ch/. I think the first syllable is /chil/, but I'm not sure how to pronounce the final i. I'll try /ī/—chil ī/. That's not a word I know. I have a friend named Mimi. The i has the /ē/ sound. So I say /chil' ē/. Now it's a word I know, and it makes sense in the sentence.*

☑ INFORMAL ASSESSMENT
OBSERVATION

Vocabulary Assess students' recognition and understanding of the word *spurs* as they read the selection. Did students:

✔ use picture clues to figure out the word?

✔ use context clues, such as *wear*?

Multiple opportunities to practice skills

Metacognition support

14 ▼

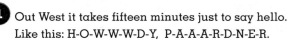

1 Out West it takes fifteen minutes just to say hello. Like this: H-O-W-W-W-D-Y, P-A-A-A-R-D-N-E-R.

Out West I'll look silly all the time. I'll have to wear **2** chaps and spurs and a bandanna and a hat so big that nobody can find me underneath it. And I'll have to ride a horse to school every day and I don't know how.

Out West everybody grows up to be a sheriff. I want to be a subway driver.

14

MODIFY Instruction

ESL/ELD

▲ Use illustrations to reinforce students' understanding of vocabulary such as *chaps, spurs, cowboy hat,* and *bandanna.* Have students compare this type of clothing with their own. Ask questions to guide them: *Do you wear chaps to school?* **(RELATE TO REAL LIFE)**

GIFTED & TALENTED

✳ Have partners role-play a dialogue between the narrator and his friend Seymour in which the narrator expresses his concerns about moving to the Southwest. **(ROLE-PLAY)**

15
▼

Teach and practice in context

My best friend is Seymour, and we like to eat
salami sandwiches together.

Out West I probably won't have any friends,
but if I do, they'll be named Tex or Slim,
and we'll eat chili and beans for breakfast. And lunch.
And dinner. While I miss Seymour and salami.

15

SKILLS AND STRATEGIES

COMPREHENSION
Compare/Contrast

TEACH/MODEL
Explain that when you compare
and contrast, you tell how
things are alike and different.

> **Look for things that are
alike and different.**

> **Notice words that signal
likeness—*like, also, too*—
and words that signal
difference—*but, however,
opposite*.**

> **Think about how the things
are alike and different.**

PRACTICE/APPLY
Ask students to use a diagram
like the one below to compare
and contrast ideas and events
in the selection as they read.

> **What does the narrator like
to eat? What does he think
he'll have to eat out West?**

> **What ideas does the
narrator have about his
friend in New York and the
friends he'll have out West?**

The East		The West
salami sandwiches	← FOOD →	chili and beans
named Seymour	←FRIENDS→	named Tex or Slim

✔ INFORMAL ASSESSMENT
OBSERVATION

Did students:

✔identify comparisons and
contrasts that the author
directly states in the text?

✔understand what is happening
in the story through
comparisons and contrasts?

See pages T38–T39 for a full
skills lesson on Compare/
Contrast.

SOCIAL STUDIES

Have students complete the
The Old West activity on
page R9, in which they will
compare the actual old West
with its reputation from the
past. Students will develop
their research skills and
learn to compare sources of
information.

Connect to content areas

WORD STUDY

To promote an interest in
words, each selection
features a Bonanza word that
is humorous or has an interesting origin. Keeping the
words on a word wall will
encourage students to use
them in conversation and
writing. The Bonanza word is
Howdy, a greeting in the West
and Southwest. It is a short-
ened form of "How do ye?"

COMPREHENSION

3 MAKE INFERENCES

> What does the boy mean when he says that his home used to be on the right side of a map, but soon it will be on the left? How does the map in the illustration help you understand what he means? *(Possible answer: He means that he used to live in the East, but soon he will be living in the West. The line and plane on the map show him flying from right to left, or east to west.)*

4 CRITICAL THINKING: ANALYZE

> How do you think the boy's feelings about moving might be different if he had been out West before? What makes you think so? *(Possible answer: He probably wouldn't be so unhappy and worried about moving there, because he would know what it was really like.)*

« 2 »

I'm on my way. Out West. It's cool in the airplane.

The desert is so hot you can collapse, and then the buzzards circle overhead, but no one rescues you because it's real life and not the movies. There are clouds out the window. No buzzards yet.

16

Check for understanding

INTERVENTION TIP

Recognize Story Transitions

Some students may have difficulty with the change in setting and the passage of time. Point out the *2* at the top of the page and remind students that a new chapter usually means a change of some kind. Help them use the context and picture clues to understand that the boy is now in the process of moving Out West.

Pacing suggestion

OPTION You may end the first day's reading here or have students continue reading the entire selection.

MODIFY Instruction

ESL/ELD

▲ Draw a compass rose on the chalkboard. Review or establish the compass points: *north, south, east, west* as well as *northeast* and *southwest.* Display a map of the U.S. and name a familiar northeastern state. Have students point to and describe its location. Ask: *Is the east at the left or the right of the map?* **(USE VISUALS)**

EXTRA HELP

■ Before asking question 3, use a map of the United States to enable students to understand the narrator's references "right," "middle," and "left". Help them see that the East is right, the Midwest is middle, and the West is left. Then guide them to locate New York City and the Southwest. **(USE VISUALS)**

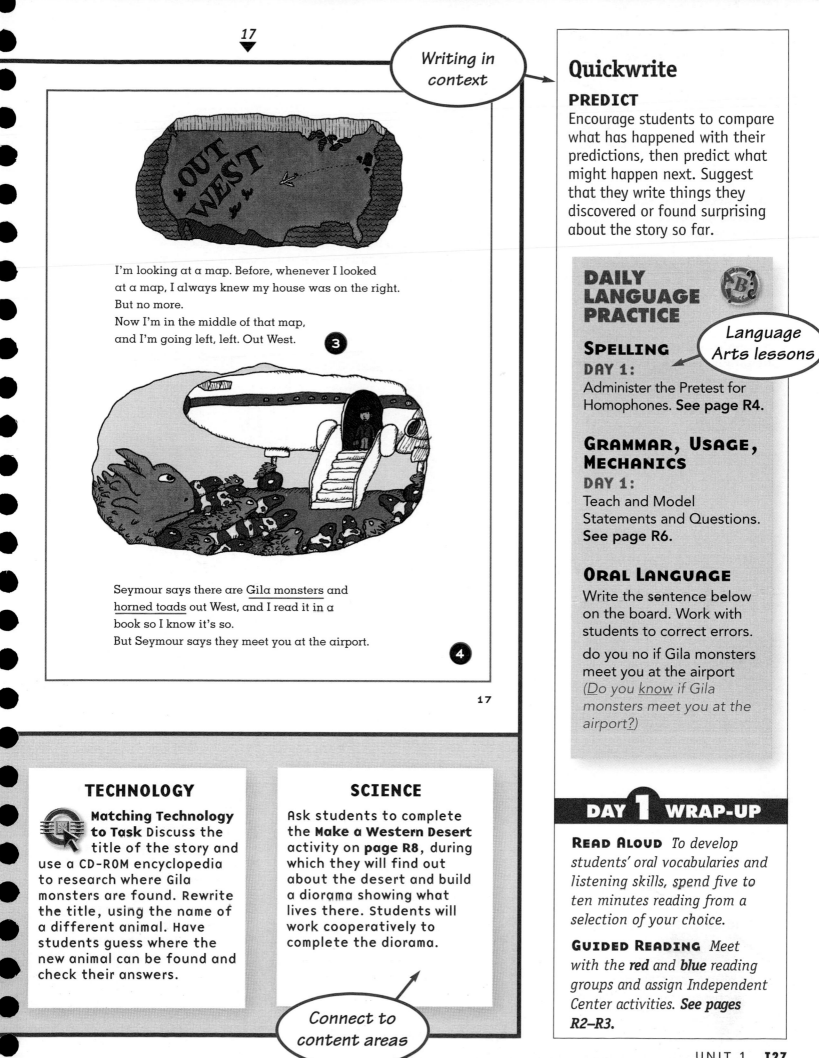

17 ▼

Writing in context

I'm looking at a map. Before, whenever I looked
at a map, I always knew my house was on the right.
But no more.
Now I'm in the middle of that map,
and I'm going left, left. Out West.

3

Seymour says there are <u>Gila monsters</u> and
<u>horned toads</u> out West, and I read it <u>in a</u>
book so I know it's so.
But Seymour says they meet you at the airport.

4

17

Quickwrite

PREDICT
Encourage students to compare what has happened with their predictions, then predict what might happen next. Suggest that they write things they discovered or found surprising about the story so far.

DAILY LANGUAGE PRACTICE

Language Arts lessons

SPELLING
DAY 1:
Administer the Pretest for Homophones. **See page R4.**

GRAMMAR, USAGE, MECHANICS
DAY 1:
Teach and Model Statements and Questions. **See page R6.**

ORAL LANGUAGE
Write the sentence below on the board. Work with students to correct errors.

do you no if Gila monsters meet you at the airport
(*Do you <u>know</u> if Gila monsters meet you at the airport?*)

TECHNOLOGY
Matching Technology to Task Discuss the title of the story and use a CD-ROM encyclopedia to research where Gila monsters are found. Rewrite the title, using the name of a different animal. Have students guess where the new animal can be found and check their answers.

SCIENCE
Ask students to complete the **Make a Western Desert** activity on **page R8**, during which they will find out about the desert and build a diorama showing what lives there. Students will work cooperatively to complete the diorama.

Connect to content areas

DAY **1** WRAP-UP

READ ALOUD *To develop students' oral vocabularies and listening skills, spend five to ten minutes reading from a selection of your choice.*

GUIDED READING *Meet with the* **red** *and* **blue** *reading groups and assign Independent Center activities.* **See pages R2–R3.**

COMPREHENSION

DAY 2 OBJECTIVES

Daily pacing suggestions

STUDENTS WILL:

READ 45 MINUTES

- Gila Monsters Meet You at the Airport, pp. 18–21
- Comprehension Skill: Fact/Opinion
- Daily Phonics: Homophones
- "Gila Monster March" and "Alligator Stomp," pp. 22–25

WRITE 25 MINUTES

- Writing Workshop: Prewrite Humorous Writing
- Spelling: Homophones
- Grammar, Usage, Mechanics: Statements and Questions
- Oral Language

EXTEND SKILLS 20 MINUTES

- Integrated Curriculum
- Read Aloud
- Guided Reading

RESOURCES

- Practice Book 1, pp. 11–12
- Spelling Resource Book, pp. 10–12

▶ Reread

You may wish to have students independently reread the first part of the story before beginning Day 2 reading.

5 SUMMARIZE

> **What has happened so far?**
(The boy has talked about what life out West will be like and has flown to his new home.)

6 FACT/OPINION

> **Do you think Tex's ideas are facts or opinions? How could you find out for sure?**
(Possible answer: Tex's ideas are opinions. To find out for sure, I could use my own knowledge, talk to someone who lives there, or read a book about the place.)

« 3 »

5

We're here.
Out West.
I don't know what a Gila monster or horned toad looks like, but I don't think I see any at the airport.

I see a boy in a cowboy hat.
He looks like Seymour, but I know his name is Tex.
"Hi," I say.
"Hi," he says. "I'm moving East."
"Great!" I say.

"*Great?*" he says. "What's so great about it? Don't you know that the streets are full of gangsters? They all wear flowers in their lapels so they look honest, but they zoom around in big cars with screeching brakes. You have to jump out of their way.

6

18

MODIFY Instruction

ESL/ELD

▲ Encourage free description and comparison of the two pieces of art. Ask: *Is Tex happy about moving East? Why not? Is Tex probably right or wrong about things in the East? Why do you think so?* **(GUIDED QUESTIONS)**

EXTRA HELP

■ Help students answer the fact/opinion question by drawing a simple two-column chart labeled **Facts** and **Opinions**. As students compare the two characters, write their ideas in the appropriate column. **(COMPARE AND CONTRAST)**

19

Model and apply in context

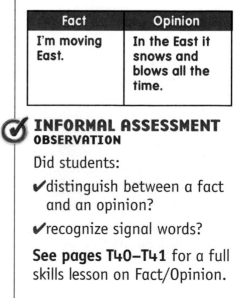

"In the East it snows and blows all the time, except for five minutes when it's spring and summer.

"And you have to live on the 50th floor. Airplanes fly through your bedroom, and you've got to duck fast.

"They ran out of extra space in the East a long time ago. It's so crowded people sit on top of each other when they ride to work.

"And alligators live in the sewers. I read it in a book so I know it's so."

Then the mother and father of the boy who looks like Seymour but isn't grab his hand, and he goes off. "Sometimes the alligators get out," he yells to me. "And they wait for you at the airport."

19

SKILLS AND STRATEGIES

COMPREHENSION
Fact/Opinion

TEACH/MODEL
Tell students that a fact is something that can be checked or proven. An opinion tells what someone thinks or feels.

> **When you are not sure if something is a fact, ask yourself: Can I check this?**

> **The words *I think, I feel, I believe* often tell you that something is an opinion. Words like *wonderful* and *funny* are also clues that an idea is an opinion.**

> **Exaggerations, such as *every day, always,* and *all the time,* are clues that an idea might be an opinion.**

Write these sentences:
I live on 95th Street in New York City.
Out West I'll look silly all the time.
Help students determine which is a fact and which is an opinion and how they know.

PRACTICE/APPLY
Help students find other facts and opinions and write them on a chart like the one below.

Fact	Opinion
I'm moving East.	In the East it snows and blows all the time.

✓ INFORMAL ASSESSMENT
OBSERVATION

Did students:

✔ distinguish between a fact and an opinion?

✔ recognize signal words?

See pages T40–T41 for a full skills lesson on Fact/Opinion.

CULTURAL CONNECTION

The cowboy hat was invented in the 1860s by John B. Stetson, a hat maker in Philadelphia. He made it large to "crown" the wealthy cattle king ranchers. Because it was practical, ranch hands adopted it, too. Have students brainstorm hats associated with other parts of the world (sombreros, berets, fezzes.)

MATH

Ask students to complete the **How Far West?** activity on **page R8**, in which they will estimate how many miles the boy traveled to reach his new home. The activity will help students learn to use a map scale and ruler to calculate the distance between points on a map.

COMPREHENSION

7 **COMPARE/CONTRAST**

> **How is the boy's new neighborhood out West different from what he thought it would be?** *(Possible answer: He thinks that everything will be different from the East, but it isn't. He doesn't see any buffalo stampedes. He sees a restaurant like one in his old neighborhood and kids playing baseball.)*

8 **DRAW CONCLUSIONS**

> **The boy seems to be changing his mind about the West now that he's there. How does he feel now? How do you know?** *(Possible answer: He is starting to feel comfortable. He calls himself a Westerner.)*

JOURNAL

Revisit Predictions

Ask students to review their predictions and record how they were or were not confirmed by the end of the story.

Metacognition support

SELF-MONITORING STRATEGY

Using Illustrations to Understand Text

THINK ALOUD *As I read, I use the illustrations to help me contrast the boy's old and new homes. For example, these illustrations show me there are palm trees in the west, and I know palm trees don't grow in New York.*

• **What other differences do the illustrations help you to understand?**

« **4** »

It's warm, but there's a nice breeze.
We're in a taxi riding to our new house.

No horses yet.
I don't see any buffalo stampedes either.

I see a restaurant just like the one in my old neighborhood.

I see some kids playing baseball.

20

MODIFY Instruction

ESL/ELD

▲ Write four key sentences about the story on sentence strips. Have students read and put the sentences in order. Then ask: *How did the boy feel before he flew west? How did he feel after he arrived?* **(GUIDED QUESTIONS)**

GIFTED & TALENTED

✳ Remind students that Tex is flying from Texas to New York. Have them look at a map to identify the states that his plane might fly over. Tell students to track the airplane's flight path on a map of the United States. **(Use Graphic Devices)**

21 ▼

Phonics practice in context

I see a horse. Hey, that's a great-looking horse!
I'm going to ask my mother and father for one like it.

Here's our house.
Some kids are riding their bikes in front of it.
I hope one of them is named Slim.

7

Tomorrow I'm writing a long letter to Seymour.
I'll tell him I'm sending it by pony express.
Seymour will believe me.
Back East they don't know much about us Westerners.

8

21

Extend the story on CD-ROM

CONNECTING TO THEME

Remind students of the unit theme—We learn about our world through new experiences. Generate a discussion in which students share what they have learned about the world through moving from one place to another.

TECHNOLOGY

FINDING THE FACTS Encourage students to go to the **Smart Place CD-ROM** and click on the Smart Spot on screen 9 to learn more about Gila monsters. Ask students to open a Sticky Note and write why they think Seymour told his friend that Gila monsters would meet him at the airport.

✓ Homophones

TEACH/MODEL

Remind students that homophones are words that sound alike but are spelled differently and have different meanings. Discuss the homophones **no/know.**

> **What word on page 21 sounds like *no* but is spelled differently and has a different meaning?**

> **How did the spelling of the word and context clues help you figure out the meaning?**

PRACTICE/APPLY

- Have students look through the story for other homophones. Write on the chalkboard the homophones they find.

- Then ask questions that can be answered by the homophones. For example: "Which word means *also*?" *(too)* Students should say and spell the word.

✓ INFORMAL ASSESSMENT
OBSERVATION

Did students:

✔ recognize homophones?

✔ use context clues and the word's spelling to determine meaning?

 IF students need more support with homophones,

THEN see the Intervention Activity on page T42.

COMPREHENSION

▶ Preview

Ask students to preview and predict by reading the titles of the poems and looking at the illustrations. Then have students read the poems.

1 MAKE PREDICTIONS

>These poems come from a book called *The Reptile Ball*. A ball is a dance. What do you think happens at a reptile ball? *(Possible answer: Snakes, lizards, Gila monsters, and alligators dance, eat, and knock things over with their tails.)*

2 COMPARE/CONTRAST 🔍

>How are all the Gila monsters in the poem alike? *(Possible answer: they are rowdy, rude, don't dance, eat a lot, and have the same shape and colors.)*

POEMS

from
The Reptile Ball
by Jacqueline K. Ogburn   pictures by John O'Brien

AWARD WINNER

22

MODIFY Instruction

ESL/ELD

▲ Have students march and clap to the rhythm as they chant the poem. Then ask if all Gila monsters are the same or different. Ask more advanced English language learners to explain how they are the same or different. **(ACT IT OUT)**

EXTRA HELP

■ Use echo reading to help students appreciate the rhyme and rhythm of the poem. Read a line and have students repeat it. Have students clap as they say aloud stressed words in the poem. **(RHYTHM)**

23 ▼

Teach and practice in context

Gila Monster March

Gilas come marching, two by two.
Gilas are black and pink and blue.
 Gilas are rowdy,
 Gilas are rude.
Gilas don't dance —
They've come for the food. **1** **2**

23

GENRE
Humorous Poetry

TEACH/MODEL
Explain to students that poems have rhythm and some poems rhyme.

> Just as songs have a beat, so do poems.

> Listen for the beat in this nursery rhyme: *A tisket, a tasket,/a green and yellow basket.*

Remind students that rhyming words sound the same.

> What word rhymes with tasket? *(basket)*

Point out that some poems are funny because they have surprises in them.

> What funny rhymes do you know?

PRACTICE/APPLY
Have students read the poem aloud.

> Which words rhyme at the end of the lines? *(two/blue; rude/food)*

> Which words repeat within the poem? *(Gilas, two)*

> What surprises in the poem do you think are funny? *(The Gilas act more like people than animals.)*

Have students answer similar questions about rhyme, rhythm, and humor when they read "Alligator Stomp" on page 25.

THE ARTS

Ask students to complete the **Make a Gila Monster Mask** activity on **page R9,** in which they will use cardboard and paint to make masks. Students will incorporate details from pictures of Gila monsters in their masks.

Connect to the arts

VISUAL LITERACY

Help students compare and contrast the illustrations of Gilas on page 17 with those in the poem. Discuss the differences in the illustrators' styles. Ask students to identify which pictures contain more detail and which pictures they think are the funniest.

Opportunity to make comparisons between stories

COMPREHENSION

3 **AUTHOR'S CRAFT: APPRECIATING LANGUAGE**

> Why do you think the poet uses the words *thomp* and *clomp*? *(Possible answer: These words rhyme with* swamp *and* stomp, *and the words sound like the noise stomping alligator feet might make.)*

4 **COMPARE/CONTRAST**

> In the poems, what's the difference between how the Gila monsters act and how the alligators and crocodiles act? *(Possible answer: The Gila monsters eat but they don't dance; the crocodiles and alligators dance.)*

> *Higher-order thinking skills*

5 **CRITICAL THINKING: EVALUATE**

> Which poem do you like best? Why? What things about this poem make it fun to read? *(Answers should reflect students' appreciation of the subject and sound of the poem.)*

SELF-MONITORING STRATEGY

Relate to Literary Experience

THINK ALOUD Kin *is an easy word to read, because I see the small word* in *in it, but I don't know what it means. I can look for clues to its meaning in the poem. For example, in the third line I read "their cousins from the swamp." Therefore, I think* kin *means relatives. Does* relatives *make sense in the sentence?*

> *Metacognition support*

24 ▼

Alligator Stomp

Suave Egyptian crocodiles
Crack wicked, toothy smiles,
When their cousins from the swamp
Start the Alligator Stomp.
Clomp!

24

MODIFY Instruction

ESL/ELD

▲ Many low frequency words appear in this poem; don't dwell on them. Focus on the rhyming words and the imagery. Have students move, crack smiles, and swing tails. They can chant, *I'm a crocodile; Here's my smile. When I romp, I go stomp, clomp, thomp!* **(ROLE-PLAY)**

GIFTED & TALENTED

✳ Suggest that students work in pairs or small groups to organize a dramatization of one of the poems. One student can read the poem while the others act it out. After they practice their presentations, take the class outdoors where students can teach the actions to the rest of the group. **(ACT IT OUT)**

25 ▼

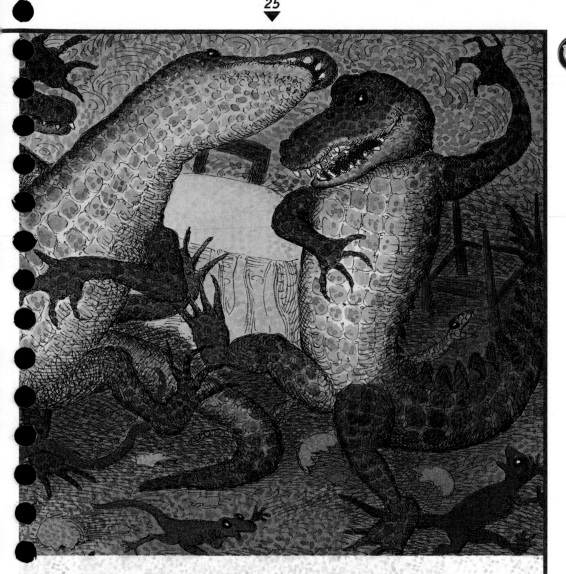

Kin from Cairo and Decatur,
Both sides of the equator,
Grinning leatherbacks thomp **3**
In the Alligator Stomp.
Clomp!

Smaller dancers have to run
From the table-smashing fun
Of the tail-swinging romp
Called the Alligator Stomp.
CLOMP!

4 **5** 25

WORKSHOP

You may wish to introduce the Workshop on this day. Set aside specific times over the next two weeks for students to work on this ongoing activity.

ORAL LANGUAGE

Have students listen while you say *stomp* and *clomp.* Point out that these words sound like the actions they describe. On the chalkboard write *horse, wolf, bee, crow.* Ask students to say aloud the onomatopoeic word they associate with each creature. For example: *neigh, stomp, howl, buzz, caw.*

Humorous Story

WRITING WORKSHOP

Using *Gila Monsters Meet You at the Airport* as a model, discuss with students elements that make a story funny, such as exaggeration and surprising events. Let students know that later they will make use of these elements when they write their own humorous stories. Have students brainstorm characters and their actions and begin to complete the prewriting organizer.

Use Practice Book 1, page 11.

DAILY LANGUAGE PRACTICE (B)

Language Arts lessons

SPELLING
DAY 2:
Practice Homophones. See page R4.

GRAMMAR, USAGE, MECHANICS
DAY 2:
Practice Statements and Questions. **See page R6.**

ORAL LANGUAGE
he will right a letter to his friend
(He will <u>write</u> a letter to his friend<u>.</u>)

DAY **2** WRAP-UP

READ ALOUD *Spend five to ten minutes reading from a selection of your choice.*

GUIDED READING *Meet with the **blue** and **green** reading groups and assign Independent Center activities.* **See pages R2–R3.**

DAY 3 OBJECTIVES

Daily pacing suggestions

STUDENTS WILL:

READ 45 MINUTES

- **Reread** *Gila Monsters Meet You at the Airport*
- **Assess Comprehension**
- **Key Comprehension Skill: Compare/Contrast**
- **Comprehension Skill: Fact/Opinion**
- **Daily Phonics: Homophones**

WRITE 30 MINUTES

- **Respond: Postcard**
- **Spelling: Homophones**
- **Grammar, Usage, Mechanics: Statements and Questions**
- **Oral Language**

EXTEND SKILLS 15 MINUTES

- **Read Aloud**
- **Guided Reading**

RESOURCES

- **Transparencies 2–3**
- **Practice Book 1, pp. 12; 12–18**
- **Spelling Resource Book, p. 11**

COMPREHENSION

▶ Think About Reading

1. *You see him in New York City at an airport, and out West.*

2. *The main character is the boy who tells the story.*

3. *He has to move out West.*

4. *He doesn't want to move. He thinks life will be different.*

5. *He sees a restaurant and kids playing baseball.*

6. *He sees a great-looking horse.*

7. *Life in the West and in the East are alike in many ways.*

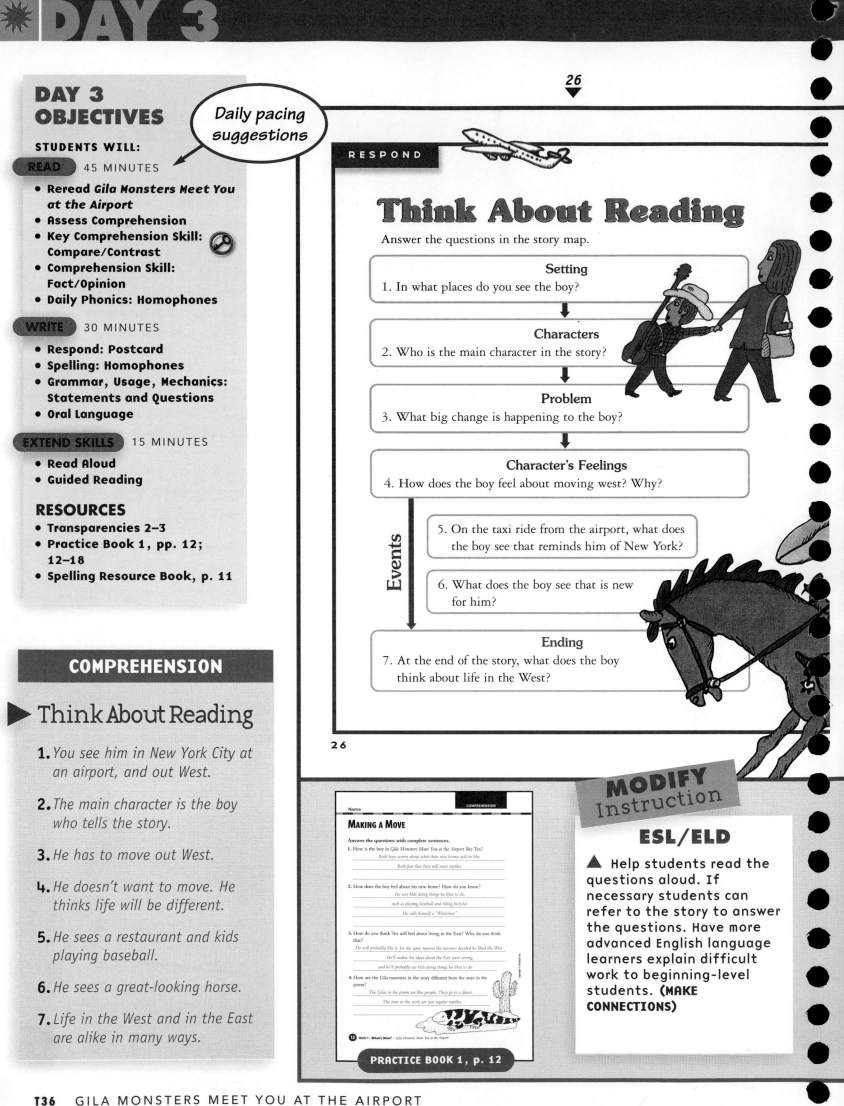

RESPOND

Think About Reading

Answer the questions in the story map.

Setting
1. In what places do you see the boy?

↓

Characters
2. Who is the main character in the story?

↓

Problem
3. What big change is happening to the boy?

↓

Character's Feelings
4. How does the boy feel about moving west? Why?

Events

5. On the taxi ride from the airport, what does the boy see that reminds him of New York?

6. What does the boy see that is new for him?

Ending
7. At the end of the story, what does the boy think about life in the West?

26

MAKING A MOVE

PRACTICE BOOK 1, p. 12

MODIFY Instruction

ESL/ELD

▲ Help students read the questions aloud. If necessary students can refer to the story to answer the questions. Have more advanced English language learners explain difficult work to beginning-level students. **(MAKE CONNECTIONS)**

27 ▼

Write A Postcard

Imagine you are the boy in the story. Write a postcard to Seymour. Tell him one interesting thing about your new home. It might be about a new friend or something fun you did. Be sure to include the date, a greeting, a short message, and a closing.

Literature Circle

The story and the poems are examples of humorous writing. Which descriptions, ideas, or events made you laugh? What made them funny?

Author
Marjorie Weinman Sharmat

Marjorie Weinman Sharmat always wanted to be a writer. She and a friend published a newspaper when she was only eight. Many of her books are about things that happened to her. In fact, she wrote *Gila Monsters Meet You at the Airport* after she moved from New York City to Arizona with her husband and sons. Did she meet any Gila monsters? You'll have to ask her.

More Books by
Marjorie Weinman Sharmat

- *Nate the Great*
- *Getting Something on Maggie Marmelstein*
- *Genghis Khan: A Dog Star Is Born*
- *I'm the Best*

27

RESPOND

✎ Write a Postcard

Before students begin to write, ask and discuss:

> **What does the boy see on the taxi ride to his new house?**

> **How does he feel about his new neighborhood?**

> **Who might become the boy's new friend?**

Literature Circle

Encourage students to participate in a conversation about the writing. Students may say that the boy's ideas of Out West and Tex's ideas of the East are funny because they exaggerate everything that is going to happen. The poems are funny because they show the Gila monsters doing things they could never possibly do.

Opportunities for speculation and interpretation

DAILY LANGUAGE PRACTICE ⓑ

Language Arts lessons

SPELLING

DAY 3:
Write Homophones. **See page R5.**

GRAMMAR, USAGE, MECHANICS

DAY 3:
Practice Statements and Questions. **See page R7.**

ORAL LANGUAGE

Wear Tex is going to live
(*Where is* Tex going to live?)

TECHNOLOGY

 **LANGUAGE DEVELOPMENT** Encourage students to go to the **Smart Place CD-ROM** and click the Smart Spot on Screen 8 to learn about places in the United States. Then have students use PlaceMaker to create a postcard to encourage people to visit a particular state.

Appropriate use of technology

🔑 COMPREHENSION
Compare/Contrast

✓ QUICKCHECK

Can students:

✔ identify comparisons and contrasts that are implied or directly stated in the text?

✔ understand what is happening in the story through comparisons and contrasts?

If **YES**, go on to Practice/Apply.

If **NO**, start at Teach/Model.

Ⓐ TEACH/MODEL

TRANSPARENCY 2

Scholastic Literacy Place

COMPARE/CONTRAST

What he thought he'd find in the West	What he found when he got to the West
Gila monsters	boys afraid of the East Coast
no baseball	nice warm weather
buffalo stampedes	restaurants like the ones
hot, uncomfortable weather	at home
cacti	baseball
horses	one horse
silly clothes	bicycles
no salami	kids who could be friends
no friends	

What was different?
nicer weather, room for horses

What was the same?
kids are like him, baseball, restaurants like the ones at home

What's New? • Gila Monsters Meet You at the Airport   ②

USE ORAL LANGUAGE

Ask students how they would describe an apple and an orange. What are they? What do you do with them? What do they look, feel, and taste like? Point out that students have been describing how the apple and orange are alike and how they are different.

When you compare, you tell how things are alike. When you contrast, you tell how they differ. Tell students that comparing and contrasting can help them better understand and remember events in a story. To compare and contrast, tell students to:

1. Look for people and things that are being compared or contrasted. Think about how they are alike and different.

2. Look for words that let you know things are alike—*also, in the same way, just like, too*—and words that let you know things are different—*but, however, opposite.*

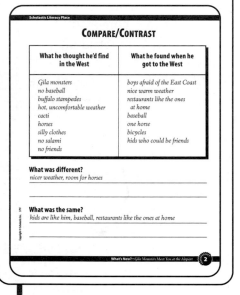

MODIFY Instruction

ESL/ELD

▲ To help students understand how the exaggeration is used in the story, have them make a comparison chart. Title one column "Out West," the other "Back East." Students can write the appropriate words or phrases and vote for the funniest exaggeration. **(GRAPHIC DEVICE)**

EXTRA HELP

■ Some students process text better by hearing it before reading it. To complete Practice Book p.14, provide an opportunity for students to listen to the audio version of the selection as they follow along in the Anthology. **(USE AUDIO)**

LITERATURE CONNECTION

Use **Transparency 2** to help students compare and contrast as they read.

THINK ALOUD *I'm going to look at what the boy thought he'd find out West and compare it to what he actually did find. Let's see . . . at first, he thought that no one would be playing baseball. While riding in the taxi, he sees that he was wrong—some kids are playing baseball. Also, he says that he sees a restaurant just like the one in his old neighborhood. Comparing and contrasting what he imagines with what he actually finds helps me better understand the story.*

Ⓑ PRACTICE/APPLY

USE PRACTICE BOOK

Have pairs of students practice the skill by completing **Practice Book 1, page 14. (PARTNERS)**

Ⓒ ASSESS

APPLY INSTRUCTIONAL ALTERNATIVES

Based on students' completion of **Transparency 2** and **Practice Book page 14** determine whether they were able to compare and contrast information in *Gila Monsters Meet You at the Airport*. The Instructional Alternatives below will aid you in pinpointing students' level of proficiency. Consider the appropriate instructional alternative to promote further skill development. To reinforce the skill, distribute **pages 15** and **16** of **Practice Book 1**.

Intervention strategies

Transfer skill to a new text

☑ INSTRUCTIONAL ALTERNATIVES

	If the student . . .	Then
Proficient	Uses story details and picture clues to make comparisons and contrasts and is able to explain them	• Have the student apply this skill independently to a more challenging story.
Apprentice	Identifies ways story details are alike and different but cannot explain the similarities and differences	• Have the student work with other students to compare and contrast story details and to explain them.
Novice	Is unable to compare and contrast story details and picture clues	• Have the student orally compare and contrast the rain forest with the Arctic or two objects in the classroom, such as the covers of two books.

PRACTICE BOOK 1, p. 14

PRACTICE BOOK 1, p. 15

PRACTICE BOOK 1, p. 16

Additional skills instruction →

COMPREHENSION
Fact/Opinion

✓ **QUICKCHECK**

Can students:
✔ distinguish between facts and opinions?
✔ recognize words that often signal opinions, such as *I think, I believe*, as well as adjectives such as *wonderful* and adverbs such as *probably*?

If **YES**, go on to Practice/Apply.

If **NO**, start at Teach/Model.

ⓐ TEACH/MODEL

USE ORAL LANGUAGE

Ask students to tell what they know about baseball or some other sport or game. Then ask students how they feel. Point out that when students described rules of the game, they were stating facts. When they told what they *felt* about the game, they were stating opinions.

A fact is a statement that can be checked in a reference source. An opinion is a statement that tells what a person thinks or believes. In *Gila Monsters*, many of the opinions used clue words like *all the time, forever*, and *always*. To evaluate fact/opinion, tell students to:

1. Read the text and ask, "Can this statement be checked and proven correct?" If so, then it is a fact.

2. Ask, "Is this a statement that cannot be proven correct and tells what someone thinks or believes?" If so, then it is an opinion.

TRANSPARENCY 3

Scholastic Literacy Place

FACT AND OPINION

Statement	Fact	Opinion	How do I know?
Out West everybody grows up to be a sheriff.		✓	The word *everybody* is a clue. This statement can't be proved.
There are Gila monsters and horned toads out West.	✓		I can look this up in an encyclopedia or on the Internet.

What's New? • *Gila Monsters Meet You at the Airport* ③

MODIFY
Instruction

ESL/ELD

▲ Play a game of True/False. Say: *True or False—you play baseball with a ball and a bat.* When students say, "True," say, *Yes, it's true. It's a fact. True or False—baseball is played in the summer.* Lead students in saying, *That's true. It's a fact.*

For an opinion, say: *True or False—Baseball is a wonderful sport.* Explain that there is no one answer to this question. Each person may have a different *opinion.* **(STEP-BY-STEP)**

LITERATURE CONNECTION

Display the chart on **Transparency 3** to help students evaluate facts and opinions as they read.

THINK ALOUD *As soon as I read the boy's ideas about the West, I realized they were his opinions. For example, when he says that everyone in the West grows up to be a sheriff, I knew this wasn't a fact. The word* **everyone** *was a clue that this is an opinion. Everyone in a place can't be a sheriff.*

B PRACTICE/APPLY

USE PRACTICE BOOK

Have students practice the skill independently by completing **Practice Book 1, page 17. (INDIVIDUALS)**

C ASSESS

APPLY INSTRUCTIONAL ALTERNATIVES

Based on students' completion of **Transparency 3** and **Practice Book 1, page 17**, determine whether they were able to evaluate facts and opinions in *Gila Monsters Meet You at the Airport*. The Instructional Alternatives below will aid you in pinpointing students' level of proficiency. Consider the appropriate instructional alternative to promote further skill development.

To reinforce the skill, distribute **pages 15** and **18** of **Practice Book 1**.

Intervention strategies

Transfer skill to a new text

C INSTRUCTIONAL ALTERNATIVES

	If the student . . .	Then
Proficient	Is able to distinguish between facts and opinions	Have the students apply this skill to a more challenging selection. Present a paragraph from a newspaper or magazine. Have the student identify facts and opinions and explain the basis for each decision.
Apprentice	Identifies facts but is unable to identify opinions or clues that signal an opinion	Have the student work with other students to identify facts and opinions and then explain the basis for their decisions.
Novice	Is unable to evaluate facts and opinions	Work with the student to identify facts and opinions in sample sentences.

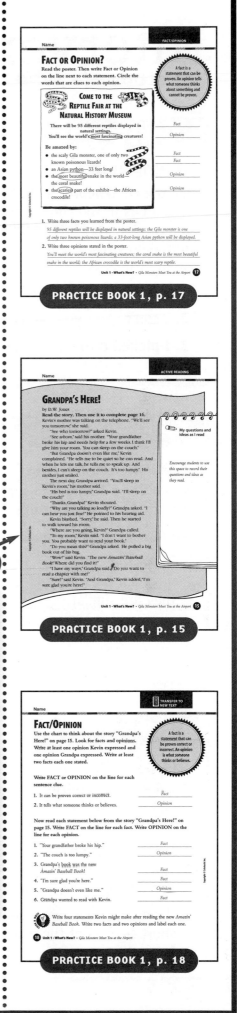

PRACTICE BOOK 1, p. 17

PRACTICE BOOK 1, p. 15

PRACTICE BOOK 1, p. 18

Intervention
For students who need extra help with. . .

PHONICS

HOMOPHONES

On the chalkboard, write the homophones and meanings in the chart. Then write the sentences below. Ask students to fill in the correct homophone and then circle a context word or phrase that they used as a clue.

1. I have a new _____ of running shoes.

2. I can't _____ your voice when you whisper.

3. I picked a piece of fruit from the _____ tree.

Homophone	Meaning
here	in this place
hear	to sense sounds
pair	a set of two things
pear	a kind of fruit

COMPREHENSION

COMPARE/CONTRAST

Use a Venn diagram to support students' ability to compare and contrast story details.

• Draw the diagram on the chalkboard for students to copy.

• Lead students in completing the diagram. Ask them for ways in which the East and the West are different and for ways they are similar.

THE EAST   BOTH   THE WEST

FLUENCY

READING ALOUD

Provide opportunities for students to improve fluency by reading aloud daily, using books in your classroom. Choose quality selections from a variety of genres.

• Model fluency by reading a short poem or the beginning of a story with expression as well as by varying your tone and pitch and emphasizing important words.

• Have volunteers practice reading the poem or continue reading a short section of the text.

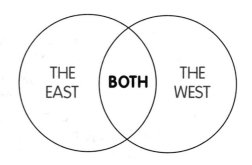

Optional Materials for Intervention

COMPREHENSION

Compare/Contrast

If students need help with compare/contrast, use the WiggleWorks Stage C book, Look-Alike Animals.

COMPARE ANIMALS

Explain to students that they will be using both the text and the pictures to learn how animals are alike and different. Have students compare and contrast two dogs or cats, or classroom animals, that they know.

READING *LOOK-ALIKE ANIMALS*

Tell students that *Look-Alike Animals* is a science book that gives information about animals. To learn about the animals in the book, they will need to use both the text and the pictures. Suggest that they look at the pictures on each page before they read the text and to look at them carefully again after they read.

Have students begin the book. Check in with them to give support as they read.

Apply to new text

LISTENING

Reading Aloud

If students need help with fluency, use the audiocassette for, Gila Monsters Meet You at the Airport.

LISTEN TO THE AUDIOCASSETTE

Have students read the story aloud together, alternating reading sections of text. Listeners should follow along and help the reading partner correct mistakes.

CHORAL READING

Student pairs could also try reading sections together, either as an echo reading or as choral reading. Pair students who need particular help reading aloud with fluent readers for echo reading.

DAY 3 WRAP-UP

READ ALOUD Spend five to ten minutes reading from a selection of your choice.

GUIDED READING Meet with the **blue** and **green** reading groups and assign Independent Center activities. *See pages R2-R3.*

DAY 4 OBJECTIVES

STUDENTS WILL:

READ 10 MINUTES

- Reread *Gila Monsters Meet You at the Airport*

WRITE 50 MINUTES

- Writing Workshop: Humorous Story
- Writer's Craft: Descriptive Details
- Spelling: Homophones
- Grammar, Usage, Mechanics: Statements and Questions
- Oral Language

EXTEND SKILLS 30 MINUTES

- Vocabulary
- Daily Phonics: Homophones
- Study Skills: Parts of a Book
- Guided Reading
- Read Aloud

RESOURCES

- Practice Book 1, pp. 11, 19, 20
- Transparency 4
- Spelling Resource Book, p. 200

Students may refer to *Putting It In Writing* and *Writing with Style.*

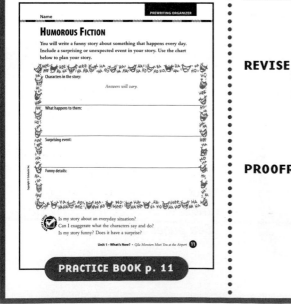

PRACTICE BOOK p. 11

✐ **WRITING WORKSHOP** *Expressive Writing*

Humorous Story

Respond to the story through writing

THINK ABOUT WRITING

Have students discuss what makes *Gila Monsters Meet You at the Airport* funny. Ask:

> **How does the writer take an ordinary situation and make it funny?**

> **What makes the boy's idea about the West humorous?**

LITERATURE CONNECTION

Have students look back at **page 21.** Ask volunteers to read aloud the parts of the page they think are the funniest. Point out the exaggeration in the boy's ideas about life in the East. Let students know that these images surprise us and help make the story humorous.

PREWRITE

COMPLETE A GRAPHIC ORGANIZER

Have students refer to the graphic organizer on **Practice Book, page 11,** that they began earlier. They might change or add characters, ideas about what happens to them, or add a surprise, and funny details.

DRAFT

TEACH WRITER'S CRAFT

Before students begin their drafts, help them understand how descriptive details can make their writing more vivid. **See Writer's Craft, page T45.**

> **Try to imagine the event and the characters. How can you exaggerate events or characters' actions to create humor? What descriptive details can you add that will paint a clear picture for the reader?**

REVISE/PROOFREAD

Note: You may wish to do Revise/Proofread on Day 5. As students revise and proofread, they might want to ask:

REVISE

- Are there any actions I can exaggerate more to make my story funnier?

- Are there any descriptive details I can add to make my event or story more interesting?

PROOFREAD

- Have I used both statements and questions in my writing?

- Did I begin each sentence with a capital letter?

- Have I used correct end punctuation?

✔ **See Students' Writing Rubric on page T52.**

Instruction in style and craft

WRITER'S CRAFT
DESCRIPTIVE DETAILS

A TEACH/MODEL

- Point out that descriptive details in writing help create a picture in the reader's mind.

  Sensory words or phrases such as *glittering red ruby* or *chewy brownies* help the reader picture what is being described.

  Precise verbs, or action words, like *leap, rush*, and *soar,* also help to make story details more lively and descriptive.

- Have students brainstorm some descriptive details.

B PRACTICE/APPLY

- **Write on the chalkboard:** *flowers in their lapels* and *zoom around in big cars with screeching brakes.* Point out that these phrases are descriptive details that help create a clear, vivid picture in the reader's mind.

- **Use Transparency 4,** or write the following sentences on the chalkboard. Ask students to choose the better one and to give reasons for their choice. Help them see why the other one is not the better choice.

> 1. The horse eats grass.
>
> 2. The brown-and-white pony grazes on the tall grass.

- Discuss that **sentence 2** is the better choice because it tells the reader exactly what the horse looks like and specifically what the horse does. **Sentence 1** does not provide any descriptive details about the horse.

Scholastic Literacy Place

DESCRIPTIVE DETAILS

1. The horse eats grass.
2. The black and white pony grazes on the tall grass.
3. Storm clouds sweep across a gray sky.
4. Clouds move across the sky.
5. Ella took a big bite of the juicy plum.
6. The girl ate a plum.

Correct choices are sentences 2, 3, and 6.

What's New? • *Gila Monsters Meet You at the Airport* 4

DAILY LANGUAGE PRACTICE B

Language Arts lessons

SPELLING
DAY 4:
Review Homophones. **See page R5.**

GRAMMAR, USAGE, MECHANICS
DAY 4:
Apply Statements and Questions. **See page R7.**

ORAL LANGUAGE
where ar the Gila monsters.
(*Where* <u>are</u> the Gila monsters<u>?</u>)

TECHNOLOGY

Writing Skills
Encourage students to use the cut and paste options in a familiar word processing program to help them revise their writing.

VOCABULARY

buffaloes	Gila monsters
chaps	horned toads
spurs	stampedes

TEACHER TIP

"I try to use the vocabulary words in other contexts during the day. For instance, I might say `I think the 100% on your spelling test spurred you on. When students line up for lunch or recess, I would suggest they not stampede.'"

Extend Vocabulary

Review Vocabulary

CLUES TO MEANING

Write or say the vocabulary words. Then read each sentence aloud and have students write or name the word it describes.

1. These small reptiles have spines that look like horns on their heads. (*horned toads*)

2. When you poke a horse with these, it runs faster. (*spurs*)

3. These animals are also called wild oxen. (*buffaloes*)

4. These leather leg coverings protect a rider's legs. (*chaps*)

5. This word names herds of animals running wildly in one direction. (*stampedes*)

6. You should keep far away from these poisonous lizards. (*Gila monsters*)

Expand Vocabulary

SYNONYMS

Remind students that synonyms are words that have the same or almost the same meaning. The boy in the story thinks that all people in the West greet each other by saying "howdy." Explain that *howdy* is a synonym for *hello*. Draw the word web and ask students to add other words for *hello*.

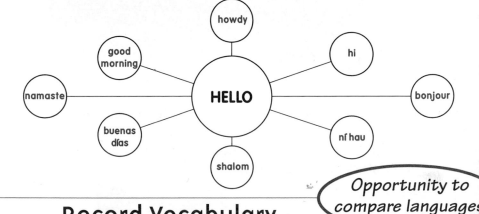

Opportunity to compare languages

Record Vocabulary

BOOK OF WORD ORIGINS FROM OTHER LANGUAGES

Tell students that many words in the story come from other languages. For example, *buffalo, chaps,* and *chili* come from Spanish. Provide students with a list of story words with foreign origins (*bandanna, salami, restaurant*). Students can look up the word origins in a dictionary. Using these and other words, students can make a book of words from other languages. They should include definitions and illustrations where possible.

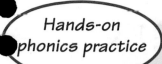

DAILY PHONICS

Homophones

PASSWORD

Prepare for the activity by making a set of word cards, each containing one word of a homophone set. Use these and other homophones:

here	hear	to	too	two
new	knew	not	knot	
right	write	their	they're	there
see	sea	know	no	

1 **SET-UP** Shuffle the cards and place them face down in a pile.

2 **TO PLAY** In turn, one student of a pair selects a card and then provides clues for his or her partner to figure out the word. For example, if a student selects the word card *right*, he or she might say, "My word rhymes with *night*. It means 'opposite of *left*.'"

- The student provides clues until the partner figures out the word and spells it.

3 **TRY THIS** Players can also use the cards to play Concentration.

MATERIALS:
Index cards, marker or pen

SUGGESTED GROUPING:
Partners

REVIEW: PHONICS: HOMOPHONES
Write the homophone that answers each clue. Then read down to find the answer to the riddle.

brake	sun	fare	creak	hear
break	son	fair	creek	here

1. you do this with your ears — hear
2. honest — fair
3. a rusty gate makes this noise — creak
4. you may use this to stop a bike — brake
5. in this place — here
6. boy child — son
7. hot shining object in the sky — sun
8. cost of a bus ride — fare
9. small stream — creek
10. smash — break

What do you call a worm that is trying to look like a reptile?
a fake snake

Unit 1 - What's New? - *Gila Monsters Meet You at the Airport* 19

PRACTICE BOOK 1, p. 19

MODIFY Instruction

ESL/ELD

▲ Help students prepare for the game by working on homophones with a fluent classmate using word cards with homophones in context (**new** shoes/I **knew** it!) Have students read the phrase, spell out the homophone, and chant the phrase. (**MULTISENSORY TECHNIQUES**)

GIFTED & TALENTED

✳ Have students brainstorm a list of more challenging homophones. For example: *flour, flower; peace, piece; plain, plane; wood, would;* and so on. Suggest that student partners write sets of sentences or dialogue, using the homophone pairs. (**MAKE CONNECTIONS**)

Supports inquiry and research

RESEARCH IDEA

Have students look at several different books on a related topic—books about reptiles, birds, or animals—to compare/contrast glossaries, tables of contents, indexes, and title pages. Suggest they note such differences as *Do glossaries contain pictures or diagrams? How is information presented in the table of contents? Why is the index longer than the table of contents?*

STUDY SKILLS
Parts of a Book

A) TEACH/MODEL

INTRODUCE PARTS OF A BOOK

Hold up a fiction and a nonfiction book and tell students that the parts of a book can help them easily find information in the book.

PRESENT THE TITLE PAGE AND TABLE OF CONTENTS

Show students the title page of the nonfiction book and identify it.

> **Why do you think it's called the title page?**

> **What information do you see on it?**

Turn to the table of contents and explain that it lists the book's chapters, in order, and gives the page number where each chapter begins.

> **How many chapters does this book have?**

> **On what page does the first chapter begin?**

Tell students that by reading the chapter titles in the table of contents, they can see what kind of information the book contains.

LOCATE THE GLOSSARY AND INDEX

Point out the glossary and index at the back of the book. Explain that the glossary is like a mini dictionary. It contains words important to the subject of the book, listed in alphabetical order.

The index is an alphabetical list of all names and subjects in the book. Page numbers tell where information about each listing can be found.

> **Where would you look to find the meaning of the word *reptile* in a science book?** *(glossary)*

> **Where would you look to find out if *buffalo* is a topic in this book?** *(index)*

B PRACTICE/APPLY

You may wish to have students work in pairs or small groups to practice using book parts in the Anthology, as well as in fiction and nonfiction trade books and other classroom textbooks. Write the book parts below on the chalkboard.

title page   table of contents

index   glossary

Have students use the books to answer the following questions:

> **Look in your Anthology. Where can you find the page number for a poem called "Gila Monster March"?** *(table of contents)*

> **Is the topic *deserts* in the social studies textbook? Where did you look?** *(index)* **What are the page references?**

> **Is there a chapter in your science book on *plants*? Where did you look?** *(table of contents)*

> **In what part of your Anthology can you find the meaning of *stampedes*?** *(glossary)* **What is its meaning?**

> **Select a story book. What is the title and the author's name? Where did you look?** *(title page)*

✓ STUDENT'S SELF-ASSESSMENT

Did I:

✔ identify the correct part of the book where information could be found?

✔ locate the correct information using book parts?

PRACTICE BOOK 1, p. 20

DAY 4 WRAP-UP

READ ALOUD *Spend five or ten minutes reading from a selection of your choice.*

GUIDED READING *Meet with the **red** and **blue** reading groups and assign Independent Center activities. See pages R2–R3.*

TECHNOLOGY

Study Skills Briefly review with students the definition and purpose of a table of contents. Discuss how it lists main ideas or chapters in a book by page number to make them easy to locate. Have students use the **Smart Place CD-ROM** to reread the Smart Book and create a table of contents using a Smart Page. Remind them to list screen or page numbers.

DAY 5 OBJECTIVES

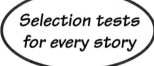

Daily pacing suggestions

STUDENTS WILL:

READ 30 MINUTES
- **Reading Assessment**
- **Daily Phonics: Homophones**

WRITE 30 MINUTES
- **Writing Assessment**
- **Spelling: Homophones**
- **Grammar, Usage, Mechanics: Statements and Questions**
- **Oral Language**

EXTEND SKILLS 30 MINUTES
- **Integrated Language Arts**
- **Read Aloud**
- **Guided Reading**

RESOURCES
- **Selection Test**
- **Spelling Resource Book, p. 202**

Selection tests for every story

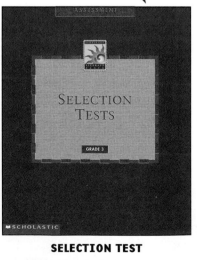

SELECTION TEST

Reading Assessment

Formal Assessment

Use the Selection Test to measure students' mastery of the week's reading skills. See the suggestions for Intervention and Modifying Assessment.

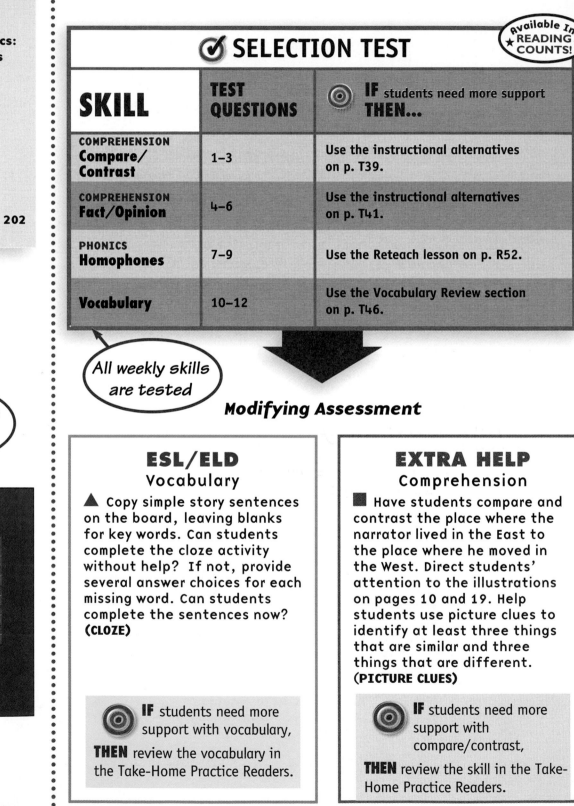

Available In ★READING★ *COUNTS!*

☑ SELECTION TEST

SKILL	TEST QUESTIONS	◎ **IF** students need more support **THEN...**
COMPREHENSION **Compare/ Contrast**	1–3	Use the instructional alternatives on p. T39.
COMPREHENSION **Fact/Opinion**	4–6	Use the instructional alternatives on p. T41.
PHONICS **Homophones**	7–9	Use the Reteach lesson on p. R52.
Vocabulary	10–12	Use the Vocabulary Review section on p. T46.

All weekly skills are tested

Modifying Assessment

ESL/ELD
Vocabulary

▲ Copy simple story sentences on the board, leaving blanks for key words. Can students complete the cloze activity without help? If not, provide several answer choices for each missing word. Can students complete the sentences now? **(CLOZE)**

◎ **IF** students need more support with vocabulary,
THEN review the vocabulary in the Take-Home Practice Readers.

EXTRA HELP
Comprehension

■ Have students compare and contrast the place where the narrator lived in the East to the place where he moved in the West. Direct students' attention to the illustrations on pages 10 and 19. Help students use picture clues to identify at least three things that are similar and three things that are different. **(PICTURE CLUES)**

◎ **IF** students need more support with compare/contrast,
THEN review the skill in the Take-Home Practice Readers.

Performance-Based Assessment

Use the assessment activities below to provide performance-based measures of students' proficiency in phonics and reading fluency. See the Conference to assess each student's progress.

Assess fluency progress

DAILY PHONICS

Dictation Sentences

HOMOPHONES Dictate the following words and sentences. Have students write them on a sheet of paper. Then write the words and sentences on the chalkboard and have students make any necessary corrections on their papers.

> here   hear   know   no
> I didn't ____ what you said.
> The boy lives ____ now.
> I ____ how to ride a horse.
> He saw cows but ____ horses.

✔ **Did students use the correct homophones in the sentences?**

IF students need more support with homophones,

THEN practice using context clues in the dictation sentences to determine which homophone is being used.

ONE-MINUTE FLUENCY

Ask students to work with a partner and read aloud to each other. Circulate and listen to individuals to assess their reading fluency.

Students can read the text on Practice Book page 15 or the text of the Take-Home Practice Readers.

✔ *Does the student read smoothly and self-correct mistakes?*

IF students need more support with fluency,

THEN have them do repeated readings of the passage to achieve an even, natural pace. Then have them tape-record themselves.

✓ CONFERENCE

Set aside time to meet with several individual students to discuss their story comprehension and to listen to them read from the story. You may wish to tape-record students as they read the section aloud.

ASSESS STORY COMPREHENSION

✔ **The narrator and Tex were both moving to new parts of the country. How are the two boys' opinions about the places they were going similar? (Compare/Contrast)**

✔ **What is one opinion the narrator had about the West? What is a fact he learned when he got there? (Fact/Opinion)**

ASSESS FLUENCY

✔ **Does the student read with correct intonation at the end of sentences?**

✔ **Does the student read at an even, natural pace?**

DAILY LANGUAGE PRACTICE

SPELLING

DAY 5:
Administer the Posttest for Homophones. **See page R5.**

GRAMMAR, USAGE, MECHANICS

DAY 5:
Assess Statements and Questions. **See page R7.**

ORAL LANGUAGE

i don't sea Gila monsters
(_I_ don't _see_ Gila monsters._)_

Language Arts lessons

PORTFOLIO

Suggest that students add their drafts and revisions to their Literacy Portfolios.

⊘ Writing Assessment

This is a good example of exaggeration because it's funny to think of Fuzzy being so tangled up in his blankets.

Look again at this paragraph. Where do you think you could have used another type of sentence?

Adding this descriptive detail—Fuzzy's neon red shirt and tie—helps the reader get a clear picture of Fuzzy.

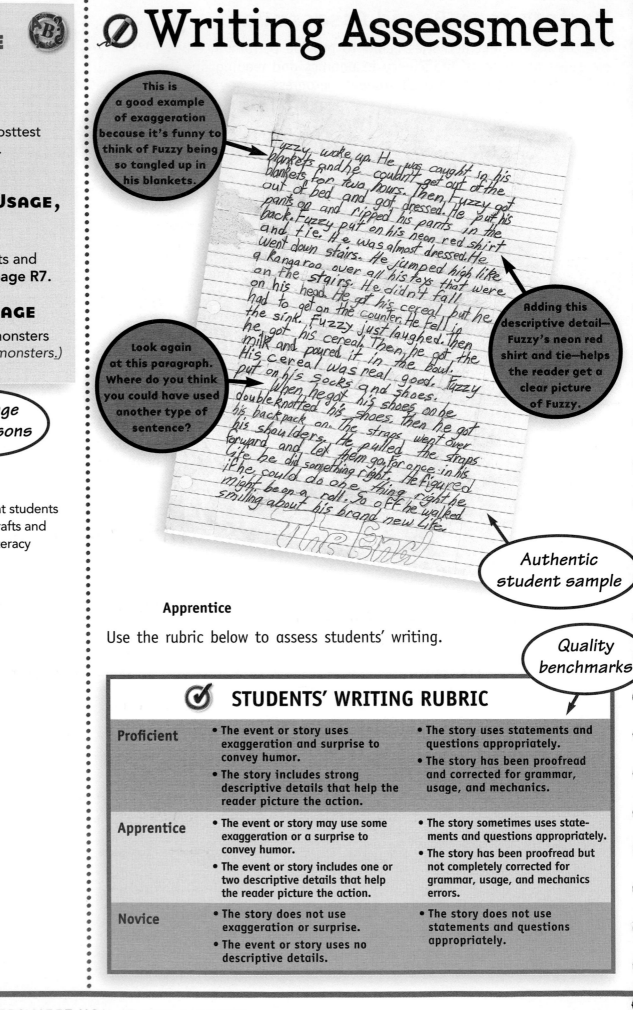

Authentic student sample

Quality benchmarks

Apprentice

Use the rubric below to assess students' writing.

☑ STUDENTS' WRITING RUBRIC

Proficient	• The event or story uses exaggeration and surprise to convey humor. • The story includes strong descriptive details that help the reader picture the action.	• The story uses statements and questions appropriately. • The story has been proofread and corrected for grammar, usage, and mechanics.
Apprentice	• The event or story may use some exaggeration or a surprise to convey humor. • The event or story includes one or two descriptive details that help the reader picture the action.	• The story sometimes uses statements and questions appropriately. • The story has been proofread but not completely corrected for grammar, usage, and mechanics errors.
Novice	• The story does not use exaggeration or surprise. • The event or story uses no descriptive details.	• The story does not use statements and questions appropriately.

Integrated Language Arts

EXPRESSIVE WRITING

Make a Poetry Book

MATERIALS:
Pencils, Paper,
Construction
Paper, Crayons

**SUGGESTED
GROUPING:**
Individuals

INTRODUCE the activity by discussing with students the two poems from *The Reptile Ball.* Point out the poet's use of rhyme, rhythm, and repetition to create a sense of movement and fun.

ASK students to write a humorous short poem of ten lines or less, describing a dance another type of animal might perform, such as a crow, a dog, or an elephant. Encourage them to use rhyme, rhythm, and repetition to enliven their poems. If they wish, they can illustrate their work.

ENCOURAGE students to share their work with classmates, perhaps reading their poems aloud.

INFORMATIVE WRITING

Nonfiction Article

MATERIALS:
Nonfiction
Science books
and articles

**SUGGESTED
GROUPING:**
Partners

INTRODUCE the activity by reminding students that the narrator of *Gila Monsters Meet You at the Airport* said that he knew that Gila monsters and horned toads live out West because he read it in a book. Point out that nonfiction books and articles give facts about subjects.

SUGGEST that students write a nonfiction article about Gila monsters, horned toads, or another unusual animal that interests them.

• •

Informative Writing

TEACH/MODEL Explain that a nonfiction article:

- contains only facts, not the writer's opinions.
- presents information in a logical order.
- uses illustrations to convey information.

PRACTICE/APPLY

> **Did I include enough information to describe the animal, where it lives, and what makes it interesting or unusual?**

> **What illustrations could I use to help readers get a picture of the animal?**

*Writing
mini-lesson*

Integrated Language Arts

SPEAKING/LISTENING

Create a Radio Show

MATERIALS:
Newspapers,
Magazines,
Pencils, Paper,
Tape recorder,
Audiocassette
tape

CHALLENGE students to create a short radio show called "Changes Happen to Everyone."

STUDENTS can read through newspapers, magazines, and their own poems for stories about changes that happen to lots of people—moving, a new job, a new school, a new sibling.

GUIDE students to choose their favorite stories to turn into a radio show. The focus should be on how change helps people to grow. Students can summarize each story in a few sentences, and have specific roles within the group dramatization. They may wish to add music or sound effects.

INVITE groups to present their dramas.

· · · · · · · · · · **TECHNOLOGY** · · · · · · · · · ·

Speaking Skills Invite students to record their radio shows on audiocassettes and present them to the class "on the air" instead of "live."

PERSUASIVE WRITING

Tell About a Trip

MATERIALS:
Pencils,
Crayons or
markers,
Paper

ENCOURAGE each student to speak for two or three minutes about a trip he or she has taken. It might be to another country, to another part of this country, or to a nearby place, such as the house of a relative or a theme park.

REMIND students to listen carefully as each story is told. Suggest that they ask questions to clarify whatever they don't understand.

ASK students to illustrate one of the stories that someone else told, after everyone has had a chance telling a story. They can work on their illustrations from memory, or, if necessary, they can continue to question the storytellers as they draw.

STUDENTS can label and briefly describe their artwork. Then, it can be placed on display for everyone to enjoy.

DAY 5 WRAP-UP

READ ALOUD *Spend five to ten minutes reading from a selection of your choice.*

GUIDED READING *Meet with the* **blue** *and* **green** *reading groups and assign Independent Center activities.* **See pages R2-R3.**

Ramona Forever

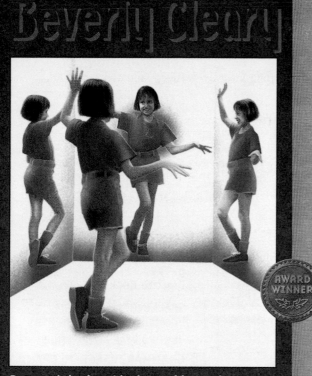

Ramona is back...with plenty of fun and surprises!

RAMONA FOREVER

Main Selection
Genre: Realistic Fiction
Award: Iowa Children's Choice Award

Paired Selection
Genre: Poem
Award-Winning Poet

Selection Summary

Ramona tries to visit her new baby sister at the hospital but the nurse won't let her. She's afraid Ramona may have a contagious disease. Ramona convinces herself that she is sick. When a doctor examines her, he diagnoses her condition as "siblingitis." Dad gives her a big hug and kiss, and Ramona's symptoms vanish. Finally, she meets her new sibling.

PAIRED SELECTION Just as Ramona exclaims at the end of the selection—"I'm wonderful me!"—this poem celebrates the singular importance of each human being.

Author

BEVERLY CLEARY
The character of Ramona was first introduced in Beverly Cleary's *Henry Huggins* series. Readers liked the character of Ramona so much they requested that she be featured in her own series of books. *Ramona the Pest* is the first in this series.

Weekly Organizer

Visit Our Web Site
www.scholastic.com

DAY 1

DAY 2

READ and Introduce Skills

- VOCABULARY
- PHONICS
- COMPREHENSION
- LITERARY ELEMENT

DAY 1

BUILD BACKGROUND, ▲ p. T61

✓ **VOCABULARY, ▲ ■** p. T62
Transparency 5
Practice Book 1, p. 21

✓ **DAILY PHONICS: ▲ ■**
Vowel /ī/ i, igh, y, i-e, ie, p. T64
Practice Book 1, p. 22

PREVIEW AND PREDICT, p. T66

READ: ▲ ☀ ■ ●
Ramona Forever, pp. T66-T71
GENRE: Realistic Fiction, p. T67

LITERARY ELEMENT:
Character, p. T69

DAY 2

READ: ▲ ☀ ■
Ramona Forever, pp. T72-T81

LITERARY ELEMENT: Suspense,
p. T73

COMPREHENSION:
Make Judgments, p. T77

DAILY PHONICS:
Vowel /ī/ i, igh, y, i-e, ie, p. T75

WRITE and Respond

- GRAMMAR
- USAGE
- MECHANICS
- SPELLING
- WRITING

DAY 1

WRITING WORKSHOP: Introduce,
p. T61

JOURNAL: Make Predictions, p. T66

✓ **SPELLING:**
Pretest: Words With Long i, p. R12
Spelling Resource Book, p. 14

✓ **GRAMMAR, USAGE, MECHANICS:**
Teach/Model: Commands and
Exclamations, p. R14

ORAL LANGUAGE, p. T71

DAY 2

WRITING WORKSHOP: Prewrite,
p. T79
Practice Book 1, p. 23

✓ **SPELLING:**
Vocabulary Practice, p. R12
Spelling Resource Book, pp. 15–17

✓ **GRAMMAR, USAGE, MECHANICS:**
Practice, p. R14

ORAL LANGUAGE, p. T79

EXTEND SKILLS and Apply to Literature

- INTEGRATED LANGUAGE ARTS
- LISTENING/SPEAKING/VIEWING
- INTEGRATED CURRICULUM
- GUIDED READING
- INDEPENDENT READING

DAY 1

READ ALOUD, p. T71

GUIDED READING, pp. R10–R11

TRADE BOOKS
- Hannah
- The Chalk Box Kid

DAY 2

READ ALOUD, p. T79

GUIDED READING, pp. R10–R11

INTEGRATED CURRICULUM:
Science, p. R16
Social Studies, p. R17
The Arts, p. R17
Math, p. R16

TRADE BOOKS
- Uncle Jed's Barbershop
- Muggie Maggie

TECHNOLOGY and REAL-WORLD SKILLS

DAY 1

SCHOLASTIC WEB SITE
Build Background, p. T71

WORKSHOP 1, pp. T99–T103

DAY 2

SMART PLACE CD–ROM
Comprehension Skills, p. T77

WORKSHOP 1, pp. T99–T103

DAY 3

READ: ▲ ■
"I Am," pp. T80–T81

✓ **LITERARY ELEMENT:** ▲ ■
Character, pp. T84–T85
Transparency 6
Practice Book 1, pp. 26–28

INTERVENTION, ● p. T86
Daily Phonics: Vowel /ī/
Literary Element: Character
Fluency: Reading Aloud

RESPOND: ▲ ■
Think About Reading, p. T82
Write An E-Mail Message, p. T83
Practice Book 1, p. 24

✓ **SPELLING:**
Write/Proofread, p. R13
Spelling Resource Book, p. 18

✓ **GRAMMAR, USAGE, MECHANICS:**
Practice, p. R15
Practice Book 1, p. 25

ORAL LANGUAGE, p. T83

RESPOND: Literature Circle, p. T83

READ ALOUD, p. T87

GUIDED READING, pp. R10–R11

OPTIONAL MATERIALS, ● p. T87
Phonics Chapter Book #9:
Kids Care about Sea Animals
Ramona Forever audiocassette

E-MAIL
Communication Through E-Mail,
p. T83

WORKSHOP 1, pp. T99–T103

DAY 4

LITERATURE CONNECTION:
Ramona Forever, T88

✓ **REVIEW VOCABULARY,** p. T90

DAILY PHONICS: ✳ ■
Vowel /ī/i, igh, y, i-e, ie, p. T91

WRITING WORKSHOP:
Realistic Description, p. T88
Writer's Craft: Vivid Verbs, p. T89
Transparency 7
Practice Book 1, p. 23

✓ **SPELLING:**
Study/Review, p. R13
Spelling Resource Book, p. 200

✓ **GRAMMAR, USAGE, MECHANICS:**
Apply, p. R15

ORAL LANGUAGE, p. T89

READ ALOUD, p. T93

GUIDED READING, pp. R10–R11

EXPAND VOCABULARY:
Invented Words, p. T90

STUDY SKILLS:
Getting Ready to Take a Test,
pp. T92–T93
Practice Book 1, p. 30

WORD PROCESSING
Writing Skills, p. T89

SMART PLACE CD-ROM
Teacher/Family Communication, T93

WORKSHOP 1, pp. T99–T103

DAY 5

READING ASSESSMENT
Selection Test, p. T94

MODIFYING ASSESSMENT, p. T94
ESL/ELD: Vocabulary
Extra Help: Comprehension

PERFORMANCE-BASED ASSESSMENT:
One Minute Fluency, p. T95
Conference, p. T95

✓ **DAILY PHONICS:** Dictation, p. T95

WRITING ASSESSMENT, p. T96
Student Model
Students' Writing Rubric

✓ **SPELLING:**
Posttest, p. R13
Spelling Resource Book, p. 202

✓ **GRAMMAR, USAGE, MECHANICS:**
Assess, p. R15

ORAL LANGUAGE, p. T96

READ ALOUD, p. T98

GUIDED READING, pp. R10–R11

INTEGRATED LANGUAGE ARTS:
Write a Persuasive Speech, p. T97
Describe Mixed Emotions, p. T97
Reenact Story Scenes, p. T98
Diagram the Story Settings, p. T98

WORD PROCESSING
Language Development, p. T97

WORKSHOP 1, pp. T99–T103

ASSESSMENT PLANNING

USE THIS CHART TO PLAN YOUR ASSESSMENT OF THE WEEKLY READING OBJECTIVES.

- **Informal Assessment** is ongoing and should be used before, during, and after reading.
- **Formal assessment** occurs at the end of the week on the selection test.
- Note that intervention activities occur throughout the lesson to support students who need extra help with skills.

YOU MAY CHOOSE AMONG THE FOLLOWING PAGES IN THE ASSESSMENT HANDBOOK.

- Informal Assessment
- Anecdotal Record
- Portfolio Checklist and Evaluation Forms
- Self-Assessment
- Second-Language Learners
- Using Technology to Assess
- Test Preparation

SKILLS AND STRATEGIES	Informal Assessment
LITERARY ELEMENT Character 🔍	**OBSERVATION p. T69** • Did students identify the character's feelings and actions? **QUICKCHECK p. T84** • Can students use what Ramona said, did, thought, or felt to identify her character traits? **CHECK PRACTICE BOOK 1, p. 26** **CONFERENCE p. T95**
GENRE Realistic Fiction	**OBSERVATION p. T67** • Did students identify realistic character traits and events that could really happen? **CONFERENCE p. T95**
DAILY PHONICS Vowel /ī/i, igh, y, i-e, ie	**OBSERVATION p. T75** • Did students identify sound-spellings of words with long *i*? **CHECK PRACTICE BOOK 1, pp. 22** **DICTATION p. T95**
VOCABULARY Selection Words contagious inflammation chickenpox ✓wheelchair ✓stethoscope ✓prescription	**OBSERVATION p. T74** • Did students use picture clues to figure out the meaning? **CHECK PRACTICE BOOK 1, p. 21**

Formal Assessment	**INTERVENTION** and Instructional Alternatives	Planning Note
SELECTION TEST • Questions 1–3 check students' mastery of the key strategy, character. **UNIT TEST**	If students need help with character, then go to: • **Instructional Alternatives, p. T85** • **Intervention, p. T86** • **Review, p. R48** • **Reteach, p. R54**	
SELECTION TEST • Questions 4–6 check students' understanding of the skill, realistic fiction.	If students need help with realistic fiction, then: • **Review the Skills and Strategies lesson on p. T67**	
SELECTION TEST • Questions 7–9 check students' ability to identify and blend words with vowel /ī/. **UNIT TEST**	If students need help identifying words with vowel /ī/, then go to: • **Intervention, p. T86** • **Review, p. R44** • **Reteach, p. R52**	
SELECTION TEST • Questions 10–12 check students' understanding of the selection vocabulary. **UNIT TEST**	If students need additional practice with the vocabulary words, then go to: • **Review Vocabulary, p. T90**	

Technology

The technology in this lesson helps teachers and students develop the skills they need for the 21st century. Look for integrated technology activities on every day of instruction.

DAY 1
Build Background

- Students look up babysitting tips in the Baby-sitters Club area at Scholastic's company web site.

www.scholastic.com

DAY 2
Comprehension Skills

- Students can use **Smart Place** PlaceMaker to compose Ramona's thought bubble about the new baby.

Oh boy! A new little thing to play with at our house. I wonder if this baby likes frogs?

Smart Place PlaceMaker CD-Rom

DAY 3
Communicating Through E-mail

- Students use E-mail to write Ramona's letter of advice to baby Roberta.

DAY 4
Teacher/Family Communication

- Design a card using **Smart Place** PlaceMaker reminding students and parents of an upcoming test.

A FRIENDLY REMINDER FROM SCHOOL

Smart Place PlaceMaker CD-Rom

DAY 5
Language Development

- Students create a table detailing the pros and cons of having a baby sister.

Build Background

Like Ramona, many youngsters have had to cope with a new brother or sister. They too have probably wondered where they'll fit in after the baby comes home. Ramona worries so much that she even gets sick—but luckily she's already in the hospital!

Activate Prior Knowledge

DISCUSS HOSPITALS

Have students share their prior knowledge about hospitals, doctors, nurses, and health care. Ask:

> Why do people go to the hospital?

> Who works in a hospital? How do they help people get better?

> Why should people be careful around newborn babies? How should they act?

 WRITING WORKSHOP *Realistic Description*

INTRODUCE Build background for writing a realistic description by having students write a brief paragraph about something they do every day. They might describe what they do when they get home from school. Tell them that they are writing a realistic description of an activity.

DAY 1 OBJECTIVES

STUDENTS WILL:

READ 45 MINUTES

- **Build Background**
- **Vocabulary**
- **Daily Phonics: Vowel /ī/ *i*, *igh*, *y*, *i-e*, *ie***
- ***Ramona Forever*, pp. 28–33**
- **Key Literary Element: Character**
- **Genre: Realistic Fiction**

WRITE 30 MINUTES

- **Writing Workshop: Introduce Writing a Realistic Description**
- **Quickwrite: Predict**
- **Spelling: Words With Long *i***
- **Grammar, Usage, Mechanics: Commands and Exclamations**
- **Oral Language**

EXTEND SKILLS 15 MINUTES

- **Read Aloud**
- **Guided Reading**

RESOURCES

- **Vocabulary Transparency 2**
- **Transparency 5**
- **Practice Book 1, pp. 21, 22**
- **Spelling Resource Book, p. 14**

ESL/ELD

▲ Lead a discussion about siblings. Ask: *Do you have any younger brothers or sisters? Can you remember when they were born? What about older brothers and sisters?* Children may bring in pictures of their siblings to make a Sisters and Brothers scrapbook. **(MAKE CONNECTIONS)**

Vocabulary

PHONICS AND SPELLING LINKS

Phonics See selection words with long *i* on page T64.

Spelling See selection words with long *i* on page R12.

Ⓐ TEACH WORD MEANINGS

INTRODUCE CONCEPT
Explain that *Ramona Forever* contains special words about hospitals, including words related to illness, and instruments, and equipment found in hospitals.

PRESENT VOCABULARY
Encourage students to discuss what each word means. Then write each word and its meaning on the chalkboard.

✔ = Tested	VOCABULARY WORDS
contagious	easily spread from one person to another (p. 31)
chickenpox	an illness that causes a fever and red itchy bumps (p. 32)
✔ **stethoscope**	an instrument used by doctors to listen to a person's heartbeat or breathing (p. 34)
inflammation	a swollen area of the body that is hot, red, and sore (p. 36)
✔ **wheelchair**	a chair on wheels that a sick or injured person uses (p. 37)
✔ **prescription**	a medical doctor's written order for medicine (p. 34)

Ⓑ BUILD ON PRIOR KNOWLEDGE

CATEGORIZE WORDS
Display the chart below. Have students use their prior knowledge and the vocabulary words to complete it.

Illness	Doctor	Hospital
cold	shots	ambulance
contagious	stethoscope	have a baby
chickenpox	prescription	emergency room
inflammation		wheelchair

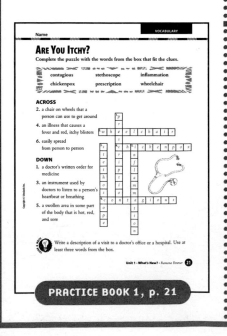

PRACTICE BOOK 1, p. 21

MODIFY Instruction

ESL/ELD

▲ Use picture cards or a picture dictionary to introduce the vocabulary and context for this story. Be sure students understand more basic vocabulary, such as *doctor*, *nurse*, and *illness*. Then have students scan to look for illustrations to describe. **(USE VISUALS)**

EXTRA HELP

■ Preview **Transparency 5** with students. Have a volunteer read each question. Discuss each category with students and have them suggest words for each question. **(USE VISUALS)**

C APPLY THROUGH MEANINGFUL SENTENCES

MODEL MEANINGFUL SENTENCES

Write or say the following. Have volunteers identify the context clues that help define the vocabulary word.

1. **Contagious** <u>diseases</u> can <u>spread</u> to other people.

2. Those <u>red, itchy bumps</u> must be **chickenpox.**

3. The doctor <u>listened</u> to his <u>chest</u> with a **stethoscope.**

4. A bee sting can cause a <u>red</u> and <u>sore</u> **inflammation.**

5. The <u>injured</u> skier <u>moved around</u> in a **wheelchair.**

6. A <u>doctor</u> wrote a **prescription** for my sore throat.

Sentences on Vocabulary Transparency 2

WORD MAP

Scholastic Literacy Place

- Why are people there?
  - they're sick
  - they're contagious
  - they have chickenpox
  - they have inflammation
- Whom do you see?
  - doctor
  - nurse
  - patient

HOSPITALS

- What do people do?
  - write prescriptions
  - take medicine
  - get better
- What equipment is used?
  - stethoscope
  - wheelchair

What's New? • *Ramona Forever* 5

WRITE MEANINGFUL SENTENCES

Students should write meaningful sentences about each word. Suggest that they ask themselves questions such as these as they write: **What is it? What does it do? Where is it found?**

USE TRANS-PARENCY 5

Have students complete the word map with vocabulary words that tell about a visit to a hospital.

SUPPORT WORDS

> **elevator** a machine that moves things between floors of a building (p.30)
> **excitement** great interest in something (p. 30)
> **unknown** not known or not familiar (p.40)*
> **blunderful** a made-up word from blunder (careless mistake) and wonderful (very good) (p.41)*
>
> ✱ Vocabulary instruction is presented where words appear in the selection.

PERSONAL WORD LIST

This excerpt from *Ramona Forever* contains many vivid verbs and precise adjectives that describe how Ramona felt and what she did. Have students record in their Journals descriptive verbs and interesting adjectives that they might like to use in future writing.

Strategy: Structural Analysis

Get Word Wise

▶**TEACH** Tell students that when they come to a new word, they can look for familiar word parts to help them figure it out. Write:

• *Ramona felt <u>excitement</u> as she stepped into the <u>elevator</u>.*

THINK ALOUD *When I see a word I don't know, I look for word parts that I recognize. In the first underlined word, I see* **ex** *as in* **extra.** *I also see* **ment** *as in* **basement.** *I can use phonics to figure out the part that's left,* **c-i-t-e.** *Because of final* **e,** *I know the syllable has a long* **i** *sound. Now I put all the parts together to pronounce the word—* **ex-cite-ment, excitement.**

APPLY Ask students to apply the same process to the second underlined word. When they have decoded it, remind them to put both words back into the sentence to see if they make sense.

HOW TO FIGURE OUT A NEW WORD

- Try to figure out the word from letter sounds.
- ▶ Look for word parts that you know.
- Try to use context clues to figure out meaning.
- Look up the word in a dictionary or ask someone.

SELECTION WORDS
With Vowel /ī/

climbed	cry
behind	time
nights	insides
excitement	

SKILLS TRACE

VOWEL /ī/ i, igh, y, i-e, ie

Introduce . . . . . .pp. T64–T65
Practice .pp. T75, T86, T91, T95
Review . . . . .p. R44
Reteach . . . . .p. R52

Vowel /ī/ i, igh, y, i-e, ie

A PHONOLOGICAL AWARENESS

RHYME Write the following rhyme on the chalkboard. Read the rhyme aloud and stress the words that contain the long *i* sound.

- Track the print as you read.

- Then isolate the words with the long *i* sound: *my, bike, kite, fine, time, ride, I'll, mile, high, pie, like.*

- Ask students to name other words that contain the same sound. Examples might include: *bite, bright, why, fly, tiny, kind, tied.*

> My bike, your kite. What a fine time!
>
> You ride, I'll ride, one at a time.
>
> Mile high pie for you and me.
>
> I like you. Do you like me?

B CONNECT SOUND-SPELLING

INTRODUCE VOWEL /ī/ i, igh, y, i-e, ie Explain to students that the long *i* sound can be spelled in many ways. For example, the letters *i, igh, y, i-e,* and *ie* can stand for /ī/ as in the words *climbed, high, by, like,* and *pie.* Write these words on the chalkboard. Have a student circle the letters that stand for the long *i* sound.

Words With Long i				
i	-igh	-y	i-e	-ie
climbed kind	sigh tight	by cry	like bike hike	pie tie lie

💭 **THINK ALOUD** *I can put the letters **h** and **igh** together to make the word **high**. Let's say the sounds slowly as I move my fingers under the letters. Listen to the sound that **igh** stands for in the word **high**.*

- Repeat with other spellings: *b* plus *y (by)*, *l* plus *ike (like)*, *p* plus *ie (pie)*. Help students add other words to the chart.

MODIFY Instruction

ESL/ELD

▲ To practice the /ī/ patterns, make matching picture and word cards for long *i* words such as *sky, fly, night, fight, mice, smile, pies, ties, child, climb.* Use the cards for Concentration and other matching, spelling, and vocabulary-building activities. **(USE PICTURE AND WORD CARDS)**

EXTRA HELP

■ Create word cards made up of words with long *i* spelled *i, igh,* or *y.* Examples might include: *mild, sigh, kind, mind, try, cry.* Distribute the cards to pairs of students. Have students take turns quizzing each other on the correct pronunciation of the words. **(WORK IN PAIRS)**

C PRACTICE/APPLY

READ WORDS To practice using the sound-spellings, list the following words and sentence on the chalkboard. Have students read each chorally. Model blending as needed.

white	bright	climbed
cry	tried	try

The room was white and bright.

DICTATION Dictate the following words for students to spell: *nine, bright, climb, night, cry, tried.* Have students write them and circle the letters that stand for the long *i* sound.

BUILD WORDS Distribute the following letter and word part cards, or have students make their own sets: *b, d, f, h, m, r, s, t, ine, ight, ie, ind.* Allow students time to build words using the cards. Students can write their words on paper. **(INDEPENDENT WORK)**

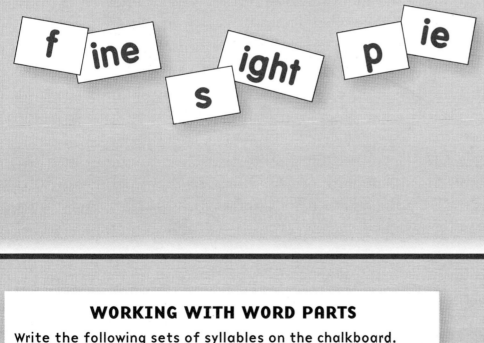

WORKING WITH WORD PARTS

Write the following sets of syllables on the chalkboard. Have students read each aloud. Point out the following:

- If a syllable ends with a vowel, the vowel usually has a long vowel sound. (open syllable)
- If a syllable ends with a consonant, the vowel usually has a short vowel sound. (closed syllable)

ov	mov	vo	li	lit	it
re	reb	eb	op	pop	po

Repeat this procedure throughout the week using these and other syllables.

PRACTICE BOOK 1, p. 22

PROFESSIONAL DEVELOPMENT

JOHN SHEFELBINE

The Nature of Systematic Instruction in Decoding Strategies

Systematic instruction in reading follows a scope and sequence for building, reviewing, and applying the content of phonological awareness, phonics, and structural analysis. Instruction (a) progresses from easier to more difficult tasks, (b) is direct and explicit, and (c) follows a predictable routine.

COMPREHENSION

▶ Preview and Predict

Read the title of the story and point out the author's name. Ask students if they have ever heard of Beverly Cleary or her character Ramona. Remind students that Ramona is a character in a popular series who gets involved in all kinds of adventures. Have students look at the pictures on the first few pages of *Ramona Forever*.

> **From what you've seen, who are the characters in the story?**

> **Where do you think the story takes place? How do you know?**

Direct students to read the first paragraph in italic type on page 29. Help them predict what might happen by asking:

> **How do you think Ramona's life will change because of the new baby in the family?**

JOURNAL

Make Predictions

Before reading further, have students record their predictions in their Journals. Students who have read other stories about Ramona may add or refine their impressions about her.

▶ Set a Purpose

Guide students to set a purpose for reading. They might read to see what happens to Ramona when a new baby joins the family and how she feels about being a "big sister." Then have students finish reading the page silently.

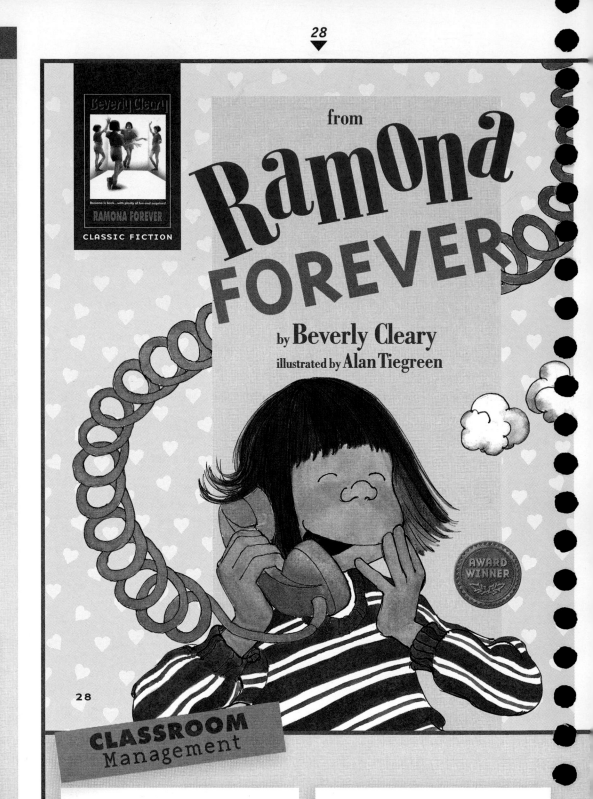

28

from
Ramona FOREVER

by **Beverly Cleary**
illustrated by **Alan Tiegreen**

Beverly Cleary
CLASSIC FICTION
RAMONA FOREVER

AWARD WINNER

28

CLASSROOM Management

WHOLE CLASS

ON-LEVEL Use the questions, Think Alouds, and Skills and Strategies lessons to guide students through the story.

BELOW-LEVEL Before students try to read the story, have them tell the story by "reading" the pictures.

COOPERATIVE

ABOVE-LEVEL You might choose to have above-level students read the story independently or with a partner and write captions for the illustrations.

29 ▼

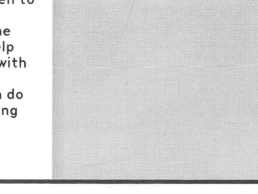

It's an exciting time for the Quimby family! Ramona's mother has just had a beautiful baby girl. Visiting her mother and baby Roberta at the hospital will be a real thrill, but Ramona is also worried. A baby around the house could change everything.

The day was long and lonely. Even a swimming lesson at the park and a trip to the library did little to make time pass. "I wonder what Roberta looks like?" said Beezus.

"And whose room she will share when she outgrows the bassinette?" worried Ramona.

29

SMALL GROUP TO WHOLE CLASS

ESL/ELD Have children listen to the story on the audiocassette prior to the class reading. This will help them to become familiar with the story sequence and vocabulary. Have children do the pre- and post-listening activities. **(AUDIO CLUES)**

SKILLS AND STRATEGIES

Revisit the selection for skills instruction.

✓ = Tested Skill

✓**GENRE**
Realistic Fiction   p. T67

✓**LITERARY ELEMENT**
Character   p. T69

✓**DAILY PHONICS**
Vowel /ī/ i, igh, y, i-e, ie   p. T75

GENRE
✓ Realistic Fiction

TEACH/MODEL
Discuss with students the key elements of realistic fiction.

> **The events in the story could really happen.**

> **The characters speak and act like real people. The setting may remind you of places you have seen in your daily life.**

PRACTICE/APPLY
Ask students to reread the first page of the story and to point out characters or events that remind them of people or experiences in their own lives.

✓ INFORMAL ASSESSMENT
OBSERVATION

Did students:

✓identify realistic character traits and events that could really happen?

◎ **IF** students need additional support,

THEN have them look for the elements of realistic fiction as they read the story.

COMPREHENSION

1 CHARACTER

> Beezus is Ramona's older sister. What do you learn about both characters from the questions each one asks about the baby? *(Possible answer: Beezus seems excited and wants time to pass quickly so that she can see what the baby looks like. Ramona seems worried that she might have to share her room with the new baby.)*

2 SUMMARIZE

> What do family members do while Mrs. Quimby is in the hospital? *(Beezus and Ramona vacuum and dust the house. When Mr. Quimby comes home, he takes the girls out for hamburgers and a visit to the hospital.)*

3 CAUSE/EFFECT

> Why does Ramona have to wait for her family in the lobby when they go to the hospital? *(Children under twelve are not allowed to visit the maternity ward because they might have contagious diseases.)*

INTERVENTION TIP

Understanding Relationships

Students who have not read any other Ramona stories may not know that Beezus is Ramona's older sister. Help students who seem unclear about characters and plot events before they read further.

①

The one happy moment in the day for the girls was a telephone call from their mother, who reported that Roberta was a beautiful, healthy little sister. She couldn't wait to bring her home, and she was proud of her daughters for being so good about staying alone. This pleased Beezus and Ramona so much they ran the vacuum cleaner and dusted, which made time pass faster until their father, looking exhausted, came home to take them out for hamburgers and a visit to the fifth Quimby.

② Ramona could feel her heart pounding as she finally climbed the steps to the hospital. Visitors, some carrying flowers and the others looking careworn, walked toward the elevators. Nurses hurried, a doctor was paged over the loudspeaker. Ramona could scarcely bear her own excitement. The rising of the elevator made her stomach feel as if it had stayed behind on the first floor. When the elevator stopped, Mr. Quimby led the way down the hall.

"Excuse me," called a nurse. Surprised, the family stopped and turned.

30

MODIFY Instruction

ESL/ELD

▲ To help students answer question 2, have volunteers take parts and role-play the hospital scene. Provide narration and encourage actors to make up dialogue. **(ROLE-PLAY)**

EXTRA HELP

■ Help students make connections by focusing on what the hospital nurse said to Ramona. Discuss with students what it means to be "coming down with something." Students might want to give examples of when they came down with something, such as a cold or the flu. **(MAKE CONNECTIONS)**

31
▼

3 "Children under twelve are not allowed to visit the maternity ward," said the nurse. "Little girl, you will have to go down and wait in the lobby."

"Why is that?" asked Mr. Quimby.

"Children under twelve might have <u>contagious</u> diseases," explained the nurse. "We have to protect the babies."

"I'm sorry, Ramona," said Mr. Quimby. "I didn't know. I am afraid you will have to do as the nurse says."

"Does she mean I'm *germy*?" Ramona was humiliated. "I took a shower this morning and washed my hands at the Whopperburger so I would be extra clean."

"Sometimes children are coming down with something and don't know it," explained Mr. Quimby. "Now, be a big girl and go downstairs and wait for us."

Ramona's eyes filled with tears of disappointment, but she found some pleasure in riding in the elevator alone. By the time she reached the lobby, she felt worse. The nurse called her a little girl. Her father called her a big girl. What was she? A germy girl.

ORAL LANGUAGE

Remind students that Ramona lost her position as the youngest child in the family. Have students poll friends about their position in the family. Are they an only child, the oldest, the youngest, or in the middle? Have volunteers share their poll results orally with the class.

CULTURAL CONNECTION

Babies are welcomed in special ways. The Baka people of Cameroon, West Africa, take a baby into the rain forest and sprinkle it with water from the bark of a tree. The water is medicinal and sacred. Ask students to share traditions they know.

LITERARY ELEMENT

✓ **Character** 🔑

TEACH/MODEL
Explain that readers can learn about characters in a story from feelings, actions, and appearance. Dialogue also shows what characters are like.

> **Think if you have ever had experiences similar to Ramona's.**

> **Notice what she says to characters in the story.**

> **Notice what Ramona does. This, too, will help you understand what she is like.**

PRACTICE/APPLY

- Let students know that what characters say and do shows what they are like. For example, if a character is always smiling, he or she is probably friendly.

- Have students make a chart. Have them write the quality that Ramona's words and actions show.

Words	Actions	What She Is Like
"Does she mean I'm germy?"	tears	*sensitive*
	rides elevator alone	*independent*

✓ **INFORMAL ASSESSMENT**
OBSERVATION

Did students:

✓ identify the character's feelings and actions?

✓ use dialogue to help them understand the characters?

See pages T84–T85 for a full skills lesson on Character.

COMPREHENSION

4 MAKE INFERENCES

> While waiting in the lobby, Ramona gets all itchy and hot. Why do you think the woman next to her moves to another couch? *(Possible answer: The woman may think that Ramona has a contagious disease because she is scratching so much. She moves because she doesn't want to catch the disease.)*

5 CHARACTER

> Why do you think Ramona is really getting more and more itchy? What does this tell you about Ramona? *(Possible answer: The nurse said that Ramona may be "germy" so she is imagining that she is sick. She feels hurt and angry because she is being left out.)*

SELF-MONITORING STRATEGY

Self-Question

THINK ALOUD *Sometimes when I'm reading and get confused, I ask myself why the character is doing something. Then I think about how the character feels. If I'm not sure about those things, I can go back to the story and reread the part that's confusing me.*

> Where might self-questioning and rereading help you better understand the story?

OPTION You may end the first day's reading here or have students continue reading the entire selection.

Ramona sat gingerly on the edge of a Naugahyde couch. If she leaned back, she might get germs on it, or it might get germs on her. She swallowed hard. Was her throat a little bit sore? She thought maybe it was, way down in back. She put her hand to her forehead the way her mother did when she thought Ramona might have a fever. Her forehead was warm, maybe too warm.

As Ramona waited, she began to itch the way she itched when she had <u>chickenpox.</u> Her head itched, her back itched, her legs itched. Ramona scratched. A woman sat down on the couch, looked at Ramona, got up, and moved to another couch.

4

32

MODIFY Instruction

ESL/ELD

▲ Ask students to think about how Ramona is feeling. Ask how they can tell. Ask students to choose words and phrases from the story that support their answers. **(KEY WORDS)**

GIFTED & TALENTED

✳ Have students work with a partner to role-play a conversation between Ramona and the woman who was sitting beside her on the couch. Ask students to write their conversation in dialogue form. **(ROLE-PLAY)**

33

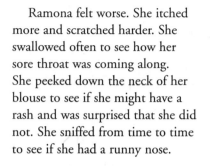

Ramona felt worse. She itched more and scratched harder. She swallowed often to see how her sore throat was coming along. She peeked down the neck of her blouse to see if she might have a rash and was surprised that she did not. She sniffed from time to time to see if she had a runny nose.

5 Now Ramona was angry. It would serve everybody right if she came down with some horrible disease, right there in their old hospital. That would show everybody how germ free the place was. Ramona squirmed and gave that hard-to-reach place between her shoulder blades a good hard scratch. Then she scratched her head with both hands. People stopped to stare.

33

CONNECTING TO THEME

What's New? Let students know that new babies are just one kind of "new face" that might enter their lives. Have students discuss their feelings when they first meet new students in their class, new neighbors, new teachers.

TECHNOLOGY

Build Background Visit the Babysitter's club Website at **www.scholastic.com** and go to Fun With the Baby-sitter area to find babysitting tips. Share the tips with students and have them add a few more. Discuss what it is like to care for small children.

Quickwrite

REVISIT PREDICTION
Students may revise predictions they made before reading and predict what will happen when Ramona finally gets to meet her new baby sister.

DAILY LANGUAGE PRACTICE

SPELLING
DAY 1:

Administer the Pretest for Words With Long *i*. **See page R12.**

GRAMMAR, USAGE, MECHANICS
DAY 1:

Teach and Model Commands and Exclamations. **See page R14.**

ORAL LANGUAGE

please don't turn the lite off
(*Please don't turn the <u>light</u> off!*)

DAY **1** WRAP-UP

READ ALOUD *To develop students' oral vocabularies and listening skills, spend five to ten minutes reading from a selection of your choice.*

GUIDED READING *Meet with the green and red reading groups and assign Independent Center activities. **See pages R10–R11.***

COMPREHENSION

DAY 2 OBJECTIVES

STUDENTS WILL:

READ 30 MINUTES

- *Ramona Forever* pp. 34–41
- Daily Phonics: Vowel /ī/ *i, igh, y, i-e, ie*

WRITE 35 MINUTES

- Writing Workshop: Prewrite
- Spelling: Words With Long *i*
- Grammar, Usage, Mechanics: Commands and Exclamations
- Oral Language

EXTEND SKILLS 25 MINUTES

- Integrated Curriculum
- Read Aloud
- Guided Reading

RESOURCES

- Practice Book 1, p. 23
- Spelling Resource Book, pp. 15–17

▶ Reread

You may wish to have students independently reread the first part of the story before beginning Day 2 reading.

6 **SUMMARIZE**

>**What has happened to Ramona so far?** *(Ramona visits her mother and baby sister in the hospital, but she is told to wait in the lobby. She feels itchy and imagines that she has a disease.)*

7 **CHARACTER**

>**What do you learn about Ramona while the doctor is examining her? Why do you think she says she feels much better?** *(Possible answer: Ramona may be getting a little worried that there really is something wrong.)*

6

A man in a white coat, with a stethoscope hanging out of his pocket, came hurrying through the lobby, glanced at Ramona, stopped, and took a good look at her. "How do you feel?" he asked.

"Awful," she admitted. "A nurse said I was too germy to go see my mother and new sister, but I think I caught some disease right here."

"I see," said the doctor. "Open your mouth and say 'ah'." Ramona *ahhed* until she gagged.

"Mh-hm," murmured the doctor. He looked so serious Ramona was alarmed. Then he pulled out his stethoscope and listened to her front and back, thumping as he did so. What was he hearing? Was there something wrong with her insides? Why didn't her father come?

The doctor nodded as if his worst suspicions had been confirmed. "Just as I thought," he said, pulling out his prescription pad.

Medicine, ugh. Ramona's twitching stopped. Her nose and throat felt fine. "I feel much better," she assured the doctor as she eyed that prescription pad with distrust.

7

34

MODIFY
Instruction

ESL/ELD

▲Help students summarize what has happened in the story so far by providing them with prompts and/or cloze sentences. For example, Ramona goes to the hospital to visit her ___. **(CLOZE)**

GIFTED & TALENTED

✳Suggest students write a letter from Beezus to a friend describing her reaction to the new baby. Encourage them to create suspense by including details that make it seem as though they are about to share an important secret. **(INNOVATE)**

35

"An acute case of siblingitis. Not at all unusual around here, but it shouldn't last long." He tore off the prescription he had written, instructed Ramona to give it to her father, and hurried on down the hall.

Ramona could not remember the name of her illness. She tried to read the doctor's scribbly cursive writing, but she could not. She could only read neat cursive, the sort her teacher wrote on the blackboard.

Itching again, she was still staring at the slip of paper when Mr. Quimby and Beezus stepped out of the elevator. "Roberta is so tiny." Beezus was radiant with joy. "And she is perfectly darling. She has a little round nose and—oh, when you see her, you'll love her."

"I'm sick." Ramona tried to sound pitiful. "I've got something awful. A doctor said so."

Beezus paid no attention. "And Roberta has brown hair—"

Mr. Quimby interrupted. "What's this all about, Ramona?"

"A doctor said I had something, some kind of *itis*, and I have to have this right away." She handed her father the prescription and scratched one shoulder. "If I don't, I might get sicker."

35

LITERARY ELEMENT
Suspense

TEACH/MODEL
Ask students to describe the way they feel while waiting to see how a particular story scene will turn out. Explain that they feel anxious or excited because the author has created suspense.

> When I am reading a story, I sometimes get tense waiting to see how things will turn out for a character.

> I feel tension because the author has created suspense in the story. Sometimes an author creates suspense by holding back information until the last possible minute.

PRACTICE/APPLY
Ask students to think about the scene in which the doctor is slowly examining Ramona.

> How do you feel when you wait to see a doctor? What do you think Ramona is feeling as she waits to hear what the doctor will say?

> How does Beverly Cleary create suspense in this scene of the story?

ORAL LANGUAGE
Have students take the parts of the doctor, Ramona, Mr. Quimby, Beezus, and a narrator. Have students give a dramatic reading of pages 34 and 35. When they are ready, they can tape-record the reading for the class.

SCIENCE
Have students work on the activity on **page R16** to complete **A Growing List of Skills** chart that will show the ages at which children learn or master skills.

COMPREHENSION

8 DRAW CONCLUSIONS

> Mr. Quimby says that *itis* means "inflammation." Ramona knows *sibling* means "brother or sister." What could *siblingitis* mean? *(Possible answer: It might mean feeling upset at not being able to see your new sister or brother, or being upset at all the attention a new sibling is getting.)*

9 CRITICAL THINKING: ANALYZE

> Why does the doctor prescribe attention to cure Ramona's disease? *(Possible answer: The doctor thought that extra attention would remind Ramona that she was loved and cared for by her family.)*

10 COMPARE/CONTRAST

> Compare Ramona's and Beezus's reactions to seeing their mother in a wheelchair. What do their reactions let you know about their characters? *(Possible answer: Ramona seems a little anxious and concerned when she sees her mother in the wheelchair. Beezus acts like the "older sister" when she reassures Ramona that their mother is all right.)*

✓ **INFORMAL ASSESSMENT**
OBSERVATION

Vocabulary Assess students' recognition and understanding of the word *wheelchair* as they read the selection.

Did students:

✓ use picture clues to figure out the meaning?

✓ pronounce the word correctly?

Mr. Quimby read the scribbly cursive, and then he did a strange thing. He lifted Ramona and gave her a big hug and a kiss, right there in the lobby. The itching stopped. Ramona felt much better. "You have acute siblingitis," explained her father. "*Itis* means inflammation." **8**

Ramona already knew the meaning of sibling. Since her father had studied to be a teacher, brothers and sisters had become siblings to him.

"He understood you were worried and angry because you weren't allowed to see your new sibling, and prescribed attention," explained Mr. Quimby. "Now let's all go buy ice-cream cones before I fall asleep standing up." **9**

Beezus said Roberta was too darling to be called a dumb word like sibling. Ramona felt silly, but she also felt better.

For the next three nights, Ramona took a book to the hospital and sat in the lobby, not reading, but sulking about the injustice of having to wait to see the strange new Roberta.

36

MODIFY Instruction

ESL/ELD

▲ Ramona's feelings go through many changes. Write these words on the chalkboard for students to pantomime: *angry, excited, disappointed, itchy, worried*. Have them take turns choosing a word and pantomiming it. The rest of the group will guess which word is being acted out. **(PANTOMIME)**

EXTRA HELP

■ Help students follow the flow of the dialogue in the story. Have them find some dialogue in the text and read it as if the character were speaking. Guide them to pay attention to punctuation and context clues as clues to how the character might speak. **(READ ALOUD)**

37
▼

On the fourth day, Mr. Quimby took an hour off from the Shop-rite Market, picked up Beezus and Ramona, who were waiting in clean clothes, and drove to the hospital to bring home his wife and new daughter.

Ramona moved closer to Beezus when she saw her mother, holding a pink bundle, emerge from the elevator in a <u>wheelchair</u> pushed by a nurse and followed by Mr. Quimby carrying her bag. "Can't Mother walk?" she whispered.

10

"Of course she can walk," answered Beezus. "The hospital wants to make sure people get out without falling down and suing for a million dollars."

Mrs. Quimby waved to the girls. Roberta's face was hidden by a corner of a pink blanket, but the nurse had no time for a little girl eager to see a new baby. She pushed the wheelchair through the automatic door to the waiting car.

"*Now* can I see her?" begged Ramona when her mother and Roberta were settled in the front, and the girls had climbed into the back seat.

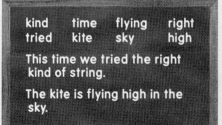

37

SOCIAL STUDIES

Ask students to do the **Old Enough** activity on **page R17** where they will discuss specific rights at certain ages.

FAMILY LITERACY RESOURCES

Recommend that families use the tips and strategies from the Family Guide to Literacy in the Home in the Literacy-At-Home Kit to improve their children's reading performance.

DAILY PHONICS

✓**Vowel /ī/ *i, igh, y, i-e, ie***

CONNECT SOUND-SPELLING

TEACH/MODEL Remind students that vowel /ī/ can have many different spellings, including *i, igh, y, i-e,* and *ie*.

• Write the story words *fine, might, tiny,* and *why* on the chalkboard.

• Pronounce each word and point out the spelling of /ī/.

• Have students underline the letters that stand for the vowel /ī/.

PRACTICE/APPLY

READ WORDS List the following words and sentences on the chalkboard. Have students read each chorally. Model blending as needed.

kind	time	flying	right
tried	kite	sky	high

This time we tried the right kind of string.

The kite is flying high in the sky.

DICTATION Dictate the following words for students to spell: *crying, tie, timeless, tighter*.

✓ **INFORMAL ASSESSMENT**
OBSERVATION

Did students:

✓identify words with /ī/

✓connect /ī/ with the letters that stand for it?

IF students need more support with vowel /ī/, **THEN** see page T91.

COMPREHENSION

11 CHARACTER

> Mrs. Quimby tells Ramona how much she's missed her. Why does Ramona think these are the most beautiful words she's ever heard? What does this tell you about Ramona? *(Possible answer: Ramona has missed her mother while she was in the hospital, and she's glad to hear that her mother missed her. She's happy to know that she is still an important member of the family.)*

12 CRITICAL THINKING: EVALUATE

> How does the new baby look to Ramona? Have you ever seen a newborn baby? What do you think about Ramona's opinion? *(She's red-faced, cross-eyed, and has wild hair. Students who have seen newborn babies may agree with Ramona's opinion. Some may feel that she was expressing her opinions honestly.)*

13 CHARACTER

> Mrs. Quimby says that Ramona looked like that when she was a baby. How do you think this makes Ramona feel? How have her feelings about the baby changed since the beginning of the story? *(Possible answer: It makes her feel closer to the baby. She begins to notice how the baby really looks—"She's so little . . . her eyes are crossed.")*

"Dear Heart, of course you may." Mrs. Quimby then spoke the most beautiful words Ramona had ever heard, "Oh, Ramona, how I've missed you," as she turned back the blanket.

Ramona, leaning over the front seat for her first glimpse of the new baby sister, tried to hold her breath so she wouldn't breathe germs on Roberta, who did not look at all like the picture on the cover of *A Name for Your Baby*. Her face was bright pink, almost red, and her hair,

38

MODIFY Instruction

ESL/ELD

▲ Ask students to look at the bubble on page 34. Explain that this shows what Ramona imagined her baby sister would look like. Then have volunteers reread aloud the description of how baby Roberta really looks. Help students fill in a chart comparing the imaginary baby to the real one. **(COMPARE AND CONTRAST)**

GIFTED & TALENTED

✳ Have students brainstorm a list of character traits. Then have them write a short paragraph about a character who displays one or two of those traits. The character can be someone they know or it can be an imaginary character. **(INNOVATE)**

39
▼

unlike the smooth pale hair of the baby on the cover of the pamphlet, was dark and wild. Ramona did not know what to say. She did not feel that words like darling or adorable fitted this baby.

"She looks exactly like you looked when you were born," Mrs. Quimby told Ramona.

"She does?" Ramona found this hard to believe. She could not imagine that she had once looked like this red, frowning little creature.

"Well, what do you think of your new sister?" asked Mr. Quimby.

"She's so—so *little*," Ramona answered truthfully. Roberta opened her blue gray eyes.

"Mother!" cried Ramona. "She's cross-eyed."

Mrs. Quimby laughed. "All babies look cross-eyed sometimes. They outgrow it when they learn to focus." Sure enough, Roberta's eyes straightened out for a moment and then crossed again. She worked her mouth as if she didn't know what to do with it. She made little snuffling noises and lifted one arm as if she didn't know what it was for.

"Why does her nightie have those little pockets at the ends of the sleeves?" asked Ramona. "They cover up her hands."

"They keep her from scratching herself," explained Mrs. Quimby. "She's too little to understand that fingernails scratch."

12

13

39

THE ARTS

Ask students to do the **Life Collage** activity on **page R17** where they will make collages showing their favorite activities or major events in their lives.

TECHNOLOGY

 Comprehension Skills Use **Smart Place**, Place Maker to draw a picture of Ramona and a bubble showing her thoughts. Think about Ramona's descriptions of how Roberta will look and act. Put the ideas into the bubble. Students might create a thought poster for Beezus, too.

COMPREHENSION
Make Judgments

TEACH/MODEL
Help students see that just as they have different feelings and opinions about the people they know and the actions those people take, they make judgments about characters and events in stories.

> Sometimes I agree with a character's actions and decisions in a story, and sometimes I don't.

> Often I ask myself, "What would I do if I were in the character's place?"

PRACTICE/APPLY
Ask students:

> What do you like most and least about Ramona? Why?

> If you were Ramona, would you have said Baby Roberta was adorable, or would you have told the truth, as she did? Explain.

COMPREHENSION

14 CHARACTER

> **Why does Ramona suddenly feel love and sympathy for the baby? How is her attitude changing?** *(Possible answer: Ramona thinks about all the changes babies go through as they grow. She thinks about ways she has changed and grown.)*

15 CRITICAL THINKING: APPLY

> **Mr. Quimby says growing up is hard, too. Ramona thinks about all the things that were hard for her. What do you think is hard about growing up?** *(Students may mention doing chores, homework.)*

16 SUMMARIZE

> **What are some things Ramona has learned since her sister was born?** *(Possible answer: She has learned about hospital rules, newborn babies, and people caring about her feelings.)*

SELF-MONITORING STRATEGY

Structural Analysis

 THINK ALOUD *I don't know u-n-e-x-p-e-c-t-e-d, so I look at the word parts to figure it out. It begins with the prefix un- which usually means "not." I know that expect means "to plan for," so unexpected probably means "not planned for."*

> **How can you figure out the word u-n-k-n-o-w-n?**

JOURNAL

Revisit Predictions

Ask students to look back at their predictions and record whether they were confirmed.

Ramona sat back and buckled her seat belt. She had once looked like Roberta. Amazing! She had once been that tiny, but she had grown, her hair had calmed down when she remembered to comb it, and she had learned to use her eyes and hands. "You know what I think?" she asked and did not wait for an answer. "I think it is hard work to be a baby." Ramona spoke as if she had discovered something unknown to the rest of the world.

14 With her words came unexpected love and sympathy for the tiny person in her mother's arms.

"I hadn't thought of it that way," said Mrs. Quimby, "but I think you're right."

"Growing up is hard work," said Mr. Quimby as

15 he drove away from the hospital. "Sometimes being grown-up is hard work."

"I know," said Ramona and thought some more. She thought about loose teeth, real sore throats, quarrels, misunderstandings with her teachers, longing for a bicycle her family could not afford, worrying when her parents bickered, how terrible she had felt when she hurt Beezus's feelings without meaning to, and all the long afternoons when Mrs. Kemp looked after her until her mother came from work. She had survived it all. "Isn't it funny?" she remarked as her father steered the car into their driveway.

"Isn't what funny?" asked her mother.

40

MODIFY Instruction

ESL/ELD

▲ Help students summarize the story by discussing all the different ways Ramona has felt toward the baby. List the words *confused, angry, worried* and *happy.* Ask students to tell why Ramona had each of those feelings. Have them point to a passage that supports their answer **(RETELL)**

EXTRA HELP

■ Brainstorm with students what Ramona used to be like and what she's like at the end of the story. Have each student write a "Ramona used to be . . . but now she is . . ." sentence to show how Ramona has changed and grown up. **(KEY STRATEGY)**

41

"That I used to be little and funny-looking and cross-eyed like Roberta," said Ramona. "And now look at me. I'm wonderful me!"

"Except when you're blunderful you," said Beezus.

Ramona did not mind when her family, except Roberta, who was too little, laughed. "Yup, wonderful, blunderful me," she said and was happy. She was winning at growing up.

16

41

MATH

Ask students to complete the **Graph Growth** activity on **page R16.** Students will graph average heights of young children.

WORD STUDY

Point out that the Bonanza word *blunderful* on p. 41 is a word Beezus invented from two other words. Ask students what those two words might be. *(blunder* and *wonderful)* Students may enjoy making up their own combination words.

Realistic Description
WRITING WORKSHOP

PREWRITE Using *Ramona Forever* as a model, discuss realistic details such as Ramona sitting back and buckling her seatbelt in the car. Tell students that they will be developing and writing a realistic description of a character doing an activity in which they might include such details. Have them begin to develop their description on the prewriting organizer.

Use Practice Book 1, page 23.

DAILY LANGUAGE PRACTICE

SPELLING
DAY 2:
Practice Words With Long i. See page R12.

GRAMMAR, USAGE, MECHANICS
DAY 2:
Practice Commands and Exclamations. See page R14.

ORAL LANGUAGE
Wow. I can't believe that candy costs only a diem? *(Wow! I can't believe that candy costs only a dime.)*

DAY **2** WRAP-UP

READ ALOUD *Spend five to ten minutes reading from a selection of your choice.*

GUIDED READING *Meet with the **red** and **blue** reading groups and assign Independent Center activities. **See pages R10–R11.***

COMPREHENSION

DAY 3 OBJECTIVES

STUDENTS WILL:

READ 35 MINUTES
- "I Am," pp. 42–43
- Assess Comprehension
- Key Literary Element: Character
- Daily Phonics: Vowel /ī/ i, igh, y, i-e, ie

WRITE 35 MINUTES
- Respond: Description
- Spelling: Words With Long i
- Grammar, Usage, Mechanics: Commands and Exclamations
- Oral Language

EXTEND SKILLS 20 MINUTES
- Read Aloud
- Guided Reading

RESOURCES
- Transparency 6
- Practice Book 1, pp. 24–28
- Spelling Resource Book, p. 18

▶ ## Preview

Invite students to preview and predict by reading the title and studying the photographs. Then have students read the poem.

1 DRAW CONCLUSIONS
> What feeling is the poet expressing in the poem? *(joy, feeling good about yourself)*

2 COMPARE/CONTRAST
> Ramona expresses a similar feeling at the end of the story. What words does she use? *("I'm wonderful me.")*

POETRY COLLECTION

from *It's Raining Laughter*
by Nikki Grimes
photographs by
Myles C. Pinkney

AWARD WINNER

I Am
I laugh
shout
sing
smile
whisper
hum
howl
gurgle
giggle
sigh.

I am joy.

❶ ❷

42

MODIFY Instruction

ESL/ELD

▲ Pairs of students can create dramatized readings. One student reads the poem, the other makes the appropriate sounds/actions for each line. Help students write their own versions, changing some or all of the verbs, and perform again. **(WORK IN PAIRS)**

EXTRA HELP

■ Help students make connections between the poem and the photographs. Discuss various details in the photographs that illustrate the specific words in the poem. Ask students which photographs they think best express the joyous mood of the poem. **(MAKE CONNECTIONS)**

43
▼

43

ORAL LANGUAGE

Have students take turns giving a reading of the poem "I Am." Encourage them to vary the tone of their voices to express the meaning of the words. For example, the word *whisper* might be read in a hushed tone. After students have practiced, they can tape-record their readings.

WORD STUDY

Ask students to think of another emotion, such as excitement or love. Students can create a similar poem or a semantic map showing what goes with that feeling.

```
family          friends
        ╲    ╱
       (love)
        ╱    ╲
hugs            kisses
```

AUTHOR'S CRAFT
Word Choice

TEACH/MODEL
Explain to students that because many poems are brief, poets have to choose just the right words.

> Poets often choose words that suggest a strong feeling or mood. For example, *gray sky* might suggest *sadness*, while *blooming roses* might suggest happiness.

> Poets also choose words that create a certain kind of sound. For example, including many words that have the same beginning sound, such as *The big, black dog barked,* creates a pleasing sound.

THINK ALOUD *When I read the poem "I Am," each word makes me think of a different emotion. For example, the word* shout *makes me think about raising my voice and calling out happy sounds.*

PRACTICE/APPLY
Reread the poem to the class.

> Which words did the author choose to create the same beginning sounds? *(sing, smile, sigh; hum, howl; gurgle, giggle)*

> Which words express feelings of joy? Why?

COMPREHENSION

▶ ## Think About Reading

Below are the **answers** to the story map *Think About Reading* questions.

1. *The story takes place in Ramona's house and in the hospital.*

2. *Some students may suggest that the main characters are Ramona, Ramona's father, and the doctor. Other students may include Beezus and the girls' mother.*

3. *The hospital rules said that children under twelve were not allowed to visit.*

4. *Ramona imagined that she was getting sick. She itched and scratched.*

5. *The doctor understood that Ramona felt worried, angry, and left out. He let Mr. Quimby know by writing "siblingitis" on the prescription and prescribing attention.*

6. *Ramona got over feeling worried and left out. She let her feelings of love and sympathy come through.*

7. *Ramona saw that she had grown up a lot. She felt wonderful.*

RESPOND

Think About Reading

Answer the questions in the story map.

Setting
1. Where does the story take place?

Characters
2. Who are the main characters in the story?

Problem
3. Why couldn't Ramona see her new baby sister in the hospital?

Events

4. What did Ramona do as she sat in the waiting room?

5. How did the doctor help her?

Ending
6. How did Ramona's feelings about baby Roberta change at the end of the story?

7. What did Ramona think about herself at the end of the story?

44

MODIFY Instruction

ESL/ELD

▲ Go over the comprehension questions with English language learners to make sure they understand each one. Then allow time for students to listen to the audio recording of the story. Go over the questions and answers in a small group. Rephrase questions and clarify story events as needed. **(AUDIO CLUES)**

EXTRA HELP

■ Some students may have difficulty using a character's words and actions to identify personality traits. Before completing the graphic organizer on Practice Book page 24, have students list what Beezus says and does in the story. Discuss what each item suggests about Beezus' character. **(KEY POINTS)**

45
▼

Write an E-Mail Message

Ramona wants to E-mail all her friends about baby Roberta. Write an E-mail message that Ramona might send. Tell what Roberta looks like and how she acts. Be sure to describe Ramona's feeling about the new member of the Quimby family.

Literature Circle

Are there any characters who change during the story? If so, how do they change? What makes them different? Make a chart to show what you think.

Author
Beverly Cleary

Books have always been important to Beverly Cleary and her family. Her mother opened the first lending library in the town where the Clearys lived. Beverly Cleary couldn't wait to learn how to read. When she did learn, she found that the stories were very different from her own life. "I wanted to read funny stories about the sort of children I knew, and I decided that someday when I grew up I would write them."

More Books by
Beverly Cleary

- *Ramona and Her Father*
- *Henry Huggins*
- *Muggie Maggie*

45

✏ Write an E-Mail Message

Remind students that e-mail messages are usually brief, informal pieces of writing. The tone of most e-mail is casual and friendly. Have students address these questions in their e-mail:

> How does baby Roberta look and behave when she first comes home?

> How does Ramona feel about the new family member at first? How do her feelings change?

Literature Circle

Small groups of students can record their ideas on a chart.

Character	Beginning of Story	End of Story
Ramona		
Father		

DAILY LANGUAGE PRACTICE

SPELLING
DAY 3:
Write Words With Long *i*. See page R13.

GRAMMAR, USAGE, MECHANICS
DAY 3:
Practice Commands and Exclamations. See page R15.

ORAL LANGUAGE
the new baby really liks me
(*The new baby really <u>likes</u> me!*)

TECHNOLOGY

 Communication Through E-mail Have students use a word processor to write an E-mail from Ramona to baby Roberta explaining two growing up things that Ramona has mastered. Remember to describe Ramona before and after learning each skill.

LITERARY ELEMENT
Character

SKILLS TRACE

Character **TESTED**

Introduce . . . . pp. T84–T85
Practice . . . . . pp. T69, T80, T94
Review . . . . . . p. R48
Reteach . . . . . p. R54

TRANSPARENCY 6

Scholastic Literacy Place

CHARACTER

Who is _____ *Ramona* _____ ?

trait: worrier
clue: She worries about how her life will change with the baby.

trait: excitable
clue: She can't wait to see her baby sister.

trait: *loving*
clue: _____

trait: *frightened*
clue: She's afraid of getting sick and not being able to see her sister.

trait: *curious*
clue: _____

trait: *independent*
clue: She likes riding the elevator alone.

What's New? • *Ramona Forever* 6

✓ QUICKCHECK

Can students:

✔ use what Ramona said, did, thought, or felt to identify her character traits?

✔ apply what other characters said about Ramona to determine what she is like?

If **YES**, go on to Practice/Apply.

If **NO**, start at Teach/Model.

Ⓐ TEACH/MODEL

USE ORAL LANGUAGE

Ask students to describe their favorite TV character. What is the character like? What kinds of things does this character say, feel, think, and do? Point out that they have identified a character's qualities, or traits.

Character traits are the special qualities of a character's personality. Tell students that authors give clues about a character by describing what the character thinks, says, does, or feels. Knowing what kind of person a character is makes it easier to understand the character's behavior. It also helps you make better sense of the story. To identify character traits, tell students to:

1. Look for words the author uses to describe the character.

2. Think about what the character thinks, says, or does.

3. Be aware of what other characters say about the character, and consider what you already know about people.

MODIFY Instruction

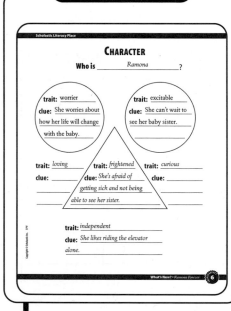

Ramona

good imagination

friendly

sometimes angry

ESL/ELD

▲ Draw an outline of a girl on a chart. Label it *Ramona*. Write phrases on word strips: *good imagination, friendly, always sick, often impatient, usually patient, unfriendly, sometimes happy, sometimes angry, loves her family.* Have students read each strip aloud and place the ones that describe Ramona on the chart. **(KEY POINTS)**

EXTRA HELP

■ Before students begin pages 26, 27, and 28 in the Practice Book, help them complete the pages orally, and discuss how they arrived at their answers. This oral preview will help students complete the pages with greater confidence. **(PREVIEW)**

LITERATURE CONNECTION

Use **Transparency 6** to help students analyze character.

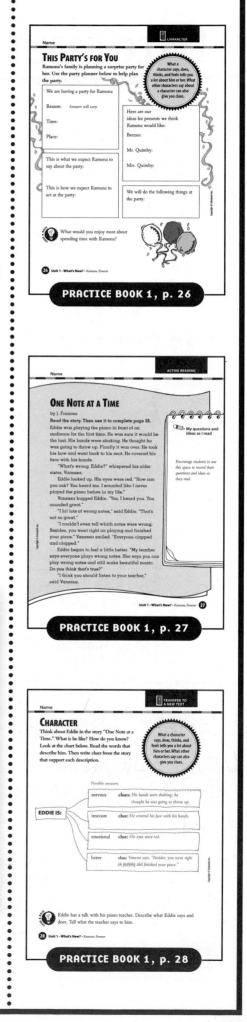

THINK ALOUD *There are lots of clues in the story that tell me about Ramona. I know she is helpful and considerate because of the way she and her sister clean the house after hearing about the new baby. I know she's independent because she enjoyed riding the elevator alone. I can tell that she's a lively and curious person when the author describes her as being hardly able to "bear her own excitement."*

Ⓑ PRACTICE/APPLY

USE PRACTICE BOOK

Have pairs of students practice the skill by completing **Practice Book 1, page 26.** (Partners)

Ⓒ ASSESS

APPLY INSTRUCTIONAL ALTERNATIVES

Based on students' completion of **Transparency 6** and **Practice Book 1, page 26,** determine whether they were able to analyze characters in the selection. The Instructional Alternatives below will aid you in pinpointing students' level of proficiency. Consider the appropriate instructional alternative to promote further skill development.

To reinforce the skill, distribute **pages 27 and 28** of **Practice Book 1.**

✅ INSTRUCTIONAL ALTERNATIVES

	If the student . . .	Then
Proficient	Identifies specific character traits by accurately analyzing picture clues and story information	• Have the student apply this skill independently to a more challenging story. • Ask the student to write a new Chapter of the story of which a character reveals himself or herself through words and thoughts.
Apprentice	Provides a partial description of the character	• Have the student find emotion words in the text, such as *happily* and *angrily,* and decide which character's feelings they refer to.
Novice	Provides information from the story, but the information does not relate to the character	• Provide details about a well-known cartoon character, and work with the student to create a character map. • Complete the Reteach lesson on page R54.

PRACTICE BOOK 1, p. 26

PRACTICE BOOK 1, p. 27

PRACTICE BOOK 1, p. 28

Intervention
For students who need extra help with . . .

PHONICS

IDENTIFYING SPELLING PATTERNS
Give students additional practice identifying words with vowel /ī/.

behind

nine

tight

- Say a word with /ī/ and have students come up with rhyming words. Write the words on word cards as students say them.

- Ask students to sort the words on the cards according to the spelling of the vowel /ī/: *i, igh, y, i-e, ie,* or any other spelling.

- Have students write a couplet that uses two rhyming words.

PARTNERS: Ask students to work with a partner to write a series of couplets that use rhyming words with vowel /ī/.

LITERARY ELEMENT

CHARACTER
Help students use clues to analyze character by relating the skill to characters from real life. Have students play "Who Is It?"

tall
funny
movie star

- Divide students into two groups. Group 1 thinks of a famous person and writes three character-trait clues on the chalkboard.

- Group 2 asks questions about the mystery person and records the person's traits on the chalkboard.

- After asking 20 questions, Group 2 must figure out who the person is. Then groups switch roles.

FLUENCY

READING ALOUD
Provide students with opportunities to read aloud daily, using books in your classroom.

- Choose from a variety of selections from all genres.

- Model fluent reading by reading to students with expression, varying tone and pitch, and emphasizing important words.

- Then ask student volunteers to practice reading a selection.

Optional Materials for Intervention

PHONICS

Vowel /ī/

If students need help with long /ī/ words, use **Phonics Chapter Book #9,** Kids Care about Sea Animals.

CONNECT SOUND–SPELLING

TEACH/MODEL Read aloud a list of words with /ī/ at the beginning, middle, or end. Ask students to listen for the sound and identify the position of the sound. For example, *ice* (beginning); *like, nice, spine* (middle); *fly, by, try* (end). Help students suggest other words with /ī/ in the same position and help them begin a chart.

Beginning	Middle	End
ice	like	fly
	nice	by
	spine	try

PRACTICE/APPLY Assign Chapter 1 of the book. Check in with students and provide support as necessary. Have students continue reading chapter by chapter.

LISTENING

Echo Reading

If students need help with fluency, use the audiocassette for **Ramona Forever.**

LISTEN TO THE AUDIOCASSETTE

Ask students to listen to an audiocassette version of the story as they follow along in their books. Tell them to listen to two or three sentences, stop the tape, and "echo" read the same sentences aloud. Suggest that students use the reader on the tape as a model for their own reading, imitating his or her expression, speed, and pronunciation.

AFTER LISTENING

RETELL THE STORY Encourage students to orally retell the story of *Ramona Forever* by briefly summarizing the main events.

DAY 3 WRAP-UP

READ ALOUD *Spend five to ten minutes reading from a selection of your choice.*

GUIDED READING *Meet with the* **blue** *and* **green** *reading groups and assign Independent Center activities.* **See pages R10–R11.**

DAY 4 OBJECTIVES

STUDENTS WILL:

READ 20 MINUTES

- Reread *Ramona Forever*

WRITE 40 MINUTES

- Writing Workshop: Realistic Description
- Writer's Craft: Vivid Verbs
- Spelling: Words With Long *i*
- Grammar, Usage, Mechanics: Commands and Exclamations
- Oral Language

EXTEND SKILLS 30 MINUTES

- Vocabulary
- Daily Phonics: Vowel /ī/ *i*, *igh*, *y*, *i-e*, *ie*
- Study Skills: Test-Taking
- Oral Language
- Read Aloud
- Guided Reading

RESOURCES

- Transparency 7
- Practice Book 1, pp. 23, 29, 30
- Spelling Resource Book, p. 200

Students may refer to *Checking Your Grammar* and *Writing With Style*.

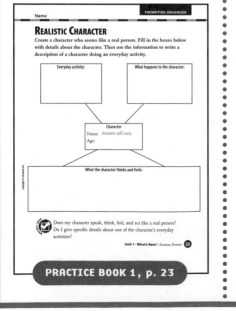

PRACTICE BOOK 1, p. 23

WRITING WORKSHOP *Expressive Writing*
Realistic Description

THINK ABOUT WRITING	Ask students what they like about Beverly Cleary's *Ramona* series. > **Why does Ramona seem real?** > **Why do the everyday events in the story seem real?**
LITERATURE CONNECTION	Draw students' attention back to the first few pages of *Ramona Forever*. Point out details about everyday life and descriptions that show how Ramona thinks and feels. For example, Ramona was excited about going to the hospital to see the new baby. Point out everyday events such as vacuuming and dusting.

PREWRITE

COMPLETE A GRAPHIC ORGANIZER	Have students refer to the graphic organizer on **page 23** of **Practice Book 1** that they began earlier. They might add more details to the Everyday activity box or change some of the character's traits.

DRAFT

TEACH WRITER'S CRAFT	Before students begin their drafts, help them understand the importance of using vivid action verbs in their writing. See **Writer's Craft, page T89**. > **Try to describe what your character thinks and feels during the everyday activity. What vivid action verbs will tell the reader what your character is doing?**

REVISE/PROOFREAD

Note: You may wish to do Revise/Proofread on Day 5. As students revise and proofread, they might want to ask themselves or a writing partner:

REVISE	• Did I use vivid verbs to describe the character's actions and feelings? • Are there any details I can add to make my everyday activity seem real?
PROOFREAD	• Have I correctly punctuated exclamations and commands? • Did I begin each sentence with a capital letter? ✔ See Students' Writing Rubric on page T96.

 **WRITER'S CRAFT**

VIVID VERBS

Ⓐ TEACH/MODEL

Tell students why it is important to use vivid verbs in their writing. Vivid verbs:

- create clear, precise pictures in the reader's mind.
- describe exactly what is happening.
- let readers know what a character is feeling, thinking, or doing.

Have students compare the final sentence of paragraph 1 on **page 35** of the selection with the following sentence: *He took off the prescription he had written, told Ramona to give it to her father, and walked down the hall.*

Discuss why Beverly Cleary's verb choices are better than the underlined words above. Explain that *tore off* describes exactly what the doctor did, whereas *took* does not. Ask students to tell why *instructed* and *hurried* give the reader a more vivid picture of what happened than *told* and *walked*.

Ⓑ PRACTICE/APPLY

- **Write on the chalkboard:** *He lifted Ramona and gave her a big hug and a kiss.* Point out that this sentence clearly describes Mr. Quimby's actions because it uses vivid words.

- **Use Transparency 7,** or write the following sentence on the chalkboard. Ask students to select the verb that best describes what is happening. Help them to see why the other verb is less precise.

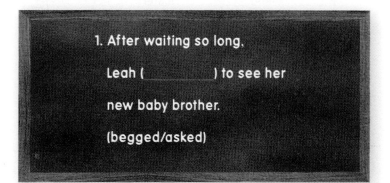

1. After waiting so long,
Leah (_____) to see her
new baby brother.
(begged/asked)

Explain that *begged* is the best choice because it describes Leah's eagerness to see her baby brother. The word *asked* is more general and does not let readers know how Leah feels.

DAILY LANGUAGE PRACTICE Ⓑ

SPELLING
DAY 4:
Review Words With Long *i*. **See page R13.**

GRAMMAR, USAGE, MECHANICS
DAY 4:
Apply Exclamations and Commands. **See p. R15.**

ORAL LANGUAGE
look at the brite star above
(*Look at the <u>bright</u> star above.*)

Technology

Writing Skills
Encourage students to use the grammar-check option in a familiar word processing program to help them proofread their writing.

VOCABULARY

contagious	chickenpox
stethoscope	inflammation
wheelchair	prescription

TEACHER TIP

"When I introduce new vocabulary words, I have students make their own set of 'flash cards.' They write the words on index cards that have a hole punched in one corner. The cards are then put on a ring that holds all their vocabulary words. They can then practice and review vocabulary words with partners."

Extend Vocabulary

Review Vocabulary

CLUES TO MEANING

Say or write the vocabulary words. Read each sentence aloud and have students name the word it describes.

1. This special chair can be used to move a patient in a hospital. *(wheelchair)*

2. A doctor might use this instrument to listen to your heartbeat. *(stethoscope)*

3. Someone with this disease might have a fever and red itchy bumps. *(chickenpox)*

4. This medical order from a doctor might make you feel better. *(prescription)*

5. This sore red swelling on your arm could be from an injury. *(inflammation)*

6. This describes an illness that is spread easily. *(contagious)*

Expand Vocabulary

INVENTED WORDS

Review with students the invented word *blunderful*. Remind them that it combines parts of two other words—*blunder* and *wonderful*. Have students think of other invented words. Put their suggestions on a Venn diagram.

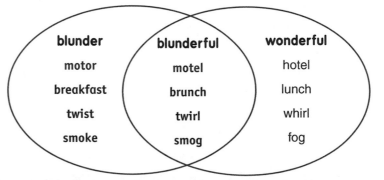

Record Vocabulary

MULTIPLE-MEANING WORDS

Remind students that some words have more than one meaning. Point out the word *mean* on page 31 and explain that it can be used to describe an unfriendly person or "to define." Ask students to find other words that have two meanings. Some examples are *trip* (p. 29), *right* (p. 35), and *hard* (p. 40). Have students write sentence pairs for each word and ask a partner to figure out the meanings from context clues.

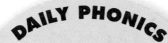

Vowel /ī/ i, igh, y, i-e, ie

RIDDLE GAME

Prepare for the activity by composing a number of riddles about words that have different spellings for long *i*.

1 **SET UP** Give students clues about the words. For example, you might say **I have a long *i* spelled *igh*. I am the opposite of day. What am I?**

2 **TO PLAY** Have students work in small groups. They should use the letter cards to build the word that answers the riddle. The group that solves the most riddles wins.

| n | i | g | h | t |

3 **TRY THIS** Ask students to make up their own riddles for words with long *i* spellings. They can play the game with a partner or ask the class the riddle.

MATERIALS:
letter cards

SUGGESTED GROUPING:
Small Groups

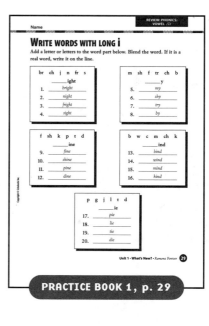

PRACTICE BOOK 1, p. 29

GIFTED & TALENTED

✳Students might enjoy the challenge of making up long sentences containing long *i* words. For example: *I might find a nice bright kite to fly.* Have students write their sentences and then read them aloud. **(INNOVATE)**

EXTRA HELP

■Provide phonogram cards for the spellings of long *i*: *i, igh, y, i-e, ie.* Put these into a pocket chart, and encourage students to use them, along with their letter cards, to build words. They can work individually or with a partner. **(USE VISUALS)**

STUDY SKILLS
Getting Ready to Take a Test

Ⓐ TEACH/MODEL

TALK ABOUT TESTS

Discuss with students the purpose of taking a test. Ask them this question:

> **Why do you take tests?**

Then tell students that there are different kinds of tests. Point out that some tests have several different answer choices for each question. These tests may also have a separate answer sheet.

GET READY FOR THE TEST

Display the following example of a standardized test.

Directions: Find the word that means the same or almost the same as the underlined word.

    1. a <u>tiny</u> baby

        ○ big   ○ small
        ○ happy ○ hungry

    Explain that it is important to listen to the directions carefully before beginning a test like this. Ask one volunteer to read the directions aloud and another to tell what the directions mean. Then ask students:

> **Why is it important to understand the directions?**

Tell students they should ask questions if they don't understand the test directions. Once the test begins, they will not have another chance.

READ THE QUESTIONS

Tell students that they should read the question and all the answer choices before they mark their answer. Point out the four answer choices in the display question. Tell students that only one word means the same as *tiny,* but any of the words in the choices can describe a baby.

MARK THE ANSWERS

Present these strategies for marking answers on a standardized test:

> **Be sure to completely fill in each circle.**

> **Mark only one answer for each question.**

> **Use a ruler to help you keep your place, if you have a separate answer sheet.**

Ⓑ PRACTICE/APPLY

PRACTICE TEST-TAKING STRATEGIES

Distribute Practice Book page 30 to students and point out the separate answer column on the right of the test. Remind them to mark their answers on this sheet. Then ask students:

> **What should you do if you don't understand the directions?**

> **What should you do before you mark your answer?**

Then have students practice the strategies by taking the test. After they have finished, have them check that they have used the separate answer sheet and have completely filled in each answer circle.

✓ STUDENT'S SELF-ASSESSMENT

Did I:

✔ understand the directions?

✔ try all choices to see which one best fit the question?

✔ correctly mark answers?

Name _____

STUDY SKILLS/ TEST TAKING

GETTING READY TO TAKE A TEST

Directions: Find the word that means the same as the underlined word.

Answer Sheet

1. a beautiful day
   ⓐ bright   ⓒ smart
   ⓑ pretty   ⓓ excited

   1. ⓐ ⓑ ⓒ ⓓ

2. a happy child
   ⓐ angry   ⓒ joyful
   ⓑ kind   ⓓ tall

   2. ⓐ ⓑ ⓒ ⓓ

Directions: Find the word that best completes each sentence.

3. The doctor used a _____ to listen to her heartbeat.
   ⓐ stethoscope   ⓒ prescription
   ⓑ wheelchair   ⓓ library

   3. ⓐ ⓑ ⓒ ⓓ

4. Ramona was _____ at the end of the story.
   ⓐ disappointed   ⓒ worried
   ⓑ happy   ⓓ angry

   4. ⓐ ⓑ ⓒ ⓓ

30 Unit 1 - What's New? • *Ramona Forever*

PRACTICE BOOK 1, p. 30

TECHNOLOGY

Teacher/Family Communication Use your creativity and **Smart PlaceMaker** to design a card to be sent home reminding students and parents of an upcoming test. Use patterns, colors, and humorous graphics to accompany test preparation hints.

DAY **4** WRAP-UP

READ ALOUD *Spend five to ten minutes reading from a selection of your choice.*

GUIDED READING *Meet with the green and blue reading groups and assign Independent Center activities. See pages R10–R11.*

DAY 5 OBJECTIVES

STUDENTS WILL:

READ 30 MINUTES

- Reading Assessment
- Daily Phonics: Vowel /ī/ *i, igh, y, i-e, ie*

WRITE 30 MINUTES

- Writing Assessment
- Spelling: Words With Long *i*
- Grammar, Usage, Mechanics: Commands and Exclamations
- Oral Language

EXTEND SKILLS 30 MINUTES

- Integrated Language Arts
- Read Aloud
- Guided Reading

RESOURCES

- Selection Test
- Spelling Resource Book, p. 202

SELECTION TEST

Reading Assessment

Formal Assessment

Use the Selection Test to measure students' mastery of the week's reading skills. See the suggestions for Intervention and Modifying Assessment.

Available In ★ READING ★ COUNTS!

☑ SELECTION TEST

SKILL	TEST QUESTIONS	IF students need more support THEN...
LITERARY ELEMENT Character	1–3	Use the Reteach lesson on p. R54.
GENRE Realistic Fiction	4–6	Use the Take-Home Practice Readers.
DAILY PHONICS Vowel /ī/	7–9	Use the Reteach lesson on p. R52.
Vocabulary	10–12	Use the Review Vocabulary section on p. T90.

Modifying Assessment

ESL/ELD
Vocabulary

▲ List the words: *prescription, stethoscope, wheelchair* on the chalkboard. Have the student complete these sentences:

The doctor listened to my heart with a ___.

I needed medicine so the doctor wrote a ___.

When you can't walk, you might need a ___. **(BUILD VOCABULARY)**

◎ **IF** students need more support with vocabulary, **THEN** review the vocabulary in the Take-Home Practice Readers.

EXTRA HELP
Comprehension

■ Write the following character traits on the chalkboard: *shy, quiet, curious, lively, mean, kind, dull.* Ask a student to circle the traits that apply to Ramona.

➤ **Can the student identify some of the character's key traits? (CHARACTER)**

◎ **IF** students need more support in identifying character traits, **THEN** review the skill in the Take-Home Practice Readers.

Performance-Based Assessment

Use the assessment activities below to provide performance-based measures of students' proficiency in phonics and reading fluency. See the Conference to assess individual students' progress.

DAILY PHONICS

Dictation

Vowel /ī/ i, igh, y, i-e, ie
Dictate the following words and sentences. Have students write them on a sheet of paper. When students are finished, write the words and sentences on the chalkboard and have students make any necessary corrections on their papers.

behind right by while tie

He wore a very bright tie .

Try to be on time .

Can you find the book?

✔ **Did students use the correct spellings for vowel /ī/?**

IF students need more support with the vowel /ī/,

THEN practice oral blending of the words with /ī/ in the dictation.

ONE-MINUTE FLUENCY

Ask students to sit in pairs and read aloud to each other. Circulate and listen to individuals to assess their reading fluency. Students can read the text on **Practice Book 1, page 27** or the text of a Mini-Book

✔ *Does the student read smoothly and self-correct mistakes?*

IF students need additional support with fluency,

THEN have them do a repeated reading of the passage and tape-record themselves.

◉ CONFERENCE

Take this time to meet with several individual students to discuss their story comprehension and to listen to them read from the story. You may wish to tape-record students as they read the section aloud.

ASSESS LITERARY ELEMENT
✔ **Did Ramona change throughout the story? What does that tell you about her character? (Character)**

ASSESS GENRE
✔ **Why does Ramona seem like a real person? (Realistic Fiction)**

ASSESS FLUENCY
✔ **Does the student read with correct intonation at the end of sentences?**

✔ **Does the student recognize and read dialogue with expression?**

DAILY LANGUAGE PRACTICE

SPELLING

DAY 5:
Administer the Posttest for Words With Long *i*.
See p. R13.

GRAMMAR, USAGE, MECHANICS

DAY 5:
Assess Commands and Exclamations. **See p. R15.**

ORAL LANGUAGE

don't ever touch a wilde animal

(*D*on't ever touch a *wild* animal!)

PORTFOLIO

Suggest that students add their drafts and revisions to their Literacy Portfolios.

⊘ Writing Assessment

This is a good example of a character doing an everyday activity.

Some verbs could be more vivid. For example, instead of I ate a big breakfast, I devoured a big breakfast.

Write complete sentences with subject and verb.

You made good use of exclamations here and at the begining of the writing sample.

TEST DAY

I just kept thinking to myself, oh no, test day! I wanted to give myself a positive attitude so I got up on time. I put on a blue jean skirt and blouse, a vest and my sneakers. I combed my hair real nice. I looked good. I ate a big breakfast. I ate eggs, sausages, orange juice and toast. I was full, but not over full. So far so good. I picked up Karen and we walked to school. The sun was shining and it looked like a great day. First subject was English. We read a good story about a lady who threw seeds over the hills to make flowers.

Recess was fun. We played jumprope and now I can finally jump double-dutch like the other girls. Back to class and this test. I studied. I know my multiplication and division facts. I'm so nervous I can feel my stomach turning upside down. Just call me Nervous Nellie. My palms are getting sweaty. Can anybody see how wet my face is. Oh my goodness. here it comes. I'm gonna faint. Ms. Crane, my teacher was looking at me. She's so nice. She always wears long skirts and glasses. Ms. Crane told Carl to leave me alone. She told us to settle down. Then she gave me my math test. I looked at those problems and almost fell to the floor. I knew this stuff! I could do this! Yes! It was a great school day after all.

Apprentice

Use the rubric below to assess students' writing.

☑ STUDENTS' WRITING RUBRIC

Proficient	• A realistic description is given of a character doing an everyday activity.	• A variety of sentences, and commands and exclamations are included.
	• Vivid verbs have been used to describe what is happening.	• The description has been proofread and corrected.
Apprentice	• A realistic description is given of a character doing an everyday activity, but details may be sketchy or incomplete.	• The realistic description contains some variety in sentences, and some commands and exclamations are used.
	• The verbs may not be vivid.	
Novice	• The description is incomplete and there are few vivid verbs.	• The description does not contain a variety of sentences and has not been proofread.

Integrated Language Arts

PERSUASIVE WRITING

Write a Persuasive Speech

MATERIALS:
Paper, pencils

SUGGESTED GROUPING:
Individuals

CHALLENGE students to write a persuasive speech.

INTRODUCE this activity by reminding students how Ramona felt at the hospital when she was told to go downstairs and wait in the lobby.

BRAINSTORM Ask students to list some reasons telling why they feel as they do.

· ·

Persuasive Writing

TEACH/MODEL Explain that persuasive writing tries to get the reader to agree with what is being said. Authors of persuasive writing

> state their opinion.
> support their opinion with reasons why they feel as they do.

PRACTICE/APPLY Tell students that they will be writing a short persuasive speech telling how they feel about the hospital rule. Suggest that they review their list of reasons supporting their opinion and decide in what order they will present them.

WRITING/VIEWING

Describe Mixed Emotions

MATERIALS:
Paper, pencil

SUGGESTED GROUPING:
Individuals

SUGGEST that students write about an experience that inspired mixed emotions.

REMIND students of how Ramona felt when her baby sister arrived. Encourage them to recall that she both liked and disliked the event. Then ask students to think of experiences they've felt two ways about--for example, they may have been nervous before giving a speech, but felt great when they received applause afterward.

ASK students, before writing, to list words that convey how they felt about the experience. They can consult this "word bank" as they write.

 Students may wish to include their "mixed-feelings" stories in their Literacy Portfolios.

· · · · · · · · · (TECHNOLOGY) · · · · · · · · ·

Language Development have the students use a word processor to create a table with the headings: Idea, Good News, Bad News. Suggest students consider the idea of having a baby sister and use the three columns to help them explore mixed emotions. How would they feel about a baby brother?

Integrated Language Arts

SPEAKING/LISTENING

SPEAKING/LISTENING

Reenact Story Scenes

MATERIALS:
Found props

SUGGESTED GROUPING:
Cooperative groups

STUDENTS can work in groups to choose a scene from *Ramona Forever* and act it out.

INVITE the class to name several memorable scenes from the story. Then, ask each cooperative group to select one of the scenes to reenact.

REMIND students to use nonverbal communication such as hand gestures and other movements to make their scenes more interesting.

SUGGEST a few episodes, such as these:

• **Mother calls Ramona and Beezus on the phone to tell them about their sister**

• **Ramona sits in the hospital waiting room.**

• **The family takes Roberta home.**

ENCOURAGE each group to find classroom items to use as props. Give each group time to rehearse and preform its scene for the class.

EXPRESSIVE WRITING

Diagram the Story Settings

Good For Grading

MATERIALS:
Large sheet of mural paper,
Pencil
Markers or crayons
Glue or paste

SUGGESTED GROUPING:
Partners

INVITE students to create a diagram of the settings and events in *Ramona Forever.*

REVIEW with the class where story events take place: maternity ward, elevator, waiting room, car, home. Partners can use cut-out pictures or found objects to indicate each place as they create a "picture diagram" of the selection. Have them label the places, and number each sequence.

CHALLENGE students to find creative ways to represent the various locations and to show the connecting pathways. Display the completed diagrams.

HOW TO GRADE Grade students on the clarity and accuracy of their story diagrams.

• •

Sequence

TEACH/MODEL Remind students that the order in which story events take place is often signaled by words, such as *until, finally, when, now, then, by the time,* and so on. These words are clues that the time and order of story events are changing.

APPLY Before students diagram the story, suggests that they review it for signal words, and make a numbered list of places and events. They can decide on a diagram layout based on the information on their list.

DAY **5** WRAP-UP

READ ALOUD *Spend five to ten minutes reading from a selection of your choice.*

GUIDED READING *Meet with the* **red** *and* **blue** *reading groups and assign Independent Center activities.* **See pages R10–R11.**

How to Make a Milestone Chart

WHY DO THIS WORKSHOP?

A milestone was originally a stone posted a mile from a similar post. It was a way for travelers to mark off their progress. In a person's life, a milestone is a figurative marker of that person's development. Students are aware of such milestones when they move from one grade to another but may be less aware of the significance of other markers of their growth.

In this Workshop, students recall important events in their lives. By reflecting on past history, each student identifies what is unique about his or her life. Then, as students compare their own milestones to those of their classmates, they'll recognize the experiences that are unique to each of them and the experiences they share with others. This Workshop gives students a chance to reflect on their past and feel pride in their progress.

WORKSHOP OBJECTIVES

STUDENTS WILL:
- Reflect on their past
- Create a milestone chart

MATERIALS
- Paper and pencil
- Tape
- Small pieces of paper or index cards

WORKSHOP

Reflect on the Past

Discuss with the class the milestone chart on pages 46–47 of the Anthology. Ask students why the writer included "starting school" and "meeting a new friend" in a milestone chart. How are these events milestones? You could also ask any of the following questions:

> Why does the writer include his or her age at each milestone?

> How is the chart organized? How do you know the order in which the milestones occurred?

> Do you think the events listed on the chart are milestones for everyone? Do you remember your first day of school?

TECHNOLOGY

Presentation Tools Encourage students to use an art program such as **Smart Place PlaceMaker** to create the panels of their milestone charts. Ask them to fully explore the clip art available as well as all the art tools.

WORKSHOP 1

How to

Make a Milestone Chart

Think of all the things you have learned and done since you were small. Each of these important events is a milestone in your life. These events can be shown on a milestone chart.

What is a milestone chart? A milestone chart lists important events. It shows the order in which each event happened.

the writer's age when the events happened ●

Met my best friend Heather

5

Got Great Dane puppy

Got Marvel the Musta... toy horse

My first... of Kindergaste...

chart runs from left to right

Teacher Mrs. Martin

46

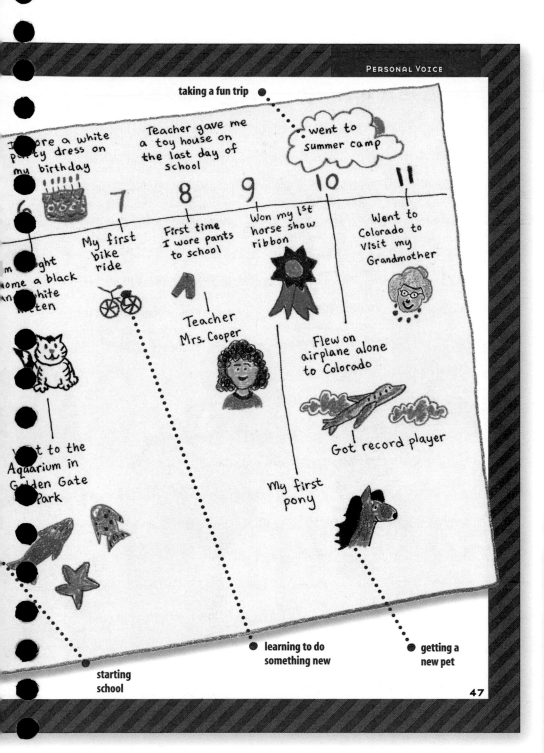

PERSONAL VOICE

taking a fun trip ●

I wore a white party dress on my birthday

Teacher gave me a toy house on the last day of school

went to summer camp

My first bike ride

First time I wore pants to school

Teacher Mrs. Cooper

Won my 1st horse show ribbon

Went to Colorado to visit my Grandmother

Flew on airplane alone to Colorado

Got record player

My first pony

Brought home a black and white kitten

Went to the Aquarium in Golden Gate Park

● learning to do something new

● getting a new pet

starting school

47

Home Involvement

Have students talk to family members about what they consider to be milestones in students' lives. Students may find that parents or guardians will mention such things as first step and first words—milestones students will have no memory of. Students may also want to discuss any shared milestones with siblings.

Troubleshooting

If students want to illustrate their time lines with photographs, you'll want to send a letter home telling parents about the Workshop. Parents should only provide pictures they're willing to part with.

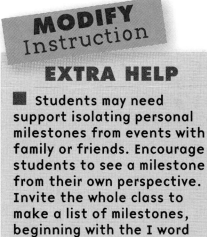

MODIFY Instruction

EXTRA HELP

■ Students may need support isolating personal milestones from events with family or friends. Encourage students to see a milestone from their own perspective. Invite the whole class to make a list of milestones, beginning with the I word and a verb: "I went . . . , I won . . . ," etc. **(KEY WORDS)**

Real-World Skills

1 WHICH MILESTONES?

Encourage students to consider the milestone categories in the Anthology as well as brainstorming a new list. Remind students that a milestone is not getting a present they wanted or something fun they did yesterday; it's an event that marks a new stage of their learning or development.

2 WHICH WAS FIRST?

Explain to students how to use birthdays and school years as markers to help identify dates. If students bring pictures from home to illustrate their charts, they may be able to use picture clues, such as the number of candles on a cake, to determine a date.

1 Which Milestones?

Make a list of some important events that have happened to you. You might begin with your first day in kindergarten. Think of things you've learned, new places you've seen, and new people in your life.

Here are some ideas: a new baby, a trip, learning to do something, moving, making a friend, or special holidays or events.

TOOLS

- pencil and paper
- tape
- small pieces of paper or index cards

2 Which Was First?

Now you need to put your milestones in order. There is an easy way to do this. Write each milestone on an index card or small piece of paper. If you know the year it happened, write that on the card, too.

Spread the cards out on a table. Put them in the order they happened. Then, number the cards so you will always know their order.

48

WORK

❸ Make the Chart

Now it's time to make your milestone chart.

- Tape two large pieces of paper together.
- Draw a line across the paper going the long way.
- Decide if you want to make your chart run from left to right or from top to bottom.
  - Begin at the top or left side of the paper. Next to the line, write your first milestone.

Tip Use your numbered index cards to write the rest of your milestones in order. You may want to illustrate some of your milestones.

❹ Show It!

Display your milestone chart on the class bulletin board. Discuss your chart with your classmates. Tell which milestones were most important to you. Look at the other charts. Do you share any of the same milestones with your classmates?

If You Are Using a Computer ...

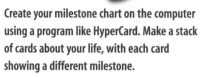

Create your milestone chart on the computer using a program like HyperCard. Make a stack of cards about your life, with each card showing a different milestone.

THINK

Learning to do something new is one kind of milestone. What would you want to learn next?

Keith Jardine
Wilderness Guide ▶

❸ MAKE THE CHART

Remind students to order the events on their time lines. They might also show different time spans by the distances between the numbered index cards. For example, two events that occurred within six months of one another would be closer together than two events that occurred several years apart.

❹ SHOW IT!

As the class reviews their charts, students could list those events that all or more of them shared. You might also want to discuss how one milestone can have different meanings for different people.

SELF-SELECTION

When students complete this Workshop, they may want to keep their milestone chart in their Literacy Portfolios.

PRACTICE BOOK 1, p. 31

PRACTICE BOOK 1, p. 32

Use **Practice Book 1, pages 31** and **32** as practice for the Workshop or as a separate activity to strengthen your students' skills.

✓ ASSESSMENT

INFORMAL ASSESSMENT
OBSERVATION

Review students' work. Ask yourself:

✓ Did students think of events in their lives that could be categorized as "milestones"?

✓ Were students able to place their milestones in chronological order?

✓ What similarities and differences did students notice as they compared their milestone charts?

STUDENT SELF-ASSESSMENT

Ask yourself:

✓ Was I able to think of milestones in my life, and put them in order on my time line?

Use the rubric below to assess students' Workshop performance.

✓ STUDENTS' WORKSHOP RUBRIC

Proficient	Students recall and record many milestones from their lives. They organize their milestones in sequence and their charts are attractive and readable.
Apprentice	Students recall and record a satisfactory number of milestones from their lives. The milestones are in sequence, but the charts may be hard to read.
Novice	Students recall and record a few milestones from their lives, but only with outside help. Their charts aren't chronological or easy to read.

WORKSHOP

How My Family Lives in America

Main Selection
Genre: Photo Essay
Award: IRA Children's Choice Award

Paired Selection
Genre: Magazine Article
Award: EDPRESS Distinguished
Achievement Award-Winning
magazine

Selection Summary

In this photo essay, the young narrator April shares information about her Chinese-American family and its traditional customs. In particular, she highlights the Chinese school she attends and the differences between Chinese and English writing. She also discusses Chinese food and games. Her essay includes a recipe.

PAIRED SELECTION This selection discusses an important issue for recent immigrants—how to keep native languages alive.

Author

SUSAN KUKLIN not only writes her books—she takes the pictures for them as well. She has a particular talent for writing books that are both readable and informative. Her first foray into children's literature was *The Story of Nim: The Chimpanzee Who Learned Language.*

Weekly Organizer

Visit Our WebSite
www.scholastic.com

How My Family Lives in America

DAY 1

DAY 2

READ and Introduce Skills

- VOCABULARY
- PHONICS
- COMPREHENSION
- LITERARY ELEMENT

DAY 1

BUILD BACKGROUND, ▲ p. T111

✓ **VOCABULARY, ▲ ■ p. T112**
Transparency 8
Practice Book 1, p. 33

✓ **DAILY PHONICS: ▲ ✳**
Words With /ə/, p. T114
Practice Book 1, p. 34

PREVIEW AND PREDICT, p. T116

READ: ▲ ✳ ■ ●
How My Family Lives in America,
pp. T116–T123

TEXT STRUCTURE: Photo Essay, p. T117

✓ **COMPREHENSION:**
Evaluate Author's Purpose, p. T119

DAY 2

READ: ▲ ✳ ■
"Kids Speak Up to Save Native Languages," pp. T124–T127

✓ **DAILY PHONICS:**
Words With /ə/, p. T125

WRITE and Respond

- GRAMMAR
- USAGE
- MECHANICS
- SPELLING
- WRITING

WRITING WORKSHOP: Introduce, p. T111

JOURNAL: Make Predictions, p. T116

✓ **SPELLING:**
Pretest: Words With *a-* and *be-*, p. R20
Spelling Resource Book, p. 19

✓ **GRAMMAR, USAGE, MECHANICS:**
Teach/Model: Common and Proper Nouns, p. R22

ORAL LANGUAGE, p. T123

WRITING WORKSHOP: Prewrite, p. T127
Practice Book 1, p. 35

✓ **SPELLING:**
Vocabulary Practice, p. R20
Spelling Resource Book, pp. 20–22

✓ **GRAMMAR, USAGE, MECHANICS:**
Practice, p. R22

ORAL LANGUAGE, p. T127

EXTEND SKILLS and Apply to Literature

- INTEGRATED LANGUAGE ARTS
- LISTENING/SPEAKING/VIEWING
- INTEGRATED CURRICULUM
- GUIDED READING
- INDEPENDENT READING

READ ALOUD, p. T123

GUIDED READING, pp. R18–R19

INTEGRATED CURRICULUM:
The Arts, p. R25
Social Studies, p. R25
Math, p. R24
Science, p. R24

TRADE BOOKS
- *Hannah*
- *The Chalk Box Kid*

READ ALOUD, p. T127

GUIDED READING, pp. R18–R19

TRADE BOOKS
- *Uncle Jed's Barbershop*
- *Muggie Maggie*

TECHNOLOGY and REAL-WORLD SKILLS

SCHOLASTIC NETWORK
Finding the Facts, p. T121

SMART PLACE CD-ROM
Presentation Tools, p. T125

WORKSHOP 2, pp. T195–T200

DAY 3

REREAD:
How My Family Lives in America

☑ **COMPREHENSION:** ▲ ■
Evaluate Author's Purpose, p. T130
Transparency 9
Practice Book 1, pp. 38–40

INTERVENTION, ● p. T132
Daily Phonics: Words With /ə/
Comprehension: Evaluate Author's Purpose
Fluency: Reading Aloud

RESPOND: ▲
Think About Reading, p. T128
Write A Caption, p. T129
Practice Book 1, p. 36

☑ **SPELLING:**
Write/Proofread, p. R21
Spelling Resource Book, p. 23

☑ **GRAMMAR, USAGE, MECHANICS:**
Practice, p. R23
Practice Book 1, p. 37

ORAL LANGUAGE, p. T129

RESPOND: Literature Circle, p. T129

READ ALOUD, p. T133

GUIDED READING, pp. R18–R19

OPTIONAL MATERIALS, ● p. T133
Phonics Chapter Book #13:
The Internet
How My Family Lives in America
audiocassette

SMART PLACE CD-ROM
Language Development, p. T129

WORKSHOP 2, pp. T195–T200

DAY 4

LITERATURE CONNECTION:
How My Family Lives in America,
p. T134

☑ **REVIEW VOCABULARY,** P. T136

☑ **DAILY PHONICS:** ▲
Words With /ə/, p. T137

WRITING WORKSHOP:
Nonfiction Description,
p. T134
Writer's Craft: Logical Order,
p. T135
Transparency 10
Practice Book 1, p. 35

☑ **SPELLING:**
Study/Review, p. R21
Spelling Resource Book, p. 200

☑ **GRAMMAR, USAGE, MECHANICS:**
Apply, p. R23

ORAL LANGUAGE, p. T135

READ ALOUD, p. T139

GUIDED READING, pp. R18–R19

EXPAND VOCABULARY:
Compound Words with *eye*, p. T136

☑ **STUDY SKILLS:**
Alphabetical Order, pp. T138–T139
Practice Book 1, p. 42

WORD PROCESSING
Writing Skills, p. T135

SPREAD SHEET
Study Skills, p. T139

WORKSHOP 2, pp. T195–T200

DAY 5

READING ASSESSMENT:
Selection Test, p. T140

MODIFYING ASSESSMENT, p. T140
ESL/ELD: Vocabulary
Extra Help: Comprehension

PERFORMANCE-BASED ASSESSMENT:
One-Minute Fluency, p. T141
Conference, p. T141

☑ **DAILY PHONICS:** Dictation, p. T141

WRITING ASSESSMENT, p. T142
Student Model
Students' Writing Rubric

☑ **SPELLING:**
Posttest, p. R21
Spelling Resource Book, p. 202

☑ **GRAMMAR, USAGE, MECHANICS:**
Assess, p. R23

ORAL LANGUAGE, p. T142

READ ALOUD, p. T144

GUIDED READING, pp. R18–R19

INTEGRATED LANGUAGE ARTS:
Interview a Character, p. T143
Make a Book of Traditions, p. T143
Make a Picture Cookbook, p. T144
Book Review, p. T144

AUDIO/VIDEO
Speaking Skills, p. T143

WORKSHOP 2, pp. T195–T200

ASSESSMENT PLANNING

USE THIS CHART TO PLAN YOUR ASSESSMENT OF THE WEEKLY READING OBJECTIVES.

- Informal Assessment is ongoing and should be used before, during, and after reading.
- Formal assessment occurs at the end of the week on the selection test.
- Note that intervention activities occur throughout the lesson to support students who need extra help with skills.

YOU MAY CHOOSE AMONG THE FOLLOWING PAGES IN THE ASSESSMENT HANDBOOK.

- Informal Assessment
- Anecdotal Record
- Portfolio Checklist and Evaluation Forms
- Self-Assessment
- English Language Learners
- Using Technology to Assess
- Test Preparation

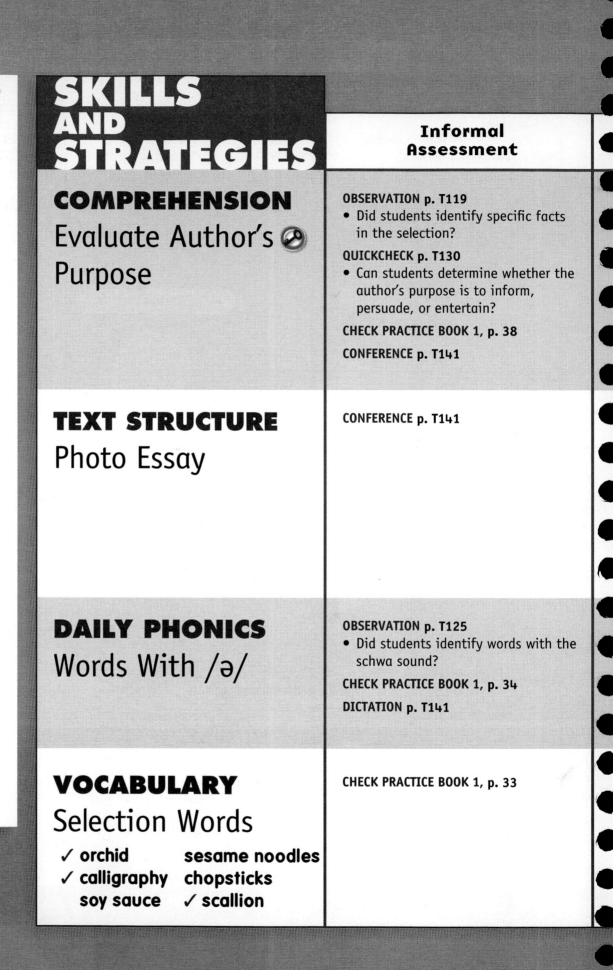

SKILLS AND STRATEGIES	Informal Assessment
COMPREHENSION Evaluate Author's Purpose 🔍	**OBSERVATION p. T119** • Did students identify specific facts in the selection? **QUICKCHECK p. T130** • Can students determine whether the author's purpose is to inform, persuade, or entertain? **CHECK PRACTICE BOOK 1, p. 38** **CONFERENCE p. T141**
TEXT STRUCTURE Photo Essay	**CONFERENCE p. T141**
DAILY PHONICS Words With /ə/	**OBSERVATION p. T125** • Did students identify words with the schwa sound? **CHECK PRACTICE BOOK 1, p. 34** **DICTATION p. T141**
VOCABULARY Selection Words ✓ orchid sesame noodles ✓ calligraphy chopsticks soy sauce ✓ scallion	**CHECK PRACTICE BOOK 1, p. 33**

Formal Assessment	INTERVENTION and Instructional Alternatives	Planning Notes
SELECTION TEST • Questions 1–3 check students' mastery of the key strategy, evaluate author's purpose.	If students need help with evaluate author's purpose, then go to: • **Instructional Alternatives, p. T131** • **Intervention, p. T132**	
SELECTION TEST • Questions 4–6 check students' understanding of the skill, photo essay.	If students need help with photo essay, then: • **Review the Skills and Strategies lesson on p. T117**	
SELECTION TEST • Questions 7–9 check students' ability to identify words with the schwa sound. **UNIT TEST**	If students need help identifying words with the schwa sound, then go to: • **Intervention, p. T132** • **Review, p. R45** • **Reteach, p. R53**	
SELECTION TEST • Questions 10–12 check students' understanding of the selection vocabulary.	If students need additional practice with the vocabulary words, then go to: • **Review Vocabulary, p. T136**	

Technology

The technology in this lesson helps teachers and students develop the skills they need for the 21st century. Look for integrated technology activities on every day of instruction.

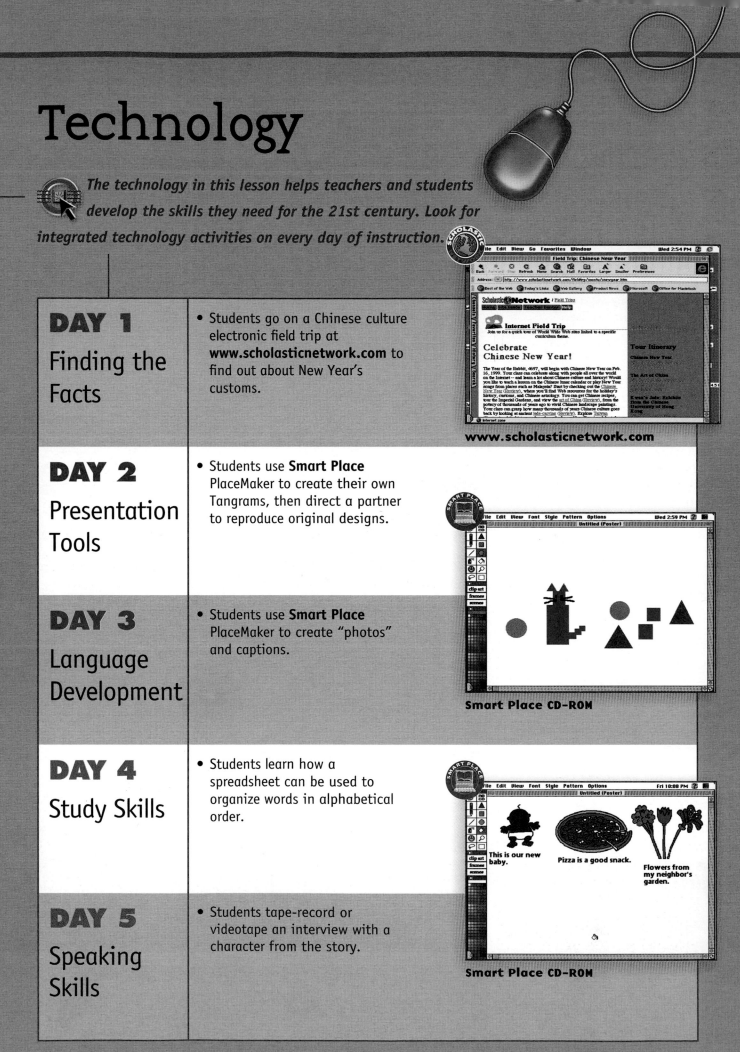

DAY 1
Finding the Facts

- Students go on a Chinese culture electronic field trip at **www.scholasticnetwork.com** to find out about New Year's customs.

www.scholasticnetwork.com

DAY 2
Presentation Tools

- Students use **Smart Place** PlaceMaker to create their own Tangrams, then direct a partner to reproduce original designs.

DAY 3
Language Development

- Students use **Smart Place** PlaceMaker to create "photos" and captions.

Smart Place CD-ROM

DAY 4
Study Skills

- Students learn how a spreadsheet can be used to organize words in alphabetical order.

This is our new baby.

Pizza is a good snack.

Flowers from my neighbor's garden.

DAY 5
Speaking Skills

- Students tape-record or videotape an interview with a character from the story.

Smart Place CD-ROM

Build Background

Where we come from is an important part of who we are. In How My Family Lives in America, *students will meet a Chinese-American girl who learns about herself by finding out about her family's heritage and traditional customs.*

Activate Prior Knowledge

DISCUSS CHINESE CULTURE

Ask students what they know about China and the way of life of its people. Have students locate China on a world map or globe.

SHARE OBSERVA-TIONS

If possible, display pictures of China, and provide time for students to share their observations.

> **What movies or television programs have you seen about China or that are set in China?**

> **What Chinese dishes have you eaten? How do these dishes compare with other food you eat?**

> **What Chinese game have you played? Describe it to the class.**

 WRITING WORKSHOP *Nonfiction Description*

INTRODUCE Build background for writing a nonfiction description by asking students to describe what they know about their own culture, including holidays.

DAY 1 OBJECTIVES

STUDENTS WILL:

READ 35 MINUTES

- **Build Background**
- **Vocabulary**
- **Daily Phonics: Words With /ə/**
- *How My Family Lives in America*, **pp. 50–57**
- **Key Comprehension Skill: Evaluate Author's Purpose**

WRITE 30 MINUTES

- **Writing Workshop: Introduce Writing a Nonfiction Description**
- **Quickwrite: Return to Purpose**
- **Spelling: Words With** *a-* **and** *be-*
- **Grammar, Usage, Mechanics: Common and Proper Nouns**
- **Oral Language**

EXTEND SKILLS 25 MINUTES

- **Integrated Curriculum**
- **Read Aloud**
- **Guided Reading**

RESOURCES

- **Vocabulary Transparency 3**
- **Transparency 8**
- **Practice Book 1, pp. 33–34**
- **Spelling Resource Book, p. 19**

MODIFY Instruction

ESL/ELD

▲ Show students where China is on a world map. Ask them to share any experiences they may have had with Chinese culture (perhaps knowing about a concept like eating with chopsticks). **(MAKE CONNECTIONS)**

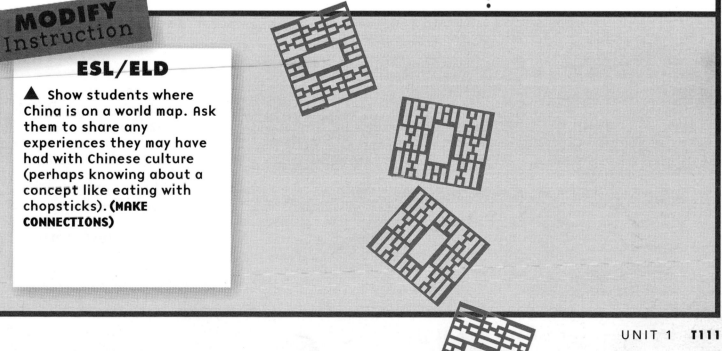

Vocabulary

Ⓐ TEACH WORD MEANINGS

INTRODUCE CONCEPT Explain that *How My Family Lives in America* contains some special words about Chinese culture.

PRESENT VOCABULARY Discuss the meaning of each word with students. Then write the word and its meaning on the chalkboard.

✔ = Tested	VOCABULARY WORDS
✔ orchid	a plant with colorful flowers found in warm, damp places (p. 50)
✔ calligraphy	the art of beautiful writing (p. 53)
sesame noodles	flat thin strips of dough covered with a sauce made from sesame seeds (p. 54)
chopsticks	a pair of small sticks used to lift food to the mouth (p. 54)
soy sauce	a dark, salty liquid made from soybeans (p. 57)
✔ scallion	a green onion (p. 57)

Ⓑ BUILD ON PRIOR KNOWLEDGE

CATEGORIZE WORDS Draw the chart below. Have students use prior knowledge and the vocabulary words to complete it.

Foods	Writing	Holidays	Other
Scallion, egg roll, sesame noodles, soy sauce	calligraphy	Chinese New Year	orchid, chopsticks

---

VOCABULARY TRACE

Build Background for
Vocabulary Words . . . . p. T112
Categorize Words . pp. T112, T132
ESL/ELD . . . . p. T112
Cloze Paragraph . . . . p. T113
Structural Analysis . . . . p. T113
Bonanza Word . . . . p. T127
Structural Analysis . . . p. T133
Extend Vocabulary . . . . p. T136

PHONICS AND SPELLING LINKS

Phonics See Selection Words With /ə/ on p. T114.

Spelling See Selection Words With *a-* and *be-* on p. R20.

MODIFY Instruction

ESL/ELD

▲ Collect pictures and realia as suggested in the Extra Help activity. Create word cards for each vocabulary word. Help students to match the words on the cards to the objects and pictures. One idea is to offer alternative phrasing: For example: orchid—a pretty flower. **(VISUAL CLUES)**

EXTRA HELP

■ Have on hand pictures of items the vocabulary words name. Display these items along with vocabulary word cards: *orchid, calligraphy, sesame noodles, soy sauce, scallion, chopsticks.* Help students identify and then match each word to its picture. **(USE REALIA)**

Name

VOCABULARY

HERITAGE OF WORDS

Read the words and their definitions. Then use the words to complete the map.

orchid: a plant with colorful flowers that grows in warm, damp places

calligraphy: fancy penmanship, or a kind of beautiful writing

sesame noodles: flat strips of dough covered with a sauce made from sesame seeds

scallion: a green onion

chopsticks: a pair of small sticks used to lift food to the mouth

soy sauce: a dark, salty liquid made from soybeans that is used as a flavoring in some Asian foods

FLOWER
orchid

TOOLS FOR EATING
chopsticks

CHINESE-AMERICAN HERITAGE

FOODS
sesame noodles
soy sauce
scallion

WRITING
calligraphy

Write a description of a meal in a Chinese restaurant. Use two words from the box.

Unit 1 · What's New? · *How My Family Lives in America* 33

PRACTICE BOOK 1, p. 33

C APPLY THROUGH MEANINGFUL SENTENCES

MODEL MEANINGFUL SENTENCES

Write the following sentences. Ask volunteers to name the context clues that help define the vocabulary word.

1. Dad grows unusual <u>flowers</u>, such as the **orchid**.
2. April uses a brush to <u>write</u> **calligraphy**.
3. **Sesame noodles** remind me of <u>spaghetti</u>.
4. The cook uses **soy sauce** to <u>flavor the Chinese food</u>.
5. The noodles had **scallions**, or <u>green onions</u>, on top.
6. We used **chopsticks** instead of a <u>fork</u>.

Sentences on Vocabulary Transparency 3

WRITE MEANINGFUL SENTENCES

Suggest that students ask themselves these questions about each word to help them write meaningful sentences: *What is it? What does it look like? How is it used?*

USE TRANS- PARENCY 8

Have students complete the cloze activity on **Transparency 8**.

SUPPORT WORDS

eyebrows	the hair above each of a person's eyes (p. 55)
tablespoon	a measuring spoon (p. 57)
powwow	a Native American get-together (p. 60)*

★ Vocabulary instruction is presented where words appear in the selection.

TRANSPARENCY 8

Scholastic Literacy Place

A FAMILY GATHERING

soy sauce	sesame noodles	chopsticks
calligraphy	scallions	orchid

Grandma's birthday party was held at her favorite Chinese restaurant. The family sent out invitations written in beautiful _____calligraphy_____. When Grandma arrived, we presented her with a sweet-smelling _____orchid_____ to pin on her dress. To begin her meal, Mei Ling ordered _____sesame noodles_____. Later, the waiter brought _____soy sauce_____ to flavor the egg rolls. Grandma enjoyed the fried rice made with chopped _____scallions_____. Naturally, everyone ate with _____chopsticks_____!

What's New? • *How My Family Lives in America* **8**

PERSONAL WORD LIST

As they read *How My Family Lives in America* and "Kids Speak Up to Save Native Languages," ask students to look for interesting or unfamiliar compound words. Encourage them to identify the word by looking at the two smaller words that make it up. Students can add the compound words and their meanings to their Journals.

Strategy: Structural Analysis

Get Word Wise

▶**TEACH** Tell students: *When you come to a word you don't know, look for clues to help you figure out what it is.* Write the following:

• *The man's <u>eyebrows</u> were thick and blond.*

THINK ALOUD *I see that the underlined word has two smaller words in it, **eye** and **brows**, so the long word must be **eyebrows**. It must be a compound word. When I put **eyebrows** back in the sentence, it makes sense.*

APPLY Write the following. Ask students to look for smaller words they know to help them identify the underlined word.

• *The recipe calls for 1 <u>tablespoon</u> of soy sauce.*

HOW TO FIGURE OUT A NEW WORD

• Try to figure out the word from letter sounds.

▶ Look for word parts that you know.

• Try to use context clues to figure out meaning.

• Look up the word in a dictionary or ask someone.

How My Family Lives in America

Susan Kuklin

SELECTION WORDS
With /ə/

America

another

about

parents

spoken

SKILLS TRACE

WORDS WITH /ə/ **TESTED**

Introduce . . . . .pp. T114–T115
Practice . . . . . . pp. T125, T132, T133, T137, T141
Review . . . . .p. R45
Reteach . . . . .p. R53

DAILY PHONICS

Words With /ə/

A PHONOLOGICAL AWARENESS

RHYME Read aloud the poem, stressing the words **ago, away,** and **asleep.** Write these words on the chalkboard and read them aloud. Ask students to repeat the words and identify the beginning sound in each.

- Write the words **person** and **happen** on the chalkboard. Have students repeat the words, listening for the same sound they heard at the beginning of **ago, away,** and **asleep.**

- Ask students to identify in which part of the word they heard the sound. (*the last syllable*)

Long Ago

Long ago and far away
An elephant came out to play.
She danced a dance,
And played a tune,
Then fell asleep beneath
the moon.

B CONNECT SOUND-SPELLING

INTRODUCE schwa /ə/ Explain to students that the letter **a** stands for the sound /ə/ in the words **ago, away,** and **asleep.** Tell them that this sound is called the schwa sound. Then write the word **wisdom** on the chalkboard and point out the letter **o.** Explain that in this word this letter also stands for the schwa sound. Point out that the letters **e** and **i** can also stand for the schwa sound, as in **taken** and **divide.**

Words With Schwa	
Schwa a	Schwa e
ago	oven
about	happen
ahead	taken

MODIFY Instruction

ESL/ELD

▲ Model common classroom commands and common English names in which students will hear the schwa sound: *Look around the room. Marie put your books away. Try again.* Have students take turns playing teacher and giving these commands to one another. **(TOTAL PHYSICAL RESPONSE)**

GIFTED & TALENTED

✷ Ask students to expand upon the Read Words activity page T115 by suggesting other words with the schwa sound. Challenge them to use these words to make up a short rhyme. **(INNOVATE)**

PHONICS MAINTENANCE Review the following sound-spellings: /ī/*i,* *igh, y, i-e, ie* and the *schwa* /ə/.

ⓒ PRACTICE/APPLY

READ WORDS To practice using the sound-spellings and review previous sound-spellings, write the following words and sentence on the chalkboard. Have students read each chorally. Model blending as needed.

ago	sudden	around
person	tonight	divide
mind	flying	supplied

We will try to eat dinner around seven o'clock tonight.

DICTATION Dictate the following words for students to spell: *ago, spoken, grind, alive, tight.*

BUILD WORDS Distribute the following letter cards, or have students use their own sets: *h, a, b, g, t, u, n, e, v, o, d, r, p.* Allow students time to build words using the cards. Students can write their words on paper. **(INDEPENDENT WORK)**

WORKING WITH WORD PARTS

Write the following common syllables on the chalkboard, one at a time. Have students read each aloud. When completed, review the syllables in random order.

ad	ple	ish	ent
ible	mid	quad	sym
est	mis	pend	dle
re	ize	un	gle
less	non	ur	ness

Repeat this procedure throughout the week using these and other syllables.

PRACTICE BOOK 1, p. 34

PROFESSIONAL DEVELOPMENT

JOHN SHEFELBINE

What Is a Schwa Sound?

The schwa sound appears in most multisyllabic words and is the most common sound in English. All vowels can stand for this sound. The schwa sound only appears in unaccented syllables.

COMPREHENSION

Preview and Predict

Let students know that in *How My Family Lives in America,* a Chinese-American girl tells us about herself and her family. Have them preview the selection by browsing through the photographs and looking at the Chinese writing shown in blue.

> **Which pictures especially interest you? Why? What do they tell you about the little girl?**

> **What would you like to learn about this little girl's life?**

Direct students to read the paragraph on page 50. Help them make predictions about the selection by asking a question:

> **How do you think this little girl's life might be the same as yours? How might it be different?**

JOURNAL

Make Predictions

Encourage students to develop predictions about the story. As they read, ask students to list facts they have discovered about Chinese culture. Students might prefer to make a semantic map, using words from the selection.

Set a Purpose

Discuss with students a purpose for reading. They may want to learn what the symbols stand for or what game the family is playing. Then have them read page 51 silently.

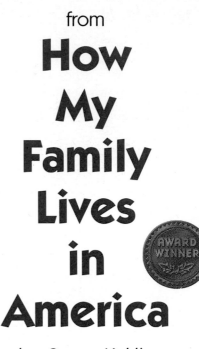

PHOTO ESSAY

from

How My Family Lives in America

AWARD WINNER

by Susan Kuklin

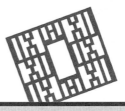

M y name in America is April. I also have a Chinese name: *Chin* (ching), which means "admire" and *Lan* (lan), which means "<u>orchid</u>."

50

CLASSROOM Management

WHOLE CLASS

On-Level Use the questions, think alouds, and Skills and Strategies lessons to guide students through a reading of the story.

Below-Level Have students listen to the story on audiocassette to familiarize themselves with the story sequence and vocabulary.

INDEPENDENT

Above-Level You may choose to have above-level students read the story independently or with a partner while you do a guided reading with the rest of the class. Students may also complete *Think About Reading* and compare their answers. Include students in the end-of-selection instruction.

51
▼

Both my parents are Chinese and were born in Taiwan. Taiwan is an island on the other side of the world. My papa came to New York without his parents to go to school and my mama moved here with her family. Because Julius, my older brother, and May, my older sister, and I were born in America, we are called Chinese Americans.

There are many Chinese Americans. But we do not all speak the same Chinese language. The way my family speaks Chinese is called Mandarin.

欽
Admire

蘭
Orchid

51

TEXT STRUCTURE
Photo Essay

TEACH/MODEL
Discuss with students the key elements of photo essays.

> A photo essay is a book or article containing many photographs about a subject.

> The photographs present detailed visual information.

> Text and captions add factual information about the photos.

PRACTICE/APPLY
Ask students to identify elements of a photo essay in parts of the story they have previewed so far.

> What can you learn from the photos that the words alone don't tell you?

> The text tells you who in the picture is telling the story. Describe the narrator and tell how you know who it is.

SMALL GROUP TO WHOLE CLASS

ESL/ELD Have children who need extra help or who are acquiring English listen to the story on the audio cassette prior to the class reading. This will help them to become familiar with the story sequence and vocabulary. Have children do the pre- and post-listening activities. **(AUDIO CLUES)**

COMPREHENSION

1 **EVALUATE AUTHOR'S PURPOSE** 🔊

> **The author gives many details about writing in Chinese. Why does she do this?** (*Possible answer: The author wants the reader to know the difference between writing in English and writing in Chinese.*)

INTERVENTION TIP ◎

Adjust Reading Rate

The idea of writing with special marks may be a new idea for some students. If they are having trouble understanding how this writing is done, have them read the description again slowly to make sure they understand all the details. After they have read it again, it may be easier for them to picture how Chinese writing is done.

✓INFORMAL ASSESSMENT
OBSERVATION

Vocabulary Assess students' recognition and understanding of the vocabulary word *calligraphy* as they read the selection.

Did students:

✔ use picture clues to figure out the word?

✔ use the context clue "special kind of writing"

✔ pronounce the word correctly?

Father

Mother

In Mandarin, I call my daddy *baba* (bah-bah) and my mommy *mama* (mah-mah). It sounds something like English, but when we write the words they look very different. Another thing that's different in Chinese is that words aren't made with letters. Each word has its own special marks.

During the week we go to public school, but on Saturday we go to Chinese school. There we learn how to speak and write in Chinese, like my parents learned in Taiwan. When I write English letters, I write from the left side of the page to the right. When I write in Chinese, I write from the right to the left. And I write in rows from the top of the page to the bottom. For us Chinese-American kids there are many things **1** to remember.

52

MODIFY Instruction

ESL/ELD

▲ To help students with the Intervention Tip, show them pictures of Chinese text. Then ask two students to stand at the chalkboard. Have one write a word left to right in English, while the other writes the same word right to left. **(KINESTHETIC)**

GIFTED & TALENTED

✳ Challenge students to create a glossary of names for family members that represents all the languages of the class. Suggest that they list the English words in one column and set up as many other columns as needed. Ask them to use language dictionaries to make their glossary. **(RESEARCH)**

53
▼

In Chinese school we also learn a special kind of writing called <u>calligraphy</u>. We use a brush instead of a pen, black ink, and special paper made from stalks of rice. Our teacher shows us the right way to hold the brush.

53

SKILLS AND STRATEGIES

✔ **COMPREHENSION**
Evaluate Author's Purpose

TEACH/MODEL
Explain to students that the three reasons why an author writes a selection is: to persuade, to inform, or to entertain.

THINK ALOUD *In this selection, the author has given me many facts. Therefore, I can conclude that the purpose is to inform.*

PRACTICE/APPLY
Ask students to complete the graphic organizer using the facts the author has given.

	Facts
Family	1. parents born in Taiwan 2. father came to New York for school; mother came with family
Language	1. family speaks Chinese 2. baba means daddy; mama means mama

> **Based on all the facts you've read so far, what do you think the author's purpose is?**

✔ **INFORMAL ASSESSMENT**
OBSERVATION
Did students:

✔ identify specific facts in the selection?

✔ use clues from the selection to help them determine the author's purpose?

See pages T130–T131 for a full skills lesson on Evaluate Author's Purpose.

THE ARTS
Ask students to complete the **Chinese Writing** activity on **page R25**, where they'll use calligraphy to make a greeting card for a friend. Students will learn what greetings some Chinese characters stand for.

TIME MANAGEMENT
Encourage family members to set up regular routines for completing homework. Each day they should ask their child what homework has been assigned and help set up a schedule for completing it. Family members can check to find out if the child is following the schedule.
(1-MINUTE LITERACY BYTE)

COMPREHENSION

2 **CRITICAL THINKING: ANALYZE**

> Look at the symbols—the Chinese words in blue. Why are they included? How do they help you understand what Chinese writing is like?

(Possible answer: The marks are included to show how different Chinese writing is from English writing and why it might be hard to learn.)

3 **EVALUATE AUTHOR'S PURPOSE**

> April loves to eat noodles. Why do you think the author shares this information? What does it tell you about the author's purpose?

(Possible answer: The author wants to give information about the girl, her Chinese-American family, and popular Chinese dishes.)

INTERVENTION TIP

Different Text Structures

Some students may need help deciding what to read or look at first on a page. Suggest that they first look at the photographs and the Chinese writing on the side, and then read the text. Then have them explain first what they learn from the text and next explain what they learn from the pictures.

54
▼

芝
蘇
涼
麵

Cold Sesame
Noodles

2 My favorite part of Chinese school is snack time. Today, Mama made me cold sesame noodles, *tsu ma liang mein* (tsu mah leeang mee-en). I eat them with a fork, but most Chinese people eat their noodles with chopsticks. I'm just **3** learning to eat with chopsticks.

Papa told us that an Italian explorer named Marco Polo discovered noodles in China a long time ago and introduced them to his country.

When Mama brought home takeout, Julius asked if a Chinese explorer discovered pizza in Italy.

Mama and Papa laughed and said, "No."

54

MODIFY Instruction

ESL/ELD

▲ Encourage students to name favorite snack foods from their own cultures. How many of them name noodle dishes? Help students to see that the author wants readers to see the ways that cultures are alike, as well as different. **(MULTICULTURAL)**

EXTRA HELP

■ Help students review the page to find factual information. Lead them to understand that the factual information can be proven, and that sometimes informative writing can sound like a story. Then, have them point out parts of the selection that "sound" like a story. **(KEY POINTS)**

55
▼

While we eat our pizza we play a game to test our wits. Papa asks us to look for letters hidden in the picture on the pizza box. Julius sees a *V* in the pizza man's shoe. May finds an *L*.

Oh, look! I can even see the Chinese letter *Ba* (bah), in the pizza man's eyebrows. *Ba* means "eight" in Chinese.

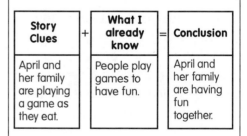

Eight

55

SKILLS AND STRATEGIES

COMPREHENSION
Draw Conclusions

TEACH/MODEL
Explain to students that in a photo essay they can find clues in both the text and photographs to draw conclusions about people and events.

> **Think about what the pictures show and the text describes.**

> **Ask yourself if you have ever done the same or a similar thing.**

> **Combine what you learn through the pictures and text with what you already know to draw conclusions.**

PRACTICE/APPLY
Ask students to use the graphic organizer below to draw a conclusion about April and her family.

Story Clues	+	What I already know	=	Conclusion
April and her family are playing a game as they eat.		People play games to have fun.		April and her family are having fun together.

> **What does the game mean to April and her family?**

TECHNOLOGY

Finding the Facts
Students can learn about traditional celebrations by visiting **www.scholasticnetwork.com.** Take the Internet field trip called *Celebrate Chinese New Year!* Note similarities between these New Year's customs and those observed by the students.

SOCIAL STUDIES

Ask students to do the **Find a Route to China** activity on **page R25**. Students will trace the route that Marco Polo took when he traveled to China. The activity will develop students' map skills.

COMPREHENSION

4 **TEXT STRUCTURE**

> **In a photo essay, text and photographs tell a nonfiction story. How would the selection be different without photos?** (*Possible answer: Without photos it would be more difficult to create a picture of April's family, learn how calligraphy is done, and understand the games the family plays.*)

5 **EVALUATE AUTHOR'S PURPOSE**

> **What parts of the story are the most informative?** (*Possible answer: The most informative parts are when April tells about calligraphy and about the Mandarin language.*)

6 **CRITICAL THINKING: SYNTHESIZE**

> **How do you think the information April learns will change her? Why do you think this? How can learning about your cultural heritage help you appreciate your customs and traditions?** (*Possible answer: April will be proud of her cultural heritage as a Chinese American. She enjoys learning about her culture. Customs and traditions tell us about ourselves and our family.*)

JOURNAL

Revisit Predictions

Ask students to look back at their predictions and record how the predictions were or were not confirmed by the end of the story.

七
巧
板

Chi chiao bang

At night when we have finished all our chores and all our homework, we play *Chi chiao bang* (chee chow bang). In America some people call it Tangram. This is a popular game in Taiwan, like checkers is in America. My grandparents and even my great-grandparents played this game. To play, you move seven different shapes to build a new shape. I like to make a pussycat. It is very difficult, but I can do it. Papa says, "Go slowly and think about a cat. After a while your mind will start to run and you will see the cat in the shapes." He's right.

There is an old Chinese saying, "The older you are the wiser you become." When I become a grown-up, I will remember to tell this to my family.

5 **6**

56

MODIFY Instruction

ESL/ELD

▲ Ask students to describe the photograph of April's family. Include all students by asking multi-level questions: *Point to April. Is this her brother? Does April have an older sister or a younger sister? What are they all doing? Have you ever tried to play this game?* (**MULTI-LEVEL QUESTIONS**)

GIFTED & TALENTED

✳ April's family likes to play *tangram*. Have students find out how to play some games from other cultures, such as *wari*, from West Africa; *pachise*, known as the national game of India; or *dominoes*, originally from China. Have students teach the class some of these new games. (**RESEARCH**)

57
▼

April's Cold Sesame Noodles

(1 serving)

2 ounces cooked Chinese noodles or spaghetti
1 tablespoon sesame sauce or peanut butter
1 teaspoon <u>soy sauce</u>
1 teaspoon chopped <u>scallion</u>

In a bowl mix the sesame sauce (or peanut butter) with 1 tablespoon warm water and soy sauce. Add to the cooked, cooled noodles and sprinkle scallion on top. Stir before eating.

57

Quickwrite

RETURN TO PURPOSE

Now that students have read *How My Family Lives in America* on pages 50–57, ask them to write a list. Have them copy onto a piece of paper the head *What I Have Learned.* Encourage them to write at least five items.

DAILY LANGUAGE PRACTICE

SPELLING

DAY 1:
Administer the Pretest for Words With *a-* and *be-*, **See page R20.**

GRAMMAR, USAGE, MECHANICS

DAY 1:
Teach and Model Common and Proper Nouns. **See page R22.**

ORAL LANGUAGE

many peopul have come from china. (*Many <u>people</u> have come from <u>China</u>.*)

DAY **1** WRAP-UP

READ ALOUD *To develop students' oral vocabularies, spend five to ten minutes reading from a selection of your choice.*

GUIDED READING *To extend reading, meet with the* **blue** *and* **green** *reading groups and assign Independent Center activities.* ***See pages R18–R19.***

MATH

Ask students to complete the **Chinese Puzzle** activity on **page R24**, where they'll use tangram pieces to make different shapes, as April does in the selection. The activity will develop students' awareness of spatial relationships.

SCIENCE

Ask students to complete the **Classify a Chinese Recipe** activity on **page R24**, where they'll use a food pyramid to classify the ingredients in the recipe in *How My Family Lives in America.* Students will learn to select foods for a balanced meal.

COMPREHENSION

DAY 2 OBJECTIVES

STUDENTS WILL:

READ 35 MINUTES

- "Kids Speak Up to Save Native Languages," pp. 58–61
- Daily Phonics: Words With /ə/

WRITE 35 MINUTES

- Writing Workshop: Prewrite Nonfiction Description
- Spelling: Words With *a-* and *be-*
- Grammar, Usage, Mechanics: Common and Proper Nouns
- Oral Language

EXTEND SKILLS 20 MINUTES

- Read Aloud
- Guided Reading

RESOURCES

- Spelling Resource Book, pp. 20–22

▶ Preview

Ask students to preview the article by looking at the pictures and reading the captions and headings. Prompt discussion:

> How might a language be saved? What will you learn about languages from this selection?

1 MAIN IDEA/DETAILS

> What is the most important idea on this page? How do the captions support this idea? *(The Hupa language is dying out. The captions tell about people who are helping to keep the Hupa language alive.)*

MAGAZINE ARTICLE

AWARD WINNER

Kids Speak Up to Save Native Languages

BY SARAH JANE BRIAN

58

MODIFY Instruction

ESL/ELD

▲ Encourage students to look at the photographs and the captions. Remind them what a proper noun is. Then ask them to pick out two proper nouns that give a clue about the children. *(Cherokee, Navajo)* Where are these children from? What languages do they speak? **(PICTURE CLUES)**

GIFTED & TALENTED

✳ Reinforce the idea of keeping native languages alive by having students write advertisements for a Hupa language course. Suggest that they write their ads for children, including three reasons why the course is important. Ask volunteers to read their ads to the class. **(INNOVATE)**

59
▼

◄ **Wearing colorful handmade costumes and dancing are two ways that Native Americans keep their traditions alive.**

"*Hey-yung*!"

That means "hello" in the Native American language of Hupa (HOOP-ah). For thousands of years, Hupa people used this language to share their thoughts, feelings, and ideas. Today, only 20 people speak Hupa well enough to hold a conversation. All of them are older members of the tribe, called elders. Most children and young adults in the tribe speak English, and know only a few Hupa words.

▲ **This Cherokee storyteller passes on traditional tales to interested listeners.**

Fourth grader David Drake wants to make sure his tribe's language doesn't die out. He is one of many Hupa kids who are trying to learn Hupa before it is too late. Last summer, David and his family went to a special language camp. There, they cooked and ate traditional foods, sang songs, and listened to stories in Hupa. "It was fun," David said. "During everything that we did, we learned new words in Hupa."

1

◄ **A young Navajo girl is learning her native language in school.**

59

TECHNOLOGY

Presentation Tools Guide students as they use **Smart Place** PlaceMaker to create their own tangrams. Use the shapes available in the software to make a set of paper tiles. Print copies of each set and cut them out. Students might take turns helping one another make designs.

CULTURAL CONNECTION

During World War II, Navajo soldiers were radio operators in the U.S. Army. Because their language could not be translated, top-secret messages could be sent and received without the code being broken.

DAILY PHONICS

☑ Words With /ə/

TEACH/MODEL Review with students that in the word *America* the first letter *a* stands for the schwa sound. That same sound is represented by the letter *e* in **happen,** *i* in **direct,** *o* in **gallop,** and *u* in **circus.**

• Write the words on the chalkboard and have volunteers circle the letter *a, e, i, o,* or *u.*

• Ask students to suggest words that contain the schwa sound, spelled *a, e, i, o,* or *u.*

PHONICS MAINTENANCE Review the following sound-spellings: /ī/ *i, igh, y, i-e, ie* the schwa /ə/.

PRACTICE/APPLY

READ WORDS List these words on the chalkboard. Have students read each chorally. Model blending as needed.

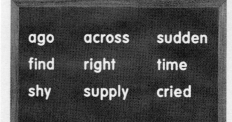

ago	across	sudden
find	right	time
shy	supply	cried

☑ INFORMAL ASSESSMENT
OBSERVATION

Did students:

✔ identify words with the schwa sound?

✔ connect /ə/ with the letters *a, e, i, o,* and *u*?

◉ **IF** students need additional support with the schwa sound,

THEN see page T132.

COMPREHENSION

2 MAKE INFERENCES

> This article explains that over one thousand native languages were spoken in North America at one time. Now most of them are forgotten. Why do you think this happened? *(Possible answer: In the past, Native Americans were not allowed to speak their native languages.)*

3 EVALUATE AUTHOR'S VIEWPOINT

> How do you think the author feels about Native American languages? What clues in the selection make you think this? *(She doesn't want Native American languages to die out. She includes reasons why it's important to keep them alive.)*

4 CRITICAL THINKING: EVALUATE

> Why do you think it's important to save native languages? *(Possible answer: Native languages are an important part of the heritage and culture of all people.)*

60
▼

▲ During a 4th of July powwow, or get-together, these Kiowa boys and girls learn traditional dances and stories.

Lost Languages

Hupa is not the only language that is in trouble. According to expert Dr. Clay Slate, more than 1,000 different native languages were once spoken in North America. Most of them have been forgotten. Today, there are only 206 of these languages left.

In the past, the U.S. government wanted Native Americans to give up their languages. David's great-grandmother was punished when she spoke Hupa in school. Today, that has changed. In 1990, the U.S. Congress passed a law to help protect native languages. Soon, a new law may provide money for tribes that want to save their languages. **2**

Getting Tongues Un-tied

Navajo teacher Andrew Becenti says we must save native languages because they are important parts of Native American cultures. "If you don't have the **3**

60

MODIFY Instruction

ESL/ELD

▲ Help all students in the class participate in the discussion about "forgotten languages." Make a class chart showing grandparents or friends who share another language or culture with students. Ask students if they hear other languages besides English at home. **(RELATE TO REAL LIFE)**

EXTRA HELP

■ Help students understand that this map is a population map, showing places where groups of people live—in this case, Native Americans. Ask them to identify the state with the largest American Indian reservation (AZ). Continue identifying larger areas. **(GRAPHIC DEVICE)**

61 ▼

language, and you try to teach the culture, it's like food without any salt. Something's missing. It's just flat," he said.

All across the U.S., many Native Americans are already working to preserve their languages. In some places, elders work to teach younger people. On the Navajo reservation in Tuba City,

Arizona, kids can take Navajo language classes in school.

Learning to speak a new language is not easy. It can take years. But people like David and his family plan to study hard for as long as it takes. "Our language is part of our heritage. We can't just let it die off," said David's mom.

❹

WHERE AMERICAN INDIANS LIVE

Long before Columbus arrived, nearly a million people lived in America. Columbus called them Indians. They belonged to different tribes across the land. Today nearly two million American Indian people live in the U.S. states shown on this map.

Most live in towns and cities. But many live on reservations—pieces of land that have been set aside for native tribes. The large blue areas on the map show the larger reservations. The small blue areas show smaller reservations and other places where American Indians live.

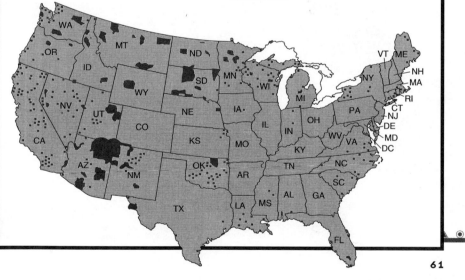

61

CONNECTING TO THEME

Discuss with students that both April Chen and the Native American boys and girls are learning about their traditional worlds from studying their culture and language. Have them describe a tradition, such as birthdays or holidays, that they have learned from their family or culture.

WORD STUDY

Powwow, the Bonanza word, is one of many words borrowed from Native American languages. Originally *powwow* meant "a ceremony for a particular event." Now it means a get-together. Students can record or "bank" their Bonanza words in a milk carton with a slit in it.

Nonfiction Description

WRITING WORKSHOP

Prewrite

Discuss family gatherings and family recipes. Let students know that later they will be writing a nonfiction description of a family celebration that includes a traditional recipe. Have them think of a family celebration and recipe and begin to complete the prewriting organizer.

Use Practice Book 1, page 35.

DAILY LANGUAGE PRACTICE

SPELLING

DAY 2:
Practice the Spelling Words With *a-* and *be-*. **See page R20.**

GRAMMAR, USAGE, MECHANICS

DAY 2:
Practice Common and Proper Nouns. **See page R22.**

ORAL LANGUAGE

Have you ever spokin in hupa
(*Have you ever* <u>spoken</u> *in* <u>Hupa</u>?)

DAY **2** WRAP-UP

READ ALOUD *Spend five to ten minutes reading from a selection of your choice.*

GUIDED READING *Meet with the* **green** *and* **red** *reading groups and assign Independent Center activities.* *See pages R18–R19.*

COMPREHENSION

DAY 3 OBJECTIVES

STUDENTS WILL:

READ 40 MINUTES

- Reread *How My Family Lives in America*
- Assess Comprehension
- Key Comprehension Skill: Evaluate Author's Purpose
- Daily Phonics: Words With /ə/

WRITE 30 MINUTES

- Respond: Caption
- Spelling: Words With *a-* and *be-*
- Grammar, Usage, Mechanics: Common and Proper Nouns
- Oral Language

EXTEND SKILLS 20 MINUTES

- Read Aloud
- Guided Reading

RESOURCES

- Transparency 9
- Practice Book 1, pp. 36–40
- Spelling Resource Book, p. 23

▶ Think About Reading

Below are the **answers** to the Think About Reading questions.

1. *She goes to a special school where she learns to speak and write in Mandarin Chinese.*

2. *Because both her parents were born in Taiwan, China, they want her to know the language and culture of China.*

3. *Answers will vary.*

4. *Possible answer: Photos make the best illustrations because they show that April is a real person.*

5. *Accept all reasonable responses.*

62

RESPOND

Think About Reading

Write your answers.

1. What does April do each Saturday?

2. Why do April's parents want her to learn calligraphy and to play Tangram?

3. How is April's Saturday school like your school? In what ways is it different?

4. Why do you think Susan Kuklin used photos to illustrate this story?

5. In what way does David Drake in "Kids Speak Up to Save Native Languages" remind you of April in *How My Family Lives in America*?

MODIFY Instruction

ESL/ELD

▲ Go over these pages orally with students. Provide guidance by writing captions and making a Venn diagram. Model and prompt as much as you need to; students may enjoy captioning photos of their own families, and making a Venn diagram comparing April to themselves. **(STEP-BY-STEP)**

PRACTICE BOOK 1, p. 36

Write a Caption

Even a great photograph needs a caption. Look at the photographs that Susan Kuklin took of April. Choose three of them. Write a caption for each one. Tell who is pictured. In a few words, tell what is happening.

Literature Circle

Think about *How My Family Lives in America* and "Kids Speak Up to Save Native Languages." How are the two articles alike? How are they different? Talk about the kinds of information in each article. Think about each author's purpose. Use a Venn diagram to record your ideas.

Author
Susan Kuklin

Photographer and author Susan Kuklin has always been interested in art and people's stories. After college she acted in plays and even taught school for a while. Her interest in art led her to photography. Then she put all her interests—people, photography, and stories—together and began to make nonfiction books for children. Her goal is to help people better understand each other.

More Books by
Susan Kuklin

- *Fighting Fires*
- *Kodomo: Children of Japan*
- *Taking My Dog to the Vet*

63

TECHNOLOGY

Language Development Have students use **Smart Place** PlaceMaker to create "photos" and captions. Select clip art, frame it, and write a caption for the picture. Encourage students to use common nouns when writing the captions. Next, have them exchange pictures and recaption the pieces.

AUTHOR/ILLUSTRATOR STUDY

Have students check out Susan Kuklin's web site at **www.penguinputnam.com** and use "author search" to find her page. They can learn all about the author and find out about projects she is working on right now.

Write a Caption

Before students begin to write, have them think about these questions:

> **What information will help readers understand the photos?**

> **Which *who, what, where, when,* and *why* details should I include in my captions?**

Students may want to read their captions aloud.

Literature Circle

Students may record some of the following ideas in their Venn diagrams: *How My Family Lives in America* is about a Chinese family, whereas "Kids Speak Up" is about Native Americans.

DAILY LANGUAGE PRACTICE

SPELLING
DAY 3:
Write the Spelling Words With *a-, be-*. **See page R21.**

GRAMMAR, USAGE, MECHANICS
DAY 3:
Practice Common and Proper Nouns. **See page R23.**

ORAL LANGUAGE
Its good for april to learn ubout China.
(*It's* good for *April* to learn *about* China.)

COMPREHENSION
Evaluate Author's Purpose

✓ QUICKCHECK

Can students:

✔ determine whether the author's purpose is to inform, persuade, or entertain?

✔ explain why they chose a particular author's purpose?

If **YES**, go on to Practice/Apply.

If **NO**, start at Teach/Model.

ⓐ TEACH/MODEL

USE ORAL LANGUAGE

Ask students to explain what they know about an *author's purpose* for writing a story or an article. Reinforce that authors have three basic purposes for writing a selection: to persuade, to inform, or to entertain.

Present students with the mnemonic device **P.I.E.** to help them remember an author's three possible purposes. If they are unsure of an author's purpose, they can review in order each of the letters.

P is for "persuade"—the author tries to convince the reader to believe as he or she does.

I is for "inform"—the author has information to present.

E is for "entertain"—the author mainly wants the reader to enjoy the piece of writing.

MODIFY Instruction

ESL/ELD

▲ Make sure students understand the terms *persuade, inform,* and *entertain.* Guide them with questions: *Does a speech inform or persuade? How about a comic book?* Discuss how a newspaper can persuade, inform, and entertain. **(EVALUATE)**

EXTRA HELP

■ Have students list at least three facts the author of *How My Family Lives in America* presents in the selection. This focused review will help them recall that the author wrote the selection to inform the reader. **(KEY POINTS/SUMMARIZE)**

LITERATURE CONNECTION

Display **Transparency 9** to help students learn how to evaluate the author's purpose.

THINK ALOUD *On page 51 of* How My Family Lives in America, *the author told me where April's parents are from and why her father came to America. I also found out that April's family speaks Mandarin Chinese. I think that the author wanted me to know about the Chinese people, so she included these facts. After reading some more important facts on page 52, I decide that the author's main purpose is to inform. Knowing this helped me decide to read the selection slowly so I don't miss any information.*

Ⓑ PRACTICE/APPLY

USE PRACTICE BOOK 1

Have pairs of students practice the skill by completing **Practice Book 1, pages 38 and 39.** (PARTNERS)

Ⓒ ASSESS

APPLY INSTRUCTIONAL ALTERNATIVES

Based on students' completion of **Transparency 9** and **Practice Book 1, pages 38** and **39**, determine if they were able to evaluate the author's purpose in *How My Family Lives in America*. The Instructional Alternatives below will aid you in pinpointing students' level of proficiency. Consider the appropriate instructional alternative to promote further skill development.

To reinforce the skills, distribute **Practice Book 1, page 40.**

☑ INSTRUCTIONAL ALTERNATIVES

	If the student . . .	Then
Proficient	Accurately determines the author's purpose	• Have students choose one of the author's purposes and make up a short story that reflects that purpose. Then they tell their story to another group, who determines the first group's purpose for telling it.
Apprentice	Determines the author's purpose but cannot provide text clues to help them support that purpose	• Pair learners with proficient readers to talk about a selection they've read. Have one student briefly retell the story. Then students can talk about the purpose of the selection.
Novice	Determines an author's purpose that does not fit the selection and the clues provided within the text	• Provide the student with clues from the text and work together to select the purpose based on the clues.

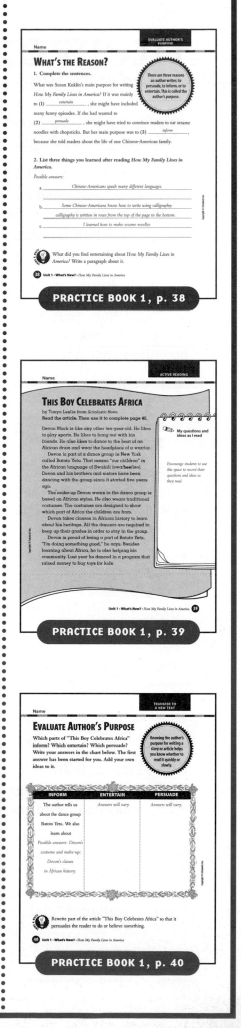

PRACTICE BOOK 1, p. 38

PRACTICE BOOK 1, p. 39

PRACTICE BOOK 1, p. 40

Intervention

For students who need extra help with. . .

PHONICS

IDENTIFYING SPELLING PATTERNS

Say pairs of words and ask students to repeat the word that contains a schwa *a* or *e*. For example, say *again, airplane*. Students should respond with *again*. Use these and other sets of words:

- <u>pizza</u>, pony
- chili, <u>spoken</u>
- English, <u>Hupa</u>
- <u>money</u>, rope

PARTNERS Have partners make an accordion book of words with schwa. Have the students fold a sheet of construction paper accordion style and write one word on each folded section.

COMPREHENSION

EVALUATE AUTHOR'S PURPOSE

Help students understand the author's purpose. Have them find places in the selection where the author provides information.

- Have students add the information to the chart.
- Display the chart for students to copy.
- Help students find information from the text that reveals the author's purpose.

Information from the story:

Taiwan is an island.

Chinese Americans speak different languages.

Chinese words are not made with letters.

FLUENCY

READING ALOUD

Provide your students with opportunities to read aloud daily, using books and magazines in your classroom.

Choose from a variety of quality selections of all genres. Model fluent reading by reading to students with expression, varying your tone and pitch, and emphasizing important words. Divide the class into small groups. Have groups read in "round-robin" fashion, with each student reading one or more paragraphs and passing the selection to her or his neighbor.

Optional Materials for Intervention

PHONICS

Schwa /ə/

If students need help with schwa sound, use the **Phonics Chapter Book, The Internet.**

CONNECT SOUND–SPELLING

TEACH/MODEL Explain to students that they will be focusing on words with the *schwa* sound. Have students blend the following words and listen for the *schwa* sound in the first or last syllable.

In first syllable	In last syllable
a bout	hap pen
a bove	gal lop

PRACTICE/APPLY Write the following words and have students identify the syllable that contains the schwa sound:

ago   awful   lemon   cabin

READ THE INTERNET

Assign Chapter 1 of the book. Check with students and provide support as they continue the story, chapter by chapter.

LISTENING

If students need help with fluency, use the audiocassette for How My Family Lives in America.

MODEL FLUENT READING

Use *How My Family Lives in America,* or another selection, to model fluent reading for your students.

CHORAL READING

Have students read a passage with you. Support them by reading more quietly when they are sustaining fluent reading, and by increasing volume when they are having difficulty sustaining fluency.

DAY **3** WRAP-UP

READ ALOUD *Spend five to ten minutes reading from a selection of your choice.*

GUIDED READING *Meet with the* **red** *and* **blue** *reading groups and assign Independent Center activities.* **See pages R18–R19.**

DAY 4 OBJECTIVES

STUDENTS WILL:

READ 20 MINUTES
- Reread *How My Family Lives in America*

WRITE 40 MINUTES
- Writing Workshop: Nonfiction Description
- Writer's Craft: Logical Order
- Spelling: Words With *a-*, *be-*
- Grammar, Usage, Mechanics: Common and Proper Nouns
- Oral Language

EXTEND SKILLS 30 MINUTES
- Vocabulary
- Daily Phonics: Schwa /ə/
- Study Skills: Alphabetical Order
- Read Aloud
- Guided Reading

RESOURCES
- Transparency 10
- Practice Book 1, pp. 35, 41–42

Students may refer to *The Scholastic Spelling Dictionary* and *Writing With Style*.

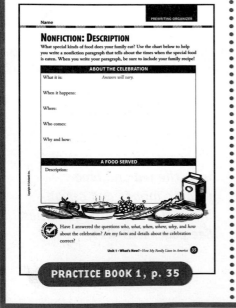

PRACTICE BOOK 1, p. 35

WRITING WORKSHOP *Expressive Writing*
Nonfiction Description

THINK ABOUT WRITING
Refer students to *How My Family Lives in America*. Ask:

> **What family gatherings does the story describe?**

> **What recipe does it include? Does your family have any special recipes?**

LITERATURE CONNECTION
Have students look back at **page 56**. Point out that April gives details about *when* the family gets together and *what* they do. Suggest that students include similar details in their own descriptions.

PREWRITE

COMPLETE A GRAPHIC ORGANIZER
Have students refer to the graphic organizer on **Practice Book 1, page 35** that they began earlier. They might list details for another family celebration and recipe.

DRAFT

TEACH WRITER'S CRAFT
Before students begin their drafts, help them understand how to organize the information. See **Writer's Craft**, page **T135**.

> **Imagine that you are describing a family celebration and recipe to someone. What facts and details will you include? In what order will you present the information?**

REVISE/PROOFREAD

REVISE
Note: You may wish to do Revise/Proofread on Day 5.
As students revise and proofread, they might want to ask themselves:

- Do I arrange my details in logical order?

- Have I included all the ingredients and directions needed to make my dish?

PROOFREAD
- Have I used common nouns correctly, writing them in all lowercase letters?

- Does each proper noun begin with a capital letter?

✔ See Student's Writing Rubric on page T142.

WRITER'S CRAFT
LOGICAL ORDER

A TEACH/MODEL

Ask students why it would not make sense for them to put on their boots before they stepped into their pants. Help them to recognize that when writing, it is as important to follow a logical or sensible order as when they get dressed in the morning.

Refer students to the recipe *April's Cold Sesame Noodles* on page 57. Point out that the recipe is presented in a logical order because by the time readers get to the directions, they will know how much of each ingredient to use.

B PRACTICE/APPLY

- **Use Transparency 10,** or write the following recipe on the chalkboard.

- Tell students that the directions in the recipe(s) are not in logical order. Ask them to renumber the directions to make the order logical. (Stuffed Eggs: 2, 4, 5, 1, 3) Have volunteers explain why the new order makes sense.

Stuffed Eggs

Ingredients	Directions
5 hard-boiled eggs 2 tablespoons plain yogurt paprika	1. Sprinkle the finished eggs with paprika. 2. Cut eggs in half, lengthwise. 3. Serve. 4. Scoop out yolks. 5. Mix with yogurt.

Scholastic Literacy Place

Stuffed Eggs

Ingredients
5 hard-boiled eggs
2 tablespoons plain yogurt
paprika

Directions
1. Sprinkle the finished eggs with paprika.
2. Cut eggs in half, lengthwise.
3. Serve.
4. Scoop out yolks.
5. Mix with yogurt.

Grilled Cheese Sandwich

Ingredients
1 slice Swiss cheese
1 slice whole wheat bread

Directions
1. Place cheese on bread.
2. Unwrap cheese slice.
3. Toast bread and cheese.
4. Remove single slice of bread from package.

What's New? • *How My Family Lives in America* 10

DAILY LANGUAGE PRACTICE

SPELLING
DAY 4:
Review Spelling Words With *a-, be-.* **See page R21.**

GRAMMAR, USAGE, MECHANICS
DAY 4:
Apply Common and Proper Nouns. **See page R23.**

ORAL LANGUAGE

Do americans twirl noodles eround their forks.
(Do <u>Americans</u> twirl noodles around their forks<u>?</u>)

TECHNOLOGY

Writing Skills
Encourage students to use the spell-check option in a familiar word processing program to help them proofread their writing.

TEACHER TIP

"I encourage students to collect interesting words for a once-a-week Name That Word game. Students write each word on an index card along with its definition. To play, students take turns giving three hints about a word. Other players can ask questions to help them guess the word. Students can read the definition of any word that stumps the players, provide additional clues, or spell part of the word."

Extend Vocabulary

Review Vocabulary

CLUES TO MEANING

Write or say the vocabulary words. Then read each sentence aloud and have students write or name the missing word.

1. Rows of long, skinny onions called _____ were growing in the garden. *(scallions)*

2. Did you use _____ or a fork to eat your Chinese food? *(chopsticks)*

3. If the meat needs flavoring, pour some _____ on it. *(soy sauce)*

4. The boy's Chinese grandmother taught him how to hold the brush when writing _____. *(calligraphy)*

5. We cut the dough into narrow strips and sprinkled it with special sauce to make _____. *(sesame noodles)*

6. A colorful _____ grows wild in the rain forest. *(orchid)*

Expand Vocabulary

COMPOUND WORDS WITH *eye*

Write the word ***eyebrows*** on the chalkboard and point out that it is a compound word. Explain that several compound words in the English language begin with the word ***eye***. Draw a word web and encourage students to add some of those words.

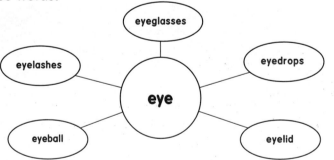

Students can make additional webs for compound words in "Kids Speak Up to Save Native Languages" (for example, ***handmade, storyteller, grandmother, something***).

Record Vocabulary

MENU OF FAVORITE WORDS

Ask students to make a menu of favorite foods that include some of the Chinese and Italian foods mentioned in *How My Family Lives in America*. Each item will be numbered and include a brief description. Students can exchange their menus and tell which items they would order.

Words With /ə/

LETTER TIC-TAC-TOE

Draw a tic-tac-toe grid on the chalkboard. In each square, write an incomplete word that contains a schwa sound. Leave a blank for the letter. Use these and other words of your choice.

_go	lem_n	awf_l	forgott_n	_mong
circ_s	d_vide	spok_n	_lone	ev_n

MATERIALS:
Oaktag,
Marker or Pen,
Pencils

SUGGESTED GROUPING:
Partners

1 SET-UP Have pairs of students copy from the chalkboard the tic-tac-toe grid, including the incomplete words.

spok_n	_lone	lem_n
circ_s	_go	_mong
d_vide	awf_l	ev_n

2 TO PLAY Each player chooses to be X or O. In order to mark a square with an X or an O, the player must complete the square's word by filling in the missing letter, and then reading the word aloud.

Next, players must identify the schwa sound in the completed word.

The object of the game is to get three X's or three O's in a row horizontally, vertically, or diagonally. The first player to do so wins the game.

3 TRY THIS Provide only two incomplete words per card—one with schwa in the first syllable and one with schwa in the second syllable. Players must complete the two words and then write other words with schwa in the first or second syllables.

PRACTICE BOOK 1, p. 41

MODIFY Instruction

ESL/ELD

▲ Provide several word cards containing words with schwa sound in the first syllable, such as *above*, and schwa sound in the second syllable, such as *happen*. Have partners say each word aloud and then sort the words according to the position of the schwa sound. **(WORK IN PAIRS)**

GIFTED & TALENTED

✳ Have pairs of students search for schwa words in reading materials in the classroom. Ask them to make lists of these words for use in playing the Tic-Tac-Toe game. Some students may want to devise a game of their own. **(WORK IN PAIRS)**

STUDY SKILLS
Alphabetical Order

Ⓐ TEACH/MODEL

ALPHABETICAL ORDER | **TESTED**
Introduce . . . . .p. T138
Practice . . . . .p. T139
Review . . . . .p. R46
Reteach . . . . .p. R53

SKILLS TRACE

RESEARCH IDEA

Have students use an encyclopedia and other reference materials to create an alphabetized list of Native American groups of North America. Remind students to include the Native Americans mentioned in the article "Kids Speak Up to Save Native Languages."

DISCUSS ALPHABETICAL ORDER

Ask students why they think all the names in a phone book are listed in alphabetical order. (*It is much easier to find a name if it is listed by its first letter.*) Point out that people also use alphabetical order to find information in other reference sources, such as a dictionary, a glossary, an index, and an encyclopedia.

REVIEW ALPHABETIZ-ING TO THE THIRD LETTER

List the following sets of names on the chalkboard. Work with students to alphabetize the names in List 1 to the first letter. Lead students to notice that in order to alphabetize the names in List 2, they must look at the second letter. Ask volunteers to alphabetize the list. Then use the words in List 3 to demonstrate when they must alphabetize to the third letter.

1	2	3	4
Chang	Lyons	Riskal	Mahoney
Adams	Lee	Riley	Maher
Williams	Landry	Rivera	Mahmood

TEACH ALPHABETIZ-ING TO THE FOURTH LETTER

Model how to alphabetize the words in List 4 to the fourth letter.

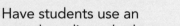 **THINK ALOUD** *I see that each name begins with the same three letters—**M, a, h**. In order to alphabetize the names, I need to look at the fourth letter—**o, e, m**. When I alphabetize these letters as **e, m, o**, I know to put the full names in this order: **Maher, Mahmood, Mahoney**.*

SHOW GUIDE WORDS

If possible, show guide words in a dictionary, an encyclopedia, and a telephone book. Explain that in these reference books, guide words are usually found at the tops of the pages. Point out that the guide words help readers find the entry they want. All the entries on a page fall alphabetically between the two guide words on that page.

ⓑ PRACTICE/APPLY

List the following words on the chalkboard and ask students to write the words alphabetically in each column.

1	2	3	4
mansion	hermit	parent	tangram
Mandarin	herder	parlor	tank
mantle	heritage	park	tandem

Now have students look up the selection words *Mandarin, heritage, parent,* and *tangram* in a dictionary and tell what guide words they used to locate them.

✔ INFORMAL ASSESSMENT: PERFORMANCE-BASED

Did Students:

✔ alphabetize to the fourth letter?

✔ explain how to use alphabetical order to locate words in a dictionary, telephone book, encyclopedia, and other reference sources?

✔ use guide words to find specific entries in a dictionary?

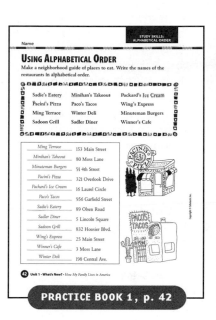

PRACTICE BOOK 1, p. 42

TECHNOLOGY

Study Skills Have students organize a two-column, ten-row spreadsheet. Ask them to type the story vocabulary into column one. Next, have them type the words into column two in alphabetical order. Now, ask them to highlight the words in column one and use the sort function to arrange the words alphabetically. Have students compare the words they alphabetized to the ones the computer alphabetized.

DAY 4 WRAP-UP

READ ALOUD *Spend five to ten minutes reading from a selection of your choice.*

GUIDED READING *Meet with the* **blue** *and* **green** *reading groups and assign Independent Center activities.* **See pages R18–R19.**

DAY 5 OBJECTIVES

STUDENTS WILL:

READ 30 MINUTES

- Reading Assessment
- Daily Phonics: Schwa /ə/

WRITE 30 MINUTES

- Writing Assessment
- Spelling: Words With a- and be-
- Grammar, Usage, Mechanics: Common and Proper Nouns
- Oral Language

EXTEND SKILLS 30 MINUTES

- Integrated Language Arts
- Read Aloud
- Guided Reading

RESOURCES
- Selection Test
- Spelling Resource Book, p. 202

SELECTION TEST

Reading Assessment

Formal Assessment

Use the Selection Test to measure students' mastery of the week's reading skills. See the suggestions for Intervention and Modifying Assessment.

Available In ★ READING COUNTS! ★

✓ SELECTION TEST		
SKILL	**TEST QUESTIONS**	◎ **IF** students need more support **THEN...**
COMPREHENSION **Evaluate Author's Purpose**	1–3	Use instructional alternative on p. T131.
TEXT STRUCTURE **Photo Essay**	4–6	Review skills lesson on p. T117.
DAILY PHONICS **Schwa /ə/**	7–9	Use the Reteach lesson on p. R53.
Vocabulary	10–12	Use the Review Vocabulary on p. T136.

Modifying Assessment

ESL/ELD
Vocabulary

▲ Evaluate students' understanding of the food vocabulary in this story by asking them to act out a restaurant scene. Have pairs order sesame noodles from one another, taking turns being the server and the customer. Tell them to use as many vocabulary words as possible. **(ACT IT OUT)**

 IF students need more support recognizing vocabulary,

THEN have them work with the visual clues you gathered earlier.

EXTRA HELP
Comprehension

■ Review both selections together, noting what the student has learned about two cultures.

Language	Mandarin is one Chinese language but there are others.	Many native languages are in danger of being lost.

 IF students need more support understanding author's purpose,

THEN work together to chart information in the texts.

Performance-Based Assessment

Use the assessment activities below to provide performance-based measures of students' proficiency in phonics and reading fluency. See the Conference to assess individual students' progress.

DAILY PHONICS

Dictation

WORDS WITH /ə/ Dictate the following words and sentences. Have students write them on a sheet of paper. When completed, write the words and sentences on the chalkboard and have students make any necessary corrections on their papers.

| ago | across | circus |
| taken | adult | elephants |

How long   was the first held?.

The picture of the was taken from across the plain.

✔ **Did students make the appropriate sound/letter correspondences for /ə/?**

 IF students need more support with schwa /ə/,

THEN practice oral blending of the words with /ə/ from the dictation.

ONE-MINUTE FLUENCY

Ask students to sit in pairs and read aloud to each other. Circulate and listen to individuals to assess their reading fluency.

Students can read the text on **Practice Book 1, page 39** or the text of the Take-Home Practice Readers.

✔ *Does the student read smoothly and self-correct mistakes?*

 IF students need more support with fluency,

THEN have them listen to you read aloud a passage before they do repeated readings themselves. Students may wish to tape-record themselves to mark improvements.

✓ CONFERENCE

Set aside time to meet with several students individually to discuss their story comprehension and to listen to them read from the story. You may wish to tape-record students as they read the section aloud.

ASSESS STORY COMPREHENSION

✔ **Why do you think the authors of both selections chose to write about different cultures? What point were they trying to make?**
(Evaluate Author's Purpose)

ASSESS TEXT STRUCTURE

✔ **How do the photographs help you understand each selection? (Photo Essay)**

ASSESS FLUENCY

✔ **Does the student read at a rate of speed appropriate for the text?**

✔ **Does the student use pronunciation guides in the text to read the Chinese and Hupa words?**

DAILY LANGUAGE PRACTICE

SPELLING

DAY 5:
Administer the Posttest for Words with *a-, be.* **See page R21.**

GRAMMAR, USAGE, MECHANICS

DAY 5:
Assess Common and Proper Nouns. **See page R23.**

ORAL LANGUAGE

david and his Family went to a special language camp

(David and his family went to a special language camp.)

PORTFOLIO

Suggest that students add their drafts and revisions to their Literacy Portfolios.

Writing Assessment

MY FAMILY TRADITION

Every year for the 4th of July weekend we go to my aunts houses on Long Island. All the family comes from all over the country for our family reunion. It is a great weekend. We eat a lot of food. One of my favorite foods is South Carolina Potatoe Salad. It is sooo good! First you peel and cut the white potatoes in fours. Then you wash and boil the potatoes and eggs together. While they are boiling you cut up onions, green peppers and celery. You get out salt and pepper, mayo and mustard. When the potatoes and eggs are finished boiling you run them under cold water. Then you put everything in a big bowl and cut up the eggs in the bowl and mix. Then put in your salt and pepper. Then add mayo and mix everything again. Now add a little mustard and mix again. My mom said the egg yolks and mustard give the potatoe salad its yellow color. Now you whip it all up, so it gets yellowy, but don't whip too much because you don't want yellow mush. I like my potatoe salad warm with bar-be-que chicken and tossed salad and rolls. Mmmm good eating. It's my favorite time and one of my favorite foods.

This description is off to a good start. Remember to use apostrophes with possessives.

I can easily follow this recipe because you're stating the steps in a logical order.

The recipe sounds yummy! But it would be helpful to state all the ingredients first.

You need to remove this sentence because it isn't part of the recipe.

Apprentice

Use the rubric below to assess students' writing.

STUDENTS' WRITING RUBRIC

Proficient	• The student effectively describes a family celebration and tells how to make a special recipe. • The description is detailed and follows a logical order.	• The student uses common and proper nouns correctly. • The description has been proofread and corrected for grammar, usage, mechanics, and spelling errors.
Apprentice	• The student has written a description that includes a family recipe. • The description could use more details.	• The student does not always use common and proper nouns correctly. • The description has been proofread but not completely.
Novice	• The student does not effectively describe a family celebration or explain how to make a family recipe.	• The student does not use common and proper nouns correctly.

Integrated Language Arts

ORAL LANGUAGE

Interview a Character

MATERIALS:
Audiocassette recorder and microphone, Video camera

SUGGESTED GROUPING:
Partners

STUDENTS work in pairs to role-play either April Chen or David Drake and an interviewer.

REVIEW the selections for details, and have students jot down questions they might want to ask April or David. Help students recall what these two children did to keep their traditions alive.

INVITE partners to come up with questions for April or David, then play the roles of the interviewer and the child interviewed.

········· TECHNOLOGY ·········

Speaking Skills Suggest that students tape-record the interview, or have a third student videotape it. Play the tapes for the class, and discuss the various questions and answers.

WRITING/VIEWING

Make a Book of Traditions

Good For Grading

MATERIALS:
Books about different cultures, Encyclopedia, Old magazines, Paste, Scissors, Markers, Crayons or pencils, Construction paper

SUGGESTED GROUPING:
Interest Groups

CHALLENGE students in small groups to write descriptions of family traditions or general traditions from another culture that interest them.

REMIND the class that they learned about some traditions of a Chinese family and of Native Americans. Have them mention activities they learned about, such as playing tangram or dancing in a powwow.

SUGGEST that students use research materials to learn about the topic they've chosen, and to help them write descriptions of the traditions.

ASK each group to enliven their descriptions with illustrations or models of things—a tangram game or a sample origami. Display the descriptions and models.

HOW TO GRADE Grade students on the completeness of their descriptions and on their ability to gather information.

Integrated Language Arts

WRITING/VIEWING

Make a Picture Cookbook

MATERIALS:
Old cookbooks, Construction paper, Index cards, Scissors, Paste, Glue or Tape, Markers

SUGGESTED GROUPING:
Individuals

ENCOURAGE students to create a class cookbook, as an extension of the "How My Family Eats in America" activity.

BRAINSTORM with students their favorite foods. Ask them to cut out or draw pictures of these foods.

SUGGEST that students label their pictures in the appropriate language, and describe on an index card how to make each dish. They can compile all the recipes into a cookbook, to be kept in the classroom library.

PREPARE a few of the foods in class, as time allows. Remind students to follow the recipe as they prepare a dish.

DANNY'S FAMOUS TACOS
lettuce cheese tomato bean shell

DAY 5 WRAP-UP

READ ALOUD *Spend five to ten minutes reading from a selection of your choice.*

GUIDED READING *Meet with the green and red reading groups and assign Independent Center activities.* See **pages R18–R19.**

PERSUASIVE WRITING

Book Review

MATERIALS:
Paper, Pencils

SUGGESTED GROUPING:
Individuals

STUDENTS work to write a book review of "How My Family Came to America." Begin by helping students to come up with a class list of reasons why others their age might like the book.

REMIND students that in a book review a writer presents a brief summary of the book, including interesting details from it. A book review also gives opinions, such as, "I think the photos in this book do a great job of telling what April's daily life is like."

Book Review

TEACH/MODEL Read aloud the following statements, and ask students to identify which is a detail and which is an opinion.

1. "April is a great narrator because she is so eager to tell readers about her culture."

2. "When I write in Chinese, I write from the right to the left."

Explain that when writing a book review students should choose details that will really interest their readers. They should support their opinions with good reasons.

PRACTICE/APPLY Have students:

• identify facts in the selection that they think would most interest readers.

• discuss with a partner their opinion of the story and write a lively book review.

On the Pampas

ON THE PAMPAS
María Cristina Brusca

AWARD WINNER

Main Selection
Genre: Personal Narrative
Award: Notable Children's Trade Book
in the Field of Social Studies

Paired Selection
Genre: Profile

Selection Summary

In this personal narrative, a young girl
spends a summer as a gaucho at her
grandparents' *estancia* in the country. She
learns how to take care of horses, how to lasso,
and how to corral the horses. As her summer
draws to a close, the girl says good-bye to life
as a gaucho but looks forward to returning next
summer.

PAIRED SELECTION River guide Keith Jardine
helps adults and children meet adventure head
on—just like the narrator did in *On the Pampas.*

Author/Illustrator

MARÍA CRISTINA BRUSCA
grew up in Argentina. She
spent her summers first on
her grandparents'
estancia and then on the
small ranch that her
mother purchased nearby. Ms.
Brusca currently lives in New York,
where she writes and illustrates
children's books inspired by her love
for the pampas.

Weekly Organizer

Visit Our Web Site
www.scholastic.com

	DAY 1	**DAY 2**
READ and Introduce Skills • VOCABULARY • PHONICS • COMPREHENSION • LITERARY ELEMENT	**BUILD BACKGROUND, ▲** p. T151 ☑ **VOCABULARY, ▲ ■** p. T152 Transparency 11 Practice Book 1, p. 43 ☑ **DAILY PHONICS: ▲ ■** 1-, 2-, 3-Syllable Words, p. T154 Practice Book 1, p. 44 **PREVIEW AND PREDICT,** p. T156 **READ: ▲ ✴ ■** On the Pampas, pp. T156–T161 **GENRE:** Personal Narrative, T157 ☑ **LITERARY ELEMENT:** Setting, p. T159	**READ: ▲ ✴ ■ ●** On the Pampas, pp. T162–T173 **ILLUSTRATOR'S CRAFT:** Details, p. T163 ☑ **DAILY PHONICS:** 1-, 2-, 3-Syllable Words, p. T165 **LITERARY ELEMENT:** Mood, p. T167 Character, p. T169 **AUTHOR'S CRAFT:** Descriptive Language, p. T171
WRITE and Respond • GRAMMAR • USAGE • MECHANICS • SPELLING • WRITING	**WRITING WORKSHOP:** Introduce, p. T151 **JOURNAL:** Make Predictions, p. T156 ☑ **SPELLING:** Pretest: Words With ng and nk, p. R28 Spelling Resource Book, p. 24 ☑ **GRAMMAR, USAGE, MECHANICS:** Teach/Model: Singular and Plural Nouns, p. R30 **ORAL LANGUAGE,** p. T161	**WRITING WORKSHOP:** Prewrite, p. T173 Practice Book 1, p. 46 ☑ **SPELLING:** Vocabulary Practice, p. R28 Spelling Resource Book, pp. 25–27 ☑ **GRAMMAR, USAGE, MECHANICS:** Practice, p. R30 **ORAL LANGUAGE,** T173
EXTEND SKILLS and Apply to Literature • INTEGRATED LANGUAGE ARTS • LISTENING/SPEAKING/VIEWING • INTEGRATED CURRICULUM • GUIDED READING • INDEPENDENT READING	**READ ALOUD,** p. T161 **GUIDED READING,** pp. R26–R27 **INTEGRATED CURRICULUM:** Social Studies, p. R33 **TRADE BOOKS** • Hannah • The Chalk Box Kid	**READ ALOUD,** p. T173 **GUIDED READING,** pp. R26–R27 **INTEGRATED CURRICULUM:** The Arts, R33 Science, R32 Math, R32 **TRADE BOOKS** • Uncle Jed's Barbershop • Muggie Maggie
TECHNOLOGY and **REAL-WORLD SKILLS**	**SMART PLACE CD-ROM** Comprehension Skills, p. T161 **WORKSHOP 2, pp. T195–T200**	**WORD PROCESSING** Communicating Through Letters, p. T167 **WORKSHOP 2, pp. T195–T200**

DAY 3

READ: ▲ ✳
"Keith Jardine," pp. T174–T177

☑ **COMPREHENSION:**
Paraphrase, p. T177

☑ **LITERARY ELEMENT:** ▲ ■
Setting, pp. T180–T181
Transparency 12
Practice Book 1, pp. 50-52

INTERVENTION, ● p. T182
Daily Phonics: 1-, 2-, 3-Syllable Words
Literary Element: Setting
Fluency: Echo Reading

RESPOND: ▲ ■
Think About Reading, p. T178
Write an Interview, p. T179
Practice Book 1, p. 48

☑ **SPELLING:**
Write/Proofread, p. R29
Spelling Resource Book, p. 28

☑ **GRAMMAR, USAGE, MECHANICS:**
Practice, p. R31
Practice Book 1, p. 49

ORAL LANGUAGE, p. T179

RESPOND: Literature Circle, p. T179

READ ALOUD, p. T183

GUIDED READING, pp. R26–R27

OPTIONAL MATERIALS, ● p. T183
Phonics Chapter Book #17,
History Mystery
On the Pampas audiocassette

VIDEO
Speaking Skills, p. T179

WORKSHOP 2, pp. T195–T200

DAY 4

LITERATURE CONNECTION:
"Keith Jardine," p. T184

☑ **REVIEW VOCABULARY,** p. T186

☑ **DAILY PHONICS:** ▲ ✳
1-, 2-, 3-Syllable Words, p. T187

WRITING WORKSHOP:
Brochure, p. T184
Writer's Craft: Opinion and
Supporting Facts, p. T185
Transparency 13
Practice Book 1, p. 46

☑ **SPELLING:**
Study/Review, p. R29
Spelling Resource Book, p. 200

☑ **GRAMMAR, USAGE, MECHANICS:**
Apply, p. R31

ORAL LANGUAGE, p. T185

READ ALOUD, p. T189

GUIDED READING, pp. R26–R27

EXPAND VOCABULARY:
Irregular Plurals, p. T186

☑ **STUDY SKILLS:**
Using a Dictionary, pp. T188–T189
Practice Book 1, p. 54

WORD PROCESSING
Writing Skills, p. T185

FIRST THOUSAND WORDS CD-ROM
Study Skills, p. T189

WORKSHOP 2, pp. T195–T200

DAY 5

READING ASSESSMENT:
Selection Test, p. T190

MODIFYING ASSESSMENT, p. T190
ESL/ELD: Vocabulary
Extra Help: Literary Element

PERFORMANCE-BASED ASSESSMENT:
One-Minute Fluency, p. T191
Conference, p. T191

☑ **DAILY PHONICS:** Dictation, p. T191

WRITING ASSESSMENT, p. T192
Student Model
Students' Writing Rubric

☑ **SPELLING:**
Posttest, p. R29
Spelling Resource Book, p. 202

☑ **GRAMMAR, USAGE, MECHANICS:**
Assess, p. R31

ORAL LANGUAGE, p. T192

READ ALOUD, p. T194

GUIDED READING, pp. R26–R27

INTEGRATED LANGUAGE ARTS:
Personal Narrative, p. T193
Create an Adventure Story, p. T193
Give a Persuasive Talk, p. T194
Map Story Locales, p. T194

SMART PLACE CD-ROM
Presentation Tools, p. T193

WORKSHOP 2, pp. T195–T200

ASSESSMENT PLANNING ✓

USE THIS CHART TO PLAN YOUR ASSESSMENT OF THE WEEKLY READING OBJECTIVES.

- **Informal Assessment** is ongoing and should be used before, during, and after reading.
- **Formal Assessment** occurs at the end of the week on the selection test.
- Note that intervention activities occur throughout the lesson to support students who need extra help with skills.

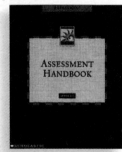

YOU MAY CHOOSE AMONG THE FOLLOWING PAGES IN THE ASSESSMENT HANDBOOK.

- Informal Assessment
- Anecdotal Record
- Portfolio Checklist and Evaluation Forms
- Self-Assessment
- Second-Language Learners
- Using Technology to Assess
- Test Preparation

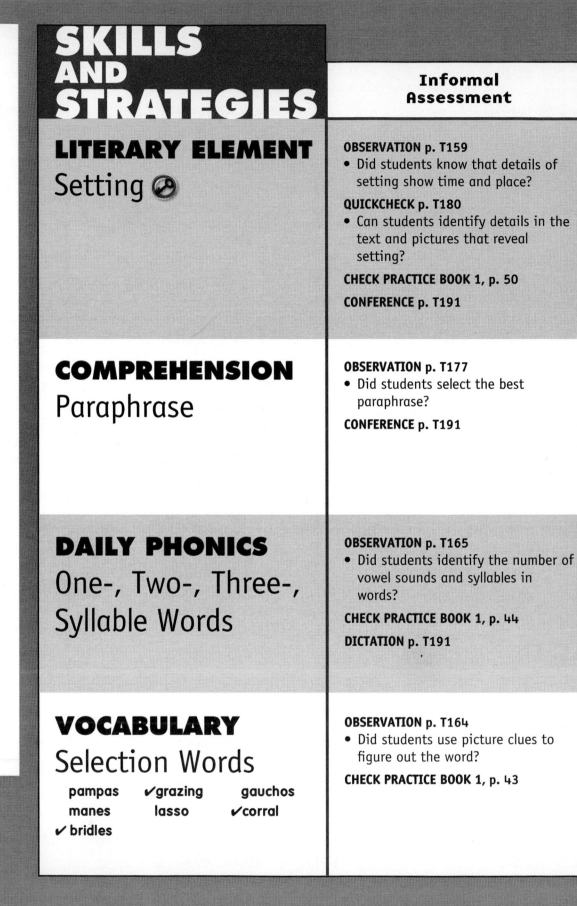

SKILLS AND STRATEGIES	Informal Assessment
LITERARY ELEMENT Setting	**OBSERVATION p. T159** • Did students know that details of setting show time and place? **QUICKCHECK p. T180** • Can students identify details in the text and pictures that reveal setting? **CHECK PRACTICE BOOK 1, p. 50** **CONFERENCE p. T191**
COMPREHENSION Paraphrase	**OBSERVATION p. T177** • Did students select the best paraphrase? **CONFERENCE p. T191**
DAILY PHONICS One-, Two-, Three-, Syllable Words	**OBSERVATION p. T165** • Did students identify the number of vowel sounds and syllables in words? **CHECK PRACTICE BOOK 1, p. 44** **DICTATION p. T191**
VOCABULARY Selection Words pampas ✓grazing gauchos manes lasso ✓corral ✓bridles	**OBSERVATION p. T164** • Did students use picture clues to figure out the word? **CHECK PRACTICE BOOK 1, p. 43**

Formal Assessment	**INTERVENTION** and Instructional Alternatives	Planning Notes
SELECTION TEST • Questions 1–3 check students' mastery of the key strategy, setting. **UNIT TEST**	**If students need help with setting, then go to:** • Instructional Alternatives, p. T181 • Intervention, p. T182 • Review, p. R50 • Reteach, p. R55	
SELECTION TEST • Questions 4–6 check students' understanding of the skill, paraphrase.	**If students need help with paraphrase, then:** • Review the Skills and Strategies lesson on p. T177	
SELECTION TEST • Questions 7–9 check students' ability to identify one-, two-, three-syllable words. **UNIT TEST**	**If students need help identifying one-, two-, three-syllable words, then go to:** • Intervention, p. T182 • Review, p. R47 • Reteach, p. R54	
SELECTION TEST • Questions 10–12 check students' understanding of the selection vocabulary. **UNIT TEST**	**If students need additional practice with the vocabulary words, then go to:** • Review Vocabulary, p. T186	

Technology

The technology in this lesson helps teachers and students develop the skills they need for the 21st century. Look for integrated technology activities on every day of instruction.

DAY 1 Comprehension Skills	• Students use **Smart Place** to compare the mentor's adventures to the girl's pampas adventure.
DAY 2 Communicating Through Letters	• Students play the role of the girl and share details of the visit to the ranch in a word processed letter.
DAY 3 Speaking Skills	• Students videotape an interview in which the girl describes life in the pampas.
DAY 4 Study Skills	• Students use **Usborne's Animated First Thousand Words** to define and research the story vocabulary.
DAY 5 Presentation Tools	• Students use a word processor and an art program such as **Smart Place** PlaceMaker to present their own adventure stories.

Smart Place CD-ROM

First Thousand Words CD-ROM

Smart Place CD-ROM

Build Background

Imagine learning to be a gaucho on the Argentine pampas! In the next selection, the author tells about her childhood summers on her grandparents' ranch.

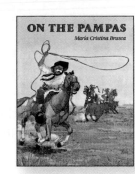

ON THE PAMPAS
María Cristina Brusca

Activate Prior Knowledge

LOCATE ARGENTINA

Explain that the next selection takes place in South America, in an area of Argentina called the *pampas*. Have students locate Argentina on a map or a globe.

Explain that the pampas is a flat grassland that stretches for hundreds of miles and is sometimes used for cattle ranching.

DISCUSS RANCH LIFE

If possible, display pictures of ranch scenes. Use questions such as these to prompt discussion:

> **Who works on a ranch? What jobs do they do?**

> **What might be fun about living on a ranch?**

 WRITING WORKSHOP *Brochure*

INTRODUCE Build background for writing a brochure by asking students to imagine they are trying to convince their family to join an adventure group for a vacation. Have them jot down and share ideas.

DAY 1 OBJECTIVES

STUDENTS WILL:

READ 40 MINUTES

- Build Background
- Vocabulary
- Daily Phonics: One-, Two-, Three-Syllable Words
- *On the Pampas*, pp. 64-69
- Key Literary Element: Setting

WRITE 25 MINUTES

- Writing Workshop: Introduce Writing a Brochure
- Quickwrite: Return to Purpose
- Spelling: Words With *ng* and *nk*
- Grammar, Usage, Mechanics: Singular and Plural Nouns
- Oral Language

EXTEND SKILLS 25 MINUTES

- Integrated Curriculum
- Read Aloud
- Guided Reading

RESOURCES

- Vocabulary Transparency 4
- Transparency 11
- Practice Book 1, pp. 43, 44
- Spelling Resource Book, p. 24

MODIFY Instruction

ESL/ELD

▲ Ask whether any students have ever lived in or visited Argentina and what language is spoken there. Have students look through the illustrations. Help them brainstorm a list of action words that describe what people in the story are doing. Define words as necessary. **(BRAINSTORM)**

Vocabulary

PHONICS AND SPELLING LINKS

Phonics See one-, two-, and three-syllable selection words with *ng* and *nk* on page T154.

Spelling See selection words with *ng* and *nk* on page R28.

Ⓐ TEACH WORD MEANINGS

INTRODUCE CONCEPT
Explain that *On the Pampas* has many vocabulary words related to ranching on the Argentine pampas.

PRESENT VOCABULARY
List the words and their definitions on the chalkboard. Encourage students to discuss what each word means.

✔ = Tested	**VOCABULARY WORDS**
pampas	vast grasslands in South America, especially Argentina (p. 66)
✔ **grazing**	eating grass or other plants (p. 66)
gauchos	South American cowhands who work on the pampas (p. 67)
manes	long, thick hair that grows on the neck and head of horses (p. 68)
lasso	a rope with a loop, used to catch cattle and horses (p. 69)
✔ **corral**	a fenced-in place to keep large animals (p. 70)
✔ **bridles**	the straps, bits, and reins put over horses' heads (p. 72)

Ⓑ BUILD ON PRIOR KNOWLEDGE

SEE RELATIONSHIPS
Draw the word web. Have students use prior knowledge about the American West and the vocabulary words to complete it.

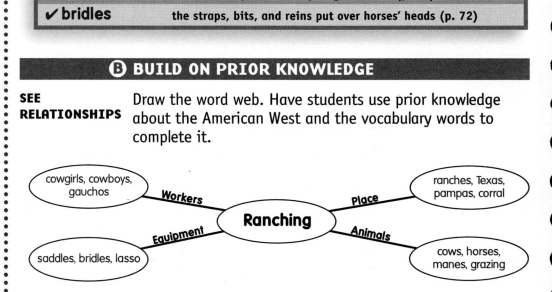

MODIFY Instruction

ESL/ELD

▲ Have students look for pictures of the vocabulary words in the text and take turns locating a specific illustration. Say one of the vocabulary words, and ask a student to point to its illustration. Repeat with other students. **(TOTAL PHYSICAL RESPONSE)**

EXTRA HELP

■ As students share what they know about ranching, encourage them to act out concept words such as *lasso, grazing,* and *bridles.* **(ACT IT OUT)**

Name _____ VOCABULARY

ROUNDUP ON THE RANCH
Study the words and their definitions. Then complete each group of words with the correct word from the box.

pampas: a Spanish word that describes huge flat, grassy areas

grazing: feeding on grass or other plants

corral: a place to fence in large animals

gauchos: South American cowhands who work on the pampas

manes: the long patches of hair that grow along the back of horses' necks

lasso: a long rope with a loop at one end, used to catch cattle or horses

bridles: the straps, bits, and reins that fit over horses' heads and are used to guide them

1. fence—cattle—area— *corral*
2. herd—nibbling—field— *grazing*
3. neck—hair—horses— *manes*
4. rope—loop—catch— *lasso*
5. workers—ranches—horseback— *gauchos*
6. leather—reins—control— *bridles*
7. grass—flat—vast— *pampas*

Write your own clues to the words in this lesson. Ask a partner to guess the words.

Unit 1 - What's New? • *On the Pampas* **43**

PRACTICE BOOK 1, p. 43

ⓒ APPLY THROUGH MEANINGFUL SENTENCES

MODEL MEANINGFUL SENTENCES

Write or say the following sentences. Call on volunteers to underline or name the context clues that help define the vocabulary word.

1. The train crossed the <u>vast grasslands</u> of the **pampas**.
2. The <u>hungry</u> cattle were **grazing** on the tall <u>grass</u>.
3. **Gauchos** on <u>horseback herded cattle</u>.
4. I <u>combed</u> the horses' <u>thick, wavy</u> **manes**.
5. The gaucho's **lasso** <u>dropped around the cow's neck</u>.
6. The horses <u>were kept</u> in the **corral** at night.
7. Before we rode, we put the **bridles** on the <u>horses' heads</u>.

Sentences an Vocabulary Transparency 4

WRITE MEANINGFUL SENTENCES

Suggest that students ask themselves these questions about each word to help them write meaningful sentences: *What is it? What does it look like? What is it used for?*

USE TRANS-PARENCY 11

Have students choose pairs of vocabulary words and write sentences to show how they're related.

SUPPORT WORDS

convinced	persuaded (p. 68)
coconuts	hard-shelled fruit of the coconut palm (p.72)*
generator	a machine that produces electricity (p. 76)
frightened	made afraid (p.76)*

✱ Vocabulary instruction is presented where words appear in the selection.

Strategy: Context Clues

Get Word Wise

▶**TEACH** Tell students that when they come to an unfamiliar word, they can look for clues to help figure out its meaning.

• *I heard the hum of the <u>generator</u> that made electricity for the house.*

THINK ALOUD *I don't know what the underlined word means, so I look for clues in the sentence. The words* hum *and that* made electricity *tell me that a generator must be a machine that makes electricity. This makes sense in the sentence.*

APPLY Write the following and ask students to use context clues to figure out the meaning of the underlined word.

• *Susan swam in the creek holding her horse's mane. At first I was afraid to follow her, but she finally <u>convinced</u> me. It was a lot of fun!*

Scholastic Literacy Place

RANCHING ON THE PAMPAS WORD CONNECTION CHART

pampas	grazing	gauchos	lasso
corral	bridles	manes	

Word	Word	Connection
grazing	gauchos	Gauchos watch cattle grazing on the pampas.

What's New? • On the Pampas 11

PERSONAL WORD LIST

As they read, have students look for interesting or unfamiliar words. Encourage them to use the steps in the How to Figure Out a New Word chart to determine the meanings of the words. Students can add these words to their Journals.

HOW TO FIGURE OUT A NEW WORD

• Try to figure out the word from letter sounds.

• Look for word parts that you know.

▶ Try to use context clues to figure out the meaning.

• Look up the word in a dictionary or ask someone.

**SELECTION WORDS
With One-, Two-,
Three- Syllables**

younger

everything

something

things

long

drank

morning

SKILLS TRACE

ONE-, TWO-, **TESTED**
THREE-SYLLABLE WORDS

Introduce . . .pp. T154–T155
Practice pp. T165, T182, T187
Review . . . . .p. R47
Reteach . . . . .p. R54

DAILY PHONICS

One-, Two-, Three-Syllable Words

Ⓐ TEACH/MODEL

INTRODUCE POLYSYLLABIC WORDS Tell students that every syllable, or word part, has just one vowel sound. List the vowels on the chalkboard. Then write the following words: *miles, tiny*. Say *miles* and *tiny*. Ask students to tell how many vowels they hear in each word.

💭 **THINK ALOUD** *I know that every syllable, or word part, has just one vowel sound. When I say* **miles***, I hear only one vowel sound, /ī/. When I say* **tiny***, I hear two vowel sounds—/ī/ and /ē/. Since* **tiny** *has two vowel sounds, I can tell the word has two syllables.*

Explain that by using what they know about sounds and letters, students can figure out how to read a word that has more than one syllable.

- Have students identify the number of syllables in *afternoon* and *ranch*.

- Read the following words and have students call out the number of syllables in each word: *cowboy, drank, adventure, long, vaccinate, morning.*

SYLLABLES IN WORDS		
One	**Two**	**Three**
ranch	pampas	family
drank	cowboy	adventure
long	morning	vaccinate

MODIFY Instruction

ESL/ELD

▲ Write column heads for 1, 2, and 3-syllable words on the chalkboard. Then write the words **ranch**, **leg**, **adventure**, **summer**, **vacation**, and **morning** to one side. Say each word aloud. Then have students clap out the syllables. Ask students to help you place each word in the correct category. **(CATEGORIZE)**

EXTRA HELP

■ Prepare students who need help connecting sound and symbol to participate in the Blend Words activity by taking a two- or three-syllable word and presenting one syllable at a time for them to decode. Then put the syllables together and have students blend them to say the whole word. **(ASSIST IN PROCESS)**

PHONICS MAINTENANCE Review the following sound-spellings: /ī/ *i*, *igh*, *y*, *i-e*, *ie*; and words with /ə/ such as <u>a</u>nother, happ<u>e</u>ns, poss<u>i</u>ble, gall<u>o</u>p, circ<u>u</u>s.

B PRACTICE/APPLY

READ WORDS To practice reading one-, two-, and three-syllable words, list the following words and sentence on the chalkboard. Have students read each chorally. Model blending as needed.

> horse   cattle   together
> admire   arrive   happening
> applied   skylight   climb
>
> The gauchos taught the girls how to handle a lasso.

DICTATION Dictate the following words for students to spell: **flying, afternoon, frighten, alive.**

BUILD WORDS Distribute the following syllable cards, or have students make their own sets using index cards: *play, morn, cat, bot, sad, bri, ad, ven, pic, sta, ac, ing, tle, dle, mire, ture, tion.* Allow time for students to build words using the cards. Suggest that students write their words on paper. **(INDEPENDENT WORK)**

WORKING WITH WORD PARTS

Write the following common syllables on the chalkboard, one at a time. Have students read each aloud. When completed, review the syllables in random order.

er	tion	fore	tle
ev	con	ex	ful
morn	ward	ture	pro
ing	be	ly	en
ad	pas	dle	de

Repeat this procedure throughout the week using these and other syllables.

PROFESSIONAL DEVELOPMENT

JOHN SHEFELBINE

Why Are Strategies Needed for Polysyllabic Words?

Studies indicate that polysyllabic words are read by syllables. Students who successfully figure out single-syllable words by sounding them out left to right need to be taught to focus on possible syllable units when reading polysyllabic words. Skilled readers easily read most polysyllabic words by their extensive knowledge of which spelling patterns are more likely to occur within a syllable.

COMPREHENSION

▶ **Preview and Predict**

Read the first paragraph of the selection with students, and ask them to look at the first few illustrations. Explain that this selection is a true story about the author's childhood, and that the author is also the illustrator. Discuss students' expectations of the story.

> **How do you think the girl feels about spending the summer in the country?**

> **What might she do on her grandparents' estancia?**

Help students make predictions before they read by asking the question below. Then have them read page 66.

> **What might happen during the girl's visit to the pampas?**

JOURNAL

Make Predictions

Have students write in their Journals what they think will happen in *On the Pampas*. Encourage them to speculate about the girl's adventures and then refine their ideas and opinions about the story as they read.

▶ **Set a Purpose**

Discuss with students a purpose for reading. They may want to find out what life on an Argentine ranch is like.

64 ▼

ON THE PAMPAS
María Cristina Brusca

PERSONAL NARRATIVE

AWARD WINNER

ON THE PAMPAS

by María Cristina Brusca

64

CLASSROOM Management

WHOLE CLASS

On-Level Have students read the selection in two sittings. Use the questions, Think Alouds, and Skills and Strategies lessons to guide students through the story.

Below-Level Have students preview each day's reading by looking at the illustrations and having a conversation about the Argentine setting.

COOPERATIVE

Above-Level Have small groups read the selections together, stopping periodically to retell sections in their own words. After reading, ask them to summarize what they read.

65
▼

65

Revisit the selection for skills instruction.

☑ Tested Skill

GENRES

Personal Narrative	T157
Profile	T175

LITERARY ELEMENTS

☑ Setting	🔧	T159
Character		T169

DAILY PHONICS

☑ One-, Two-, Three-Syllable Words	T165

COMPREHENSION

☑ Paraphrase	T177

GENRE
Personal Narrative

TEACH/MODEL

Have students describe writing they have done about a real-life event. Explain that this writing is called a personal narrative. Discuss the key elements of the genre.

> A personal narrative tells about the writer's own experiences.

> It is written from the first-person point of view.

> The writer expresses personal feelings about his or her experiences.

PRACTICE/APPLY

Have students read the first page of the story and identify elements of personal narrative.

> How do you know this story is written in the first person?

> How would you expect this selection to be different from a made-up story?

SMALL GROUP TO WHOLE CLASS

ESL/ELD Have students listen to the story on the audiocassette prior to the whole class reading. This will help them to become familiar with the story sequence and vocabulary. Make sure that they pay attention to the pre- and post-listening activities. **(AUDIO CLUES)**

COMPREHENSION

1 DRAW CONCLUSIONS

> The first word in this story is *I.* Who is telling this story? How can you tell? *(Possible answer: The young girl in the picture is telling the story. She says that she spends the summer at her grandparents' estancia.)*

2 SETTING

> The author gives a lot of information about the pampas. What words and phrases help you picture the setting of this story? *(Possible answer: Words such as* flattest land in the world, fences, windmills, *and* millions of cattle grazing *describe the setting.)*

3 CRITICAL THINKING: EVALUATE

> Why do you think Susanita knows so much about horses? *(Possible answer: Since she lives on the ranch year-round, she probably has learned by listening to and watching the gauchos, and by riding and taking care of horses herself.)*

66

I grew up in Argentina, in South America. I lived with my family in the big city of Buenos Aires, but we spent our summers in the country, at my grandparents' *estancia.* One summer my parents and brother stayed in the city, so I went without them.

My grandmother met me at the station in Buenos Aires, and we had breakfast as we rode through miles and miles of the flattest land in the world—the pampas. All around us, as far as we could see, were fences, windmills, and millions of cattle grazing.

Our station, San Enrique, was at the end of the line, where the train tracks stopped. My grandfather was there to meet us in his pickup truck and take us the five miles to the estancia.

66

MODIFY Instruction

ESL/ELD

▲ Instruct a student mentor to read aloud the first sentence of the story: *I grew up in Argentina, in South America.* The student mentor points to him- or herself and says "I grew up in _____." Each student in the group repeats the sentence, giving information about themselves. **(RELATE TO REAL LIFE)**

GIFTED & TALENTED

✳ To help students answer question 1, draw a circle labeled *Narrator* with "I" in parentheses. Draw spokes from the circle and label them as students name other family members. Keep the map on display and add new names as they are introduced. **(GRAPHIC DEVICE)**

67

The ranch was called La Carlota, and the gates were made of iron bars from a fort that had been on that very spot a hundred years before. As we drove up to the gates, we were greeted by a cloud of dust and a thundering of hooves—it was my cousin Susanita, on her horse.

Susanita lived at the estancia all year round. She knew everything about horses, cows, and all the other animals that live on the pampas. Even though she was three years younger than me, she had her own horse, La Baya. Susanita was so tiny, she had to shimmy up La Baya's leg to get on her back. But she rode so well that the gauchos called her La Gauchita—"The Little Gaucho." **3**

67

SOCIAL STUDIES

Ask students to complete the **Find Other Pampas** activity on **page R32**, where they will use a world map to find other regions with geography similar to the Argentine pampas. Students will interpret information on a topographical map.

CULTURAL CONNECTION

Gauchos are cowboys from Argentina and Uruguay. A gaucho's work tools consist of a lasso, a knife, and bolas (leather cords weighted with iron balls that wrap an animal's legs together). Have students compare gauchos with what they have read about the cowhands of the western United States.

LITERARY ELEMENT
Setting

TEACH/MODEL
Ask students to describe a place that they have visited. Point out that this time and place could be the setting for a personal narrative or a make-believe story.

Explain that in both nonfiction and fiction, setting is where and when a story takes place. To figure out the setting:

> **Use picture clues and story details.**

> **Search for details that tell *where*, such as names of places and scenery.**

> **Find details and clues that tell *when*, such as the time of day, dates, and season.**

PRACTICE/APPLY
Write on the chalkboard: *day, ranch, pampas, summer*. Have students copy and complete the chart.

SETTING	
Place	**Time**
ranch	day
pampas	summer

INFORMAL ASSESSMENT
OBSERVATION

Did students:

✔ know that details of setting show time and place?

✔ enter details under the appropriate headings?

See pages T180–T181 for a full skills lesson on Setting.

COMPREHENSION

4 CHARACTER

> How does the girl feel about trying new things? What does this tell you about her character? *(Possible answer: Sometimes she is afraid at first, but she's always willing to try; she is an adventurous person.)*

5 DRAW CONCLUSIONS

> Based on the pictures you've seen, what conclusions can you draw about the kinds of skills a gaucho needs to work on a ranch? *(Possible answer: A gaucho needs to know how to ride a horse, use a lasso, and take care of horses and cattle.)*

SELF-MONITORING STRATEGY

Adjust Reading Rates

THINK ALOUD *When I'm reading something that contains a lot of new words, I read more slowly to keep track of what I'm reading. I've come across many new words in the story, and some of them are not in English. When this happens, I slow down until I get a better sense of the setting and events. When the text I'm reading seems familiar, I can start reading more quickly again.*

OPTION You may end the first day's reading here or have students continue reading the entire selection.

I didn't have a horse of my own, but old Salguero, the ranch foreman, brought me Pampita, a sweet-tempered mare, to ride. She wasn't very fast, but she certainly was my friend.

Susanita and I did everything together that summer. She was the one who showed me how to take care of the horses. We would brush their coats, trim their hooves, and braid their <u>manes</u> and tails.

4 Susanita was always ready for an adventure, no matter how scary. She used to swim in the creek holding on to La Baya's mane. At first I was afraid to follow her, but when she finally convinced me, it was a lot of fun.

68

MODIFY Instruction

ESL/ELD

▲ Ask students to think about the main characters and compare the two cousins. Help them by asking questions. Ask: *Is Susanita adventurous? Is her cousin? Which of the cousins is a real gaucho?* Students may elaborate on their responses according to ability. **(COMPARE/CONTRAST)**

EXTRA HELP

■ For students who need help answering the comprehension questions, review the story with them, paragraph by paragraph. Use questions to lead students to an understanding of what the narrator is thinking and feeling. **(GUIDED QUESTIONS)**

69

I wanted to learn all the things a gaucho has to know. I wanted to ride out on the pampas every day, as Salguero did, and to wear a belt like his, with silver coins from all over the world and a buckle with my initials on it. Salguero said I'd have to begin at the beginning, and he spent hours showing Susanita and me how to use the lasso.

69

TECHNOLOGY

Comprehension Skills Have students open **Smart Place** and Meet the Mentor, Keith Jardine. Ask them to consider how Keith's adventures and the girl's pampas adventure can be scary and fun at the same time.

CONNECTING TO THEME

Remind students of the unit theme: *We learn about our world through new experiences.* Have students bring in photographs or draw pictures of themselves doing something new in a new place. Ask them to write picture captions, using the pronouns *I, me,* or *my.*

Quickwrite

RETURN TO PURPOSE
Encourage students to review their purpose for reading. Have them describe anything they found interesting about the story so far or new information they have learned. Students may also want to set a purpose for reading the rest of the selection.

DAILY LANGUAGE PRACTICE

SPELLING

DAY 1:
Administer the Pretest for Words With *ng* and *nk*.
See page R28.

GRAMMAR, USAGE, MECHANICS

DAY 1:
Teach and Model Singular and Plural Nouns.
See page R30.

ORAL LANGUAGE

she was rideing a tall, strong horses.
(*She was* <u>riding</u> *a tall, strong* <u>horse</u>.)

DAY **1** WRAP-UP

READ ALOUD *To develop students' oral vocabularies and listening skills, spend five to ten minutes reading from a selection of your choice.*

GUIDED READING *Meet with the* **red** *and* **blue** *reading groups and assign Independent Center activities.* **See pages R26–R27.**

COMPREHENSION

DAY 2 OBJECTIVES

STUDENTS WILL:

READ 40 MINUTES

- *On the Pampas,* pp. 70–81
- Daily Phonics: One-, Two-, Three-Syllable Words

WRITE 20 MINUTES

- Writing Workshop: Prewrite a Brochure
- Spelling: Words With *ng* and *nk*
- Grammar, Usage, Mechanics: Singular and Plural Nouns
- Oral Language

EXTEND SKILLS 30 MINUTES

- Integrated Curriculum
- Read Aloud
- Guided Reading

RESOURCES

- Practice Book 1, pp. 45, 46
- Spelling Resource Book, pp. 25–27

▶ Reread

You may wish to have students independently reread the first part of the story before beginning Day 2 reading.

6 SUMMARIZE

> **What has happened so far in the story?** *(The narrator has gone to spend the summer on her grandparents' ranch. She has learned how to take care of horses and has begun to learn to do the things gauchos do.)*

7 SETTING

> **What details in the illustration and the text help you picture the eucalyptus grove?** *(Possible answer: It is a quiet, shady place. The text says that it was nice and cool; the illustration shows tall trees and the girls sitting on a log.)*

---

70 ▼

6 It was going to take a while for me to become a gaucho. The first time I lassoed a calf, it dragged me halfway across the <u>corral</u>. But Salguero told me that even he had been dragged plenty of times, so I kept trying, until I got pretty good at it.

Whenever the gauchos were working with the cattle, Susanita was there, and before long I was too. Sometimes the herd had to be rounded up and moved from one pasture to another. I loved galloping behind hundreds of cattle, yelling to make them run. I never got to yell like that in the city!

One day we separated the calves from the cows, to vaccinate them and brand them with "the scissors," La Carlota's mark. That was more difficult—and more

70

MODIFY Instruction

ESL/ELD

▲ Have groups role-play the morning and afternoon activities of the two cousins. Ask them to state what they are doing right now. Remind them to use the progressive, or *ing,* form. For example, *I'm riding my horse. I'm lassoing a calf. I love galloping!* **(ROLE-PLAY)**

GIFTED & TALENTED

✳ Point out the metaphor *sea of cattle* and the two things being compared: *sea* and *cattle.* Remind students that when an author compares two unlike things without using the words *like* or *as,* it is called a *metaphor.* Challenge students to create metaphors about ranch life. **(INNOVATE)**

71 ▼

exciting, too. I tried to do what Salguero told me to, but sometimes I got lost in the middle of that sea of cattle.

At noon, everybody would sit down around one big table and eat together. I was always hungry. Grandma, Susanita's mother, and Maria the cook had been working hard all morning too. They would make soup, salad, and lamb stew or pot roast, or my favorite, *carbonada*, a thick stew made of corn and peaches.

After lunch the grown-ups took a *siesta*, but not us. We liked to stay outdoors. Some afternoons, when it was too hot to do anything else, we rode out to a eucalyptus grove that was nice and cool, and stayed there until it got dark, reading comic books or cowboy stories. ❼

71

ORAL LANGUAGE

Have students give a dramatic reading of pages 70 and 71. Encourage them to focus on the phrases or words that they will emphasize and how they will show changes of mood. When students are ready, they can tape-record their readings for the class.

WORD STUDY

Explain that the endings *-ito* and *-ita* in Spanish mean "little" and are often used affectionately. The ending *-ito* is masculine, while *-ita* is feminine. Thus, *Susanita* means "little Susana" and *gauchita* means "little gaucha." Ask students to think of other *-ito/-ita* words they may have heard.

ILLUSTRATOR'S CRAFT
Details

TEACH/MODEL
Ask students to imagine what *On the Pampas* would be like without any pictures.

> **How do the pictures help you understand the story, characters, and setting?**

Explain that the text and illustrations work together to tell a story. Often an illustrator adds details that are not stated in the text.

> **If you do not get a clear picture of a scene from the text, details in the illustrations can help you understand what is happening.**

PRACTICE/APPLY
Tell students the illustrator has included details about the traditional dress of gauchos on pages 69 and 70. Have them use the chart to organize details of how gauchos dress.

> **What do gauchos seem to wear all the time?**

Text Details	Picture Details
belt with silver coins	wide hat
	neckerchief
buckle with initials	baggy pants
	boots

COMPREHENSION

8 **SETTING**

> At what time of day do the girls find the *ñandú* egg? What clues in the text and picture help you figure out when this happened? *(It is late in the day; text clue: "After riding around all afternoon"; picture clue: the sun is setting.)*

9 **AUTHOR'S CRAFT: SIMILES**

> The author says that the eggs were "as big as coconuts." When the word *like* or *as* is used to make a comparison, this is called a *simile*. Why do you think the author uses this simile? *(Possible answer: She uses the simile to help the reader understand just how big the eggs were by comparing them to something the reader knows.)*

10 **MAKE JUDGMENTS**

> How do you feel when the girls take the egg? Why do you feel that way? *(Answers should reflect an understanding of why the girls took the egg and what they used it for.)*

☑ INFORMAL ASSESSMENT
OBSERVATION

Vocabulary Assess students' recognition and understanding of the vocabulary word *bridles* as they read the selection. Did students:

✔ use picture clues to figure out the word?

✔ use the context clue *saddles*?

✔ pronounce the word correctly?

Other times we would gallop for two hours to the general store and buy ourselves an orange soda. Then, while we drank it, we'd look at all the saddles and <u>bridles</u> we planned to have when we were grown up and rich. Sometimes the storekeeper would take down a wonderful gaucho belt like Salguero's, and we would admire the silver coins and wonder where each one came from.

One day we rode far away from the house, to a field where Susanita thought we might find *ñandú* eggs. They are so huge, you can bake a whole cake with just one of them. After riding around all afternoon, we found a nest, well hidden in the tall grass, with about twenty pale-yellow eggs as big as coconuts.

8
9

72

MODIFY Instruction

ESL/ELD

▲ Work with students on understanding how similes are formed. Write the phrase *eggs as big as coconuts* on the chalkboard, and underline *as big as*. Ask more proficient students to describe the eggs using other similes (*as big as baseballs; as yellow as lemons*). **(FOLLOW PATTERNS)**

EXTRA HELP

■ Prepare students to answer the question about setting. In small groups, have them make simple, two-column charts with the columns labeled *Text Clues* and *Picture Clues*. Guide them to find information in the text and picture clues and write it in the appropriate columns. **(GRAPHIC DEVICE)**

Salguero had warned us to watch out for the ñandú, and he was right! The father ñandú, who protects the nest, saw us taking an egg. He was furious and chased us out of the field.

The next day we used the ñandú egg to bake a birthday cake for my grandmother. We snuck into the kitchen while she was taking her siesta, so it would be a surprise. The cake had three layers, and in between them we put whipped cream and peaches from the trees on the ranch.

10

CONNECTING TO NATURE GUIDES

Tell students that the *ñandú* is one example of the fascinating wildlife of the pampas. Ask them to use a nature guide to find out more about the *ñandú*, *mulita* (a kind of armadillo), and other creatures that live in the pampas. Then have them compare personal narratives to nature guides.

WORD STUDY

Call attention to and discuss the meaning of the Bonanza word *coconuts* on page 72. Generate excitement about learning new words that are fun to say. You may wish to have students create a mobile to which they can add Bonanza words as they come up.

DAILY PHONICS

✓ One-, Two-, Three-Syllable Words

TEACH/MODEL
Review with students that words may have one, two, three, or more syllables and that each syllable has just one vowel sound.

- Say the word *furious*. Point out that the word has three vowel sounds and therefore three syllables.

- Repeat for the words *storekeeper*, *hidden*, *grass*, and *coconuts*.

PRACTICE/APPLY
Have students find the word *gallop* on page 72.

- Ask a volunteer to say the word, then tell how many vowel sounds and syllables it has.

- Have students look in the story for words with specific numbers of syllables.

✓ INFORMAL ASSESSMENT
OBSERVATION

Did students:

✔ identify the number of vowel sounds and syllables in words?

✔ identify words with a specific number of syllables?

 IF students need more support with syllabication, **THEN** see the Intervention Activity on page T182.

COMPREHENSION

11 **ILLUSTRATOR'S CRAFT: DETAILS**

> The author gives only a few details about the birthday party. What could you add, based on details in the picture, that would help a reader get a sense of what this birthday party was like?
> *(Possible answers: Gauchos turn meat on spits around a fire while people sit at a long table, eating. A gaucho plays a guitar while people dance.)*

12 **MOOD**

> What is the mood of the party? What picture clues help get this mood across?
> *(Possible answers: The mood is happy. Everyone is smiling and gathered in groups talking, eating, and dancing.)*

INTERVENTION TIP ◎

Words from Other Languages

María Cristina Brusca has included many Spanish words in this story. Some students may have difficulty understanding these words. Point out that words in another language are sometimes printed in italics, as they are in this story. As students encounter these words in the text, help them use context and picture clues to understand them.

We had a wonderful party for my grandmother's birthday. The gauchos started the fire for the *asado* early in the evening, and soon the smell of the slowly cooking meat filled the air.

74

MODIFY Instruction

ESL/ELD

▲ Ask students to use picture clues to help them tell you in their own words what is happening at the party. Are there words in Spanish that students can explain? Encourage students to compare what they see here to birthday celebrations in their own families. **(RELATE TO REAL LIFE)**

EXTRA HELP

■ Students may need support keeping track of new information about Argentine customs. Help them answer question 11 by showing them how to make a simple list called "Birthday Parties in Argentina." Have them create categories such as Food, Clothes, and Music. **(KEY POINTS)**

75

There was music, and dancing, too. We stayed up almost all night, and I learned to dance the *zamba*, taking little steps and hops, and twirling my handkerchief.

11

12

75

THE ARTS

Ask students to complete the **Dance the Zamba** activity on **page R33**, in which they will learn the steps to an Argentinean dance. Students will follow the basic steps and add their own touches and interpretations of the dance.

TECHNOLOGY

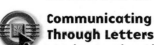

Communicating Through Letters Have students play the role of the girl in the story and write a letter to a friend at home. Have them use a word processor to create the letter. Encourage them to include lots of details describing the settings in which the girl finds herself.

SKILLS AND STRATEGIES

LITERARY ELEMENT
Mood

TEACH/MODEL
Display photographs of funny, sad, and happy scenes. Ask students to describe the feeling or atmosphere of each scene.

Explain that in stories, **mood** is the feeling or atmosphere an author creates. Point out that authors use mood to give a story a particular feeling, such as happiness or excitement, and to make the reader have certain feelings.

Discuss ways to pick up on the mood of a story.

> **Look for words that the author uses to help create a mood. Think about how these words make you feel.**

> **Look at details in the illustrations, such as expressions on people's faces.**

PRACTICE/APPLY
Ask students to use the graphic organizer below to help them determine the mood on pages 74–75.

Descriptive Words	Picture Details	Mood
wonderful party	People are smiling, dancing, talking, and eating.	happy, joyous, lively

COMPREHENSION

13 MOOD

> What mood does the picture on page 76 help to create? What picture details help convey this atmosphere? *(Possible answer: The mood is scary; picture details include the owl and the dark colors.)*

14 CHARACTER

> If you were Salguero, why would you lend your horse to the narrator? What character traits of hers would lead you to trust her? *(Possible answer: She has shown that she is hard-working, eager, and willing to learn new things.)*

INTERVENTION TIP ◎

Understand Time Frame

Remind students that the author describes events that happened to her over a whole summer. Some events, such as eating dinner, happened regularly while others, such as the birthday party, happened only once.

SELF-MONITORING STRATEGY

Decoding

💭 **THINK ALOUD** *If I don't know the word f-r-i-g-h-t-e-n-e-d, here's what I do: First I look for letter sounds I know. I know that the letters igh together can stand for a long i sound. Then, I look for other parts I know such as fr and ed. I put the parts together and say the word—frightened. Now the word makes sense in the sentence.*

13

Most evenings were much quieter. There was just the hum of the generator that made electricity for the house. We liked to go out to the *mate* house, where the gauchos spent their evenings.

We listened to them tell ghost stories and tall tales while they sat around the fire, passing the gourd and sipping mate through the silver straw. We didn't like the hot, bitter tea, but we loved being frightened by their spooky stories.

76

MODIFY Instruction

ESL/ELD

▲ Focus on the mood in the illustration on page 76. Ask: *Is it morning or night? How do you know? Do you know the name of this bird?* (Point to the owl.) *What do you know about owls? What else makes this picture look dark?* **(PICTURE CLUES)**

EXTRA HELP

■ Some students may not be familiar with what the picture suggests. Help them participate in the discussion of mood by talking about some of the characteristics of an owl: It is out at night, it makes an eerie sound, and it has large, staring eyes. Help students verbalize the feelings an owl evokes. **(KEY POINTS)**

The summer was drawing to a close, and soon I would be returning to Buenos Aires. The night before I was to leave, Salguero showed me how to find the Southern Cross. The generator had been turned off, and there was only the soft sound of the peepers. We could see the horses sleeping far off in the field.

The next morning, my last at the estancia, Susanita and I got up before dawn. Pampita and the other horses were still out in the field. Salguero handed me his own horse's reins. He told me he thought I was ready to bring in the horses by myself. I wasn't sure I could do it, but Susanita encouraged me to try.

77

WORD STUDY

Remind students that homophones sound exactly alike but are spelled differently and have different meanings. Ask them what word on page 76 is a homophone of *tails*, the part that sticks out from the end of an animal's body. *(tales)* What does tales mean? Start a class homophone list.

SCIENCE

Ask students to complete the **Stars in Argentina** activity on **page R32**, during which they will discover the differences in the night sky as seen from the Northern and Southern hemispheres. Students will find the Southern Cross on a map of the night sky and notice the differences between maps of the two hemispheres.

SKILLS AND STRATEGIES

LITERARY ELEMENT
Character

TEACH/MODEL
Remind students that character traits are special qualities of a character's personality. Authors give information about character traits in several ways:

• words that describe a character directly.

• what the character does, says, thinks, or feels.

• how other characters feel about the character.

PRACTICE/APPLY
Ask students to fill in the chart. They should enter an example from the story and name the trait the example shows.

Susanita	
Description	
Example:	**Character trait:**
She knew everything about horses, cows, and the other animals.	intelligent
Actions	
Example:	**Character trait:**
She used to swim in the creek holding on to La Baya's mane.	adventurous
Other Characters' Reactions	
Example:	**Character trait:**
She rode so well that the gauchos called her La Gauchita.	skillful

Assign **Practice Book 1, page 45** for skill maintenance.

◎ **IF** students need more support with character,

THEN see the review lesson on page R48.

DAY 2

COMPREHENSION

15 **AUTHOR'S CRAFT: DESCRIPTIVE LANGUAGE**

> What details in the text help you visualize what it is like when horses are herded into a corral? *(Possible answers: The author describes the foals as frisky. She says that they kept running away and that they were trotting.)*

16 **CHARACTER**

> The narrator doesn't notice that everyone is watching her round up the horses. What does this statement tell you about her character? *(Possible answer: She is concentrating on what she is doing, not on what other people might think of her; she wants to succeed at her job.)*

17 **DRAW CONCLUSIONS**

> What important gifts does the girl receive from her grandparents? What does this tell you about how her family and the gauchos feel about her? *(Possible answer: She receives a gaucho belt and a horse of her own. Her family and the gauchos are proud of what she has learned during the summer.)*

I remembered what I'd seen Salguero do. I tried to get the leading mare, with her bell, to go toward the corral, and the others would follow her. It wasn't easy. The foals were frisky and kept running away. But I stayed behind **15** them until finally the little herd was all together, trotting in front of me.

16 I was so busy trying to keep the foals from running off that I didn't notice the whole household waiting in the corral with Salguero. Everyone cheered as I rode in, and before I knew it, my grandfather was helping me off the horse. "You've become quite a gaucho this summer," he said.

78

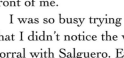
MODIFY Instruction

ESL/ELD

▲ Explain such phrases as *leading mare* and *gaucho belt*. Ask students to look for words that describe herding. Ask them to organize the information they find, for example: *The most important part of herding is making sure the horses will follow the leading mare.* **(KEY WORDS)**

GIFTED & TALENTED

✷ Encourage groups of students to choose one of the story events or scenes, such as the journey to the *estancia*, the birthday party, or finding the *ñandú* egg. Challenge them to develop dialogue written from the narrator's point of view. **(INNOVATE)**

My grandmother held out a wonderful gaucho belt like Salguero's, with silver coins from around the world—and my initials on the buckle!

"And," she added, "there's something else every gaucho needs. Next summer, when you come back, you'll have your very own horse waiting for you!" She pointed to the leading mare's foal, the friskiest and most beautiful of them all. **17**

Before I could say a word, the foal pranced over to me, tossing his head. I would have the whole winter to decide what to name him, and to look forward to my next summer on the pampas.

CULTURAL CONNECTION

The gauchos of the Argentine pampas could not do their jobs without horses. For centuries people have bred horses for speed, strength, and endurance. One of the hardiest breeds is the Criollo, the small, sturdy horse of the gauchos. Ask students to pretend that they are gauchos choosing a horse. Have them draw the horse they want. At a "horse show" students can introduce their horse to the class. For ideas, students may want to check out books or videos on horses from the library.

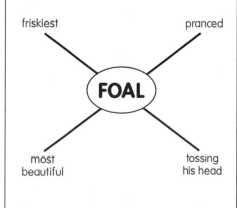

AUTHOR'S CRAFT
Descriptive Language

TEACH/MODEL
Ask students to describe a special gift they have received.

> **How do descriptive words help others picture the gift?**

Discuss with students the author's use of descriptive language.

> **The author's style in this selection is to tell what action is taking place and to give one or two important details to help you picture the scene.**

> **Noticing the words the author uses can help you enjoy the story.**

PRACTICE/APPLY
Encourage students to identify descriptive details in the text and use them to build a word web.

> **What details in the text help you picture the foal the narrator's grandparents gave her?**

friskiest   pranced

FOAL

most
beautiful   tossing
his head

COMPREHENSION

18 **INTERPRET GRAPHIC DEVICES**

> **What new information can you learn from the map that the rest of the story doesn't teach you?** *(Possible answer: The map shows where the pampas is in South America, and it gives the names of other countries, rivers, and oceans.)*

JOURNAL

Revisit Predictions

Ask students to look back at their predictions and record how they were or were not confirmed by the end of the selection.

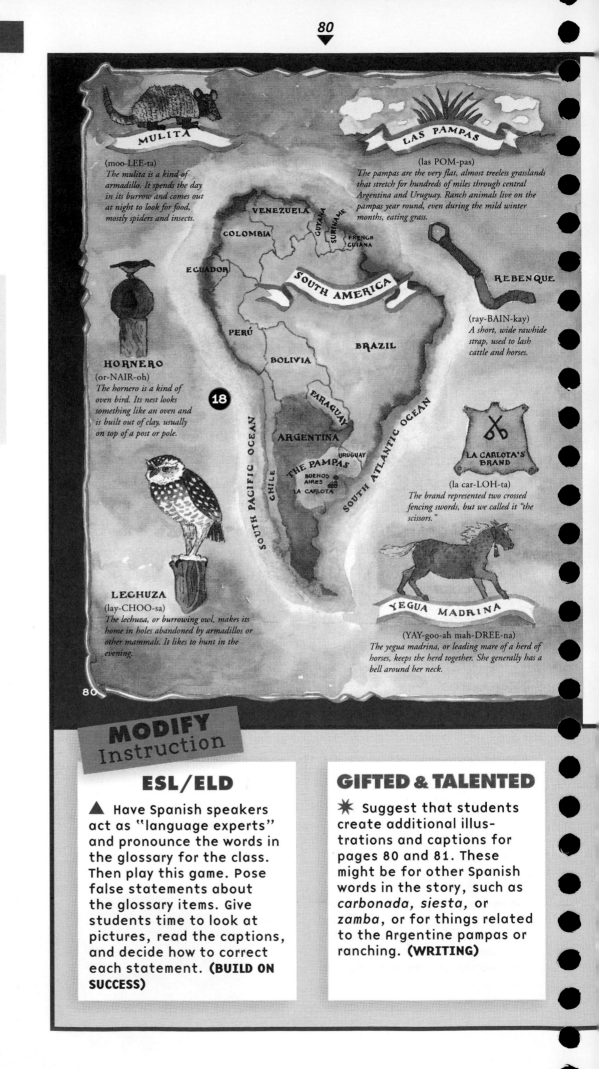

80 ▼

MULITA

(moo-LEE-ta)
The mulita is a kind of armadillo. It spends the day in its burrow and comes out at night to look for food, mostly spiders and insects.

LAS PAMPAS

(las POM-pas)
The pampas are the very flat, almost treeless grasslands that stretch for hundreds of miles through central Argentina and Uruguay. Ranch animals live on the pampas year round, even during the mild winter months, eating grass.

REBENQUE

(ray-BAIN-kay)
A short, wide rawhide strap, used to lash cattle and horses.

HORNERO

(or-NAIR-oh)
The hornero is a kind of oven bird. Its nest looks something like an oven and is built out of clay, usually on top of a post or pole.

LA CARLOTA'S BRAND

(la car-LOH-ta)
The brand represented two crossed fencing swords, but we called it "the scissors."

LECHUZA

(lay-CHOO-sa)
The lechuza, or burrowing owl, makes its home in holes abandoned by armadillos or other mammals. It likes to hunt in the evening.

YEGUA MADRINA

(YAY-goo-ah mah-DREE-na)
The yegua madrina, or leading mare of a herd of horses, keeps the herd together. She generally has a bell around her neck.

VENEZUELA · COLOMBIA · GUYANA · SURINAME · FRENCH GUIANA · ECUADOR · SOUTH AMERICA · PERÚ · BRAZIL · BOLIVIA · PARAGUAY · SOUTH PACIFIC OCEAN · ARGENTINA · THE PAMPAS · URUGUAY · BUENOS AIRES · LA CARLOTA · CHILE · SOUTH ATLANTIC OCEAN

MODIFY Instruction

ESL/ELD

▲ Have Spanish speakers act as "language experts" and pronounce the words in the glossary for the class. Then play this game. Pose false statements about the glossary items. Give students time to look at pictures, read the captions, and decide how to correct each statement. **(BUILD ON SUCCESS)**

GIFTED & TALENTED

✳ Suggest that students create additional illustrations and captions for pages 80 and 81. These might be for other Spanish words in the story, such as *carbonada*, *siesta*, or *zamba*, or for things related to the Argentine pampas or ranching. **(WRITING)**

81 ▼

ASADO
(ah-SAH-doh)
Meat, usually beef, roasted outdoors over a fire.

MATE
(MAH-tay)
Mate is a bitter, greenish tea. It is sipped through a silver straw called a bombilla (bome-BEE-yah) from a hollow gourd that is passed around.

FACÓN
(fah-KONE)
A gaucho knife. Gauchos used to carry them as weapons, but now they are used for ranch work.

GAUCHO CLOTHES

BOLEADORAS
(boh-lay-ah-DOOR-ahs)
Gauchos used to catch ñandús and other animals with boleadoras, which they threw in such a way that the animals' legs were tangled up in them.

RASTRA
(RAH-stra)
A gaucho belt made from a wide strip of leather decorated with silver coins, usually from different countries. Some gauchos have their initials on the buckle.

BOMBACHA
(bome-BAH-cha)
Loose gaucho pants.

RECADO
(ray-KAH-doh)
The gaucho saddle, made of many layers of leather and wool, with a sheepskin on the top.

ÑANDÚ
(nyon-DOO)
The ñandú, or South American ostrich, is the largest bird in the Americas. It grows to be five feet tall and to weigh about fifty pounds. Although it cannot fly, it can run very fast. The male ñandú guards the nest, hatches the eggs, and takes care of the chicks.

ESTANCIA
(eh-STAHN-see-ah)
A South American cattle ranch.

81

Brochure
WRITING WORKSHOP

PREWRITE Ask students to imagine that they have a chance to take an exciting adventure trip. Tell them that later they will be developing a brochure to persuade people to go on such a trip. Have them think of reasons people should take an adventure trip. Then have students begin the prewriting organizer.

Use Practice Book 1, page 46.

DAILY LANGUAGE PRACTICE

SPELLING
DAY 2:
Practice Words With *ng* and *nk*. **See page R28.**

GRAMMAR, USAGE, MECHANICS
DAY 2:
Practice Singular and Plural Nouns. **See page R30.**

ORAL LANGUAGE
One day thay took a long rides on the pampas? *(One day <u>they</u> took a long <u>ride</u> on the pampas<u>.</u>)*

DAY **2** WRAP-UP

READ ALOUD *Spend five to ten minutes reading from a selection of your choice.*

GUIDED READING *Meet with the* **blue** *and* **green** *reading groups and assign Independent Center activities.* **See pages R26–R27.**

MATH
Ask students to do the **How Big Is Argentina?** activity on **page R32**, where they will use a map to compare the areas of the United States and Argentina. Students will make plans to compare areas and follow their plans to reach reasonable solutions.

VISUAL LITERACY
Discuss the illustrations and captions that surround the map. Point out that these give information on wildlife of the Argentine pampas and the meanings of Spanish words the author used. Have students discuss how pages 80–81 add to their enjoyment and understanding of the story.

COMPREHENSION

DAY 3 OBJECTIVES

STUDENTS WILL:

READ 30 MINUTES

- "Keith Jardine: Wilderness Guide," pp. 82–85
- Comprehension Skill: Paraphrase
- Assess Comprehension
- Key Literary Element: Setting
- Daily Phonics: One-, Two-, Three-Syllable Words

WRITE 30 MINUTES

- Respond: Interview
- Spelling: Words With *ng* and *nk*
- Grammar, Usage, Mechanics: Singular and Plural Nouns
- Oral Language

EXTEND SKILLS 30 MINUTES

- Read Aloud
- Guided Reading

RESOURCES

- Transparency 12
- Practice Book 1, pp. 47–52
- Spelling Resource Book, p. 28

▶ Preview

Have students preview the selection by looking at the photographs and captions. Ask students to read pages 82–83.

1 **CRITICAL THINKING: ANALYZE**

> What might be dangerous about a river trip? What are some possible benefits to such a trip? *(Possible answers: Dangers might include falling overboard. Benefits might include learning a new skill and finding out you can do something you've never done before.)*

82

MENTOR

Keith Jardine

Wilderness Guide

River rafting is full of new experiences! **1**

Wilderness guide Keith Jardine works for a wilderness school. But his workplace isn't an indoor classroom. Instead, he grabs a paddle, puts on a life jacket, and jumps into a rubber raft. Jardine's job is taking adults and kids on adventure trips down some of California's fastest-moving rivers And he loves every minute of it!

MODIFY Instruction

ESL/ELD

▲ Use the visuals on the page to clarify the key vocabulary words *wilderness* and *river rafting*. Then pair English language learners with peers who are first language speakers. Have them create a graphic device to illustrate the dangers and benefits of a river trip. **(GRAPHIC DEVICE)**

GIFTED & TALENTED

✳ Suggest that students create a profile of themselves, modeled on the profile of Keith Jardine on page 83. For *Job*, they should write "student." Encourage students to post their profiles on a bulletin board for classmates to read. **(INNOVATE)**

83

PERSONAL VOICE

PROFILE

Name: Keith Jardine

Born: Sonoma, California

Job: wilderness guide

Hobby: river rafting

First wilderness experience: exploring his own backyard

Favorite wilderness place: California's Clavey River. He even named one of his sons Klavey, spelled with a *K*.

Fantasy adventure trip: rafting on a wild Alaskan river

Horizon Line
Recirculating Hole
Rock
Direction of Current

83

ORAL LANGUAGE

Have students give a reading of the text on page 82 as if they were a radio or television announcer introducing Keith Jardine as a guest on a talk show. Remind them to read with enthusiasm to grab the attention of their audience and to use hand gestures appropriately during the introduction. When students are ready, they can tape-record their readings for the class. Encourage students to replay their recordings and, as they listen, to note at what point and /or how they might improve their speaking techniques.

GENRE
Profile

TEACH/MODEL

Tell students that this selection is a profile of the mentor Keith Jardine. Have students recall profiles they have read of movie stars and athletes. Ask them to describe the kinds of information such profiles contain. Explain the key elements of a profile.

> **A profile is a short biography.**

> **It provides facts about the person, as well as his or her opinions and feelings.**

PRACTICE/APPLY

As students read, have them identify some facts as well as some of Keith Jardine's opinions and feelings. They can record them on a chart like the one below.

> **What do his opinions tell us about the kind of person Keith Jardine is?**

Keith Jardine	
Facts	**Opinions**
Born in Sonoma, California	River rafting is fun.

COMPREHENSION

2 PARAPHRASE

> Keith Jardine tells us how he deals with youngsters who are nervous about rafting. Retell in your own words how he handles this situation. (*Possible answer: He tells them that they can decide not to go, but he asks them to take a chance and see how they feel about it after they've tried it.*)

3 CHARACTER

> What kind of person is Keith Jardine? Why do you think he enjoys taking river trips and teaching people how to raft? (*Possible answer: He loves the outdoors and wants to share his knowledge and love with other people and get them to feel the same way he does about the wilderness.*)

4 CAUSE/EFFECT

> When the young rafters feel successful, they feel more confident. Why would succeeding cause you to feel more confident? (*Possible answer: When people succeed at something, they feel better about themselves. Thinking more highly of themselves makes them more confident.*)

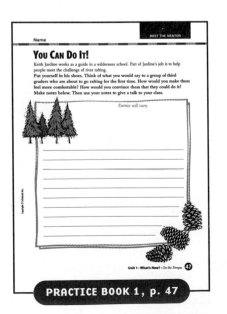

Name _____

MEET THE MENTOR

YOU CAN DO IT!

Keith Jardine works as a guide in a wilderness school. Part of Jardine's job is to help people meet the challenge of river rafting.
Put yourself in his shoes. Think of what you would say to a group of third graders who are about to go rafting for the first time. How would you make them feel more comfortable? How would you convince them that they could do it? Make notes below. Then use your notes to give a talk to your class.

Entries will vary.

Unit 1 - What's New? - *On the Pampas* ㊼

PRACTICE BOOK 1, p. 47

ALL ABOUT
Keith Jardine

Here's how wilderness guide Keith Jardine teaches kids to meet adventure head on.

"River rafting is a lot of fun," says Keith Jardine. "But it also takes a willingness to learn. You can't just jump in a boat and float down the river."

Jardine especially likes taking kids in raft trips. He finds that they are willing to listen and learn about the wilderness experience.

"Some kids already know a lot about the wilderness," says Jardine. "They're usually the ones who come from small towns and have spent time hiking or camping. But rafting is a different experience for city kids," he explains. "For many of them, the adventure is new and even scary."

What happens when kids are nervous about rafting? "I'm there to help them out," says Jardine. If kids are afraid to get into the raft, he tells them that they don't have to go. But he always asks them to give it a try. "By the time they're down the river a half mile, their attitudes usually change. They really start to enjoy it."

84

MODIFY Instruction

ESL/ELD

▲ To help students answer question 4, reread the quote on page 85 from the girl who was afraid to ride on the river. At the end of the trip she said, "I can really do this!" Ask: *How does this girl feel?* Define the words proud/confident. Ask: *What makes you feel proud or gives you lots of confidence?* **(PERSONALIZE)**

GIFTED & TALENTED

✳ Challenge groups of students to plan their own adventure trips. When they have made their plans, encourage them to act out the adventures for the whole class, complete with sound effects and props. **(ACT IT OUT)**

85 ▼

PERSONAL VOICE

Jardine feels that wilderness adventures, on and off the river, can help kids find out about themselves. "They learn that it is okay to get out in the world and explore new things."

Exploring and looking for adventure have always been a part of Keith Jardine's life. As a kid he went hiking and camping with his parents. They taught him how to get along by himself in the woods. Meeting these challenges gave Jardine lots of self-confidence.

As a wilderness guide, Keith Jardine is still meeting challenges and learning about himself, And so are the kids who go rafting with him. A girl who was frightened about riding on the river discovered that she could help steer the big rubber raft. When she finished the trip, she said, "I can really do this!"

Keith Jardine thinks that new experiences like river rafting are good for kids. He says, "It's one of my goals to help these kids succeed. They can use that feeling of success in whatever they do." ③ ④

Keith Jardine's Tips
for Meeting New Challenges

1 Learn all you can about what you're going to do. Ask questions.

2 Make sure you have all the gear or materials you need.

3 Tell yourself, "I can do this!"

4 Even if you're afraid, give it a try.

85

HELP WITH HOMEWORK

Encourage family members to read aloud the directions on a homework paper with their child. Then they should ask the child to rephrase the directions in his or her own words. **(1-MINUTE LITERACY BYTE)**

ORAL LANGUAGE

Have pairs of students plan an interview between a TV reporter and Keith Jardine. They should first think of questions that can be answered by what Jardine says in the article. Have students present their interviews to the class from the text.

SKILLS AND STRATEGIES

COMPREHENSION
Paraphrase

TEACH/MODEL
Explain to students that retelling what they read will help them understand and remember information.

> **Paraphrasing means telling in your own words what you have read.**

> **Keep the meaning of the original text and don't add your own opinions.**

Model paraphrasing the first paragraph of the selection.

💭 **THINK ALOUD** *First, I reread the passage and think about its meaning. Then I retell it in my own words:* Keith Jardine says that river rafting is fun, but you have to be ready to learn the skills you'll need.

PRACTICE/APPLY
Write the following sentence on the chalkboard and have students work together to paraphrase it. *Jardine feels that wilderness adventures, on and off the river, can help youngsters find out about themselves. (Jardine believes wilderness adventures help youngsters.)*

✓ INFORMAL ASSESSMENT
OBSERVATION

Did students:

✔ select the best paraphrase?

✔ use paraphrasing to monitor their comprehension?

◎ **IF** students need more practice, **THEN** have them paraphrase the first paragraph on page 85.

COMPREHENSION

▶ Think About Reading

Below are the **answers** to the *Think About Reading* questions.

1. *She wants to learn how to be a gaucho.*

2. *She is brave, willing to try new things, and doesn't give up. She swims in the creek, rounds up cattle, and spends hours learning to use a lasso.*

3. *Accept all reasonable responses that relate to the types of work and play that take place on an Argentine estancia.*

4. *Possible answers: The ranch hands are called gauchos, their clothes are different from those of American cowhands, the people take afternoon siestas.*

5. *Possible answers: The narrator would probably enjoy going on the raft trip because she likes new adventures and is willing to learn how to do new things.*

RESPOND

Think About Reading

Write your answers.

1. What does the girl want to learn from Salguero?

2. What kind of person is the girl? How do you know?

3. If you visited the estancia, what would you most like to do? Why?

4. In what ways is life in *On the Pampas* different from life on a ranch in the United States?

5. How do you think the girl in *On the Pampas* would feel about going on one of Keith Jardine's raft trips? Explain your answer.

86

MODIFY
Instruction

ESL/ELD

▲ Have students work in small groups to write the interview questions for the Write an Interview activity. Those who are not ready to write independently may dictate their questions to you or to a peer mentor. **(WORK IN GROUPS)**

EXTRA HELP

■ For the writing activity, students can work in pairs to brainstorm a list of questions and answers. Students can use an outline or a graphic organizer to record their ideas. **(VISUAL AID)**

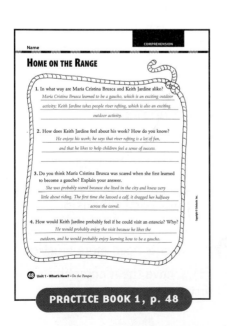

PRACTICE BOOK 1, p. 48

Write an Interview

You are a reporter for your class newspaper. Your job is to interview the girl in *On the Pampas* about her summer on the estancia. First, write two or three questions you want to ask the girl about her adventures. Then write the answers she might give. Be sure to include colorful details in the answers to questions.

Literature Circle

Ranch life and river rafting are both filled with challenges. What advice do you think the girl in *On the Pampas* might give to young people who are going river rafting? How would Keith Jardine feel about her advice?

Author
María Cristina Brusca

María Cristina Brusca really did visit her grandparents' estancia while she was on vacation. Like the girl in *On the Pampas*, she also dreamed of becoming a gaucho! Her dream came true when she wrote and illustrated the book based on her adventures. Now she lives in Kingston, New York, but she still has time to ride her horse in the nearby countryside.

More Books by María Cristina Brusca
• *My Mama's Little Ranch on the Pampas*
• *The Cook and the King*

87

RESPOND

Write an Interview

Remind students that interviews follow a question/answer format. Have students think about these questions:

> **What questions would you like to ask the girl?**

> **What answers might she give, based on what you know from the selection?**

Literature Circle

Students may say that the girl would tell river rafters to try something, even if they are afraid, and that Keith Jardine would agree with her. Students might enjoy role-playing a conversation between the girl and Keith Jardine and recording it.

DAILY LANGUAGE PRACTICE

SPELLING
DAY 3:
Write Words With *ng* and *nk*. See page R29.

GRAMMAR, USAGE, MECHANICS
DAY 3:
Practice Singular and Plural Nouns. See page R31.

ORAL LANGUAGE
The girl think they cood be gauchos?

(The girls think they could be gauchos.)

TECHNOLOGY

SPEAKING SKILLS
Have students use the questions they've written to interview the girl on videotape. Have students play the parts of the interviewer, the girl, and a studio audience, who also ask questions.

AUTHOR/ILLUSTRATOR STUDY

Author María Cristina Brusca is one of many talented members of the Brusca clan. Send students to this web site: **www.kingsfield.com.** Tell them to look for the keyword *brusca*, and they will find out how this family got its last name.

🔑 LITERARY ELEMENT
Setting

SKILLS TRACE

SETTING **TESTED**

Introduce . . . .pp. T180–T181
Practice . . . . . .pp. T159, T182, T190
Review . . . . . . .p. R50
Reteach . . . . .p. R55

✓ QUICKCHECK

Can students:

✔ identify details in the text and pictures that reveal setting?

✔ understand how the story's events and setting are linked?

If **YES**, go on to Practice/Apply.

If **NO**, start at Teach/Model.

Ⓐ TEACH/MODEL

USE ORAL LANGUAGE

Have students describe a favorite place outside. What does it look like? How big are nearby trees or bushes? How close is a road or street? Where is the nearest pond or river or fountain? Point out that they have described a setting.

A setting is where and when a story takes place. To identify setting, tell students to:

1. Look at the cover illustration and all the pictures in the story.

2. Find out the place where the story occurs and identify story details that relate to that place.

3. Find out the time when the story happens and identify story details related to time.

4. Remember that the setting can change in different parts of the story.

TRANSPARENCY 12

Scholastic Literacy Place

SETTING

Part of a Selection	When	Where
page 66	summer, morning	train crossing the Argentine pampas
page 71	afternoon	a eucalyptus grove
pages 74–75	night	outside the ranch house
page 76	evening	the mate house
page 77	dawn or morning	field and corral

What's New? • On the Pampas 12

MODIFY Instruction

ESL/ELD

▲ Draw on the chalkboard a T-chart with the headings **Words** and **Pictures**. Remind students that in a story, words and pictures help readers understand the setting. Ask volunteers to use the chart and help you list items from the story that demonstrate setting. **(WORD CLUES/PICTURE CLUES)**

EXTRA HELP

■ Provide additional support to students during Teach/Model. If necessary, find and identify story details that show time and place and make a distinction between the two. After the Think Aloud, you may also wish to reread those parts of the story that reveal setting. **(MAKE CONNECTIONS)**

LITERATURE CONNECTION

Use Transparency 12 to help students identify the setting changes on the selection pages indicated.

THINK ALOUD *The first paragraph on page 66 tells me that the characters are in Argentina. Outside the window are cattle on a grassy plain. These clues tell me where this scene takes place—on a train crossing the Argentine pampas—and when—on a summer morning. I'll use what the story tells me about the Argentine pampas to help me understand the events. As I read I'll also pay attention to changes in the setting.*

B PRACTICE/APPLY

USE PRACTICE BOOK 1

Have students work independently to practice the skill by completing **Practice Book 1, page 50. (Independent)**

C ASSESS

APPLY INSTRUCTIONAL ALTERNATIVES

Based on students' completion of **Transparency 12** and **Practice Book 1, page 50**, determine whether they were able to identify setting in *On the Pampas*. The Instructional Alternatives below will aid you in pinpointing students' level of proficiency. Consider the appropriate instructional alternative to promote further skill development.

To reinforce the skill, distribute **pages 51 and 52** of **Practice Book 1.**

✓ INSTRUCTIONAL ALTERNATIVES

	If the student . . .	Then
Proficient	Identifies details in the pictures and text that show the story setting	• Have the student apply this skill independently to a more challenging story.
Apprentice	Identifies some details of setting but can't connect the setting to story events	• Work with the student to make a chart linking specific events with a specific setting. For example, kitchen—cooking, eating, noon—siesta, reading.
Novice	Misidentifies details of setting and doesn't understand how setting affects plot	• Provide the student with a less challenging story and work with the student to identify details of setting. • Complete the Reteach lesson on page R55.

PRACTICE BOOK 1, p. 50

PRACTICE BOOK 1, p. 51

PRACTICE BOOK 1, p. 52

ON THE PAMPAS
Maria Cristina Brusca

Intervention
For students who need extra help with . . .

PHONICS

ONE-, TWO-, THREE-SYLLABLE WORDS
Create syllable cards by writing single syllables on index cards. Do this for two- and three-syllable words in the selection, such as *an-i-mal, puz-zle, wa-ter, cat-tle,* and *sum-mer.*

- Hold up each syllable of a word until you make the whole word.

- Ask students to say each syllable as you hold up its card.

- Individually or chorally, students can pronounce the whole word.

an   i   mal   puz   zle

LITERARY ELEMENT

SETTING
Support students' understanding of how the setting of *On the Pampas* affects the story.

- Put the chart on the chalkboard for students to copy.

- Guide students in completing the chart, asking how the setting determines the kinds of animals in the story, the workers, and the kinds of work they do.

Setting of Story *Pampas of Argentina*		
Kinds of Animals	Kinds of Workers	Kinds of Work That's Done
horses	gauchos	raising cattle
cattle	cook	branding cattle
dog		vaccinating cattle
		cooking for workers
		riding horses

FLUENCY

ECHO READING
Use echo reading to model fluency by reading aloud short sections of text.

- Have a student or a small group of students repeat or echo the same text section after you.

- Use your oral reading to provide students with an immediate, positive, and fluent model.

- Begin with short text sections and build up to larger chunks.

Use the Take-Home Practice Readers to build fluency.

Optional Materials for Intervention

PHONICS

Polysyllabic Words

If students need help with polysyllabic words, use Phonics Chapter Book #17, History Mystery.

BEFORE READING

READ WORDS Explain to students that they will be focusing on 3-syllable words. Have students chorally read the following words syllable by syllable as you reveal each syllable.

- history
- family
- understand
- carefully
- exercise
- minerals

TEACH STRUCTURAL ANALYSIS Write the following suffixes on the chalkboard: *-ly, -y, -er, -est.* Have students chorally read each of the following words syllable by syllable.

- sugary
- explorer
- family
- highest

READ *HISTORY MYSTERY*

Assign Chapter 1 of the book. Check in with students and provide support as they continue reading the story.

LISTENING

Repeated Reading

If students need help with fluency, use the audiocassette for On the Pampas.

LISTEN TO THE AUDIOCASSETTE

Encourage students to listen to the audiocassette of *On the Pampas,* following along in the text as the narrator reads.

SUMMARIZE EVENTS

Remind students that the setting of a story can change in different parts of the story. Have pairs of students listen to the audiocassette and stop the tape when the setting shifts. Students can take turns summarizing the events that took place in the setting.

DAY **3** WRAP-UP

READ ALOUD *Spend five to ten minutes reading from a selection of your choice.*

GUIDED READING *Meet with the* **green** *and* **red** *reading groups and assign Independent Center activities.* **See pages R26–R27.**

DAY 4 OBJECTIVES

STUDENTS WILL:

READ 15 MINUTES

• Reread the Mentor Profile

WRITE 45 MINUTES

• Writing Workshop: Brochure
• Writer's Craft: Opinion and Supporting Facts
• Spelling: Words With *ng* and *nk*
• Grammar, Usage, Mechanics: Singular and Plural Nouns
• Oral Language

EXTEND SKILLS 30 MINUTES

• Vocabulary
• Daily Phonics: One-, Two-, Three-Syllable Words
• Study Skills: Using a Dictionary
• Read Aloud
• Guided Reading

RESOURCES

• Transparency 13
• Practice Book 1, pp. 46, 53, 54
• Spelling Resource Book, p. 200

Students may refer to *Putting It In Writing* and *Writing With Style*.

PRACTICE BOOK 1, p. 46

✎ WRITING WORKSHOP *Persuasive Writing*
Brochure

THINK ABOUT WRITING

Remind students that Keith Jardine's job is taking people on adventure trips down rivers.

> **How do you think people find out about these rafting trips?**

> **What might persuade people to go river rafting?**

LITERATURE CONNECTION

If possible, display a variety of travel brochures and have students examine them. Then have students look back at pages 84 and 85. Guide them to find statements that might persuade people to go on a river rafting trip, such as "River rafting is a lot of fun" on page 84. Explain that a brochure advertising a river rafting trip would include ideas such as these.

PREWRITE

COMPLETE A GRAPHIC ORGANIZER

Have students refer to the graphic organizer on **Practice Book 1, page 46** that they began earlier. They might add more facts and opinions to include in their brochure.

DRAFT

TEACH WRITER'S CRAFT

Before students begin their drafts, help them understand the use of opinions, supporting facts, and examples. **See Writer's Craft, page T185.**

> **Now that you have organized your ideas for a persuasive brochure, use your ideas to write a first draft.**

REVISE/PROOFREAD

Note: You may wish to do Revise/Proofread on Day 5.

As students revise and proofread, they might want to ask themselves:

REVISE

• Have I included opinions and supported them with facts and examples?

• Did I state my position at the beginning and restate it at the end?

PROOFREAD

• Have I used singular and plural nouns correctly?

• Do all my sentences begin with capital letters?

✔ **See Students' Writing Rubric on page T192.**

WRITER'S CRAFT
OPINION AND SUPPORTING FACTS

(A) TEACH/MODEL

Point out that in persuasive writing, it is important to include facts and examples that support your opinions. A good opinion—one that is persuasive—has lots of good facts to support it.

(B) PRACTICE/APPLY

- **Write on the chalkboard:** *Hiking in Yosemite National Park is a thrilling experience. You will pass mountain lakes and streams and see Yosemite Falls—one of the highest waterfalls in the world.* Point out that the examples of what you will see and the fact about Yosemite Falls support the opinion that hiking in Yosemite is thrilling.

- **Use Transparency 13,** or write the following sentences on the chalkboard. Ask students to choose the better passage and give reasons for their choice. Help them see why the other passage is not the better choice.

> 1. Glacier National Park is a paradise for nature lovers. Located in northern Montana, the park contains 10,000-foot-tall mountains and more than 200 lakes.
>
> 2. You'll feel you're on top of the world when you climb the mountain trails in Glacier National Park. It's a great feeling! You'll want to stay forever.

- Discuss that **passage 1** is the better choice because the second sentence offers facts to support the opinion expressed in the first sentence. **Passage 2** is not good because all of the sentences are opinions; no examples are given to support the opinions.

Scholastic Literacy Place

WRITER'S CRAFT

1. Glacier National Park is a paradise for nature lovers. Located in northern Montana, the park contains 10,000-foot-tall mountains and more than 200 lakes.

2. You'll feel like you're on top of the world when you climb a mountain. It's a great feeling! You'll want to stay forever.

3. You'll see some amazing wildlife on a photo safari. You'd better bring a lot of film!

4. Many travel companies offer ten day and twenty-one day photo safaris. Most safaris visit the large animal preserves in Africa.

5. Scuba divers explore the waters of lakes, rivers, and oceans. Special breathing gear lets them stay underwater for an hour at a time.

6. You'll have the time of your life when you scuba dive! It's fun, and it's educational, too.

Correct choices are 1, 4, 5.

What's New? • On the Pampas 13

DAILY LANGUAGE PRACTICE

SPELLING
DAY 4:
Review Words With *ng* and *nk*. **See page R29.**

GRAMMAR, USAGE, MECHANICS
DAY 4:
Apply Singular and Plural Nouns. **See page R31.**

ORAL LANGUAGE
The horses named jocko has strong, wite teeth.
(The horse *named Jocko has strong,* white *teeth.)*

TECHNOLOGY

Writing Skills
Encourage students to use the cut and paste options in a familiar word processing program to help them revise their writing.

VOCABULARY WORDS

pampas	corral
grazing	bridles
gauchos	manes
lasso	

TEACHER TIP

"When the vocabulary words we are working with are almost all picturable, I encourage students to create a mini picture dictionary — one word and picture to a page. Sometimes we develop a 'pix-dix' display first, on a wall or bulletin board, and then later compile all the pages into a class book to keep on hand for ready reference."

Extend Vocabulary

Review Vocabulary

CLUES TO MEANING

Write or say the vocabulary words. Then read each sentence aloud and have students write or name the word it describes.

1. This is a vast, flat grassland area in South America. *(pampas)*

2. Horses have this thick, heavy hair on their necks. *(manes)*

3. Cowhands use this long rope to catch cattle. *(lasso)*

4. Cattle are doing this when they eat grass. *(grazing)*

5. These South American cowhands work on the pampas. *(gauchos)*

6. These go over horses' heads so that their riders can control them. *(bridles)*

7. You might see horses or cows in this fenced-in place. *(corral)*

Expand Vocabulary

IRREGULAR PLURALS

Remind students that the plural of most nouns is formed by adding *-s* or *-es*. However, some nouns in the plural stay the same or change their spelling. Point out *calf* and *calves* on page 70 of the story, and write the words on the chart. Encourage students to find and brainstorm other examples and add them to the chart.

Irregular Plurals	
Singular	**Plural**
calf	**calves**
child	children
sheep	sheep
tooth	teeth

Record Vocabulary

HORSE DIAGRAM

Students can work together to create a diagram of a horse, saddled and bridled. After they draw the horse, they can label it with the appropriate vocabulary words, *mane* and *bridle*. Students can add other terms for parts of a horse and its tack as they learn them.

One-, Two-, Three-Syllable Words

BOWLING FOR WORDS

Prepare for the activity by making a bowling score sheet for each student as shown. Then make a set of large tagboard or construction paper bowling pins. On each pin, write a one-, two-, or three-syllable word and a number from 1 to 10. Assign the highest numbers to the most difficult words. Use these and other words:

younger	morning	everything
long	drank	something

Bowling for Words											Total
Matt	6	0	7	8	1	0	3	9	0	2	36

1 SET-UP Divide the class into two teams. Place the bowling pins in a bag or box so that students cannot see them.

2 TO PLAY One player from each team reaches in and selects a pin.

- If players can correctly read the word and tell the number of syllables it has, they record the score on their score sheets.

- If a player cannot read the word, he or she receives a "gutter ball"—a score of 0.

- The game ends when all ten frames of the bowling game have been played and the scores tallied.

3 TRY THIS Players must also use the words in sentences.

ESL/ELD

▲ Help students create a chalkboard bar graph to track how many one-, two-, and three-syllable words were used in the bowling game. Help volunteers write each word within the correct bar of the graph. **(GRAPHIC DEVICE)**

GIFTED & TALENTED

✳ Suggest that students use the words on the bowling pins to create crossword puzzles. Encourage them to use a dictionary to help them write clues to the words. **(BUILD ON SUCCESS)**

MATERIALS:
Tagboard or construction paper
Scissors
Marker or pen

SUGGESTED GROUPING:
Whole class

PRACTICE BOOK 1, p. 53

 IF students need more support with one-, two-, three-syllable words,

THEN see the review lesson on page R42.

STUDY SKILLS
Using a Dictionary

SKILLS TRACE

USING A DICTIONARY `TESTED`

Introduce . . . . p. T188
Practice . . . . p. T189
Review . . . . p. R49
Reteach . . . . p. R55

RESEARCH IDEA

Use the dictionary to look up the meaning of the following words: *eucalyptus, ostrich,* and *gourd*.

Ⓐ TEACH/MODEL

DEFINE DICTIONARY

Tell students that a dictionary is a book containing an alphabetical listing of words, their pronunciations, parts of speech, meanings, and other information.

DISCUSS ALPHABETICAL ORDER AND GUIDE WORDS

Open a student dictionary and call attention to the guide words at the top of a page. Explain that these are the first and last entry words that are found on that page. All the words on the page come between the two guide words. They are in alphabetical order.

> **How do you think the guide words can help you quickly and easily find the entry word you want?**

USE GUIDE WORDS TO LOCATE AN ENTRY WORD

If students have their own dictionaries, ask them to use the guide words to help them find the entry for *pampas*. Otherwise, ask a volunteer to locate the word and identify the guide words it falls between.

DISCUSS PARTS OF AN ENTRY

Point out and explain the various parts of an entry:

- The entry word is divided into syllables by dots or spaces.

- The pronunciation in parentheses after the entry uses special symbols that are explained in a pronunciation key. Accent marks show which syllables are stressed. Some dictionaries may use boldface type for an accented syllable.

- The part of speech of the word is given, either as an abbreviation or in full.

- The definition tells what the word means. Some definitions include sentences or phrases.

> **What part of speech is the word *pampas*?**

> **How does the dictionary define *pampas*?**

--- Guide words ---

one   Part of speech   **Pronunciation**   **ongoing**

Entry word —— **one** (wun) *adjective* **1** a single unit or thing **2** united; forming a whole **3** a certain, not named, person or thing – *noun* **1** the number that names a single unit **2** a person or thing

one·fold (wun′fōld′) *adjective* whole; complete

O·nei·da (ō nī′də) *noun* **1** a member of the Iroquois people formerly of the region east of Oneida Lake **2** the Iroquois language of the Oneida **3** a city in central New York

on·er·ous (on′ər əs, ō′ nər–) *adjective* **1** burdensome or troublesome; causing hardship **2** having or involving responsibilities that outweigh the advantages

Definition ——

EXPLAIN THE PRONUNCIATION KEY

Go over the pronunciation key with students. Point out the pronunciation symbols and the example words that go with them.

PRESENT BACKMATTER

Explain that in the back of many dictionaries students will find additional information, such as biographical entries, geographical entries, and maps. Point out this section and discuss with students how they might make use of the information it contains.

> **What information can you find about Argentina?**

Ⓑ PRACTICE/APPLY

Ask students to use a dictionary to answer these questions:

> **What guide words are on the same page as the word *gaucho*?**

> **What word in the pronunciation key has the same vowel sound as the first syllable in *across*?**

> **Look up the word *lasso*. How many definitions are given for the word? What parts of speech can *lasso* be used as?**

✔ INFORMAL ASSESSMENT: PERFORMANCE-BASED

Did students:

✔ understand how to use the guide words to locate an entry word?

✔ use the pronunciation key to determine how to pronounce a word?

✔ understand the information presented in each part of an entry?

TECHNOLOGY

Study Skills Have students use a CD-ROM dictionary such as **Usborne's Animated First Thousand Words** to define vocabulary and other story words. If using Usborne's, have them look up the Spanish terms also.

Name _____

STUDY SKILLS: DICTIONARY

LOOK IT UP

Read the dictionary entries below. Then use the dictionary skills you have learned to answer each question.

raft (raft, räft) *noun* a floating platform made of wood, air-filled rubber, or other material

rain·y (rā'nē) *adjective* having much rain; *April is a rainy month.*

ram (ram) *noun* 1 a male sheep 2 something that strikes heavy blows *verb* butt against; strike head on

rang·er (rān'jar) *noun* a person employed to guard a forest

rap·id (rap'id) *adjective* very quick; swift

rasp·ber·ry (raz'ber·ē) *noun* a small red or black fruit that grows on bushes

1. Circle the guide words for this page.
   railroad/rainy   (raft/raspberry)   rabbit/radio
2. Write the entry words that have one syllable.
   raft, ram
3. Write the entry words in which the first syllable is stressed, or accented.
   rainy, ranger, rapid, raspberry
4. What two parts of speech can the word *ram* be used as?
   noun, verb
5. Write the entry word that has three syllables.
   raspberry
6. Write the entry words that are adjectives.
   rainy, rapid

Write a secret message. Then rewrite it using dictionary respellings. Exchange secret messages with a friend. Use the pronunciation key to decode each other's message.

54   Unit 1 - What's New? • *On the Pampas*

PRACTICE BOOK 1, p. 54

IF students need more support using a dictionary,

THEN see the review lesson on page R49.

DAY **4** WRAP-UP

READ ALOUD *Spend five or ten minutes reading from a selection of your choice.*

GUIDED READING *Meet with the **red** and **blue** reading groups and assign Independent Center activities.* **See pages R26–R27.**

DAY 5 OBJECTIVES

STUDENTS WILL:

READ 30 MINUTES

- **Reading Assessment**
- **Daily Phonics: One-, Two-, Three-Syllable Words**

WRITE 30 MINUTES

- **Writing Assessment**
- **Spelling: Words With *ng* and *nk***
- **Grammar, Usage, Mechanics: Singular and Plural Nouns**
- **Oral Language**

EXTEND SKILLS 30 MINUTES

- **Integrated Language Arts**
- **Read Aloud**
- **Guided Reading**

RESOURCES

- **Selection Test**
- **Spelling Resource Book, p. 202.**

Reading Assessment

Formal Assessment

Use the Selection Test to measure students' mastery of the week's reading skills. See the suggestions for Intervention and Modifying Assessment.

Available In ★**READING COUNTS!**★

✓ SELECTION TEST		
SKILL	**TEST QUESTIONS**	◎ **IF** students need more support **THEN...**
LITERARY ELEMENT **Setting**	1–3	Use the Reteach lesson on p. R55.
COMPREHENSION **Paraphrase**	4–6	Review the skills lesson on p. T177.
DAILY PHONICS **1-, 2-, 3- Syllable Words**	7–9	Use the Reteach lesson on p. R54.
Vocabulary	10–12	Use the Review Vocabulary on p. T186.

Modifying Assessment

SELECTION TEST

ESL/ELD
Vocabulary

▲ Help students show understanding by breaking the long story into three parts: Arriving at the Ranch/During the Summer/End of Summer. Each student should be able to tell at least one story event for each part. Ask students to use key vocabulary words and sequence words. **(STEP-BY-STEP)**

 IF students need more support with vocabulary,

THEN review the vocabulary in the Take-Home Practice Readers.

EXTRA HELP
Literary Element

■ Ask students to describe the setting of *On the Pampas*, telling both when and where the story takes place. **(GUIDED QUESTIONS)**

> **What time of year is it?**

> **Where is the ranch?**

> **What work is done there?**

> **What kinds of animals are in the story?**

◎ **IF** students need more support with setting,

THEN review the skill in the Take-Home Practice Readers.

Performance-Based Assessment

Use the assessment activities below to provide performance-based measures of students' proficiency in phonics and reading fluency. See the Conference to assess each student's progress.

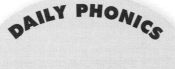

DAILY PHONICS

Dictation

ONE-, TWO-, THREE-SYLLABLE WORDS Direct students to divide a sheet of paper into three columns labeled 1, 2, and 3. Dictate the words on the chalkboard. Ask students to write each word in the correct column, depending on its number of syllables.

coconuts	gaucho	pampas
drink	horses	manes
younger	everything	belt
cattle	morning	together

✔ **Did students identify the correct number of syllables?**

IF students need more support with syllabication,

THEN practice reading words one syllable at a time and have students identify the number of vowel sounds.

ONE-MINUTE FLUENCY

Ask students to sit in pairs and read aloud to each other. Circulate and listen to individuals to assess their reading fluency.

Students can read the text on **Practice Book 1, page 51** or the text from the Take-Home Practice Readers.

✔ *Does the student vary tone and pitch and emphasize important words?*

IF students need more support with fluency,

THEN have them read a passage with a partner, alternating reading and listening.

✔ CONFERENCE

Set aside time to meet with several students individually to discuss their story comprehension and to listen to them read from the story. You may wish to tape-record students as they read the section aloud.

ASSESS LITERARY ELEMENT
✔ **How would this story have been different if it were set at another time of year, such as winter? (Setting)**

ASSESS STORY COMPREHENSION
✔ **How would you describe in your own words what happened when the author found a ñandú egg? (Paraphrase)**

ASSESS FLUENCY
✔ **Does the student read in clauses and sentences with proper expression?**

✔ **Does the student read at a natural and consistent pace?**

Writing Assessment

DAILY LANGUAGE PRACTICE

SPELLING

DAY 5:
Administer the Posttest for Words With *ng* and *nk*. **See page R29.**

GRAMMAR, USAGE, MECHANICS

DAY 5:
Assess Singular and Plural Nouns. **See page R31.**

ORAL LANGUAGE

the girl thankd the gauchoses.
(*The* girl *thanked* the *gauchos*.)

PORTFOLIO

Suggest that students add their drafts and revisions to their Literacy Portfolios.

This nicely follows the form of a brochure. I like the way you call out the points you want to make.

You state several opinions about camping, but you don't support your opinions.

Look again at this paragraph. You spelled *Yellowstone* as two words. It should be one word.

There's a lot of repetition. Instead of repeating words, try using different words.

Camping

Go camping and experience new adventures and challenges to learn self-confidence

I've been camping in a lot of places including Maine, Arizona, and Yellow Stone National Park. So take my advice when you read this brochure.

Camping can be a lot of fun if you put your heart into it. You have to have confidence in yourself, and you have to say you will have fun. To camp you should feel like you really want to do it, and you won't get scared. If you want to camp you should think positively. Camping can be a lot of fun only if you put your heart in to it. GO CAMPING AND HAVE A LOT OF FUN!!!

Apprentice

Use the rubric below to assess students' writing.

✓ STUDENTS' WRITING RUBRIC

Proficient	• The writing follows the form of a brochure. • The brochure is persuasive. Opinions are supported by facts.	• Student uses singular and plural nouns correctly. • The brochure has been proofread and corrected for grammar, usage, and mechanics.
Apprentice	• The writing follows the form of a brochure. • The brochure does not make a clear distinction between opinion and fact.	• Student sometimes misses singular and plural nouns. • The brochure has been proofread but not completely corrected for errors.
Novice	• The form is not a brochure. • It is not persuasive, and no clear distinction is made between opinion and fact.	• The student misses singular and plural nouns. • The brochure has not been corrected for errors.

Integrated Language Arts

Personal Narrative

MATERIALS:
Pencils
Paper

SUGGESTED GROUPING:
Individuals

INTRODUCE the activity by reminding students that *On the Pampas* was a personal narrative in which the author wrote about things that happened to her one summer when she was a young girl.

INFORM students that they will be writing their own personal narratives about a memorable experience they had in another place.

Expressive Writing

TEACH/MODEL Explain that in expressive writing, an author is free to express his or her feelings, thoughts, or personal responses to experiences. When students write expressively, they respond in a personal way to the world around them. Expressive writing takes various forms, such as poems, journal entries, and personal narratives.

PRACTICE/APPLY Encourage students to decide on a special experience they might have had while visiting a friend or relative in another place or while on vacation. As they prepare to write their personal narratives, they might ask themselves what happened, how they acted, and what they felt. A personal narrative uses the first-person pronouns *I, me, my,* and *mine* when referring to the author.

Create an Adventure Story

MATERIALS:
Pencils
Paper

SUGGESTED GROUPING:
Individuals

Good For Grading

STUDENTS will write their own short adventure stories, set on the pampas.

RETURN to page 76 of *On the Pampas,* where the gauchos sip *mate* and tell stories around the fire. Discuss how this passage contributes to the scary feelings the narrator experienced. How can something that is frightening also be fun? Encourage students to write an adventure that has a strong mood, like that of the passage mentioned. Suggest that they use Spanish terms from the selection when possible.

GATHER groups of five or six into "campfire" circles. Give each student time to tell his or her story to the others. A volunteer from each group can then read or retell one of the stories to the entire class.

GRADE students on their ability to create a mood of adventure and a feasible story line.

· · · · · · · (**TECHNOLOGY**) · · · · · · · ·

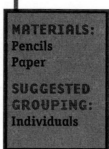

Presentation Tools Have students use a word processor to type their adventure stories. Ask them to use an art program such as **Smart Place** PlaceMaker to create the cover page. Or, they might find photos in a CD-ROM or online encyclopedia to use on the cover.

Integrated Language Arts

LISTENING/SPEAKING

Give a Persuasive Talk

MATERIALS:
Pencils
Paper

SUGGESTED GROUPING:
Whole class

HAVE students make a speech to convince their principal to allow them to go on a class trip.

REVIEW with students some of the challenges faced by the narrator in *On the Pampas*, and by the children in the mentor profile of Keith Jardine. What uncertainties or fears did they have? How did they conquer them? Ask students to jot down some of the challenges faced, as well as some of the factors that helped the children in both cases put aside their fears and go on the trip or do something new.

IMAGINE with the class that they've been invited to a local nature preserve, but they must convince their principal that the trip is a good idea. What benefits of the trip could they state? What might they learn? How might they assure the principal that the trip will be safe?

STUDENTS can take turns role-playing student and principal in front of the class. Allow time for feedback from other students.

DAY 5 WRAP-UP

READ ALOUD *Spend five to ten minutes reading from a selection of your choice.*

GUIDED READING *Meet with the **blue** and **green** reading groups and assign Independent Center activities.* **See pages R26–R27.**

VIEWING

Map Story Locales

MATERIALS:
Drawing paper
Pencils
Crayons

SUGGESTED GROUPING:
Whole class
Individuals

DISCUSS maps with students. When is a map more descriptive than words? Point out the map at the back of *On the Pampas,* and locate Argentina, Buenos Aires, and the pampas.

LIST on the chalkboard places mentioned in *On the Pampas:* the creek, the eucalyptus grove, the general store, and so on. Emphasize that the story tells *what* the places are but not *where* they are. Ask students to imagine where these spots are in relation to one another.

ENCOURAGE students to create maps of La Carlota. Display the completed maps and discuss similarities and differences among them.

Maps

TEACH/MODEL Explain that maps are drawings that show where places or landmarks are located. Most maps include a title, a key to the symbols used, a scale to show distance, and a compass rose to show direction. Display a map and discuss its features with students.

PRACTICE/APPLY As students develop their maps of La Carlota, encourage them to choose symbols and to incorporate map features that help viewers to visualize the place.

How to Write a Friendly Letter

WHY DO THIS WORKSHOP?

Many of us, not just students, might ask, "Why write a friendly letter?" In an age of immediacy, when telephones and electronic messaging predominate, who needs pen and paper? The key term may be "friendly." A letter may travel a few miles or many before it reaches the hand of another friend. There is a personal, and even tactile, satisfaction to finding, holding, and reading a letter addressed just to you. And, of course, if you want to get such a letter, you have to write one.

Unlike telephone messages, letters can be saved and referred to later. Letters written over many years may record a person's life, a family's history, or the progress of a friendship. This Workshop gives students a chance to share their achievements with someone who welcomes the communication. It also prepares them for the upcoming Project, in which they'll write a personal anecdote.

WORKSHOP OBJECTIVES

STUDENTS WILL:
- Make a record of their personal achievements
- Use the record as the basis of a friendly letter

MATERIALS
- Paper and pencil
- Textbooks
- Envelope addresses (optional)
- Pen (optional)
- Envelope (optional)
- First-class stamp (optional)

WORKSHOP

Note Achievements

Ask students if they've ever received a letter. What did the letter tell you about? How was reading a letter or having it read to you different from talking to someone over the phone? You could also ask any of the following questions:

> **What does Hal tell Jim about summer camp?**

> **What has Hal learned to do?**

> **What are the parts of the letter?**

TECHNOLOGY

Communicating Through E-mail Encourage students to use e-mail to send their letters. You might want to go to the Teacher Center at **www.scholasticnetwork.com** and use the bulletin boards to find another classroom interested in e-mail exchange.

WORKSHOP 2

How to Write a Friendly Letter

People like to keep in touch with friends and relatives who live far away. One way to do this is by writing a friendly letter.

What is a friendly letter? A friendly letter is a message written to someone you know and like. In it, you can describe events in your life.

The greeting names the person you are writing to.

The closing signals the letter's e...

88

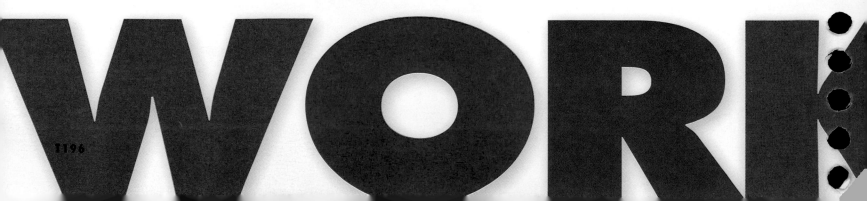

PERSONAL VOICE

CAMP SUNRISE
Dubois, WY 82000
July 20

Dear Jim,
How's your summer going? Mine's great so far. Camp is cool. There's a lake for swimming and other stuff, lots of hiking trails, and most of my friends are here from last year. I went canoeing yesterday for the first time. I worked the back paddle, the one that changes directions, so I'm the boat-master. We've got to find a lake when I get back home. I have to end this letter because we're going hiking. I'm going to the top this time! See you in a month.

Your buddy,
Hal

P.S. Write me back. I don't get much mail, except from my parents.

● The heading includes your address and the date.

● The body of the letter tells your news.

● The signature is your name, printed or written in cursive.

89

Home Involvement

Students may enjoy becoming pen pals with residents at a Senior Citizen Center in your community. Contact a local center and find out the names of people who would like to receive such letters. Students could write about what they're studying in class, field trips they go on, or their own interests. They could also ask the center's members about their own lives and interests.

Troubleshooting

Depending on how you decide to send students' letters, you may need to have envelopes and stamps available for students. You may also want to inform parents about the Workshop so that they can provide the addresses of the persons students write to.

MODIFY Instruction

ESL/ELD

▲ Reinforce the organization of a friendly letter. Write sample parts of a friendly letter on individual index cards. (Sample heading, body, greeting, closing and signature) Have students paste the cards on a sheet of paper in the places they belong to create a friendly letter. **(MULTISENSORY TECHNIQUES)**

1 WHAT TO WRITE ABOUT

Students might also consider activities that they've done as part of a group, including team sports achievements, school projects, and presentations.

2 MAKE A ROUGH DRAFT

Remind students to think of their audience when they write friendly letters. What would the person reading your letter want to know about you? What details about your achievement should you include? Also point out to students that it's customary in friendly letters to ask about the other person. What has he or she been doing? What interesting things has the person done or learned?

---

1 What to Write About

Think of some things you have learned to do recently, or a job you have finished or done well. Maybe you learned to use a computer, or built a birdhouse, or wrote a funny poem. List some of your achievements. Choose one achievement to write about in a friendly letter.

TOOLS

• pencil and paper

• envelope

90

2 Make a Rough Draft

Decide who will receive your letter. Will it be a best friend who moved away? a classmate at school? a favorite relative? Then, make a rough draft of what you want to say and include the following:

• Describe your achievement. Was it hard to learn? How long did it take you to do?

• Tell why it is important to you.

Now go back and reread what you have written. Are your thoughts clear? Is there anything else you want to say? Make your corrections.

 Remember, a rough draft doesn't have to be perfect. You can go back and make changes after you have finished it.

WORK

PERSONAL VOICE

3 Write the Letter

Now write the final version of your letter. Use your best handwriting. You want your friend or relative to be able to read it. Remember, this is a letter to someone you know well. Make it warm and friendly.

Does your letter have:

- the date and your address?
- a greeting?
- a closing?
- your signature?

4 Send Your Letter

If you wish, you can show your letter to your teacher and classmates. Share your achievement with them, too. Then, address an envelope for the letter and put a stamp on it. Mail your letter to your friend or relative. If you're lucky, you'll receive a reply.

If You Are Using a Computer ...

As you revise your letter, use the electronic thesaurus to help you find just the right words. Choose a letterhead you like to create your own personal stationery. Then, use E-mail to send your letter on-line.

w to get
o t terfall

Hal Wong

CAMP SUNRISE
Dubois, WY 82000

Jim Smith
1 Main Street
Anytow

THINK

Most days are filled with achievements, big or small. What is one thing you have done well today?

Keith Jardine
Wilderness Guide ▶

3 WRITE THE LETTER

Remind students that they can refer to the example of the letter on Anthology pages 88–89 as they are writing their own letters.

4 SEND YOUR LETTER

As students share and read each other's letters, ask them if they found out all they wanted to know about the topic. Could the writer have included more details in the description of the achievement? Was the writer clear about how the achievement made him or her feel? If students get replies to their letters at a later date, they may enjoy sharing them with their classmates.

SHOP

SELF-SELECTION

Students may want to keep copies of their letters in their Literacy Portfolios as examples of work done well.

PRACTICE BOOK 1, p. 55

Name   WORKSHOP 2

WHAT IS A FRIENDLY LETTER?
A friendly letter is the kind you write to someone you know well.
A formal letter is the kind you write to someone you don't know very well.

Study the examples below. Then answer the questions that follow the two letters.

January 12

Dear Crispin,
I just wanted to let you know that I got the sweater you and your parents sent me. Thanks! I love it! You remembered that I like big sweaters with buttons. And you picked colors I just love. Thank you, thank you, thank you.

Love you!
Ilana

6074 West Pine
North Snowdrift, VT 05111-1279
February 12

Martin Heep, Mayor
Town Hall
North Snowdrift, VT 05111

Dear Mayor Heep:
When you ran for office last year, you told me that West Pine would be one of the first roads you would have paved. You lived up to your promise, and I wish to thank you. Driving has been so much easier since the road was paved.
Sincerely,
Seth Garner

1. Which is the friendly letter? How can you tell?
    The first one—it's a personal message to someone the writer knows.

2. The formal letter has three things that the friendly letter doesn't. What are they?
    return address, recipient's address, first and last names

3. Two things are the same in both letters. What are they?
    dates, salutations

Unit 1 • What's New? • Workshop 2 **55**

PRACTICE BOOK 1, p. 56

Name   WORKSHOP 2

WRITE A FRIENDLY LETTER
Write a letter to a friend or relative. Tell what you've been doing recently. Mention any accomplishments that you're proud of, or something you've enjoyed doing lately.

Answer will vary.

56 Unit 1 • What's New? • Workshop 2

Use **Practice Book pages 55** and **56** as practice for the Workshop or as a separate activity to strengthen your students' skills.

✓ ASSESSMENT

INFORMAL ASSESSMENT
OBSERVATION
Review students' work. Ask yourself:

✓ Did students express themselves clearly as they described their achievements?

✓ Did students include all the parts of a friendly letter?

✓ What other information did students include in their letters?

STUDENT SELF-ASSESSMENT

✓ **Did I say all I wanted to say about my achievement?**

✓ **What other details could I add to improve my letter?**

Use the rubric below to assess students' Workshop performance.

✓ STUDENTS' WORKSHOP RUBRIC

Proficient	Students clearly describe a personal achievement and its relevance to them. They make revisions to improve the final letter and follow the correct format.
Apprentice	Students include details in their letters, but may not be able to explain the relevance of their personal achievements. Students need only a minor amount of guidance in formatting the letter.
Novice	Students are not able to describe personal achievements clearly. They may not understand the purpose of a friendly letter, and their letters may be missing important events.

WORKSHOP

How the World Got Wisdom

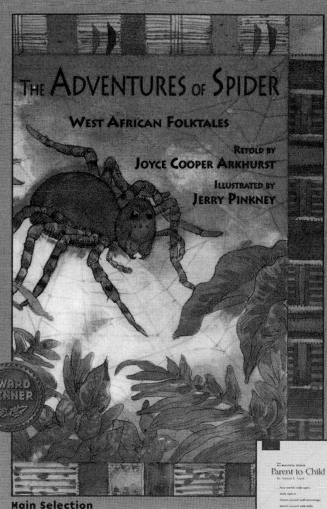

Main Selection
Genre: Folk Tale
Award: Two-time Caldecott Honor
Award-winning illustrator

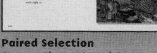

Paired Selection
Genre: Fine Art and Poem

Selection Summary

Nyame the Sky God gives all the wisdom in the world to Spider who puts it in a pot. He tries to hide the pot in a tall tree. When Spider's son offers advice, Spider realizes that the pot doesn't contain all the wisdom of the world. He angrily breaks the pot. People rush to collect the wisdom.

PAIRED SELECTION In the poem, a parent encourages a child to take advantage of all the wisdom the world has to offer.

Illustrator

JERRY PINKNEY'S first experience with art came as a young boy, when he began copying drawings from comic books and photo magazines. Today he is an accomplished artist and teaches art at numerous universities. One of the many award-winning books he has illustrated is *The Tales of Uncle Remus*.

Weekly Organizer

Visit Our WebSite
www.scholastic.com

How the World Got Wisdom

	DAY 1	**DAY 2**
READ and Introduce Skills • PHONICS • VOCABULARY • COMPREHENSION • LITERARY ELEMENT	**BUILD BACKGROUND,** ▲ p. T207 ☑ **VOCABULARY,** ▲ ✹ p. T208 Transparency 14, p. T209 Practice Book 1, p. 57 ☑ **DAILY PHONICS:** ▲ ■ Vowel /ô/a, au, aw, p. T210 Practice Book 1, p. 58 **PREVIEW AND PREDICT,** p. T212 **READ:** ▲ ✹ ■ How the World Got Wisdom, pp. T212–T217 ☑ **COMPREHENSION SKILL:** Cause/Effect, p. T215	**READ:** ▲ ✹ ■ How the World Got Wisdom, pp. T218–T221 "Parent to Child," pp. T222–T223 ☑ **DAILY PHONICS:** Vowel /ô/a, au, aw, p. T221 **LITERARY ELEMENT** Setting, p. T219
WRITE and Respond • GRAMMAR • USAGE • MECHANICS • SPELLING • WRITING	**WRITING WORKSHOP,** p. T207 **JOURNAL:** Make Predictions, p. T212 **QUICKWRITE:** Predict, p. T217 ☑ **SPELLING:** Pretest: Words With the Vowel Sound in saw, p. R36 Spelling Resource Book, p. 29 ☑ **GRAMMAR, USAGE, MECHANICS:** Teach/Model: Singular and Plural Pronouns, p. R38 **ORAL LANGUAGE,** p. T217	**WRITING WORKSHOP,** p. T223 ☑ **SPELLING:** Practice, p. R36 Spelling Resource Book, pp. 30–32 ☑ **GRAMMAR, USAGE, MECHANICS:** Practice, p. R38 **ORAL LANGUAGE,** p. T223
EXTEND SKILLS and Apply to Literature • INTEGRATED LANGUAGE ARTS • LISTENING/SPEAKING/VIEWING • INTEGRATED CURRICULUM • GUIDED READING • INDEPENDENT READING	**READ ALOUD,** p. T217 **GUIDED READING,** pp. R34–R35 **INTEGRATED CURRICULUM:** Science, p. R40 The Arts, p. R41 **TRADE BOOKS** • Hannah • The Chalk Box Kid	**READ ALOUD,** p. T223 **GUIDED READING,** pp. R34–R35 **INTEGRATED CURRICULUM:** Social Studies, p. R41 Math, p. R40 **TRADE BOOKS** • Uncle Jed's Barbershop • Muggie Maggie
TECHNOLOGY and **REAL-WORLD SKILLS**	**SMART PLACE CD-ROM** Presentation Tools, p. T215	**SCHOLASTIC NETWORK** Matching Technology to Task, p. T219 **PROJECT,** pp. T248–T255

DAY 3

✓ **COMPREHENSION:** ▲ ■
Cause/Effect, p. T226
Transparency 15
Practice Book 1, pp. 63–65

✓ **DAILY PHONICS:**
Vowel /ô/a, au, aw, p. T228

INTERVENTION, ● p. T228
Daily Phonics: Vowel /ô/ a, au, aw
Comprehension: Cause/Effect
Fluency: Reading Aloud

RESPOND: ✳
Think About Reading, p. T224
Write a Folk Tale Review, p. T225
Practice Book 1, p. 61

✓ **SPELLING:**
Write/Proofread, p. R37
Spelling Resource Book, p. 33

✓ **GRAMMAR, USAGE, MECHANICS:**
Practice, p. R39
Practice Book 1, p. 62

ORAL LANGUAGE, p. T225

RESPOND: Literature Circle, p. T225

READ ALOUD, p. T229

GUIDED READING, pp. R34–R35

OPTIONAL MATERIALS, ● p. T229
Phonics Chapter Book #16:
The Great Time Travel Ride
How the World Got Wisdom
audiocassette

🖳 **VIDEO**
Viewing Skills, p. T225

PROJECT, pp. T248–T255

DAY 4

LITERATURE CONNECTION:
How the World Got Wisdom, p. 230

VOCABULARY REVIEW, p. T232

✓ **DAILY PHONICS:**
Vowel /ô/a, au, aw, p. T233

WRITING WORKSHOP:
Character Sketch for a Folk Tale, p. T230

WRITER'S CRAFT:
Precise Adjectives, p. T231
Transparency 16
Practice Book 1, p. 60

✓ **SPELLING:** Review, p. R37
Spelling Resource Book, p. 200

✓ **GRAMMAR, USAGE, MECHANICS:**
Apply, p. R39

ORAL LANGUAGE, p. T231

READ ALOUD, p. T235

GUIDED READING, pp. R34–R35

EXPAND VOCABULARY:
Homophones, p. T232

ORAL LANGUAGE:
Tell a Story to Entertain,
pp. T234–T235
Practice Book 1, p. 67

📖 **SMART PLACE CD-ROM**
Speaking Skills, p. T235

PROJECT, pp. T248–T255

DAY 5

READING ASSESSMENT: Selection Test,
p. T236

MODIFYING ASSESSMENT, p. T236
ESL/ELD: Vocabulary
Extra Help: Comprehension

PERFORMANCE-BASED ASSESSMENT:
One-Minute Fluency, p. T237
Conference, p. T237

✓ **DAILY PHONICS:** Dictation, p. T237

WRITING ASSESSMENT, p. T238
Student Model
Students' Writing Rubric

✓ **SPELLING:**
Posttest, p. R37
Spelling Resource Book, p. 202

✓ **GRAMMAR, USAGE, MECHANICS:**
Assess, p. R39

ORAL LANGUAGE, p. T238

READ ALOUD, p. T240

GUIDED READING, pp. R34–R35

INTEGRATED LANGUAGE ARTS:
Interview Spider and Kuma, p. T239
Write: Persuasive Letter, p. T239
Writing Slogans, p. T240
Compare Folk Tales, p. T240

🖳 **WORD PROCESSING**
Communicating Through Letters,
p. T239

PROJECT, pp. T248–T255

ASSESSMENT PLANNING

USE THIS CHART TO PLAN YOUR ASSESSMENT OF THE WEEKLY READING OBJECTIVES.

- Informal Assessment is ongoing and should be used before, during, and after reading.

- Formal assessment occurs at the end of the week on the selection test.

- Note that intervention activities occur throughout the lesson to support students who need extra help with skills.

YOU MAY CHOOSE AMONG THE FOLLOWING PAGES IN THE ASSESSMENT HANDBOOK.

- Informal Assessment
- Anecdotal Record
- Portfolio Checklist and Evaluation Forms
- Self-Assessment
- English Language Learners
- Using Technology to Assess
- Test Preparation

SKILLS AND STRATEGIES	Informal Assessment
COMPREHENSION Cause/Effect	**OBSERVATION p. T215** • Did students identify events and why they happened? **QUICKCHECK p. T226** • Can students identify a cause as why something happens and an effect as what happens? **CHECK PRACTICE BOOK 1 p. 63** **CONFERENCE p. T237**
GENRE Folk Tale	**PERFORMANCE p. T237** • How did you know this was a folk tale? **CONFERENCE p. T237**
DAILY PHONICS Vowel /ô/a, au, aw	**OBSERVATION p. T221** • Did students identify words with /ô/? **CHECK PRACTICE BOOK 1 p. 58** **DICTATION p. T237**
VOCABULARY Selection Words ✓ idea ✓ knowledge ✓ wise thought wisdom skills sense	**OBSERVATION p. T220** • Did students recognize context clues that came after the word? **CHECK PRACTICE BOOK 1 p. 57**

Formal Assessment	INTERVENTION and Instructional Alternatives	Planning Notes
SELECTION TEST • Questions 1–3 check students' mastery of the key strategy, cause/effect. **UNIT TEST**	**If students need help with cause/effect, then go to:** • Instructional Alternatives, p. T227 • Intervention, pp. T228, T229	
SELECTION TEST • Questions 4–6 check students' understanding of the genre folk tale.	**If students need help with genre folk tale, then:** • Review the Skills and Strategies lesson on p. T213	
SELECTION TEST • Questions 4–6 check students' ability to identify and blend words with vowel /ô/. **UNIT TEST**	**If students need help identifying words with vowel /ô/, then go to:** • Intervention, p. T228 • Review, p. R51 • Reteach, p. R56	
SELECTION TEST • Questions 7–9 check students' understanding of the selection vocabulary. **UNIT TEST**	**If students need additional practice with the vocabulary words, then go to:** • Vocabulary Review, p. T232 • Integrated Language Arts, p. T239	

Technology

The technology in this lesson helps teachers and students develop the skills they need for the 21st century. Look for integrated technology activities on every day of instruction.

DAY 1
Presentation Tools

- Students use **Smart Place** PlaceMaker to design a new pot for Spider.

Sunny days make the trees green and beautiful.

Smart Place CD-ROM

DAY 2
Matching Technology to Task

- Students visit the Internet site **www.scholasticnetwork.com** to find folk tales from settings around the world.

www.scholasticnetwork.com

DAY 3
Viewing Skills

- Students produce a video version of a folk tale review. Will the story get "thumbs up," or "thumbs down"?

DAY 4
Speaking Skills

- Students use **Smart Place** PlaceMaker to write and illustrate personal anecdote. They then record it using drama and creativity.

It was a wonderful day of bird watching. We walked through the fields in the morning and in the afternoon we sat at the bottom of the mountains right near a stream. Then we heard the most beautiful bird song ever. We looked up into a nearby tree and

Smart Place CD-ROM

DAY 5
Communicating Through Letters

- Students use word processing tools to format important text in a persuasive letter.

Build Background

Imagine you are sitting around a campfire in West Africa listening to folk tales. At least one of them is bound to be about Spider, the clever trickster. As clever as Spider is, he often ends up in trouble! In this selection, Spider finds that wisdom isn't something he can keep to himself.

Activate Prior Knowledge

DISCUSS POURQUOI TALES
Briefly discuss folk tales. One special type of folk tale—called a *pourquoi* tale—explains how things came to be. Give examples, such as how the elephant got its trunk. Encourage volunteers to tell about similar stories they know.

DISCUSS SPIDER TALES
Let volunteers tell what they know about Spider or Anansi. If necessary, explain that Spider is a character in folk tales from West Africa.

 WRITING WORKSHOP *Character Sketch for a Folk Tale*

INTRODUCE Ask students to think about an animal—how it acts, what it looks like, and what it likes to do. Then have them develop their ideas to write a description of that animal.

MODIFY Instruction

ESL/ELD

▲ Tell students that Anansi tales come from West Africa. Explain that Anansi is always playing tricks and getting in trouble. Ask if they know other folktale characters like this. (Students may know the famous Br'er Rabbit tales that also come from Africa.) **(MAKE CONNECTIONS)**

Vocabulary

PHONICS AND SPELLING LINKS

Phonics See selection words with /ô/ on page T210.

Spelling See selection words with the vowel sound in *saw* on page R36.

Ⓐ TEACH WORD MEANINGS

INTRODUCE CONCEPT
Tell students that *How the World Got Wisdom* has many words that are about learning.

PRESENT VOCABULARY
Encourage students to discuss what each word means. Then write the word and its definition on the chalkboard.

✔ = Tested	VOCABULARY WORDS
wisdom	knowledge, experience, and good judgment (p. 92)
sense	good judgment (p. 92)
thought	used your mind to create ideas or make decisions (p. 92)
✔ **idea**	a thought or plan you form in your mind (p. 99)
✔ **wise**	having intelligence or good judgment (p. 101)
✔ **knowledge**	the things a person knows (p. 102)
skills	abilities to do things (p. 102)

Ⓑ BUILD ON PRIOR KNOWLEDGE

GENERATE WORDS
Discuss things students need in order to learn in school. Have students complete the web below.

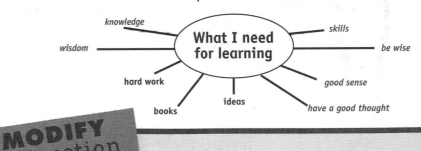

knowledge · skills · wisdom · be wise · hard work · good sense · books · ideas · have a good thought

What I need for learning

MODIFY Instruction

ESL/ELD

▲ Point out the spelling and pronunciation change from *wise* to *wisdom*. Ask students to name wise people they know, and tell why they think they are wise. Brainstorm words that have similar meanings (*smart; bright*) and words that mean the opposite (*foolish, silly*). **(KEY WORDS)**

GIFTED & TALENTED

✳ Suggest that students make a collage of magazine pictures around the theme *The Faces of Learning* and use the vocabulary words to write captions. Students should be prepared to explain the connection between the words and their visual interpretation. **(INNOVATE)**

Name _____ **VOCABULARY**

WISE THOUGHTS
Write the vocabulary word that completes each sentence.

wisdom sense thought idea
wise knowledge skills

A. s k i l l s   You need math ___ to add and subtract.
   1 2 3 4 5 6

B. w i s e   A ___ person has good judgment.
   1 2 3 4

C. i d e a   When you think, you might have an ___.
   1 2 3 4

D. k n o w l e d g e   A teacher has ___ of many subjects.
   1 2 3 4 5 6 7 8 9

E. w i s d o m   You can't put ___—knowledge and experience—in a pot.
   1 2 3 4 5 6

F. s e n s e   Spider didn't have good judgment, or ___.
   1 2 3 4 5

G. t h o u g h t   Kuma ___ and came up with an idea.
   1 2 3 4 5 6 7

What are these words about? To find out, write the letter to match each clue.
l e a r n i n g
A5 B4 C4 D2 E2 F3 G5

Write two questions you would like to ask a wise person.

Unit 1 • What's New? • *How the World Got Wisdom* ⑤⑦

PRACTICE BOOK 1, p.57

ⓒ APPLY THROUGH MEANINGFUL SENTENCES

MODEL MEANINGFUL SENTENCES

Write or say the following sentences. Ask volunteers to underline or name the context clues.

1. A person with **wisdom** has <u>knowledge</u> and <u>experience</u>.
2. Good **sense** <u>helps to tell us what to do</u>.
3. I <u>used my mind</u> and **thought** of a good plan.
4. My <u>thoughts and plans</u> were all part of my **idea** for a great science project.
5. My **wise** grandmother <u>knew exactly what to do</u>.
6. A <u>teacher</u> has **knowledge** about <u>many subjects</u>.
7. I <u>practiced</u> adding, and my **skills** in math improved.

Sentences on Vocabulary Transparency 5

WRITE MEANINGFUL SENTENCES

Suggest that students ask themselves these questions about the words to help them write meaningful sentences: *What is it? What would it mean to have this quality?*

USE TRANS-PARENCY 14

Have students use the definitions to discuss the words.

SUPPORT WORDS

> **gauze** a thin, loosely woven cloth (p. 95)
> **finger** one of the five parts at the end of the hand (p. 96)*
> **directions** the lines along which something moves (p. 99)
> **drench** to make completely wet (p. 102)*
>
> ✱ Vocabulary instruction is presented where words appear in the selection.

Strategy:Dictionary

Get Word Wise

▶**TEACH** Tell students: *When you come to a word you don't know and using word and context clues doesn't help you figure out its meaning, look the word up in the dictionary.* Write:

> *The branches were covered with soft silvery leaves and a fine <u>gauze</u> that looked like cotton.*

THINK ALOUD *I'm not sure what the word gauze means. The sentence tells me that gauze looks like cotton. Does this mean cotton fabric or cotton balls? To find out, I'll look it up in the dictionary. When I do, I see that gauze is a thin, loosely woven cloth.*

APPLY Write the following and ask students to follow the above procedure to find the meaning of the underlined word.

• *The good sense poured out in all <u>directions</u>.*

TRANSPARENCY 14 — WORDS OF WISDOM

Scholastic Literacy Place

WORDS OF WISDOM

1. A librarian has a great deal of <u>knowledge</u> about books.
2. If you are in need of advice, you can ask a <u>wise</u> person – someone who is intelligent and shows good judgment.
3. Having <u>wisdom</u>–knowledge, experience, and good judgment–can help you get ahead in life.
4. He couldn't come up with an <u>idea</u>, or plan formed in his mind, for writing a story.
5. If Spider had used <u>sense</u>, or good judgment, he wouldn't have tried to climb the smooth tree.
6. A storyteller needs good speaking <u>skills</u> to entertain people.
7. We <u>thought</u> about how to solve the problem. Then we used our ideas to come up with a plan.

What's New?–How the World Got Wisdom 14

PERSONAL WORD LIST

As they read, have students write down words they do not know. They can also write familiar words that are used in a new way or seem to have an unfamiliar meaning. Remind them to check the meaning of these words in a dictionary.

Strategies for Reading

HOW TO FIGURE OUT A NEW WORD

• Try to figure out the word from letter sounds.
• Look for word parts that you know.
• Try to use context clues and picture clues to figure out meaning.
▶ Look up the word in a dictionary or ask someone.

SELECTION WORDS
With /ô/

all

because

gauze

saw

SKILLS TRACE

VOWEL /ô/ a, au, aw

TESTED

Introduce ....pp. T210–T211
Practice .pp. T221, T228, T233, T237
Review ....p. R51
Reteach ....p. R56

DAILY PHONICS

Vowel /ô/ a, au, aw

Ⓐ PHONOLOGICAL AWARENESS

POEM Write the poem on the chalkboard and read it aloud. Stress words with /ô/, such as *saw* and *hawk*.

In August I saw a hawk
In a very tall tree.
I heard the hawk squawk.
Did the hawk see me?

- Isolate words with /ô/: *saw, hawk, tall, squawk.* Point out /ô/ in each word.

- Ask students to name other words that contain this vowel sound. Examples include: *salt, ball, because, yawn, paw.*

Ⓑ CONNECT SOUND-SPELLING

INTRODUCE VOWEL /ô/ *a, au, aw* Explain that the letters *a, au,* and *aw* can stand for /ô/ as in the words *tall, August,* and *saw.* Write *tall, August,* and *saw* on the chalkboard and underline the letters *a, au,* and *aw.*

THINK ALOUD *I can put the letters s, a, and w together to make the word* **saw.** *Let's say the sounds slowly as I move my finger under the letters. Listen to the sound that* **aw** *stands for in* **saw.** *The sound of* **aw** *is* /ô/.

- Ask students for words in which *a, au,* and *aw* stand for /ô/. When they give an example, write it on the chalkboard. If students have trouble thinking of words, have them name words that rhyme with *tall* and *saw.*

Common /ô/ Patterns		
a	au	aw
ball	August	draw
call	because	law
small	sauce	claw

MODIFY Instruction

ESL/ELD

▲ Help students with pronunciation by modeling how to drop your jaw as you say words like *thought, saw, salt, tall,* and *sauce.* Point out that the spellings are different, but the /ô/ sound is the same. Ask for more examples of words students may know. **(MODEL)**

EXTRA HELP

■ Have partners write words with /ô/ on index cards, writing the letters that stand for /ô/ in color. Students play Concentration, turning over two cards at a time, trying to match words with the same spelling for /ô/. **(HANDS-ON LEARNING)**

PHONICS MAINTENANCE Review the following sound-spellings; /ô/*a, au, aw; schwa /ə/; /ī/i, igh, y, i-e, ie.*

C PRACTICE/APPLY

READ WORDS To practice using the sound-spellings and review previous sound-spellings, list the following words and sentence on the chalkboard. Have students read each chorally. Model blending as needed.

faucet	because	saw	fallen
fault	draw	ball	August
alive	frighten	kind	America

The spider crawled up a tall tree.

DICTATION Dictate the following words for students to spell: *sauce, awful, call, around, bright.*

BUILD WORDS Distribute the following letter and word part cards, or have students use their own sets: *a, u, d, t, s, p, l, c, e, r, ight, ind, aw, all, en.* Allow students time to build as many words as possible using the letter cards. Students can write their words on a separate sheet of paper.

WORKING WITH WORD PARTS

Write each word on the chalkboard, syllable by syllable. Leave a space between syllables. Pause after each syllable for students to read it aloud. When they have finished reading each syllable, have them read the entire word aloud.

sum-mer	tight-ly	per-fect
some-times	ac-ci-dent	di-rec-tions
wis-dom	el-e-phant	an-i-mals

Repeat this procedure throughout the week using these and other syllables.

PRACTICE BOOK 1, p. 58

PROFESSIONAL DEVELOPMENT

JOHN SHEFELBINE

Phonics Maintenance: Purpose and Prodecures

In phonics maintenance, students review their phonics by chorally saying the sounds of the phonic spellings that have been taught. This is a critical daily activity which helps students not only learn but actually overlearn sound-spelling relationships. Write each spelling on a card, mix them, and have students say the sounds chorally. Avoid distorting sounds by adding an "uh" such as "suh" or "muh."

COMPREHENSION

▶ Preview and Predict

Tell students that *How the World Got Wisdom* is a folk tale from West Africa. Encourage them to preview the first four pages of the selection.

> **Who do you think the main character is?**

> **What do you think is in the pot in the illustration on page 93?**

Help students make predictions before they read by asking a question. Then have them read silently page 92.

> **What do you think Spider will do with wisdom?**

JOURNAL

Make Predictions

Ask students to write their predictions in their Journals. Encourage them to record things they discover about Spider's character as they read.

▶ Set a Purpose

Help students set their purpose for reading. They may want to discover why the story is titled *How the World Got Wisdom*.

FOLKTALE COLLECTION

FROM **THE ADVENTURES OF SPIDER WEST AFRICAN FOLKTALES**

HOW THE WORLD GOT WISDOM

RETOLD BY JOYCE COOPER ARKHURST
ILLUSTRATED BY JERRY PINKNEY

NOW, <u>WISDOM</u> is another word for good <u>sense</u>. Nowadays there is wisdom everywhere in the world, but there wouldn't be any at all if it hadn't been for Spider's accident. Would you like to hear a story about it?

When the world was very new, Nyame, the Sky God, gave all the wisdom in the world to Spider, and told him to do whatever he wished with it. Of course, Spider wanted to keep it all for himself, and so he put it in a huge clay pot and covered it up tightly.

"How lucky I am to have all this good sense," <u>thought</u> Spider. "One day I will become King, for I will be the only wise man in the world.

92

CLASSROOM Management

WHOLE CLASS

On-Level Guide students through the story by using the questions, think-alouds, and skills and strategies lessons. Encourage students to use the key strategy, cause/effect.

Below-Level Before students read the story by themselves, read it aloud to them. Encourage them to listen for details about Spider's character and why things happen in the story.

PARTNERS

Above-Level You might choose to have above-level students read the story with a partner while you do a guided reading of the story with the rest of the class. When everyone has finished, have these students rejoin the group to participate in the story discussion.

93
▼

93

Revisit the selection for skills instruction.

☑ Tested Skill

GENRE
Folk Tale T213

COMPREHENSION
☑ Cause/Effect 🔑 T215

LITERARY ELEMENT
☑ Setting T219

DAILY PHONICS
☑ Vowel /ô/ *a, au, aw* T221

GENRE
Folk Tale

TEACH/MODEL
Encourage students to tell what they know about folk tales. Be sure they mention the following key elements:

> **Folk tales are stories that have been handed down from one generation to the next by word of mouth.**

> **They often contain unusual characters, such as animals that speak.**

> **Many folk tales explain how something came to be.**

PRACTICE/APPLY
Encourage students to identify the elements of a folk tale in the part of the story they have previewed so far.

> **What clues about the characters tell you that this story is a folk tale?**

> **What event do you think the folk tale will explain?**

SMALL GROUP TO WHOLE CLASS

ESL/ELD Have students who need extra help or who are acquiring English listen to the story on the audiocassette prior to the whole class reading. This will help them to become familiar with the story sequence and vocabulary. Have students do the pre- and post-listening activities. **(AUDIO CLUES)**

COMPREHENSION

1 **CAUSE/EFFECT** 🔑
> **Why does Spider keep running when Tortoise and Hare talk to him?** *(He doesn't want to share wisdom with them.)*

2 **DISTINGUISH FANTASY/REALITY**
> **How do you know this story couldn't really have happened?** *(Possible answers: Spiders, tortoises, and hares don't talk. Wisdom isn't something that will fit in a pot.)*

SELF-MONITORING STRATEGY

Relate to Personal Experience

🗨 **THINK ALOUD** *As I read about Spider and how he wants to hide the pot of wisdom, I remember other characters I've read about in stories who didn't want to share. I think about how those characters felt, and this helps me understand how Spider feels about his pot of wisdom.*

> **How does Spider feel at the beginning of the story?**

> **How do you think he might change?**

✳

I must hide it carefully, where no one else can see it."

Spider ran through the forest as fast as his eight legs would carry him, looking for a place to hide his pot of wisdom.

"Where are you going?" asked the Tortoise.

"Where are you going?" asked the Hare. "And why are you in such a hurry?"

1 But Spider didn't answer. He just kept running, looking for a place to hide his wisdom before somebody saw it and took some of it away from him. **2**

"I know what I'll do," said Spider to himself.

94

MODIFY Instruction

ESL/ELD

▲ Help students with the Think Aloud activity. Say: *Let's think like the Spider. Spider does not like to share things. Do you like to share? Is sharing a good thing? Do you think Spider will have problems because he tries to keep the pot of wisdom for himself?* **(PREDICT)**

GIFTED & TALENTED

✳ Have students draw a picture of the tree as it is described in the story. Alternatively, have students write a description of a tree they see every day. Encourage them to use vivid words to help readers create a picture in their minds of the tree. **(INNOVATE)**

95

"I'll hide my wisdom in the top of the tallest tree in all the world."

At last he found just the tree. It was a great silk-cotton tree. At the bottom its roots came up above the ground and they were wide enough to hide an elephant. Its smooth trunk was wide enough for Spider's whole house. At the top the branches spread out like an umbrella, and they were covered with soft silvery leaves, and a fine gauze that looked like cotton. "It's the perfect hiding place," cried Spider. "No one will be able to climb it, because there are no branches near the ground."

SCIENCE

Have students complete the **Compare Characters' Characteristics** activity on **page R40**, in which they will compare the qualities of a tortoise, a hare, and a spider. Students will articulate differences among the three types of animal.

TECHNOLOGY

 Presentation Tools Look at the designs on Spider's pot and discuss their possible message about the place and people of Spider's time. Have students use **Smart Place** PlaceMaker to draw a new pot and let students explain their designs.

SKILLS AND STRATEGIES

COMPREHENSION
✓ Cause/Effect 🔑

TEACH/MODEL
Write this sentence on the chalkboard: *The tree fell over because the wind blew so hard.*

> **What happened? Why did it happen?**

- Elicit from students that the blowing wind caused the tree to fall over.

- Point out to students that they can ask themselves the two questions as they read to figure out what is happening and why it is happening.

- Point out that signal words, such as *because* and *so*, sometimes point to a cause/effect relationship.

PRACTICE/APPLY
Guide students to use what they have learned about cause/effect relationships to complete a chart as shown.

Why Did It Happen?	What Happened?
Spider wanted to keep all the wisdom.	*He put it in a clay pot.*
He was in a hurry to hide the wisdom.	Spider didn't talk to Tortoise and Hare.

✓ INFORMAL ASSESSMENT
OBSERVATION

Did students:

✔ identify events and why they happened?

✔ understand that one event caused another event to happen?

See pages T226–T227 for a full skills lesson on Cause/Effect.

COMPREHENSION

3 MAKE JUDGMENTS

> **How well does Spider prepare for his climb? Explain your answer.** *(Possible answer: He prepares very well; he ties the pot with a strong rope; he uses his middle legs to hold the pot and positions his front and back legs to climb.)*

4 CAUSE/EFFECT

> **Why does Spider fall from the tree?** *(The tree's trunk is smooth; the pot is large and heavy; Spider can use only four legs to climb.)*

INTERVENTION TIP

Decoding

Point out the word **finger** on page 96. Help students use syllabication to pronounce the word. Write the following on the chalkboard: **fing–ger**. Point out that the first syllable ends in **/ng/** and the second syllable begins with **/g/**. Have a volunteer say each syllable as you point to it. Then blend the syllables and say the whole word.

OPTION You may end the first day's reading here or have students continue reading the entire selection.

96

So Spider went back to the place where he had left the pot of wisdom, and carried it to the foot of the great tree. Now, the silk-cotton tree is very hard to climb, for its outside is as smooth as a finger. But Spider was sure *he* could climb it. For one thing he had more legs than almost anybody else. People have two and animals have four, but Spider had eight.

Spider tied the pot around his neck with a piece of strong rope, so that it hung right in front of him. Then he made ready to climb. He put his two top legs around the trunk of the tree as far as they would reach. He put the next two legs around the top of the pot, two more around the bottom of the pot, and the last two **3** under the pot. Spider pulled with his two top legs, and pushed with his two bottom legs, and held the pot with his four middle legs. My but the pot was heavy! After all it contained all the wisdom in the world. Little by little, he began to go upward. Spider was feeling very pleased, when suddenly he slipped. In fact, he fell all the way back to the ground. **4**

96

MODIFY Instruction

ESL/ELD

▲ As you read aloud, have students pretend to climb the tree like Anansi. Stop to ask questions and have students answer each time, so that they understand the cause and effect: *How do you feel now? Is the pot getting heavy? Is it slipping? Oh, no! Are you falling?* **(PANTOMIME)**

EXTRA HELP

■ When students finish reading the page, check their comprehension of the story so far. Ask what has just happened to Spider. Then ask *Why* questions: *Why did he slip? Why was he climbing the tree? Why did he want to hide the pot?* If necessary, suggest that they reread the text to find the answers. **(REVIEW)**

97

PREDICT

Encourage students to write down some of the things they have learned so far about Spider. They may also refine the predictions they made before reading and predict what will happen next.

DAILY LANGUAGE PRACTICE

SPELLING

DAY 1:
Administer the Pretest for Words With the Vowel Sound in *saw*. **See page R36.**

GRAMMAR, USAGE, MECHANICS

DAY 1:
Teach and Model Singular and Plural Pronouns. **See page R38.**

ORAL LANGUAGE

me like Spider becaws he is funny (*I like Spider* <u>because</u> *he is funny.*)

DAY 1 WRAP-UP

READ ALOUD *To develop students' oral vocabularies, spend five to ten minutes reading from a selection of your choice.*

GUIDED READING *Meet with the* **green** *and* **red** *reading groups and assign Independent Center activities.* **See pages R34–R35.**

MENTOR

Ask students to think about what advice mentor Keith Jardine might give Spider about meeting new challenges. Encourage students to role-play a meeting between Spider and Keith Jardine.

THE ARTS

Ask students to complete the **Make a Spider Design** activity on **page R41**, for which they will create a spider design that could go on a T-shirt. Students will demonstrate originality in their designs.

COMPREHENSION

DAY 2 OBJECTIVES

STUDENTS WILL:

READ 30 MINUTES

- *How the World Got Wisdom*, pp. 98-100
- "Spider Gets Around," p. 101
- "Parent to Child," pp. 102-103
- Literary Element: Setting
- Daily Phonics: Vowel /ô/ *a, au, aw*

WRITE 30 MINUTES

- Writing Workshop: Prewrite Character Sketch
- Spelling: Words With the Vowel Sound in *saw*
- Grammar, Usage, Mechanics: Singular and Plural Pronouns
- Oral Language

EXTEND SKILLS 30 MINUTES

- Integrated Curriculum
- Read Aloud
- Guided Reading

RESOURCES

- Practice Book 1, p. 59
- Spelling Resource Book, pp. 30–32

▶ **Reread**

You may wish to have students independently reread the first part of the story before beginning Day 2 reading.

5 SUMMARIZE

> **What has Spider done so far with the pot of wisdom?**

(Spider decides to hide it at the top of a tree but slips when he tries to carry it up the trunk.)

6 SETTING

> **How would the story have been different if it had occurred in a different place?**

(Possible answer: Spider would have found a different hiding place.)

---

5   **6**

"Dear me," thought Spider. "I have eight legs. Surely I can climb this tree."

So he started again. He hugged the tree as tightly as he could, and pushed and pulled with all his might. The pot was so heavy, and his two bottom legs just couldn't catch on under its weight. But this time, his luck was no better than before. He fell right back down to the ground. Spider was getting warm. And I'm afraid he was getting angry. He decided to try once again. So he pushed and pulled harder than ever. But the same thing happened. No sooner did he get off the ground than his middle leg slipped. Then his right upper leg slipped and his left top leg slipped and his right bottom leg slipped, and BOOM!

98

MODIFY Instruction

ESL/ELD

▲ Prompt students to summarize what has happened in the story so far. Go back over each page and ask: *What happened on this page?* Ask students to state one main idea and one detail each time. Then ask, *Did Anansi's son give him good advice?* **(SUMMARIZE)**

GIFTED & TALENTED

✳ The author says that Spider got warm and that he was getting angry. Have students make a list of phrases that mean "become angry." *(lose one's temper, get mad or sore, bristle, get one's dander up, flare up, see red)* Is there a phrase that combines "get warm" with anger? *(hot under the collar)* **(INNOVATE)**

99

Down came Spider, pot and wisdom and all right on the ground again.

Now all this time, Kuma, Spider's eldest son, had been watching. "Father," said Kuma, "I have an <u>idea</u>. Hang the pot behind you instead of in front of you. Then you will be able to climb the tree."

When Spider heard this, he knew that Kuma had some wisdom too, and that he did not have all the wisdom in the world to himself. This made him so angry that he threw the pot to the ground. It broke into many pieces and the good sense poured out in all directions.

99

LITERARY ELEMENT
Setting

TEACH/MODEL

Remind students that the setting is when and where a story takes place. Ask:

> **What clues show you that a story takes place in the country? In the city?**

Point out that information in a story and illustrations will help them figure out the setting.

PRACTICE/APPLY

Ask students questions to help them identify the story's setting. Have them complete a chart like the one below.

> **When does the story take place?**

> **From what part of the world does this story come?**

> **What does spider climb?**

> **What does the art show about the setting?**

When	Where
a long time ago when the world was new	West Africa a tall tree lots of flowers and trees, maybe a forest

Assign Practice Book 1, page 59 for skill maintenance.

IF students need more support with setting,
THEN see the review lesson on **page R59.**

CONNECTING TO THEME

Remind students of the What's New unit theme: *We learn about our world through new experiences.* Point out that when all the characters in the folk tale gain wisdom, they are able to learn about all kinds of things through new experiences.

TECHNOLOGY

MATCHING TECHNOLOGY TO TASK Have students compare this folk tale with others around the world. By visiting **www.scholasticnetwork.com** and looking under Folktales, Fables and Myths in the Web Guide, students will find links to sites with tales from places like Egypt, France, and Russia.

DAY 2

COMPREHENSION

7 **CAUSE/EFFECT**
> **What caused people to come running from everywhere?**
> *(The people heard the sound of the pot breaking.)*

8 **CRITICAL THINKING: HYPOTHESIZE**
> **Why do the people of West Africa put pictures of Spider on many everyday objects?**
> *(Possible answer: They want to be as wise as Spider.)*

JOURNAL

Revisit Predictions

Ask students to look back at their predictions and record how they were or were not confirmed by the end of the story.

INFORMAL ASSESSMENT
OBSERVATION

Assess students' understanding of the vocabulary word *wise* as they read *Spider Gets Around*.

Did students:

✔ recognize context clues that came after the word?

✔ use the context clues to help them understand the meaning of the word?

It made such a noise that people came from everywhere to see what it was. Old women came from the market. Men came from the farms, little boys came from their games, and little girls ran out of the round houses. And when they saw the wisdom pouring out of the pot, they all reached down and took some of it. Even the animals got some. They spread it all over the world. In India and Spain and Panama, where it is always hot or where it is always cold, everybody has some wisdom.

7 Because there was plenty to go around. Plenty for you and plenty for me.

100

MODIFY Instruction

ESL/ELD

▲ Make sure students understand why people came running. Say: *What happened to the pot when Spider fell? Did it make a noise? If you hear something break, do you run to see what happened?* Have students pantomime their response to the sound of something breaking. **(GUIDED QUESTIONS)**

EXTRA HELP

■ Help students recall the four main events of the story in sequence. Then ask them to retell the events in their own words by writing sentences, or they can retell the events by drawing four pictures in cartoon frames. **(SUMMARIZE)**

101 ▼

SPIDER GETS AROUND

Anansi the Spider is very popular in West Africa. Everyone likes this folk tale character because he is so <u>wise</u>. Anansi shows up on special beaded masks and hats. He is carved onto wooden bowls and around doorways. He appears on jewelry, stools, and walking sticks. **8**

The Akan people of Ghana even have a saying about this clever character. "No one goes to the house of the spider Anansi to teach it wisdom."

This gold-covered staff, or walking stick, is from Ghana. A wise person always carries this staff when there is something important to say.

101

DAILY PHONICS

✓ Vowel /ô/ *a, au, aw*

CONNECT SOUND-SPELLING

TEACH MODEL Review with students that the letters *a, au,* and *aw* often stand for /ô/ as in *tall, cause,* and *saw.*

Write the words *all, because,* and *paw* on the chalkboard, and have a volunteer circle the letters that stand for /ô/. Ask students to name story words that contain /ô/. *(gauze, all, saw, because)*

PHONICS MAINTENANCE Review the following sound-spellings: /ô/*a, au, aw*; schwa /ə/; long vowel /ī/.

PRACTICE/APPLY

READ WORDS To practice using the sound-spellings and review previous sound-spellings, list the following words on the chalkboard: **crawl, taller, audience, aside.** Have students read each chorally. Model blending as needed.

✓ INFORMAL ASSESSMENT
OBSERVATION

Did students:

✓ identify words with /ô/?

✓ connect /ô/ with the letters that stand for this sound, *a, au, aw*?

◎ **IF** students need more support with /ô/,

THEN see the Intervention Activity on **page T228.**

SOCIAL STUDIES

Ask students to complete the **Jobs That Spread Wisdom** activity on **page R41,** in which they will interview people to develop descriptions of jobs that spread wisdom. Students will write job descriptions.

MATH

Have students complete the **Graph Favorite Folk Tales** activity on **page R41,** in which they will survey classmates' favorite types of folk tales. Students will show the results on a pictograph.

COMPREHENSION

▶ Preview

Ask students to preview the poem by reading the title and studying the illustration that goes with it.

1 DRAW CONCLUSIONS

> Who is saying the words in the poem? Who is listening to the words? How do you know?

(The parent is talking to the child. The title tells me this.)

2 PARAPHRASE

> How would you put the poet's message in your own words?

(Possible answer: You can do anything you want. You can do anything with knowledge and skills.)

3 RESPOND TO LITERATURE

> What did you learn from the story and the poem about wisdom and knowledge?

(Possible answer: Everyone can learn things and become wise.)

SELF-MONITORING STRATEGY

Figurative Language

THINK ALOUD *I know that poems use special language, so when I read "drench yourself," I know that the poet doesn't mean "get wet." By reading the rest of the poem, I can figure out that "drench yourself" means "get a lot of."*

> Which other words have special meanings?

---

102 ▼

POEM

from
ALL BEAUTIFUL THINGS

Parent to Child

By Naomi F. Faust

Your world's wide open.

Walk right in.

Drown yourself with <u>knowledge</u>;

drench yourself with <u>skills</u>.

The world's wide open, child;

walk right in.

1 2 3

102

MODIFY
Instruction

ESL/ELD

▲ Help with figurative meanings of key words *drown* and *drench*. Explain that the poet thinks we should surround ourselves with knowledge and skills. Brainstorm ways to acquire knowledge and skills (read books/listen to elders/try new activities).
(BRAINSTORM)

EXTRA HELP

■ Help students appreciate the unique rhythm of the poem by first reading it aloud to them. Then ask students to retell, in their own words, the advice the parent is giving to the child.
(READ ALOUD/RETELL)

103 ▼

103

PREWRITE

Using Spider in *How the World Got Wisdom* as a model, discuss character traits with students. Tell them that later they will be writing a character sketch of a folk tale character. Explain that a character sketch is a description that helps make the character seem real. Have them think about a folk tale character to write about and begin the prewriting organizer.

Use Practice Book 1, page 60.

DAILY LANGUAGE PRACTICE

SPELLING

DAY 2:
Practice Spelling Words With the Vowel Sound in *saw.* **See page R36.**

GRAMMAR, USAGE, MECHANICS

DAY 2:
Practice Singular and Plural Pronouns. **See page R38.**

ORAL LANGUAGE

Him has awl the wisdom?
(*He* has *all* the wisdom*.*)

WORD STUDY

Point out that the Bonanza word **drench** comes from an Old English word that means "to drink." Over time, its meaning changed to mean "soak, or completely wet." Encourage students to make up short sentences using **drench** and share them with the class.

FAMILY READING

Invite a family member of an English language learner to school to read aloud or retell an animal folk tale from his or her country of origin. Have students prepare questions to ask their guest about the story.

DAY **2** WRAP-UP

READ ALOUD *Spend five to ten minutes reading from a selection of your choice.*

GUIDED READING *Meet with the **red** and **blue** reading groups and assign Independent Center activities. See **pages R34–R35.***

DAY 3 OBJECTIVES

STUDENTS WILL:

READ 30 MINUTES

Reread *How the World Got Wisdom*
Assess Comprehension
- **Key Comprehension Skill: Cause/Effect**
- **Daily Phonics: Vowel /ô/ a, au, aw**

WRITE 30 MINUTES

- **Respond: Folk Tale Review**
- **Spelling: Words with the Vowel Sound in *saw***
- **Grammar, Usage, Mechanics: Singular and Plural Pronouns**
- **Oral Language**

EXTEND SKILLS 30 MINUTES

- **Read Aloud**
- **Guided Reading**

RESOURCES

Transparency 15
- **Practice Book 1, pp. 61, 63–65**
- **Spelling Resource Book, p. 33**

▶ Think About Reading

Below are the **answers** to the Think About Reading questions.

1. *Spider wanted to hide the pot.*

2. *Spider was selfish; he wanted to keep wisdom for himself.*

3. *Accept reasonable responses.*

4. *Accept reasonable responses.*

5. *The poem encourages the child to gain knowledge while Spider doesn't want to share wisdom.*

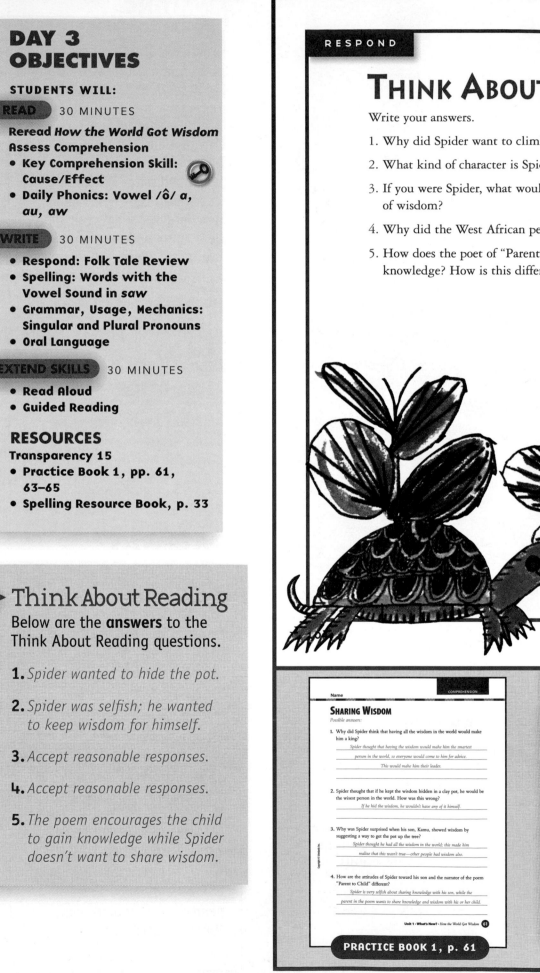

104 ▼

RESPOND

THINK ABOUT READING

Write your answers.

1. Why did Spider want to climb the tree?

2. What kind of character is Spider? How do you know?

3. If you were Spider, what would you do with the pot of wisdom?

4. Why did the West African people tell this story?

5. How does the poet of "Parent to Child" feel about knowledge? How is this different from Spider's feelings?

PRACTICE BOOK 1, p. 61

MODIFY
Instruction

GIFTED & TALENTED

✳ Let students imagine a chance meeting between two famous spider characters, such as Spider, Charlotte from *Charlotte's Web*, Spiderman, the Itsy Bitsy Spider, and the spider that scared Miss Muffet. Have students write a play or act out what the characters would say to each other. **(INNOVATE)**

105

WRITE A REVIEW

What did you like about *How the World Got Wisdom*? What would you tell another reader about it? Write a short review of this folk tale. Be sure to tell why you feel this way. Give the folk tale a rating.

LITERATURE CIRCLE

In *How the World Got Wisdom*, you meet one kind of spider. Think of songs, films, comics, stories, or other folk tales that have spiders. Tell what kind of character each spider is. Record your thoughts on a web. Then talk about how these spiders are different from the spider in the folk tale.

ILLUSTRATOR
JERRY PINKNEY

Jerry Pinkney started drawing when he was very young. He says this about his childhood: "I'd rather sit and draw than do almost anything else." Today Jerry Pinkney makes his living as an artist. He usually illustrates picture books about African Americans. He also likes the strong characters in folk tales. He says, "When I'm working on a book, I wish the phone would never ring."

MORE BOOKS ILLUSTRATED BY JERRY PINKNEY

• *Black Cowboys/Wild Horses* by Julius Lester
• *Rabbit Makes a Monkey of Lion* by Verna Aardema

105

RESPOND

Write a Folk Tale Review

Before students begin to write, have them think about these questions:

> **Which part of the story did you like the best—the characters, the setting, or what happens in the story?**
> **What details can you find to support your opinion?**

Literature Circle

Encourage students to use their completed webs to compare in a group the ways the spider is portrayed.

Spider
- Poems: Ms. Spider's Tea Party
- Songs: Itsy, Bitsy Spider
- Stories: Charlotte's Web

DAILY LANGUAGE PRACTICE

SPELLING
DAY 3: Write Words with the Vowel Sound in *saw*. **See page R37.**

GRAMMAR, USAGE, MECHANICS
DAY 3: Practice Singular and Plural Pronouns. **See page R39.**

ORAL LANGUAGE
You and me sau kim. *(You and I saw Kim.)*

AUTHOR/ILLUSTRATOR STUDY

Your students will be amazed to learn how many books Jerry Pinkney has illustrated. You'll find his bio at **www.penguinputnam.com** (click on Young Readers, then Authors and Illustrators).

TECHNOLOGY

Viewing Skills Have students make a video version of their folk tale review. Playing "thumbs up" or "thumbs down" story reviewers, have students prepare scripted reviews of the story. Brainstorm techniques and props that would make the presentation fun to watch.

COMPREHENSION
Cause/Effect

SKILLS TRACE

Cause/Effect `TESTED`

Introduce . . . . p. T226
Practice . . . . pp. T215,
                  T228–T229, T236
Review } This skill will be reviewed
Reteach } in *Big Plans* (pp. **T43**
         and R53)

TRANSPARENCY 15

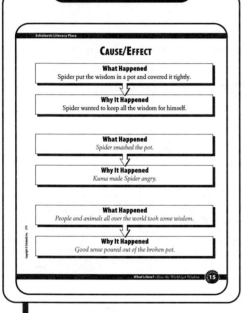

QUICKCHECK

Can students:

✔ identify a cause as why something
   happens and an effect as what happens?

✔ identify signal words and other clues
   about cause and effect?

If **YES**, go on to Practice/Apply.

If **NO**, start at Teach/Model.

Ⓐ TEACH/MODEL

USE ORAL LANGUAGE

Ask students what would happen if they knocked over a glass full of water. Discuss with them how knocking the glass over is likely to cause the water to spill. The water spilling is **what happened**. Knocking over the glass is **why it happened**. Point out that you might say, "Because I knocked over the glass, the water spilled." Call attention to the signal word *because*. Elicit from students other examples of cause/effect relationships. Encourage them to use signal words, such as *because* and *so*.

Cause/effect relationships help make up the events in a story. To help identify them, tell students they can:

1. ask, "What happened?"

2. ask, "Why did it happen?"

3. look for signal words such as *because* and *so*.

4. use what they already know.

MODIFY Instruction

ESL/ELD

▲ To help students with the cause/effect relationship, draw a T-shaped graphic on the chalkboard with columns headed "What Happened?" and "Why Did It Happen?" Help students go back over the story and fill in key events and explanations. **(GRAPHIC DEVICE)**

EXTRA HELP

■ Before they start the Practice Book pages, suggest that students write the signal words on a card to keep in front of them as a reminder of signal words that can identify a cause/effect relationship. **(USE VISUAL AIDS)**

LITERATURE CONNECTION

Display the diagram on **Transparency 15** to help students recognize cause/effect relationships.

THINK ALOUD *I can figure out how events in a story go together. When Spider puts wisdom in a pot, I know that this is what happened. Then I ask myself, "Why did it happen?" I find out that Spider wanted to keep wisdom all to himself. By asking myself what happened and why it happened, I can better understand how the events in a story go together.*

Ⓑ PRACTICE/APPLY

USE PRACTICE BOOK 1

Have students practice the skill independently by completing **Practice Book 1, page 63.** (INDIVIDUALS)

Ⓒ ASSESS

APPLY INSTRUCTIONAL ALTERNATIVES

Based on students' completion of **Transparency 15** and **Practice Book page 63**, determine if they were able to recognize cause/effect relationships in *How the World Got Wisdom*. The instructional alternatives below will help you pinpoint students' level of proficiency. Consider the appropriate instructional alternative to promote further development of the skill.

To reinforce the skill, distribute **pages 64** and **65** of **Practice Book 1.**

✓ INSTRUCTIONAL ALTERNATIVES

	If the student . . .	Then
Proficient	Understands cause/effect relationships	• Have the student apply the skill independently to a chapter of a book read outside of school.
Apprentice	Recognizes signal words but does not always identify the cause or effect	• Have pairs of students ask each other "Why did ...?" and "What happened when ...?" questions. The answering student identifies which part of a cause/effect relationship is asked for before answering.
Novice	Does not identify events as causes or effects; cannot recognize signal words	• Provide the student with simple cause/effect sentences that contain signal words and work with the student to identify the parts.

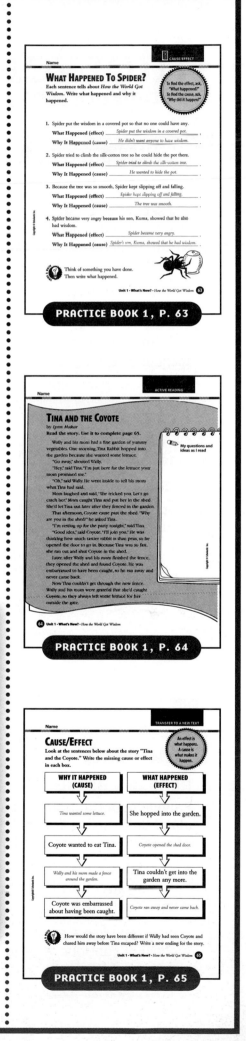

PRACTICE BOOK 1, P. 63

PRACTICE BOOK 1, P. 64

PRACTICE BOOK 1, P. 65

Intervention
For students who need extra help with . . .

PHONICS

IDENTIFYING SPELLING PATTERNS

Say sets of three words, and ask students to repeat the words that have the same vowel sound. Then write the words with /ô/ on the chalkboard, and have volunteers circle the letter(s) that stand for /ô/. Use these and other sets of words:

- dawn, saw, pay
- neat, pause, fault

PARTNERS Encourage partners to brainstorm and write words with /ô/. Have students sort the words into lists according to the spelling of the vowel sound.

call

cold

fall

COMPREHENSION

CAUSE/EFFECT

Support students' understanding of the cause/effect relationships in *How the World Got Wisdom*.

- Write the pairs of sentences on the chalkboard.

- Help students rewrite each pair as one cause/effect sentence with a signal word.

> Spider looked for a tall tree. He wanted to find a hiding place.
>
> Spider lost his footing on the smooth tree trunk. He slipped to the ground.
>
> Spider threw the pot. He was very angry.

FLUENCY

READING ALOUD

Provide opportunities for students to improve fluency by reading aloud daily, using books in your classroom. Choose from a variety of quality selections of all genres.

- Model fluent reading by reading a story with expression by varying your tone and pitch and emphasizing important words.

- Have volunteers practice reading the poem or continue reading a short section of the text.

Optional Materials for Intervention

PHONICS

Vowel /ô/ a, au, aw

If students need help recognizing words with /ô/, use Phonics Chapter Book #16, **The Great Time Travel Ride.**

CONNECT SOUND–SPELLING

TEACH/MODEL Tell students that they will be reading a story that contains words with the vowel sound /ô/. Remind them that /ô/ can be spelled *a* as in *all, au* as in *gauze,* or *aw* as in *saw.* Write the following words on the chalkboard, and have students blend them.

- almost
- automatic
- yawning
- crawling
- because
- already

READ *THE GREAT TIME TRAVEL RIDE*

PRACTICE/APPLY Assign Chapter 1 of the book. Check in with students and provide support as they continue reading the story, chapter by chapter.

LISTENING

Cause/Effect

If students need help with cause/effect relationships, use the audiocassette for **How the World Got Wisdom.**

BEFORE LISTENING

Before they begin listening, remind students that a cause/effect relationship has two parts: what happens and why it happens. Remind them that signal words such as **because** and **so** can help them identify causes and effects. Write the questions *What happened?* and *Why did it happen?* on the chalkboard.

LISTEN TO THE AUDIOCASSETTE

Have students listen to the story with a partner. Suggest that they stop the tape from time to time to talk about things that happened and why they happened.

DAY 3 WRAP-UP

READ ALOUD *Spend five to ten minutes reading from a selection of your choice.*

GUIDED READING *Meet with the* **blue** *and* **green** *reading groups and assign Independent Center activities.* **See pages R34–R35.**

DAY 4 OBJECTIVES

STUDENTS WILL:

READ 15 MINUTES

• **Reread** *How the World Got Wisdom*

WRITE 45 MINUTES

• **Writing Workshop: Character Sketch for a Folk Tale**
• **Writer's Craft: Precise Adjectives**
• **Spelling: Words With the Vowel Sound in** *saw*
• **Grammar, Usage, Mechanics: Singular and Plural Pronouns**
• **Oral Language**

EXTEND SKILLS 30 MINUTES

• **Vocabulary**
• **Daily Phonics: Vowel /ô/** *a, au, aw*
• **Oral Language**
• **Read Aloud**
• **Guided Reading**

RESOURCES

Transparency 16
Practice Book 1, pp. 60, 66, 67
Spelling Resource Book, p. 200

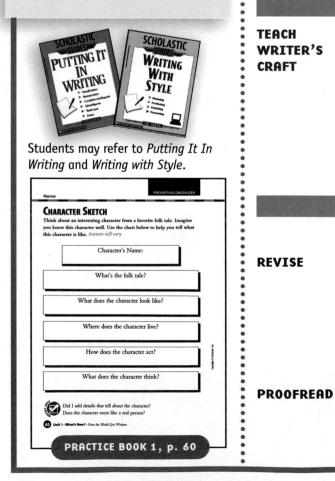

Students may refer to *Putting It In Writing* and *Writing with Style.*

PRACTICE BOOK 1, p. 60

⟲ WRITING WORKSHOP *Expressive Writing*

Character Sketch for a Folk Tale

THINK ABOUT WRITING

Ask students about the character Spider in *How the World Got Wisdom:*

> **How would you describe Spider? What is he like? How does he act?**

> **What details did the author use to help you understand him?**

LITERATURE CONNECTION

Read aloud the sentence "Of course, Spider wanted to keep it all for himself,..." on **page 92.** Ask students what that information tells about Spider. *(He was greedy.)* Explain that what characters do gives us clues that help us understand them.

PREWRITE

COMPLETE A GRAPHIC ORGANIZER

Have students refer to the chart on **Practice Book 1, page 60** that they began earlier. They might add more details about their folk tale characters.

DRAFT

TEACH WRITER'S CRAFT

Before students begin their drafts, show them how precise adjectives can make their writing clearer. See **The Writer's Craft, page T231.**

> **Now that you've recorded lots of information about your character, begin writing the character sketch as if you know the character well. Use details that are colorful and exact.**

REVISE/PROOFREAD

Note: You may wish to do Revise/Proofread on Day 5.

REVISE

As students revise and proofread, suggest that they ask themselves:

• Have I included details about what kind of person the character is?

• Did I use colorful and active adjectives?

PROOFREAD

• Did I use singular and plural pronouns correctly?

• Did I remember to capitalize the pronoun *I*?

✔See Student's Writing Rubric on page T238.

WRITER'S CRAFT
PRECISE ADJECTIVES

A TEACH/MODEL

Remind students that adjectives describe nouns. Then write the following phrases on the chalkboard:

a nice day   **a hot, sunny day**

Ask students which phrase gives a clearer picture of what kind of day it is. Explain that some adjectives, such as *nice*, are used so often they aren't meaningful.

Adjectives that are precise help make writing clearer. Precise adjectives:

- are strong and colorful.
- make writing more interesting.
- help readers see through the writer's eyes.

B PRACTICE/APPLY

- **Write on the chalkboard: The branches were covered with soft silvery leaves and a fine gauze that looked like cotton.** Ask students to identify the adjectives that make the sentence colorful. *(soft, silvery, fine)*

- **Use Transparency 16,** or write the following sentences and adjectives on the chalkboard. Ask students to read each sentence and choose the most precise adjective to complete the sentence.

> 1. We put our treasure in a _____ cave.
>   good   hidden
>
> 2. Spider had _____ slender legs.
>   many   eight

Ask students to explain why *hidden* and *eight* are more precise than *good* and *many*.

TRANSPARENCY 16

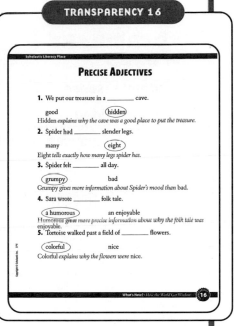

Scholastic Literacy Place

PRECISE ADJECTIVES

1. We put our treasure in a _____ cave.
   good   (hidden)
   Hidden *explains why the cave was a good place to put the treasure.*
2. Spider had _____ slender legs.
   many   (eight)
   Eight *tells exactly how many legs spider has.*
3. Spider felt _____ all day.
   (grumpy)   bad
   Grumpy *gives more information about Spider's mood than bad.*
4. Sara wrote _____ folk tale.
   (a humorous)   an enjoyable
   Humorous *gives more precise information about why the folk tale was enjoyable.*
5. Tortoise walked past a field of _____ flowers.
   (colorful)   nice
   Colorful *explains why the flowers were nice.*

What's New? · How the World Got Wisdom 16

DAILY LANGUAGE PRACTICE

SPELLING
DAY 4:
Review Words With the Vowel Sound in *saw.* **See page R37.**

GRAMMAR, USAGE, MECHANICS
DAY 4:
Apply Singular and Plural Pronouns. **See page R39.**

ORAL LANGUAGE
DAY 4:
they met Joe and I by the taul tree. *(They met Joe and me by the tall tree.)*

TEACHER TIP

"From time to time, I put a vocabulary concept category from an earlier lesson on the chalkboard and ask students to add words. I call it 'The Word Bank.' I leave the category up for a day or two and let students add words that fit. The resulting 'account' usually includes a good variety of words. Often a word that does not appear to fit is readily explained by the student depositor."

Extend Vocabulary

Review Vocabulary

CLUES TO MEANING

Write or say the vocabulary words. Then read each incomplete sentence and have students write or say the word that fits in the blank.

1. Spider _____ until he came up with a plan. *(thought)*

2. A _____ person has good judgment. *(wise)*

3. Your _____ about spiders is amazing. *(knowledge)*

4. Many people go to school to learn computer _____. *(skills)*

5. _____ is spread all over the world, to people and animals. *(Wisdom)*

6. Sometimes it's hard to think of a good _____. *(idea)*

7. Planning ahead makes good _____. *(sense)*

Expand Vocabulary

HOMOPHONES

Remind students that many words in English—called homophones—sound alike but have different spellings and meanings. Draw the chart on the chalkboard and have students think of a word that sounds like *sense*. Then have them suggest other homophone pairs that you can add to the chart.

Homophone Pairs	
sense	*cents*
pair	*pear, pare*
here	*hear*
four	*for*

Record Vocabulary

ADJECTIVE FILE

Students can begin a file of vivid adjectives with words from the story, such as *soft, silvery, smooth*. Have students write the words on index cards with a sample sentence. Students might draw or paste pictures onto the cards as well. Provide a file box for the cards, and encourage students to add words as they think of them or come across them in their reading.

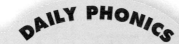

DAILY PHONICS

Vowel /ô/ a, au, aw

VOWEL TOSS

WORD TOSS Prepare for the activity by taping three plastic foam or paper cups to the floor close together, as in a carnival game. Inside one cup, write **a**; in the second cup, **au**; and in the third cup, **aw**. To make the game easier, you may wish to write words with /ô/ on the chalkboard.

fault	ball	crawl
saw	cause	wall
tall	lawn	sauce
straw	launch	small

1 SET-UP Give students buttons or other small objects to toss.

2 TO PLAY Students take turns tossing a button, trying to get one in a cup.

- When a button lands in a cup, the student looks at the spelling of /ô/ inside the cup and states a word that contains that spelling.

- If the word is correct, the student scores a point.

- Play continues until each student has had multiple turns. The player with the most points at the end of the game wins.

3 TRY THIS Players who spell the word as well as say it earn two points.

MODIFY
Instruction

ESL/ELD

▲ In playing Vowel Toss, permit English language learners to come to the chalkboard to point to one of the words that fits the spelling pattern if they do not feel comfortable pronouncing it. **(TOTAL PHYSICAL RESPONSE)**

GIFTED & TALENTED

✳ Point out that many words with /ô/ rhyme. Encourage students to list rhyming words with /ô/ and then use the words to write poems or rhyming couplets. Set aside time for a poetry reading during which students can share their rhymes. **(INNOVATE)**

MATERIALS: Plastic foam or paper cups, marker or pen, buttons

SUGGESTED GROUPING: Whole class or small groups

SPIDER'S STORY
Choose the word that best completes each sentence. Circle the word and write it on the line.

1. This (author, lawyer) wrote a story about Spider.
   author
2. Spider wanted (some, all) of the wisdom for himself.
   all
3. Spider (raw, gnawed) a silk-cotton tree.
   saw
4. He tried to climb up the (raw, tall), smooth tree.
   tall
5. Spider had a hard time (scrawl, because) the tree was so smooth.
   because
6. The slippery bark made Spider (crawl, fall).
   fall
7. Spider (paused, hauled) before trying to climb again.
   paused
8. Spider's plan for keeping the wisdom had a (claw, flaw).
   flaw
9. Spider let out a (squawk, hawk) when the pot smashed.
   squawk
10. It was Spider's (vault, fault) that the wisdom poured out of the pot.
    fault

PRACTICE BOOK 1, p. 66

ORAL LANGUAGE
Tell a Story to Entertain

You may wish to present the following example of an entertaining story to students before they begin preparing their own.

Long ago, the sun was much, much hotter than it is today. The people and animals complained so much about how hot it was that the sun got angry. "Let's see how you like having no sun!" it said. And the next morning, it didn't rise. The world was cold and dark.

The people and animals held a meeting. They decided to send the rooster to beg the sun to shine again. But the sun was still mad. It just told the rooster to go back home. Now, the clever rooster had an idea. He said to the sun, "It's very dark, and I'm afraid a tiger will catch me. If you hear me crow, please shine your light to frighten the tigers away." The sun agreed to do this. And that is why every morning, when the rooster crows, the sun comes out—to keep the tigers away!

A TEACH/MODEL

DEFINE TELLING A STORY TO ENTERTAIN

Remind students that *How the World Got Wisdom,* like other folk tales, is a story that came down to us by word of mouth. Explain that through the ages, storytellers have told stories to entertain their listeners.

> **What makes a story entertaining? The descriptions of places and characters? The events that happen in the story? A funny or surprising ending?**

Encourage volunteers to tell about stories they especially enjoyed and what made the stories entertaining.

SPEAK TO ENTERTAIN

Point out that everyone loves to hear a good story. Offer the following suggestions to students for things a speaker needs to keep in mind when telling a story:

- Speak with a lively tone of voice and use lots of expression.

- Think about what kind of story you're telling and try to make it sound exciting, funny, or scary.

- Look at your listeners as you're speaking.

- Use hand gestures and other movements to help create a mood or get across a feeling.

- Speak clearly, and pause before you tell the story's punchline or a funny ending.

> **How would you speak differently when telling a scary story from the way you'd speak when telling a funny story?**

> **How could you use your voice to show that different characters are speaking?**

Tell students that to help them feel at ease when they tell a story, they should rehearse it beforehand.

LISTEN TO AN ENTERTAINING STORY

Explain to students that listening is an important skill, just as speaking is. A good listener:

- listens quietly.

- tries to predict or guess what will happen next in a story.

- tries to picture in his or her mind what is happening.

ⓑ PRACTICE/APPLY

CHOOSE A STORY

Encourage students to decide on a story to tell. Explain that they may wish to tell a short, amusing story about something that happened to them, or they may want to tell a short version of an entertaining story that they like. Divide the class into small groups, and have group members discuss their story ideas

TELL A STORY TO ENTERTAIN

Have each group member prepare an entertaining story to tell and then present it. Encourage each group member to make a presentation. You may want to give students time to rehearse their presentations in their group before presenting to the whole class. Groups can do a quick run-through using the strategies you discussed.

DISCUSS THE PRESENTATIONS

When students finish their presentations, have group members review and discuss them.

- Did the student speak clearly and make eye contact with listeners?
- Did the student use gestures and speak expressively?

SELECTION LINK

Students can apply the speaking/listening skill when they participate in the project "Tell an Anecdote" at the end of Unit 1.

✓ STUDENTS' SELF-ASSESSMENT

Help students assess their performance as speakers and listeners by asking themselves questions such as these:

Did I:

✔ speak clearly and with expression?

✔ look at my audience while I spoke?

✔ listen quietly and attentively?

✔ try to picture the story events in my mind?

BE A BETTER SPEAKER

Use the following questions to help you be a better speaker.

☐ Did I look at my audience? Did I make eye contact and smile?

☐ Did I think about who my audience will be? Did I choose words I think they will understand?

☐ Did I think about the kinds of questions my audience might have? Was I prepared to answer them?

☐ Did I know what I was going to say and how I was going to say it?

☐ Did I practice my speech in front of a mirror?

☐ Did I use body language to help my audience understand me better?

☐ Did I remember to relax and speak slowly and clearly?

WHEN AND WHY DO I NEED TO SPEAK?	HOW CAN I BE A BETTER SPEAKER?	WHAT ADVANTAGE WILL IT GIVE ME?
Answers will vary.		

Unit 1 • What's New? • *How the World Got Wisdom* **67**

PRACTICE BOOK 1, p. 67

TECHNOLOGY

Speaking Skills Have students use **Smart Place** PlaceMaker to write and illustrate a brief, personal anecdote telling how a seemingly simple situation did not work out as planned. Ask them to italicize the sentences that create the drama, humor, or entertainment in their story. Encourage students to record themselves reading their anecdotes with special emphasis on the highlighted portions.

DAY **4** WRAP-UP

READ ALOUD *Spend five or ten minutes reading from a selection of your choice.*

GUIDED READING *Meet with the **green** and **red** reading groups and assign Independent Center activities.* **See pages R34–R35.**

DAY 5 OBJECTIVES

STUDENTS WILL:

READ 30 MINUTES

- **Reading Assessment**
- **Daily Phonics: Vowel /ô/ a, au, aw**

WRITE 30 MINUTES

- **Writing Assessment**
- **Spelling: Words With the Vowel Sound in saw**
- **Grammar, Usage, Mechanics: Singular and Plural Pronouns**
- **Oral Language**

EXTEND SKILLS 30 MINUTES

- **Integrated Language Arts**
- **Read Aloud**
- **Guided Reading**

RESOURCES

- **Selection Test**
- **Spelling Resource Book, p. 202**

SELECTION TEST

Reading Assessment

Formal Assessment

Use the Selection Test to measure student mastery of the week's reading skills. See the suggestions for Intervention and Modifying Assessment.

✅ SELECTION TEST

Available In ★READING COUNTS!★

SKILL	TEST QUESTIONS	◎ IF students need more support THEN...
COMPREHENSION Cause/Effect	1–3	Use the Reteach lesson in *Big Plans* on p. R53
GENRE Folk Tale	4–6	Review the skills lesson on p. T213.
DAILY PHONICS Vowel /ô/, a, au, ou	7–9	Use the Reteach lesson on p. R51.
Vocabulary	10–12	Use the Review Vocabulary on p. T232

Modifying Assessment

ESL/ELD
Vocabulary

▲ Do an oral cloze activity in which you retell the story, leaving out key nouns and verbs. Students supply the missing words. Have students read aloud in pairs and leave out key words. Listening partners read the missing words. **(CLOZE)**

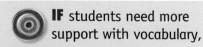 **IF** students need more support with vocabulary, **THEN** review the vocabulary in the Take-Home Practice Readers.

EXTRA HELP
Comprehension

■ Ask students to retell *How the World Got Wisdom*. Have them identify cause/effect relationships. Then ask:

> **Why did Spider put wisdom in a clay pot and cover it up?**
> **Why couldn't Spider climb the tree? What happened as a result? (RETELL)**

 IF students need more support with cause/effect, **THEN** review the skill in the Take-Home Practice Readers.

Performance-Based Assessment

Use the assessment activities below to provide performance-based measures of students' proficiency in phonics and reading fluency. See the Conference to assess individual students' progress.

DAILY PHONICS

Dictation

Words With Vowel /ô/ Dictate the following words and sentence. Have students write them on a sheet of paper. When completed, write the words and sentence on the chalkboard and have students make any necessary corrections on their papers.

> ball gauze draw author
> The small cat licked its paws.
> A hawk paused in flight.

✔ **Did students use the letters *a, au,* or *aw* to stand for /ô/?**

> **IF** students need more support with /ô/,
> **THEN** practice oral blending of the words with /ô/ from the dictation.

ONE-MINUTE FLUENCY

Ask students to sit in pairs and read aloud to each other. Circulate and listen to individuals to assess their reading fluency.

Students can read the text on **Practice Book 1, page 145** or the text of the Take-Home Practice Readers.

✔ *Does the student read with correct phrasing at the end of sentences and phrases?*

> **IF** students need more support with fluency,
> **THEN** have them practice rereading the passage and tape-record themselves.

✓ CONFERENCE

Take this time to meet with several students individually to discuss their story comprehension and to listen to them read from the story. You may wish to tape-record students as they read the section aloud.

ASSESS STORY COMPREHENSION
✔ **Why did Spider smash the pot of wisdom when his son told him what to do with it? (Cause/Effect)**

ASSESS GENRE
✔ **How did you know this was a folk tale? (Genre)**

ASSESS FLUENCY
✔ **Is the student comfortable reading aloud?**
✔ **Does the student read with expression and good pacing?**
✔ **Monitor and record student's reading rate.**

DAILY LANGUAGE PRACTICE

SPELLING

DAY 5:
Administer the Posttest for Words With the Vowel Sound in *saw*. **See page R37.**

GRAMMAR, USAGE, MECHANICS

DAY 5:
Assess Singular and Plural Pronouns. **See page R39.**

ORAL LANGUAGE

Spider grabbed the smawl pot and threw them on the ground (*Spider grabbed the* <u>small</u> *pot and threw* <u>it</u> *on the ground.*)

PORTFOLIO

Suggest that students add their drafts and revisions to their Literacy Portfolios.

Writing Assessment

You've used singular pronouns correctly. However, you didn't use any plural pronouns.

You might have described another character in this sketch instead of Spider.

The adjectives you used are too general. You repeat the word very four times. Try to use precise adjectives.

In the last paragraph you create an original sense of character by putting Spider into another setting. Good job!

Spider

The character that I am using is Spider. Spider is very greedy because he tried to steal all the wisdom in the world.

He tried to steal all the wisdom in the world because he wanted to be very smart, and he did not want anyone else to be very smart. He was being very greedy. He was being very mean to his eldest son, the animals, the people, and the whole world.

If Spider was at the circus, he would get all the stuff from the gift shops, and make a mess with the soda and popcorn. He would kick out all the performers that were out on the ring, and do all the acts himself.

The End

Apprentice

Use the rubric below to assess students' writing.

✓ STUDENTS' WRITING RUBRIC

Proficient	• The character sketch reflects an understanding of the folk tale character. • The student uses precise adjectives.	• Student uses singular and plural pronouns correctly. • The story has been proofread and corrected for grammar, usage, and mechanics.
Apprentice	• The character sketch reflects a familiarity with the folk tale character but may not be original. • The student may use some precise adjectives.	• Singular and plural pronouns are used, but there may be some errors. • The character sketch has been proofread but not completely corrected for errors.
Novice	• The character sketch does not reflect the folk tale character's traits. • Adjectives used are general rather than precise.	• The character sketch has not been corrected for grammar, usage, mechanics, and spelling errors.

Integrated Language Arts

ORAL LANGUAGE

Interview Spider and Kuma

Good For Grading

MATERIALS:
Paper, pencils

SUGGESTED GROUPING:
Small groups

INTRODUCE the activity by discussing with students how television reporters often interview people involved in news-making events.

ASK students to imagine what questions an interviewer might ask Spider and his son Kuma. Suggest that they review the story and note the details that might help them write questions and form answers.

ENCOURAGE student groups to present their interviews to the class. At the end of an interview, give the class a chance to pose questions to Spider and Kuma.

GRADE students on their presentation and how they used story material.

PERSUASIVE WRITING

Persuasive Letter

MATERIALS:
Paper, pens or pencils

SUGGESTED GROUPING:
Individuals

INTRODUCE the activity by asking students to imagine they are Nyame, the Sky God, and they have just heard that Spider intends to keep the wisdom for himself. Have them write a letter to persuade Spider to put wisdom to another use.

BRAINSTORM with students what Nyame might have wanted Spider to do with the wisdom.

············ **MINI-LESSON** ···········

TEACH/MODEL Explain that the purpose of a persuasive letter is to convince the reader to accept the writer's opinions or ideas. To do this, the writer presents logical arguments.

PRACTICE/APPLY Ask students to imagine they are Nyame. Have them come up with ideas about what Spider should do with the wisdom.

············ **TECHNOLOGY** ···········

Communicating Through Letters Have students use a familiar word processor to compose the Nyame's letter to Spider. Encourage them to use boldface, italicized, or colored text to highlight the strongest parts of Nyame's argument.

Integrated Language Arts

VIEWING/WRITING

Writing Slogans

MATERIALS:
Paper, pencils
Magazines or
newspapers

SUGGESTED GROUPING:
Partners or
individuals

INTRODUCE the activity by talking with students about slogans they have seen or heard such as "Take a look and read a book." Show examples of slogans in newspapers and magazines. Point out that slogans are usually short and are used to draw people's attention to an idea or a product.

ASK students to recall what they learned from *How the World Got Wisdom* and from the poem "Parent to Child." Have them write a slogan about knowledge: why knowledge is important, for example, or the importance of sharing what you know.

CHALLENGE students to create posters to illustrate their slogans. Some students may want to use a computer paint program to design their posters.

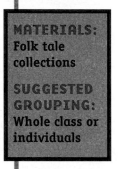

DAY **5** WRAP-UP

READ ALOUD *Spend five to ten minutes reading from a selection of your choice.*

GUIDED READING *Meet with the* **red** *and* **blue** *reading groups and assign Independent Center activities.* ***See pages R34–R35.***

LISTENING/WRITING

Compare Folk Tales

Good For Grading

MATERIALS:
Folk tale
collections

SUGGESTED GROUPING:
Whole class or
individuals

READ aloud another version of *How the World Got Wisdom*, such as the Native American version in which the main character is Turtle. Or read aloud another Spider tale from *The Adventures of Spider* by Joyce Cooper Arkhurst.

DISCUSS with students how the tales are alike and different. Help students compare and contrast theme, characters, setting, and plot events.

ENCOURAGE students to share which version of the folk tale (or which folk tale) they enjoyed more and why by having them write a critic's review. They can read their reviews aloud or post them in a Critic's Corner.

GRADE students by looking for textual support of opinions and use of comparative words.

Unit ❶ Wrap-Up

Students demonstrate independence and make meaningful connections to the real world.

WEEK 6 OBJECTIVES

WRITING PROCESS
Folk Tale
- write an original folk tale with natural dialogue

TRADE BOOK LIBRARY
- demonstrate independence

PROJECT
Write an Anecdote
- write and share a personal story

PRESENTATION SKILL
Speak to Entertain
- make an oral presentation

HOME INVOLVEMENT
- plan a family literacy night

TECHNOLOGY
- use the **Smart Place** CD-ROM to write an Adventure Log at the Meet the Mentor area

END OF UNIT ASSESSMENT
- follow-up on the baseline assessment and conduct formal and informal assessments

WEEKLY ORGANIZER

DAY 1	DAY 2	DAY 3	DAY 4	DAY 5
• WRITING PROCESS • TRADE BOOK LIBRARY • TECHNOLOGY	• WRITING PROCESS • TRADE BOOK LIBRARY • TECHNOLOGY	• WRITING PROCESS • TRADE BOOK LIBRARY • PROJECT	• TRADE BOOK LIBRARY • PROJECT • HOME INVOLVEMENT	• TRADE BOOK LIBRARY • PRESENTATION SKILL • END OF UNIT ASSESSMENT

WRAP-UP

WEEK 6 WRITING OBJECTIVES

STUDENTS WILL:
- write an original folk tale
- use natural dialogue in their folk tale
- capitalize proper nouns

MATERIALS
- Anthology pp. 92–101
- *Scholastic Dictionary of Idioms*
- *Writing With Style*
- Practice Book 1, p. 70
- Transparency 17

SUGGESTED GROUPING
- Whole class and individuals

PRACTICE BOOK 1, p. 70

FOLK TALE

THINK ABOUT WRITING

Discuss with students key characteristics of a folk tale:

- Folk tales are stories handed down through generations.
- They often contain unusual characters, such as speaking animals.
- Many folk tales teach a lesson about life.

Have students talk about folk tales they have heard or read.

LITERATURE CONNECTION

Review the elements of a folk tale in *How the World Got Wisdom*. (It is about a spider who behaves like a human and has human personality traits. It takes place a long time ago and teaches a lesson about life—the world's wisdom is meant to be shared among people and animals.)

Tell students that they will be writing their own folk tale. Suggest that their folk tale also feature an animal with human traits and a lesson about life.

PREWRITE

COMPLETE A PREWRITING ORGANIZER

Have students complete **Practice Book 1, page 70**, a chart on which they create a profile of the main character for their folk tale. Before they begin, help them make a distinction between human behavior and human traits.

> **Behavior is the character's actions, such as laughing or talking loudly.**

> **Traits are personality characteristics that tell what a person is like, such as being funny or creative.**

After students have finished their charts, suggest that they work with a partner to brainstorm other elements for their folk tales. They can ask themselves:

- What is the setting of the folk tale?
- What problem will the main character face?

WRIT

WRITER'S CRAFT
NATURAL DIALOGUE

Ⓐ TEACH/MODEL

Point out that in all kinds of stories, dialogue—a conversation between two or more people—should sound natural. It should have the same tone as people talking in real life.

Read aloud the following two lines of dialogue:

> "Where are you going?" asked the hare. "And why are you in such a hurry?"

> "To what place are you traveling?" asked the hare. "For what reason are you rushing so?"

Explain that although both lines of dialogue have the same meaning, the first is more natural. It has the same tone a person in real life would use in casual conversation.

Ⓑ PRACTICE/APPLY

Tell students that you're going to "write" natural dialogue together. Use **Transparency 17**, or write the following incomplete sentences on the chalkboard. Ask students to select the words that complete the dialogue and sound the way people actually speak.

> Dinah Cat picked up her brush. "I'm going to ___(1)___ your ___(2)___," she said to Hector Dog.
>
> 1. paint/create
> 2. likeness/picture

Explain that *paint* and *picture* are the better choices because these words make the dialogue seem natural and true-to-life.

TRANSPARENCY 17

NATURAL DIALOGUE

Dinah Cat picked up her brush. "I'm going to __1__ your __2__," she said to Hector Dog.
1 paint / create
2 likeness / picture

"I'm a __3__ artist. You should be honored that I __4__ to paint you."
3 famed / great
4 want / desire

Poor Hector did not know what to do. "She paints __5__. Let me __6__ it."
5 very well / in an excellent manner
6 ponder / think about

"There's __7__ I have to do __8__," Hector said. And off he went to take a nap.
7 another activity / something else
8 right now / at this point in time

Students may refer to the *Scholastic Dictionary of Idioms* and *Writing With Style*.

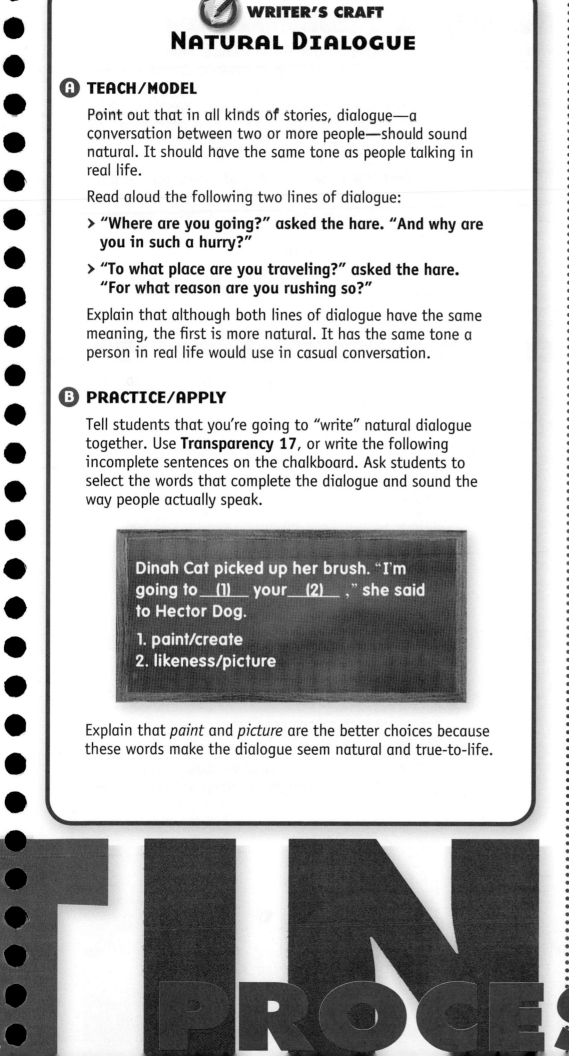

Writing Process *Expressive Writing*

TEACHER TIP

"When my students write dialogue, I suggest they read it aloud and listen to hear if it sounds natural. Some students tape-record it and play it back; others ask a classmate for an honest assessment. Classmates often give good suggestions I wouldn't have thought of."

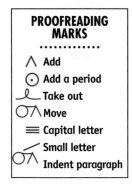

PROOFREADING MARKS

- ∧ Add
- ⊙ Add a period
- ꝶ Take out
- ◯⌒ Move
- ≡ Capital letter
- ╱ Small letter
- ◯⌒ Indent paragraph

DRAFT

WRITE

After completing the Writer's Craft, have students look back at their *Prewriting Organizer: Creating a Folk Tale Character*. Ask them to recall ideas they brainstormed with their partners in Prewrite, and begin a draft. Here is a paragraph from a draft of a folk tale:

Dinah Cat thought she was the best artist in the world. ❶ "I'm such a terrific painter," she boasted. ❷ She kept telling all the other cats and dogs about how talented she was. Dinah was starting to get on everyone's nerves. ❸	❶ An animal with human traits ❷ Dialogue that sounds natural ❸ The central problem

REVISE/PROOFREAD

Have students ask themselves or a writing partner the following questions:

REVISE

- Does my dialogue sound natural?
- Is my main character interesting or unusual?
- Did I clearly communicate the lesson my folk tale teaches?

PROOFREAD

- Have I capitalized all my proper nouns? Did I correct all my misspellings?

Help students create a list of important features to include in their writing.

PUBLISH

SPEAKING/ LISTENING

Encourage students to take the roles of storyteller and audience for dramatic readings of their folk tales.

TECHNOLOGY

Suggest students send their folk tale to some faraway friends or relatives by attaching the file to an e-mail. If possible, show students how to do this, or suggest they ask a friend or fellow student for help.

Yes, this is a proper noun. The first letter of each word should be capitalized.

How Dogs Came to Laugh

Once upon a time no dogs ever laughed. It all started when king high and mighty said that all the dogs in his kingdom had to keep there [their] mouths shut. Only people were allowed to laugh. So all the dog kept [dogs keeped their] there mouths tightly shut.

That is until Jasper the dalmation. One day there was a serious ceremony. King high and mighty was wearing his most ekspensive [expensive] black and white spotted robe. "He looks just like me!" Jasper said. He laughed. "Jasper! Put your tongue back in your mouth!" said Jaspers owner Duke Dusthead. "King high and mighty is passing."

But Jasper just could not obey. Then all the dogs stuck out there [their] pink tongues opened there [their] mouths and started to laugh. There were hundreds of them. "Shut your mouths!" yelled the king. He yelled and yelled. But he just looked like a yelling dalmation.

That's how dogs came to laugh.

THE END

Apprentice

You have captured one of the main characteristics of a folk tale. Animals can talk like people.

Good natural dialogue! Remember to add apostrophes to possessive nouns.

You were right to move this to fix the order in which the actions occurred.

TEACHER TIP

"Many students don't understand that revising is just part of the writing process. It is not a sign that they have failed. I emphasize this by saying that this is the most important stage: It's the polish that makes the writing shine."

Use the rubric below to assess students' writing.

☑ STUDENTS' WRITING RUBRIC

Proficient	• The folk tale is original and has all the genre's key characteristics. • The dialogue is natural.	• Proper nouns are capitalized. • Student corrects errors and uses proofreading marks properly.
Apprentice	• The folk tale is original but it may lack an interesting or unusual character or a lesson. • The dialogue doesn't always sound natural.	• Proper nouns are sometimes capitalized. • Student corrects some errors and uses most proofreading marks properly.
Novice	• The story lacks the key characteristics of a folk tale. • The dialogue is stilted.	• Proper nouns are not capitalized. • Student doesn't correct errors or use proofreading marks.

WRITING PROCESS

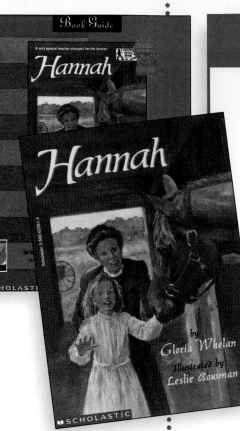

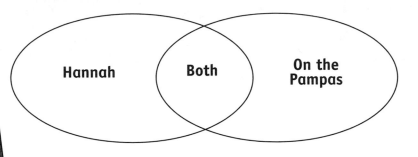

LITERARY Connection

SETTING *Hannah* and *On the Pampas* have similar settings—one a farm, the other a ranch. Students could use a Venn diagram to compare and contrast details of the settings of the two stories.

Hannah   Both   On the Pampas

Lexile Level: 740

THEME Connection

Both *How My Family Lives in America* and *The Chalk Box Kid* describe a child who grows and learns in special ways. Have students explore ways in which April and Gregory learn about the world through new experiences.

> **What is special about April and Gregory?**

> **How do April and Gregory face new and difficult experiences?**

> **What did you learn from *How My Family Lives in America* and *The Chalk Box Kid* that can help you grow as a person?**

Lexile Level: 270

TRADE

ILLUSTRATOR Connection

Uncle Jed's Barbershop and *Gila Monsters Meet You at the Airport* are realistic stories. One is told seriously, the other as humor. Have students compare the illustrations for these stories.

> By looking at the illustrations for *Uncle Jed's Barbershop,* how do you know the story is realistic? How do you know it's told in a serious way?

> By looking at the illustrations of *Gila Monsters Meet You at the Airport,* how do you know it is also realistic? What makes the illustrations humorous?

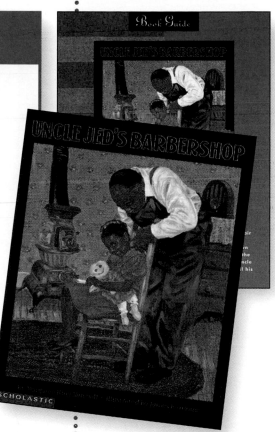

Lexile Level: 680

KEY SKILL Connection

CAUSE/EFFECT Help students practice recognizing cause/effect relationships by organizing the main events in *Muggie Maggie* and *Ramona Forever* as a series of causes and effects. Have students complete the graphic organizer below to see how each story is built.

	Cause	Effect
Muggie Maggie	⇨	
	⇨	
Ramona Forever	⇨	
	⇨	

Who needs to learn cursive writing? The other third graders are eager to learn the new skill, but Maggie doesn't even want to try. Is there anything that can make her change her mind?

Lexile Level: 730

BOOKS

Real-World Skills

PROJECT OBJECTIVES

STUDENTS WILL:
- write and speak descriptively
- write personal anecdotes

MATERIALS
- Paper
- Pencils
- Colored pencils, crayons or markers

TECHNOLOGY

Organizing Information Students should use a word processor to create the outline for their anecdotes. Guide them to list key ideas of the story with at least two supporting details beneath each idea. Model how to use the word processor's outline function to organize the ideas.

PROJECT

How to

Write an Anecdote

Tell a story about something that really happened to you.

Suppose a friend says to you, "You'll never guess what I did last weekend." When you hear these words, you expect to hear an anecdote about your friend's experience. An anecdote is a short story about an interesting or funny event. Personal anecdotes are interesting to hear, but they are even more fun to share. And everyone has at least one.

106

PERSONAL VOICE

Did I ever tell you about..

107

Elaborate Descriptions

Explain to students that an anecdote is a short story about something that happened. Ask students why people like to share anecdotes with others and if they have ever told one.

Discuss the text and pictures for the anecdote on pages 106–111.

> **What kind of experience do you think the girl is describing?**

> **Why might the girl think the experience was an exciting "adventure"?**

> **Based on the pictures and the text, how would you tell this story?**

Home Involvement

Suggest that students ask family members about anecdotes and think about these questions:

> **What kind of experiences do family anecdotes describe?**

> **What do these anecdotes tell you about yourself or a family member?**

Students can share the anecdotes they learned with the class or use one for the Project.

Troubleshooting

As students begin to write, review their ideas with them. Make sure they're not developing a story they'd be uncomfortable sharing in front of the class.

1 WHAT'S YOUR STORY?

Your students may think that an anecdote must be funny. Explain that anecdotes can have many forms and purposes. An anecdote is informative when the teller gives facts that no one knows. An anecdote can also give a lesson, or it may be sad. Stress that one reason people tell anecdotes is to reveal something about themselves. The story is important. What you learn from it is important, too.

PRACTICE BOOK 1, p. 68

Practice Book 1, pages 68 and 69 can help students plan, organize, and decide how to illustrate their anecdotes.

1 What's Your Story?

Think of something that has happened to you that would make a good story. It might be about something that surprised you.

It might be about something you didn't like and then learned to enjoy. It might even be about going to a new place or meeting new people. Jot down possible ideas. Then choose the one you like the most.

TOOLS

- pencil and paper

- colored pencils, crayons, or markers

...and when I looked around...

108

PERSONAL VOICE

2 Get the Facts

Think about your anecdote. Try to get all the facts straight. Then take notes about what happened. Make sure you know the order in which the events in your story took place.

Now go back and look at your notes. Decide which details in your story are most important or interesting. Did something surprising or funny happen to you? Did you find out something about yourself—what you can do or what you like to do? Now you have all the information you need to put your anecdote on paper.

How Am I Doing?

Before you write your anecdote, take a few minutes to answer these questions.

- Is my anecdote about something that happened to me?

- Do I remember the parts of the story that are important?

- Does my story have a good ending?

109

2 GET THE FACTS

INDIVIDUALS Remind students that like a story, an anecdote has a beginning, a middle, and an end. As they take notes about the information they'll include in their anecdote, remind them to think about the order in which they'll present those facts.

HOW AM I DOING? You and your students can use the questions in the Anthology as a check for assessing progress up to this point and for adjusting their work as needed.

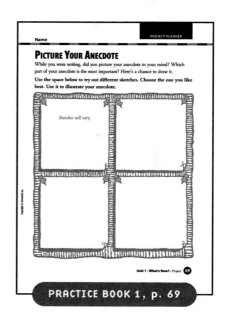

Name _____ PROJECT PLANNER

PICTURE YOUR ANECDOTE

While you were writing, did you picture your anecdote in your mind? Which part of your anecdote is the most important? Here's a chance to draw it.

Use the space below to try out different sketches. Choose the one you like best. Use it to illustrate your anecdote.

Sketches will vary.

Unit 1 - What's New? - Project 69

PRACTICE BOOK 1, p. 69

3 **WRITE YOUR STORY**

Remind students that because their listeners did not experience the event the anecdote describes, as they write they should consider these questions:

> **What do listeners need to know about the people and places involved?**

> **What facts will help listeners understand why the anecdote is particularly funny, surprising, or sad?**

4 **TELL YOUR STORY**

Use the Presentation Skill lesson plan on pages T254–T255 to support students in giving and viewing their presentations. The lesson will help students perform their anecdotes.

---

3 ## Write Your Story

Use your notes to write your story. Start out by briefly telling where the story takes place. Then tell what happened. As you write, imagine you are telling your anecdote to a friend. Try to make it lively. After you've finished, write the title and your name at the top.

Now illustrate your anecdote. Choose the part that you think is most important, and draw it. For example, if you won a prize, show yourself holding the prize.

Tip Personal anecdotes are always told in the first person. This means that you use the pronoun *I* when you tell your story.

What an ADVENTURE

110

PRO

PERSONAL VOICE

4 Tell Your Story

Everybody loves to hear a good anecdote. Read yours to the class. Use lots of expression in your voice. Try to make your story sound exciting, funny, or scary. Display your illustration, too. Answer any questions your classmates may have about your anecdote.

that was!

If You Are Using a Computer ...

Tell your anecdote using the Record and Playback Tools on the computer. You can listen to your story as you write it. You may want to share your anecdotes with friends on-line.

CONGRATULATIONS

You have learned how new experiences can change you. They can make you feel good about yourself, too.

Keith Jardine
Wilderness Guide ▶

ASSESSMENT

☑ INFORMAL ASSESSMENT
OBSERVATION

When students have completed their anecdotes, review their work. Ask yourself:

✔ Did students choose an appropriate anecdote?

✔ Did students include all the descriptive details and events important to their story?

✔ What did students learn about themselves from the anecdote?

STUDENT SELF-ASSESSMENT

> What is an anecdote? What did my anecdote tell about me?

SELF-SELECTION

Students may want to keep their anecdote in their Literacy Portfolio as an example of work well done.

☑ STUDENTS' PROJECT RUBRIC

Proficient	Students chose interesting events for their personal anecdotes. Their anecdotes are descriptive and engaging, and include all the elements of a story in a clear order.
Apprentice	Students are able to use events from their lives to write a personal anecdote. Some elements of the story may be missing, but students include enough description to make their anecdote clear.
Novice	Students have difficulty identifying events in their lives to use in an anecdote. The anecdote has few details, and the order of events may be unclear.

Presentation Skill

T254

PRESENTATION SKILL OBJECTIVE

STUDENTS WILL:
- practice telling their anecdotes to their classmates

MATERIALS
- Students' personal anecdotes from Project
- Paper and pencil (optional)
- Video of children's comedy program (optional)
- VCR (optional)

TECHNOLOGY

Presentation Tools Have your students make a videotape of each other's anecdote presentations. Using their outlines as the basis for the final presentation, students should complete the script using a word processor. Encourage them to practice their oral presentations several times before they are videotaped.

SPEAK TO ENTERTAIN

Ⓐ TEACH/MODEL

PUT IT IN CONTEXT

Explain to students that they'll be telling their anecdotes to the class. Remind them that they will need to speak clearly and slowly so that everyone in the audience can hear and understand them.

Encourage them to think about the story as they tell it.

> **If it's an exciting or scary moment, how could you communicate that with your voice? If it's sad, or happy, how could you communicate that?**

> **What gestures could you use as you tell the story?**

> **What parts could you act out?**

> **If more than one person speaks in the story, how can you show that with your tone of voice?**

Some students may want to read their anecdotes; others may want to perform them. Performers could jot down a few notes to refer to as they tell their story.

B PRACTICE/APPLY

SPEAK TO ENTERTAIN

COOPERATIVE GROUPS Ask groups to discuss how they can use the suggestions the class came up with when they read or perform their anecdotes. Have students practice presenting their anecdotes to their groups. Listeners could consider these questions:

> **Could I hear and understand the storyteller?**

> **How could the storyteller make his or her anecdote more entertaining?**

After the practice sessions, have students present their anecdotes to the class. Discuss the anecdotes together. How many different kinds of anecdotes did the class tell? Brainstorm a list of the characteristics of a good storyteller.

OPTION

TRANSFER TO A NEW MEDIUM To apply the skill to other media, have groups view at least two segments of a children's program from a public television series, then rate the speakers' or actors' ability to entertain using the list the class made.

C ASSESS

INFORMAL ASSESSMENT: OBSERVATION

When students finish the Presentation Skill activity, review their work. Ask yourself:

✔ Did students recognize what makes an anecdote interesting or entertaining?

✔ Were students able to speak clearly in front of the class?

✔ What elements from the class discussion did students use in their own presentations?

STUDENT SELF-ASSESSMENT

✔ What is important to remember when presenting an anecdote? What will I do next time I speak in front of a group of people?

MODIFY Instruction

ESL/ELD

▲ In order to better evaluate the anecdotes, have students answer the following questions: *Was the anecdote funny? Sad? Informative? Surprising? Did it have a beginning? Middle? End? Did the speaker's voice change? Did the speaker use gestures? Name one thing you learned.* **(GUIDED QUESTIONS)**

EXTRA HELP

■ Well-timed gestures and facial expressions can provoke laughter as well as help tell a story. Encourage students to bring physical expression to their presentations. After students have identified some of the qualities of good storytelling, have students play a round of charades to practice making gestures. **(PANTOMIME)**

FAMILY LITERACY NIGHT

Open the doors of your classroom Publishing Company so that students can share their work from the *What's New?* unit with family members. Try these ideas to plan, organize, and set up the event.

- **ANNOUNCEMENTS** Let students make invitations to send to other classes, family members, and people in the community announcing the family literacy night. If you have the **Smart Place** CD-ROM available, encourage them to use the PlaceMaker feature to design the invitations as well as make programs for the event itself.

- **TOUR GUIDES** Ask several students to act as tour guides or hosts to greet people at the door, pass out programs, or walk visitors through "The Place." If you set up Learning Stations, have a host at each station, too.

- **HOME/COMMUNITY** Create a special display in "The Place" by taking the Personal Voice theme into the community. Feature unique voices from the community along with unit selection characters and examples of students' activities.

Learning Stations

Set up Learning Stations so that visitors can try out Integrated Curriculum or Language Arts activities from the unit.

- **COMMUNITY MENTORS** Have students and families view the Meet the Mentor video, or talk to a community mentor—a hiker or backpacker, mountain climber, or wildlife manager, for example—who exemplifies a strong personal voice.

- **QUICKWRITE** Encourage visitors to express their own personal voice through writing. Set up a writing center with paper, pencils, and starter ideas.

CONNE

Technology

INTERACTIVE WRITING

Students can go to the Meet the Mentor area on the **Smart Place** CD-ROM to watch exciting videos and respond to them through guided writing activities. Each writing activity will become an entry in their personal Adventure Log.

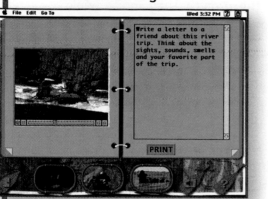

Smart Place CD-ROM

- **DESCRIBE A WHITE WATER RAFTING TRIP** After students watch a video that puts them in the center of the action during a white water rafting trip with wilderness guide Keith Jardine, they will be asked to write a letter to a friend describing the breathtaking experience. Encourage students to draw on each of their senses to describe the trip.

- **CREATE AN OUTDOOR ADVENTURE** Students have a bird's-eye view as they watch a fast-paced video that takes them from a mountain bike to a roller coaster to a hang glider. Students are then encouraged to write about an outdoor adventure, casting themselves as the main character. Some students might enjoy imagining themselves in one of the adventures shown on the video, while others will prefer to write about a new experience.

Smart Place CD-ROM

- **PLAN A SLED DOG EXPEDITION** After watching an expert musher and his team of energetic sled dogs race across Alaska's open terrain as they compete in the Iditarod, students are asked to write about how they would prepare for this challenging race. Encourage students to visit **www.scholasticnetwork.com** to meet musher Martin Buser and learn more about the Iditarod.

- **WRITE A SUMMARY** To conclude, have students use a familiar word processor to write down their thoughts about being an adventure guide. Ask them to share their feelings about whether or not they have the interest or skills to become a guide. The writing could take the form of a Pro and Con table. The piece could also be in response to the title, "Why I Want/Do Not Want to Be an Adventure Guide."

📖 SCHOLASTIC SOLUTIONS

Be sure to visit the Scholastic Solutions area on www.scholastic.com to learn more about Scholastic's many resources for teachers, including trade books, leveled libraries, phonics resources, magazines, videos, CD-ROMs, professional books, and much more.

WEEK 6 ASSESSMENT

SEE THE ASSESSMENT HANDBOOK FOR:

- **Guidelines for Assessment Planning**
- **Methods of Assessment including Observation and Portfolio**
- **Tools for Assessment including Literacy Record and Literacy Log**
- **Oral Reading Assessment**
- **Rubrics for Evaluation**
- **Grading Guidelines**

ASSESSMENT HANDBOOK

STUDENT ASSESSMENT

FOLLOW-UP ON BASELINE ASSESSMENT

The Baseline Assessment allowed you to identify which concepts students understood as they started this unit. By repeating the task, you can better understand and share with students the growth they made while exploring their personal voice.

At the beginning of the unit, students described a recent new experience. Ask them to think of and describe another new experience. Distribute the descriptions saved from the beginning of the unit, and encourage students to compare and contrast the new with the old. Discuss how new experiences are an important part of growing up. Students may decide to put one or both descriptions in their Literacy Portfolios. You could also use them as a focus during a student conference.

K-W-H-L

With the class, look back at the K-W-H-L chart you've worked on. Finish filling in the "What Did We Learn?" section. Have students form conference groups to compare what they wanted to learn about new experiences with what they actually learned in the *What's New?* unit. What would they still like to learn about new experiences?

STUDENT SELF-ASSESSMENT

Have students look back at the Unit Planner pages from Practice Book 1, then complete the "What Did I Learn?" page. Did they meet the goals they set for themselves?

OBSERVATIONAL CHECKLIST

Use the Individual and Class Unit Checklist for *What's New?* from the Classroom Management Forms, to record your end of unit evaluations and observations of each student in the class. Then complete and send home the Family Literacy Newsletter.

INFORMAL ASSESSMENT

Use the Workshops, Project, and writing activities to assess students' understanding of the importance of new experiences. You can also use the rubrics noted in the Teacher's Edition and student self-assessment pieces.

PORTFOLIO

Allow students time to sort through the material they've saved for their Literacy Portfolios. Distribute the Portfolio Checklist from the Assessment Handbook to help them decide what to keep in their *What's New?* Portfolio.

Before students use the checklist, have them decide what they want to do with their Literacy Portfolios. Do they want to save only their favorite work? What is it about these pieces that makes them important?

FORMAL TESTING

- ✔ See Practice Tests in the Spelling Resource Book.
- ✔ To prepare students for the *What's New?* Unit Test, see the Teacher's Test Manual.
- ✔ Forms A and B of the test and directions for administering, scoring, and using the tests are in the Teacher's Test Manual.

Spelling Practice Tests

Teacher's Test Manual

Unit Test Form A

Unit Test Form B

TEACHER SELF-ASSESSMENT

Spend some time critiquing your own teaching:

- ✔ Did my students learn that new experiences could make their lives more meaningful?

- ✔ Were they able to draw comparisons between new and old experiences?

- ✔ Did they learn that new experiences can change how people feel and think about things?

GLOSSARY

You will find all your vocabulary words in alphabetical order in the Glossary. Look at the sample entry below to see how to use it.

This is the **entry word** you look up. It is divided into syllables.

This part tells you how to **pronounce** the entry word. It uses the marks in the pronunciation key.

This tells you what **part of speech** the entry word is.

fos·sils (fos´əlz) *noun*
The hardened remains of plants or animals that lived a long time ago. Dinosaur bones found in the earth are *fossils*. ▲ fossil

fossil

Look here to find the **meaning** of the word. There also may be a sentence that tells more about the word or that shows how the word is used.

This is **another form** of the entry word.

a	add	o͞o	took	ə =
ā	ace	o͞o	pool	ə in *above*
â	care	u	up	e in *sicken*
ä	palm	û	burn	i in *possible*
e	end	yo͞o	fuse	o in *melon*
ē	equal	oi	oil	u in *circus*
i	it	ou	pout	
ī	ice	ng	ring	
o	odd	th	thin	
ō	open	ŧħ	this	
ô	order	zh	vision	

The **pronunciation key** will help you figure out how to pronounce the entry word.

ap·pren·tic·es
(ə pren´ ti siz) *noun*
People who learn a trade or job by working with a more skilled person.
▲ apprentice

bed·rock
(bed´ rok´) *noun*
The solid layer of rock that lies under the soil and loose rock.

bel·lowed
(bel´ ōd) *verb*
Shouted or roared. I *bellowed* when my dog ate my sandwich.
▲ bellow

bi·cus·pid
(bī kus´ pid) *noun*
A tooth with two points on its top.

blaz·es (blā´ ziz) *noun*
Large fires. ▲ blaze

bri·dles (brīd´ lz) *noun*
The straps, bits, and reins that fit over horses' heads and are used to guide the animals.
▲ bridle

buf·fa·loes
(buf´ ə lōz´) *noun*
Wild oxen of North America that have large, shaggy heads. Buffalo are also called bison.
▲ buffalo

buffaloes

cal·lig·ra·phy
(kə lig´ rə fē) *noun*
Fancy penmanship, or a kind of beautiful writing.

calligraphy

chaps
(chaps or shaps) *noun*
Leather leg coverings that are worn over pants. Chaps are worn by cowhands to protect their legs from thorns.

chick·en·pox
(chik´ ən poks´) *noun*
A childhood disease that causes red, itchy bumps on the skin.

378   379

GLOS

chop·sticks
(chop´ stiks´) *noun*
A pair of thin sticks used to lift food to the mouth. Chopsticks are used mostly in Asian countries. ▲ chopstick

chopsticks

coaxed (kōkst) *verb*
Encouraged someone gently to do something. We *coaxed* our friend to stay for lunch. ▲ coax

col·umns
(kol´ əmz) *noun*
Things having the shape of tall, upright structures that support a building. *Columns* of smoke rose from the burning forest. ▲ column

com·plained
(kəm plānd´) *verb*
Said that something was unpleasant or wrong. We *complained* that the noise was too loud. ▲ complain

con·ceit·ed
(kən sēt´ əd) *adjective*
Having too high an opinion of oneself. The *conceited* actor couldn't believe that he wasn't chosen to star in the play.

con·ta·gious
(kən tā´ jəs) *adjective*
Easily spread from one person to another. I got sick because Judy's cold was *contagious*.

con·trac·tor
(kon´ trak tər) *noun*
A person whose job is to make sure workers and supplies are at a building site.

corn·husks
(kôrn´ husks´) *noun*
The coverings on cars of corn. ▲ cornhusk

cornhusk

cor·ral (kə ral´) *noun*
A fenced area that holds large animals, especially horses or cows.

crane

cranes (krānz) *noun*
Large machines used for lifting or moving heavy objects. ▲ crane

WORD STUDY
The word **crane** has more than one meaning.
- A crane is also a large wading bird. It has long legs and a long neck and bill.
- You use *crane* as a verb, too. It means to stretch your neck so that you can see over or around something.

cu·ri·ous
(kyoor´ ē əs) *adjective*
Eager to learn about new or interesting things. The *curious* child asked many questions.

den·tine
(den´ tēn) *noun*
The hard, thick material that makes up most of a tooth. It is inside the tooth.

de·sign (di zīn´) *verb*
To draw something that could be built or made. Did you *design* the patterns on this rug?

dough (dō) *noun*
A mixture of flour, milk or water, and other ingredients that is made into bread or pastry.

drought (drout) *noun*
A long period of very dry weather.

dy·ers (dī´ ərz) *noun*
Workers who change the color of fabric by soaking it in dye.
▲ dyer

em·bers
(em´ bərz) *noun*
Small pieces of burned wood that are still hot and glowing in the ashes of a fire. ▲ ember

embers

a	add	o͞o	took	ə =
ā	ace	o͞o	pool	a in *above*
â	care	u	up	e in *sicken*
ä	palm	û	burn	i in *possible*
e	end	yo͞o	fuse	o in *melon*
ē	equal	oi	oil	u in *circus*
i	it	ou	pout	
ī	ice	ng	ring	
o	odd	th	thin	
ō	open	th	this	
ô	order	zh	vision	

Glossary

en·gi·neer
(en´ jə nēr´) *noun*
A person who is trained to design and build machines, roads, bridges, buildings, and other structures.

e·quip·ment
(i kwip´ mənt) *noun*
The tools, machines, or supplies needed for a job or activity. My fishing *equipment* includes a rod, hooks, and bait.

ex·per·i·ment
(ik sper´ ə ment´) *verb*
To try out or test an idea to prove something. The inventor wanted to *experiment* with electricity.

ex·trac·tor
(ik strak´ tər) *noun*
A machine that pulls something out with great force. We used an *extractor* to take the water out of the wet rug.

fire·storm
(fīr´ stôrm´) *noun*
A giant fire that moves very quickly—like a storm. Firestorms are often pushed by strong winds.

fos·sils
(fos´ əlz) *noun*
The hardened remains of plants or animals that lived a long time ago. Dinosaur bones found in the earth are *fossils*. ▲ fossil

---

FACT FILE

- Scientists who study **fossils** are called paleontologists.
- The oldest known fossils are more than 2 billion years old.
- One of the biggest fossil bones ever discovered came from a huge dinosaur. The bone was over six feet long, and was dug up in Colorado in 1972.

---

frame·work
(frām´ wûrk´) *noun*
The part of a building or structure that gives it shape or holds it up.

gasped (gaspt) *verb*
Took in a quick breath of air because of a surprise or shock. She *gasped* with surprise when she received the award. ▲ gasp

gau·chos
(gou´ chōz) *noun*
Cowhands from South America who work on the pampas. ▲ gaucho

gauze (gôz) *noun*
A light, thin cloth that is often used as a bandage.

fossil

Gila monster

Gi·la mon·sters
(hē´ lə mon´ stərz) *noun*
Large, poisonous lizards that live in the southwestern part of the United States and in Mexico.
▲ Gila monster

graz·ing
(grā´ zing) *verb*
Eating grass that is growing. The cows were *grazing* in the field. ▲ graze

grum·bled
(grum´ bəld) *verb*
Complained in a grouchy way. Our soccer team *grumbled* when the game was rained out. ▲ grumble

hoists (hoists) *noun*
Machines used to raise objects. ▲ hoist

horned toads
(hôrnd´ tōdz´) *noun*
Small lizards that have horn-like spines on their heads. Horned toads are also called horned lizards. They live in the western United States.
▲ horned toad

horned toad

ich·thy·o·saur
(ik´ thē ə sôr´) *noun*
A giant reptile, now extinct, with a fishlike body and a long snout. Ichthyosaurs lived millions of years ago in the oceans.

WORD HISTORY

The word **ichthyosaur** comes from two Greek words, which together mean "fish lizard." The ichthyosaur was a kind of dinosaur that lived in water, like a fish.

---

i·de·a (ī dē´ ə) *noun*
A thought or plan you form in your mind. Getting a paper route to earn money was Juan's *idea*.

a	add	o͞o	took	ə =
ā	ace	o͞o	pool	ə in *above*
â	care	u	up	ə in *sicken*
ä	palm	û	burn	i in *possible*
e	end	yo͞o	fuse	o in *melon*
ē	equal	oi	oil	u in *circus*
i	it	ou	pout	
ī	ice	ng	ring	
o	odd	th	thin	
ō	open	ŧħ	this	
ô	order	zh	vision	

im·age (im´ ij) *noun*
Something that is seen in a mirror or a picture.

in·flam·ma·tion (in´ flə mā´ shən) *noun*
A swollen area in some part of the body that is hot, red, and sore. The splinter in her finger caused an *inflammation*.

in·for·ma·tion (in´ fər mā´ shən) *noun*
Facts and knowledge. This book has lots of *information* about monkeys.

knead·ed (nē´ did) *verb*
Mixed clay or dough with the hands by pressing and squeezing it over and over. The baker *kneaded* the bread dough for five minutes.
▲ knead

knead

knowl·edge (nol´ ij) *noun*
The things a person knows; information about a particular subject. Your *knowledge* of travel will help me plan my trip.

lab·o·ra·to·ry (lab´ rə tôr´ ē) *noun*
A room or place with equipment used to do scientific experiments. The scientist looked at plant cells under the microscope in his *laboratory*.
▲ laboratories

Thesaurus
large
huge
giant
gigantic
enormous

large (lärj) *adjective*
Very big.

las·so (las´ ō or la sōō´) *noun*
A long rope with a loop at the end used to catch cattle or horses.
▲ lassos or lassoes

lasso

FACT FILE
At any one time, there are 1,800 thunderstorms happening all over the world. That means **lightning** is striking the earth 100 times every second.

light·ning (līt´ ning) *noun*
A sudden flash of light in the sky when electricity moves between clouds or between clouds and the ground.

loom (lōōm) *noun*
A machine for weaving thread or yarn into cloth.

loom

manes (mānz) *noun*
The long thick hair that grows on the heads and necks of horses.
▲ mane

ma·sa (mä´ sä) *noun*
A Spanish word for a dough made of corn flour, shortening, and water. It is used to make tamales.

mu·ti·ny (myōō´ tə nē) *noun*
A revolt or fight against the way things are.

op·ti·cal il·lu·sions (op´ ti kəl i lōō´ zhənz) *noun* Pictures that fool the eye by making something look different than how it really is.
▲ optical illusion

orchid

or·chid (ôr´ kid) *noun* A plant with colorful flowers that grows in warm, damp places.

a	add	ōō	took	ə =	
ā	ace	ōō	pool		ə in *above*
â	care	u	up		e in *sicken*
ä	palm	û	burn		i in *possible*
e	end	yōō	fuse		o in *melon*
ē	equal	oi	oil		u in *circus*
i	it	ou	pout		
ī	ice	ng	ring		
o	odd	th	thin		
ō	open	th	this		
ô	order	zh	vision		

384

385

Glossary

pampas

pam·pas (pam´ pəz)
noun A Spanish word
for large plains with
lots of grass and few
trees. Pampas are found
in South America,
especially in Argentina.
We rode our horses
across the *pampas*.

pa·tience
(pā´ shəns) *noun*
The ability to work
quietly and steadily
without getting upset
or giving up. Alex had
the *patience* to put a
jigsaw puzzle together.

perked (pûrkt) *verb*
Became more cheerful.
The sick boy *perked* up
after he watched the
funny cartoon. ▲ perk

plas·ter (plas´ tər)
noun A soft, sticky
mixture of lime, sand,
and water that hardens
as it dries. Plaster is
often used to cover walls.

pos·si·bil·i·ties
(pos´ ə bil´ i tēz) *noun*
Things that might
happen or might be
true. The two *possibilities*
for our vacation are the
beach and the woods.
▲ possibility

pre·scrip·tion
(pri skrip´ shən) *noun*
A medical doctor's
written order for
medicine. Dr. Jenkins
wrote a *prescription* for
cough syrup to help
me get well.

prove (prōōv) *verb*
To show that
something is true.
Can you *prove* that your
answer is correct?

re·vers·es
(ri vûr´ siz) *verb*
Turns a thing
backwards, upside
down, or inside out.
When I push the red
button, the toy car
reverses and goes
backward. ▲ reverse

scal·lion
(skal´ yən) *noun*
Any onion that doesn't
have a large bulb;
a green onion.

scallions

scold·ed (skōld´ əd)
verb Told someone in
an angry way that he or
she has done something
wrong. Mom *scolded*
the dog for tracking
mud into the kitchen.
▲ scold

scratch·y
(skrach´ ē) *adjective*
Rough or harsh
sounding. Grandpa's
voice sounds *scratchy*
because he has a
bad cold.

sea·shells
(sē´ shelz´) *noun*
Shells of sea animals,
such as clams or
oysters. ▲ seashell

seashells

sense (sens) *noun*
Good judgment. I have
the good *sense* to look
both ways before I cross
a street.

ses·a·me noo·dles
(ses´ ə mē nōōd´ lz)
noun Flat, thin strips
of dough covered with
a sauce made from
sesame seeds.
▲ sesame noodle

skel·e·tons
(skel´ i tnz) *noun*
All the bones of human
or animal bodies as
they fit together.
▲ skeleton

skills (skilz) *noun*
Abilities to do things.
I practice my swimming
skills in the pool and at
the beach. ▲ skill

smoke (smōk) *noun*
The gas and tiny bits
of matter that are given
off when something
burns. The *smoke* from
our campfire made
me cough.

so·lu·tion
(sə lōō´ shən) *noun*
The answer to a
problem. Dad found a
solution to the puzzle.

soy sauce
(soi´ sôs´) *noun*
A dark, salty liquid
made from soybeans.
It is used as a flavoring
in some Asian foods.

a	add	ōō	took	ə =
ā	ace	ōō	pool	ə in *above*
â	care	u	up	ə in *sicken*
ä	palm	û	burn	i in *possible*
e	end	yōō	fuse	o in *melon*
ē	equal	oi	oil	u in *circus*
i	it	ou	pout	
ī	ice	ng	ring	
o	odd	th	thin	
ō	open	ŦH	this	
ô	order	zh	vision	

386   387

GLOS

spin·ning
(spin´ ing) *verb*
Making long, thin
pieces of fiber into yarn
or thread. The worker
is *spinning* thread from
wool. ▲ spin

spoon·ful
(spōōn´ fōōl) *noun*
The amount that
a spoon will hold.
▲ spoonfuls

spoonful

spurs (spûrz) *noun*
Pointed metal pieces
worn on the heels of
boots that are used to
poke a horse to make it
move forward. ▲ spur

stam·pedes
(stam pēdz´) *noun*
Herds of animals
moving wildly in one
direction because
something has
frightened them.
▲ stampede

steth·o·scope
(steth´ ə skōp) *noun*
An instrument used
by doctors to listen
to a person's heartbeat
or breathing.

WORD HISTORY

Stethoscope comes
from two Greek words
meaning "chest"
and "examine."
Today doctors often
use stethoscopes to
listen to, or examine,
people's chests.

su·per·struc·ture
(sōō´ pər struk´ chər)
noun The part of a
building that rises
above the basement.

ta·ma·les
(tə mä´ lēz) *noun*
Mexican food made of
chopped meat and red
peppers in a cornmeal
dough. The mixture is
wrapped in corn husks
and then cooked.
▲ tamale

stethoscope

thought (thôt) *verb*
Used your mind to
create ideas or make
decisions. I *thought* of
some questions to ask
the author.

tooth·aches
(tōōth´ āks´) *noun*
Pains in or near teeth.
▲ toothache

tamales

vol·ca·noes
(vol kā´ nōz) *noun*
Openings in the earth's
surface through which
rock, gas, and steam
erupt. ▲ volcano

volcano

FACT FILE

- There are more than
  800 active **volcanoes**
  in the world.
- The hot melted rock
  that flows out of
  erupting **volcanoes** is
  called lava.
- **Volcanoes** exist in
  the oceans as well
  as on land.

whis·pered
(hwis´ pərd or wis´ pərd)
verb Talked very quietly
or softly. I *whispered* a
secret to my best friend.
▲ whisper

weav·ers
(wē´ vərz) *noun*
Workers who make
cloth or rugs on a loom
by passing threads or
yarn over and under
in a crisscross pattern.
▲ weaver

wheel·chair
(hwēl´ châr or wēl´ châr)
noun A chair on wheels
that a sick, injured, or
disabled person uses for
moving around.

wheelchair

wis·dom
(wiz´ dəm) *noun*
Knowledge, experience,
and good judgment.
The teacher has *wisdom*
because he knows a lot.

wise (wiz) *adjective*
Having or showing
intelligence or good
judgment. The *wise*
woman knew a way to
solve the problem.

yank (yangk) *verb*
To give a sudden, strong
pull. My dog can *yank*
the leash out of my
hands when she's excited.

a add	ōō took	ə =
ā ace	ōō pool	a in *above*
â care	u up	e in *sicken*
ä palm	û burn	i in *possible*
e end	yōō fuse	o in *melon*
ē equal	oi oil	u in *circus*
i it	ou pout	
ī ice	ng ring	
o odd	th thin	
ō open	ŧh this	
ô order	zh vision	

We learn about our world through new experiences.

Additional Support

ESTABLISHING A ROUTINE

- Meet with each guided reading group several times a week. Start with two groups a day and slowly increase the number as students gain more experience working independently. While meeting with one group, the rest of the students visit the Independent Centers, complete assignments, and read independently.

- To guide students through the Independent Centers, display a pocket chart. In the pocket chart, place the names of the centers shown. Above each set of centers place a colored index card showing which groups can visit those centers that day. Be sure students are assigned to one group and know the color of their group. Each day, rotate the cards so that students visit different centers throughout the week.

CONDUCTING GUIDED READING GROUPS

Meet with at least two reading groups each day. Select a book on each group's instructional reading level from the *Scholastic Guided Reading Library* or a book in your classroom library. For more information on conducting guided reading groups, see *Scholastic Guided Reading Library*, Teacher's Guide.

SETTING UP INDEPENDENT CENTERS

While meeting with each reading group, have the rest of the class work in the Independent Centers listed below. Place the appropriate center cards in a pocket chart for student reference. Rotate the cards each day. Students may also use this time to do the following:

- revise or complete writing assignments,
- complete Practice Book pages,
- write in their Journals,
- read independently.

SAMPLE MANAGEMENT PLAN FOR CENTERS

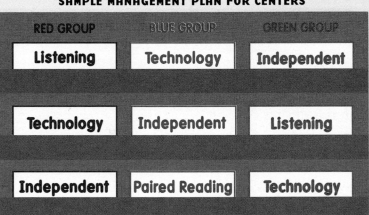

RED GROUP	BLUE GROUP	GREEN GROUP
Listening	Technology	Independent
Technology	Independent	Listening
Independent	Paired Reading	Technology

TEACHER TIP

To make the most of the Independent Centers:

- organize and clearly label each center.
- don't set up more centers than can be completed in one week.
- introduce one center at a time, and allow students time to understand it fully before introducing another center.
- be sure centers are adequately supplied with materials, but don't include more supplies than are needed.
- set up routines for using centers—days used, time allowed, number of students.

GAY SU PINNELL

INDEPENDENT CENTERS

Students can work in these centers while you meet with guided reading groups.

TECHNOLOGY

Each day, have two students from each group spend time at the computer. Have them reread *Gila Monsters Meet You at the Airport*, a **Smart Place** selection. When students are finished, they can open Smart Pages and write a paragraph summarizing the story.

INDEPENDENT READING

Choose several books for each reading group, and place them in the appropriate Browsing Box. The books can be a mix of previously read titles and ones that correspond to each group's independent reading level. Have students choose a book to read or reread independently. Afterward, ask students to write a retelling of the story in the Writing Center.

PAIRED READING

Have partners select and read a book together. Suggest that partners take turns reading the book to each other, or they can alternate reading one page at a time. Students who do not have a partner can read the selection into a tape recorder and play it back.

LISTENING

Place three stories on tape in the Listening Center. One tape should be the audiocassette version of *Gila Monsters Meet You at the Airport*. Ask students to pick one tape and follow along in the book as the story is read aloud on the tape. After listening, students can gather in a group to tell what they like about the stories they chose.

Spelling

WEEK 1 RESOURCES

SPELLING RESOURCE BOOK
- **Word Sort,** p. 9
- **Vocabulary Practice,** pp. 10-12
- **Proofread,** p. 13
- **Vocabulary Card,** p.159
- **Student Test Form,** p. 200
- **Individual Progress Chart,** p. 201
- **Class Progress Chart,** p. 202
- **Unit 1 Family Newsletter,** p. 206*

ADDITIONAL RESOURCES
- **Spelling Strategy Poster**
- **Proofreading Marks Poster**

*You may wish to send home the Unit 1 Family Newsletter.

THE SPELLING CONCEPT

weak	right
week	write

Homophones are words that sound alike but have different meanings. They have different spellings, too.

SPELLING WORDS

main	• week	side
mane	heal	sighed
• sail	heel	• road
• sale	• right	rode
• weak	• write	★ rowed

Key: • = core words
★ = exception or difficult word

SELECTION LINK

- Homophones: right
- Write the following selection words:

too   know   their
knew   right   so

Have students supply the homophone(s) for each word.

DAY 1 PRETEST/SELF-CHECK

ADMINISTER THE PRETEST

1. Walk in the **main** entrance.
2. The lion has a thick **mane**.
3. It is fun to **sail** our new boat.
4. Walking shoes are on **sale**.
5. The sick boy felt **weak**.
6. I went to camp for a **week**.
7. Medicine will **heal** my cut.
8. Only one boot needs a **heel**.
9. Turn **right** at the stop sign.
10. Please **write** me a letter.
11. The car is on a **side** street.
12. I **sighed** in relief at the test.
13. Use care to cross the **road**.
14. She **rode** the train to town.
15. We **rowed** the boat to shore.

THE SPELLING CONCEPT

- Teach the spelling concept and present the spelling words.

WORD SORT

On the chalkboard, draw the word sort chart. Ask students to sort the spelling words on the chart.

long a	long e	long i	long o
main	weak	right	road
mane	week	write	rode
sail	heal	side	rowed
sale	heel	sighed	

Have students complete **Spelling Resource Book, page 9.**

SPELLING RESOURCE BOOK p. 9

DAY 2 VOCABULARY PRACTICE

BUILD VOCABULARY: HOMOPHONES

- Review homophones. Write on the chalkboard:

  I bought a cap at the sail.

  Ask students to give the meanings of *sail* and *sale*. Help them select the spelling word that makes the sentence correct.

- Students can write sentences using other homophones on the spelling list. Tell them to remove the homophone and exchange sentences with a partner, who must insert the correct homophone.

WORD STUDY: LONG VOWEL SPELLINGS

- Write *heel* on the chalkboard. Ask students to identify the vowel sound. Call on a volunteer to underline the letters that stand for the long e. Do the same with *heal*.

- Write these homophone pairs: *rode, road; mane, main; right, write*. Have students identify the long vowel sound and the letters that stand for that sound in each pair. Challenge students to write a sentence using two homophones.

Have students complete **Spelling Resource Book, page 10, 11,** or **12.**

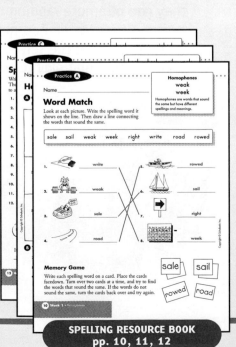

SPELLING RESOURCE BOOK pp. 10, 11, 12

DAY 3 WRITE/PROOFREAD

WRITE

- Students will write jokes and stories. They should use homophone pairs to make their jokes and stories funny. Encourage students to include spelling words as well as other words that use the spelling concept.

- Students may work together to brainstorm homophone pairs. A graphic organizer will help them record ideas.

Did What — Who — Where

Students may:

- write their stories and jokes on a word processor and illustrate them.

PROOFREAD

- Review the proofreading marks.

```
PROOFREADING
MARKS
...........
∧  Add
⊙  Add a period
⌐  Take out
○⁊  Move
≡  Capital letter
/  Small letter
¶  Indent paragraph
```

- Use the following sentence for proofreading practice:

I saw a horse with a brown ~~main~~ mane on the ~~rode~~ road⊙

Have students complete **Spelling Resource Book, page 13.**

DAY 4 STUDY/REVIEW

ALPHABETIZE

- Remind students how to find a word in the dictionary. Tell them that the words are listed in alphabetical order from **A** to **Z**.

- Write on the chalkboard:
  main   heel   sale
  week   right
  Have students focus on the first letter of each word. Then ask them to write the words in alphabetical order. *(heel, main, right, sale, week)*

TEST YOURSELF

- Review the Spelling Strategy.

- Students may work in pairs to practice for tomorrow's Posttest. One student supplies a definition or clue for the spelling word. The other writes the word. They may use the spelling word list to check each other's spelling.

- One student can use a spelling word in a sentence and challenge a partner to identify and spell a homophone for that word.

Students may use the **Student Test Form, page 200.**

DAY 5 POSTTEST/SELF-CHECK

ADMINISTER THE POSTTEST

For the Posttest, read aloud the sentences from Day 1. Have students write each spelling word.

Have students:

- self-check.

- record the results of their Posttest on the **Individual Progress Chart.**

- keep a list of their misspelled words in their spelling journals.

ASSESSMENT

Record the results of students' Posttests on the **Class Progress Chart, Spelling Resource Book, page 202.**

See **Handwriting Practice, Position, page 1.**

SPELLING RESOURCE BOOK p. 13

SPELLING RESOURCE BOOK p. 200

SPELLING RESOURCE BOOK p. 202

R5

Grammar, Usage, Mechanics

OBJECTIVES

Students will:

- **identify statements and questions.**
- **use correct word order.**
- **use correct punctuation.**
- **use statements and questions in their writing.**

RESOURCES

- **Practice Book 1,** p. 13
- **Grammar, Usage, Mechanics, Resource Book,** pp. 4–7

A **statement** is a sentence that tells something. It begins with a capital letter and ends with a period.

A **question** is a sentence that asks something. It begins with a capital letter and ends with a question mark.

MODIFY Instruction

ESL/ELD

▲ Review the correct use of capital letters, periods, and question marks in statements and questions. Demonstrate the different intonation patterns for English language learners, particularly how the voice rises at the end of yes–no questions. Then go through one or two pages of the story with students, having them identify statements and questions, read each aloud, and describe the punctuation. **(DEMONSTRATE)**

DAY 1 TEACH/MODEL

SELECTION LINK

- On the chalkboard, write the following sentence from *Gila Monsters Meet You at the Airport.*

   Out West nobody plays baseball.

   Tell students that the sentence is a statement. It tells about something. Point out that it begins with a capital letter and ends with a period.

- Write the following on the chalkboard:

   What do they play there?

   Tell students that this sentence is a question. It asks something. Point out that it begins with a capital letter and ends with a question mark.

- Write the following on the chalkboard:

   1. I want to be a subway driver.

   2. Where are they going?

   Ask students what kinds of sentences these are and how they know.

- Then write the following sentence.

   Cool in the airplane it's.

   Does the sentence make sense? Why not? Explain that word order is very important in any kind of sentence. Ask a volunteer to put the words in the correct order.

As students read:

- have them locate and list other statements.

- have them record examples of questions from **Anthology, page 18.**

DAY 2 PRACTICE

- Review the explanation of statements and questions with students. Then ask students to share some of the statements and questions they found in the story.

- Write the following sentences on the chalkboard and have students rewrite them. Remind students to begin each sentence with a capital letter and to use the correct punctuation.

   1. when will the boy move *(When will the boy move?)*

   2. the boy will make new friends *(The boy will make new friends.)*

   3. was a Gila monster at the airport *(Was a Gila monster at the airport?)*

   4. what did he see out the window *(What did he see out the window?)*

   5. the boy likes his new home *(The boy likes his new home.)*

- Ask each student to work with a partner. One student writes a question related to the story, and the other writes an answer. Then they reverse roles. Remind students to check capitalization, word order, and end punctuation.

Where is Tex going?

He's moving East.

DAY 3 PRACTICE

- Review statements and questions with students. Then remind them that word order is important in any type of sentence. Explain that word order can change the meaning of a sentence.
- Write the following on the chalkboard:

you   horse   can   ride   a

Ask students to:

1. use the words to write a statement. *(You can ride a horse.)*
2. write the words in a different order to make a question. *(Can you ride a horse?)*
3. change the word order again to write a funny question and answer. *(Can a horse ride you? A horse can ride you.)*

- Have students play "What's My Question?" Write a statement on the chalkboard and ask students to write the question that the statement answers. For example: *Cowboys wear them on their boots. (What are spurs?)* Students may continue to play "What's My Question?" in small groups.

Have students complete **Practice Book 1, page 13.**

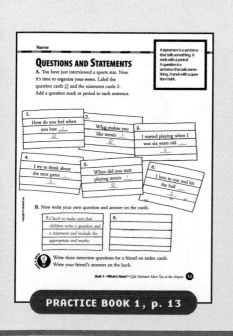

PRACTICE BOOK 1, p. 13

DAY 4 APPLY

WRITING CONNECTION

- Review statements and questions.
- Write the following words on the chalkboard:

buffaloes   airport   alligators

Ask students to choose one word and write a question that uses the word. Then have them answer the question with a statement. Remind students to begin each sentence with a capital letter and to end each sentence with the correct punctuation—a period or a question mark. Tell students to check that the word order of each sentence makes sense.

REVISE/PROOFREAD

- After students have proofread the humorous story they wrote for the Writing Workshop, have them identify two statements and any questions they may have included in their writing. Students can list them on a chart such as the one below.

My story title:_____	
Statements	Questions

DAY 5 ASSESS

- Ask students to write a question about moving. Then have them write a statement about moving.
- Write the following statement and question on the chalkboard and have students rewrite them correctly.

> many children move to a new house.
>
> Did he make new friends

(Many children move to a new house.)
(Did he make new friends?)

✓ INFORMAL ASSESSMENT OBSERVATION

Did students:

✔ identify statements and questions?

✔ use correct word order?

✔ use correct punctuation?

If students need additional support, use the **Reteach** lesson on **page R56.**

MATH

How Far West?

OBJECTIVE:
Use charts, graphs, and visual displays.

MATERIALS:
Map of the United States
Ruler

ACTIVITY

Students estimate how many miles the boy in *Gila Monsters Meet You at the Airport* traveled to reach his new home. **(VISUAL LITERACY)**

CONNECT TO THE ANTHOLOGY

The airplane that took the boy out West landed close enough to his new home for him to take a taxi from the airport. Ask students what they can tell about the boy's new town.

MAKE NEW DISCOVERIES

- Partners use the map to pick a possible location for the boy's new home. They should pick a city that is large enough to have an airport.

- They use the map scale and ruler to calculate the distance between New York City and the city they've chosen.

- Partners might try to guess the distance from New York to locations that other pairs have chosen.

✓ HOW TO ASSESS

Were students able to use the scale and a ruler to calculate the distance between points on the map?

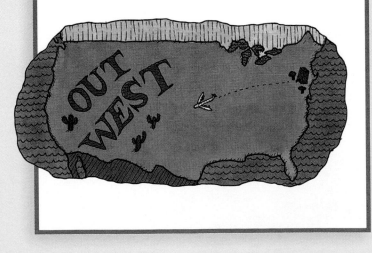

SCIENCE

Make a Western Desert

OBJECTIVE:
Use charts, graphs, and visual displays.

MATERIALS:
Modeling clay
Paper
Cardboard
Paints and paintbrushes
Markers

ACTIVITY

Students find out about the desert and build a diorama showing what lives there. **(VISUAL LITERACY)**

CONNECT TO THE ANTHOLOGY

The boy in the story thinks his new home will be in the desert, among unfamiliar animals and plants.

MAKE NEW DISCOVERIES

- Students look through the reference material to find pictures of living things from the desert.

- Each student chooses a desert animal or plant, or decides to work on the diorama background.

- Students work as a class to make the diorama. Some make forms of desert life from clay or cardboard, while others paint the background.

✓ HOW TO ASSESS

Were students able to work together to make a diorama that showed a realistic desert scene?

SOCIAL STUDIES

The Old West

OBJECTIVE:
Compare sources of information.

MATERIALS:
Paper and pencil
Reference material

ACTIVITY
Students compare the actual Old West with its "wild" reputation.

CONNECT TO THE ANTHOLOGY
The narrator believes a lot of things about today's West that aren't true. Ask students what they think the Old West was like.

MAKE NEW DISCOVERIES

• Assign each group a different aspect of Western life, based on students' responses to the question about the Old West.

• Group members research the reference material to find out facts about their subject. They write the "wild" version of the West in one column, and the true version in the second column.

• Groups combine their work in a book.

HOW TO ASSESS
Did students find factual details about the Old West and compare them with the stereotype?

THE ARTS

Make a Gila Monster Mask

OBJECTIVE:
Use charts, graphs, and visual displays.

MATERIALS:
Cardboard
Scissors
String
Paint and paintbrushes

ACTIVITY
Students use cardboard and paint to make Gila monster masks.

CONNECT TO THE ANTHOLOGY
Tell students that the Gila monster is one of only two poisonous lizards in the world. (The other is the Mexican beaded lizard.) Gila monsters are about 20 inches long.

MAKE NEW DISCOVERIES

• Students draw outlines on cardboard or posterboard, then cut out the masks.

• You may want to suggest that several students share the same paints. When they have completed the masks and the paint has dried, help students make holes where the string will be attached.

HOW TO ASSESS
Did students incorporate details from the illustrations of Gila monsters in their masks?

WEEK 2

CONDUCTING GUIDED READING GROUPS

Meet with at least two reading groups each day. Select a book on each group's instructional reading level from the *Scholastic Guided Reading Library* or a book in your classroom library. For more information on conducting guided reading groups, see *Scholastic Guided Reading Library*, Teacher's Guide.

SETTING UP INDEPENDENT CENTERS

While meeting with each reading group, have the rest of the class work in the Independent Centers listed below. Place the appropriate center cards in a pocket chart for student reference. Rotate the cards each day. Students may also use this time to do the following:

- revise or complete writing assignments,
- complete Practice Book pages,
- write in their Journals,
- read independently.

SAMPLE MANAGEMENT PLAN FOR CENTERS

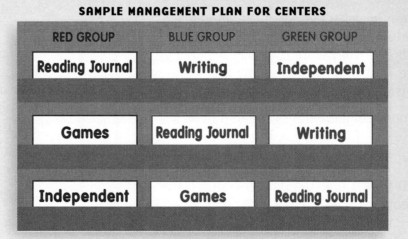

RED GROUP	BLUE GROUP	GREEN GROUP
Reading Journal	Writing	Independent
Games	Reading Journal	Writing
Independent	Games	Reading Journal

TEACHER TIP

If you choose to add other centers to the pocket chart, be sure:

- no two groups are doing the same activity simultaneously (unless there are ample materials, as in the Browsing Boxes).
- all activities involve some kind of literacy.
- quiet and noisier activities are balanced, but there are no activities that will disrupt reading groups or a student's individual work.
- there is some opportunity for students to make choices.
- there is a balance of reading and writing activities.

GAY SU PINNELL

INDEPENDENT CENTERS

Students can work in these centers while you meet with guided reading groups.

READING JOURNAL

Ask students to spend time on their reading Journals. Students should begin recording the titles of books they have read independently so far. Tell students to jot down notes about each book they list in their Journal. The notes should focus on their personal responses to the books.

WRITING

Have students spend the activity time in the Writing Center. Ask them to write a short letter to the author of one of their favorite books. Tell students to explain why they liked the book and to ask the author questions about writing stories. After students have finished writing, volunteers can read their letters to class.

GAMES

Provide several word games for students to play during the activity time. The games should be fun, instructional, and challenging. Students can play the games with a partner or in a group. Remind students to follow the rules and play fairly.

INDEPENDENT READING

Collect several books to place in the Browsing Box for each reading group. Pick books that students have read during guided reading or that match each group's independent reading level. Tell students to choose a book and read it independently. After students finish reading, they can retell the story to their partners.

Spelling

THE SPELLING CONCEPT

ind	kind
ild	child
ie	pie

The letter *i* usually has the long *i* sound in words that end in *nd* or *ld*. The letters *ie* also stand for the long *i* sound in three-letter words.

SPELLING WORDS

• find	grind	★ children
• kind	• behind	die
• mind	mild	• lie
wind	wild	pie
blind	• child	• tie

Key: • = core words
★ = exception or difficult word

SELECTION LINK

- Words with long *i*:
  behind   mind   wild
- Write these selection words on the chalkboard:
  mind   behind   wild
  thrill   itch

  Have students circle the words with the long *i* sound. *(mind, behind, wild)*

DAY 1 PRETEST/SELF-CHECK

ADMINISTER THE PRETEST

1. Did you **find** your keys?
2. I like that **kind** of cereal.
3. He changed his **mind** again.
4. I will **wind** the ball of yarn.
5. Close the window **blind**.
6. We **grind** wheat to make flour.
7. He hid **behind** the tree.
8. A **mild** cold won't last long.
9. The field is full of **wild** flowers.
10. The **child** likes her school.
11. The **children** sang a song.
12. Plants **die** without water.
13. Did the dog **lie** on the sofa?
14. Do you want a piece of **pie**?
15. She can **tie** her own shoes.

THE SPELLING CONCEPT

- Teach the spelling concept and present the spelling words.

WORD SORT

On the chalkboard, draw the word sort target. Ask students to sort the spelling words on the target.

(target diagram: ind / ild / ie)

(**ind:** *find, kind, mind, wind, blind, grind, behind;* **ild:** *mild, wild, child;* **ie:** *die, lie, pie, tie;* **Other:** *children*)

Have students complete **Spelling Resource Book, page 14.**

DAY 2 VOCABULARY PRACTICE

BUILD VOCABULARY: OPPOSITES

- Review the concept of opposites. Say *tame*, and ask students to supply a spelling word that has the opposite meaning. *(wild)*
- Continue the activity by saying these words: *adults, mean, ahead.* Students write the spelling word that is the opposite of each word.

WORD STUDY: BEGINNING CONSONANTS

- Write *kind* on the chalkboard. Ask students to identify the beginning sound. Then write *f* in place of *k*. Have students blend *f* with the rest of the word and say the new word.
- Write these sentences on the chalkboard:
  1. My uncle wears a purple p<u>ie</u>.
  2. A lion is a <u>m</u>ild animal.
  3. Do you <u>w</u>ind if I sit here?

  Ask students to replace the underlined letter with a consonant to create a spelling word that makes sense in the sentence. *(tie, wild, mind)*

Have students complete **Spelling Resource Book, page 15, 16,** or **17.**

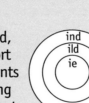

SPELLING RESOURCE BOOK p. 14

SPELLING RESOURCE BOOK p. 15, 16, 17

DAY 3 WRITE/PROOFREAD

WRITE

- Tell students that they will write a description of an imaginary animal. Students should use at least three spelling words in their descriptions.

- In class, students may brainstorm ideas with partners and list the spelling words they might use. A graphic organizer will help them record ideas.

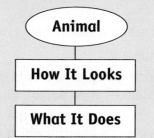

Students may:

- write their descriptions of an imaginary animal on a sheet of paper or on a word processor.

- draw their animals to illustrate their work.

PROOFREAD

- Review the proofreading marks, using the class Proofreading Chart for reference.

- Use the following sentence for proofreading practice:

We saw the ~~wilde~~ wild lion ~~li~~lie down.

Have students complete **Spelling Resource Book, page 18.**

SPELLING RESOURCE BOOK p. 18

DAY 4 STUDY/REVIEW

ALPHABETIZE

- Remind students that there are many words in the dictionary that begin with the same letter. Words with the same first letter are alphabetized by their second letter.

- Write these words on the chalkboard and ask students to alphabetize them.

car	*bat*
wind	*behind*
blind	*blind*
when	*car*
behind	*children*
bat	*when*
children	*wind*

TEST YOURSELF

- Review the Spelling Strategy.

- Students may work in pairs to practice for tomorrow's Posttest. One student says a spelling word and the other writes it.

- Suggest that students use each spelling word in a sentence.

Students may use the **Student Test Form, page 200.**

SPELLING RESOURCE BOOK p. 200

DAY 5 POSTTEST/SELF-CHECK

ADMINISTER THE POSTTEST

For the Posttest, read aloud the sentences from Day 1. Have students write each spelling word.

Have students:

- self-check.

- record the results of their Posttest on the **Individual Progress Chart.**

- keep a list of their misspelled words in their spelling journals.

ASSESSMENT

Record the results of students' Posttests on the **Class Progress Chart, Spelling Resource Book, page 202.**

See **Handwriting Practice, Cursive Basic Strokes, page 2.**

SPELLING RESOURCE BOOK p. 202

Grammar, Usage, Mechanics

OBJECTIVE

Students will:

- identify commands and exclamations.
- correctly punctuate commands and exclamations
- use commands and exclamations in their writing.

RESOURCES

- **Practice Book 1**, p. 25
- **Grammar, Usage, Mechanics, Resource Book,** pp. 8–11

An **exclamation** is a sentence that shows strong feeling. It ends with an exclamation point.

A **command** is a sentence that gives an order. It ends with a period.

MODIFY Instruction

ESL/ELD

▲ After students have an understanding of the difference between statements, commands, and exclamations, encourage them to come to the chalkboard to participate in the daily practice activities. Stress intonation patterns for English language learners, having them read aloud each completed item. Have them work with fluent peer partners to create commands and exclamations in the Day 4 Apply activity. **(WORK IN PAIRS)**

DAY 1 TEACH/MODEL

SELECTION LINK

- Write the following sentence about *Ramona Forever* on the chalkboard.

  This is the world's cutest baby!

  Tell students that this sentence is an exclamation. It shows strong feeling. It ends with an exclamation mark.

  Remind students that the first word of a sentence begins with a capital letter.

- Then write the following:

  Wait for us downstairs.

  Tell students that this sentence is a command. It gives an order. A command ends with a period.

- Point out that both groups of words are sentences because each one tells a complete thought.

- Tell students that a group of words such as "The world's cutest baby" is not a sentence because it does not tell a complete thought.

- Ask students to find an exclamation on **Anthology page 29** and a command on **Anthology page 31**.

As students read, have them:

- write down other examples of exclamations.
- keep a list of commands in the story.

DAY 2 PRACTICE

- Review with students that a sentence is a group of words that tells a complete thought, that an exclamation shows strong feeling and ends with an exclamation mark, and that a command gives an order and ends with a period.

- Ask students to share the exclamations and commands they found in the selection.

  Then write the following:

  1. **Reached the lobby quickly.**
  2. **She sat on a couch in the lobby.**

  Ask students:

  > **Which group of words is a sentence? How do you know?**

- Then have students read the following and identify which are sentences.

  1. **Ramona and Beezus cleaned the house.** *(sentence)*
  2. **Looked so serious.** *(not a sentence)*
  3. **Her mother and baby Roberta.** *(not a sentence)*
  4. **She buckled her seat belt.** *(sentence)*
  5. **Mrs. Quimby waved to the girls.** *(sentence)*

  Ask students to make the groups of words that aren't sentences into complete thoughts by adding words.

- Then ask students to read the following and identify which is an exclamation and which is a command.

  This book is great! *(exclamation)*

  Read this book. *(command)*

DAY 3 PRACTICE

- Review with students that an exclamation is a sentence that shows strong feeling and ends with an exclamation mark. A command is a sentence that gives an order and ends with a period.

- Write the following:
  1. **That was the best movie!**
     (exclamation)
  2. **Tell me about the movie.**
     (command)

  Have volunteers identify the exclamation and the command.

- Write the following. Have students write each sentence correctly and tell whether it is a command or an exclamation.
  1. **this story is great** *(This story is great! exclamation)*
  2. **open your book to page 10** *(Open your book to page 10. command)*
  3. **we love Ramona Quimby** *(We love Ramona Quimby! exclamation)*
  4. **feed the cat.** *(Feed the cat. command)*

- Have each student write a command and an exclamation. Then have students exchange papers and tell what kind of sentence each is.

Have students complete **Practice Book 1, page 25.**

Name

EXCLAMATIONS AND COMMANDS

Read each of the sentences below. If the sentence is an exclamation, add an exclamation point at the end. If the sentence is a command, add a period. Circle the *C* if the sentence is a command. Circle the *E* if it is an exclamation.

An exclamation is a sentence that shows strong feelings. It ends with an exclamation point. A command is a sentence that gives an order. It ends with a period.

1. I can't wait to go to the zoo __!__   C Ⓔ
2. Don't go near the fence ____   Ⓒ E
3. Take a picture of the giraffe ____   Ⓒ E
4. Look at the baby elephant ____   C Ⓔ
5. What fun this is __!__   C Ⓔ
6. Tell me about the tiger ____   Ⓒ E
7. The lion's roar is so loud ____   C Ⓔ
8. Show me where the snakes are ____   Ⓒ E
9. Wow, the gorilla is so big __!__   C Ⓔ
10. The zoo is really great __!__   C Ⓔ

Write a command that tells what you should not do at the zoo.
Write an exclamation that tells how you feel about going to the zoo.

Unit 1 • What's New? • *Ramona Forever* **23**

PRACTICE BOOK 1, p. 25

DAY 4 APPLY

WRITING CONNECTION

- Review exclamations and commands with students.

- Write the commands and exclamations below on index cards. Ask volunteers to say and dramatize each sentence. Have the rest of the class tell whether each sentence is an exclamation or a command. Ask what punctuation goes at the end of each.
  1. Sit down on the couch.
  2. I'm so excited!
  3. Hold the baby.
  4. Feed the baby.
  5. Gosh, I'm sick!

- Have partners write two other exclamations and commands. Remind them to begin each sentence with a capital letter and to use the correct punctuation at the end. Remind students to check that they have written sentences that are complete thoughts.

REVISE/PROOFREAD

- After students have proofread the descriptions that they wrote for the Writing Workshop, have them list any commands and exclamations that they included. Students can list their sentences on a chart like the one below. Help them correct any incomplete sentences.

Commands	Exclamations

DAY 5 ASSESS

- Ask students to write two complete sentences about a baby. One sentence should be an exclamation and show strong feeling. The other should be a command and give an order.

- Write the following two sentences on the chalkboard. Ask students to rewrite them correctly.

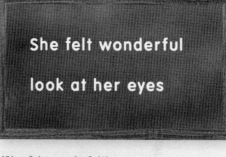

She felt wonderful

look at her eyes

(She felt wonderful!)
(Look at her eyes.)

✓ INFORMAL ASSESSMENT
OBSERVATION

Did students:

✔ write complete sentences?

✔ begin each sentence with a capital letter?

✔ use an exclamation mark to end an exclamation?

✔ use a period to end a command?

If students need additonal support, use the **Reteach** lesson on **page R56.**

MATH

Graph Growth

OBJECTIVE:
Use charts, graphs, and visual displays.

MATERIALS:
Grid paper
Pencil

ACTIVITY
Students use a table of average heights to graph the heights of Roberta and Ramona in *Ramona Forever*.
(VISUAL LITERACY)

CONNECT TO THE ANTHOLOGY

In *Ramona Forever*, Ramona is a nine-year-old girl who has a newborn baby sister, Roberta.

MAKE NEW DISCOVERIES

• Write the following average heights for American girls on the chalkboard. Stress that these are averages, and aren't meant to be ideal.

Birth	20 inches
3 years	36 inches
6 years	45 inches
9 years	52 inches

• Have students make bar graphs showing the height for each age. Ask them if a child grows at the same rate throughout its life.

✔ HOW TO ASSESS
Were children able to transfer the data into a bar graph and interpret the graph?

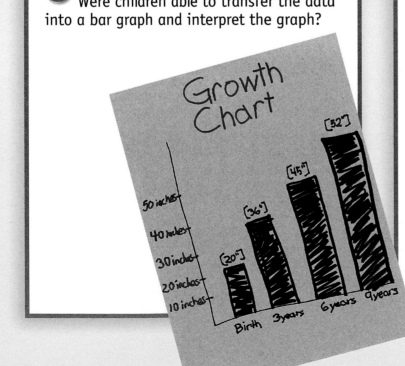

SCIENCE

A Growing List of Skills

OBJECTIVE:
Sort information.

MATERIALS:
None

ACTIVITY
Students make a chart showing the ages at which children learn or master new skills.

CONNECT TO THE ANTHOLOGY

On **Anthology page 72**, Ramona realizes that she used to be a baby, and that she has learned a lot since then.

MAKE NEW DISCOVERIES

• Draw columns or rows on the chalkboard and label them with the ages 0 through 9 years.

• For each age, ask for volunteers who have firsthand knowledge of a child who is that age. Ask them to name new skills that child has learned or mastered. For example, in its first year, a child learns to smile and crawl.

• Complete the chart, and ask students if they think Ramona is right when she says being a baby is hard work.

✔ HOW TO ASSESS
Were students able to categorize new skills and to sort the information by age?

SOCIAL STUDIES

Old Enough

OBJECTIVE:
Find problems that need solutions.

MATERIALS:
Paper
Pencils

ACTIVITY
Students make a case for having a specific right that at present they are denied due to their age.

CONNECT TO THE ANTHOLOGY
Ramona isn't allowed in the maternity ward because she is under 12 years of age. Ask students if they can think of any things they are denied because of their age.

MAKE NEW DISCOVERIES
- Groups discuss things they aren't allowed to do because of their age, such as voting, driving, and sitting on a jury.

- They pick one right they think they should have, and list their reasons.

- Each group presents its case to the rest of the class. Other class members may argue against the case and provide their reasons for doing so.

HOW TO ASSESS
Did students present reasonable justification for being given a right they don't presently have?

THE ARTS

Life Collage

OBJECTIVE:
Use charts, graphs, and visual displays.

MATERIALS:
Unwanted magazines
Paper
Markers
Glue
Posterboard
Scissors

ACTIVITY
Students make collages showing their favorite activities or major events in their lives.

CONNECT TO THE ANTHOLOGY
Ramona remembers a lot of things that have happened to her since she was a baby, and she's old enough to have her own likes and dislikes.

MAKE NEW DISCOVERIES
- Tell students that their collages can show either their favorite activities or events that have been important in their lives.

- Students browse through the magazines, and choose pictures they can use. They can also draw and cut out their own pictures.

- Students arrange and glue the images to make their collages.

HOW TO ASSESS
Did students choose or draw images that they felt represented favorite activities or events in their lives?

ASSESSMENT

Select two students in each reading group to observe. Keep anecdotal records on each student's reading performance. Consider the following questions:

✔ **What cues does the student use to figure out words and make meaning while reading?**

✔ **How well does the student retell the story?**

✔ **What sound-spellings or high-frequency words are causing the student difficulty?**

When completed, add the anecdotal records to the student's literacy folder for future use when grading or conferencing.

CONDUCTING GUIDED READING GROUPS

Meet with at least two reading groups each day. Select a book on each group's instructional reading level from the *Scholastic Guided Reading Library* or a book in your classroom library. For more information on conducting guided reading groups, see *Scholastic Guided Reading Library*, Teacher's Guide.

SETTING UP INDEPENDENT CENTERS

While meeting with each reading group, have the rest of the class work in the Independent Centers listed below. Place the appropriate center cards in a pocket chart for student reference. Rotate the cards each day. Students may also use this time to do the following:

• revise or complete writing assignments,

• complete Practice Book pages,

• write in their Journals,

• read independently.

SAMPLE MANAGEMENT PLAN FOR CENTERS

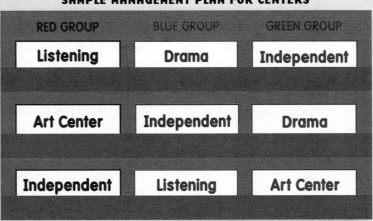

RED GROUP	BLUE GROUP	GREEN GROUP
Listening	Drama	Independent
Art Center	Independent	Drama
Independent	Listening	Art Center

TEACHER TIP

To make sure that the Independent Centers continue to meet the students' needs,

• monitor each center for a few moments as often as you can.

• confirm that students are following the correct routines and using each area independently.

• verify that each center has materials that encourage students to work independently.

• reorganize materials and prepare new labels for the centers on a regular basis.

• check that all equipment, such as computers, audiotape systems, and the overhead projector, is in proper working order.

GAY SU PINNELL

INDEPENDENT CENTERS

Students can work in these centers while you meet with guided reading groups.

LISTENING

Place three stories, including the audiocassette version of *How My Family Lives in America*, on tape in the Listening Center. Ask students to select one story and follow along in the book as it is read aloud on the tape. To close the activity, have students write a short paragraph about their favorite part of the story.

DRAMA

Have students work together to produce a play based on *How My Family Lives in America* or another story they have recently read. Students can make a set with props and create costumes for their play. If possible, schedule time for students to perform their dramatic version of the story for the class.

INDEPENDENT READING

Have students choose a book from the Browsing Box for their reading group. The books can be titles the students have read during guided reading or ones that correspond to their independent reading level. Ask students to read or reread the books independently. Afterward, each student can go to the Writing Center and write a brief retelling of the book.

ART CENTER

Ask students to draw a picture about their own lives in America. Have students depict a typical scene at home, in school, or at play. Their artwork can spotlight playing with friends, a favorite pastime, or anything they enjoy doing. When students are finished, have them write captions describing their drawings.

Spelling

WEEK 3 RESOURCES

SPELLING RESOURCE BOOK
- Word Sort, p. 19
- Vocabulary Practice, pp. 20–22
- Proofread, p. 23
- Vocabulary Card, p.160
- Student Test Form, p. 200
- Individual Progress Chart, p. 201
- Class Progress Chart, p. 202

ADDITIONAL RESOURCES
- Spelling Strategy Poster
- Proofreading Marks Poster

THE SPELLING CONCEPT

a	across	alike
be	become	beside

Many words have two syllables. Words that begin with **a-** or **be-** are often followed by a word or a group of letters you already know.

SPELLING WORDS

•about	•agree	become
•above	alike	belong
•across	alive	•below
★again	alone	beside
ago	•along	•between

Key: • = core words
★ = exception or difficult word

SELECTION LINK

- Words with **a-** and **be-**:

  about   ago   because

  across   adults   before

- Write the selection words above on the chalkboard. Have pairs of students create sentences with a blank for a selection word. Then partners exchange sentences and supply the missing word.

DAY 1 PRETEST/SELF-CHECK

ADMINISTER THE PRETEST
1. We heard **about** the library.
2. A picture is **above** the table.
3. He skated **across** the lake.
4. Come visit our school **again**.
5. Dinosaurs lived long **ago**.
6. We **agree** to return soon.
7. The twins look exactly **alike**.
8. Keep plants **alive** with water.
9. I want to be left **alone**.
10. Come **along** to the play.
11. Will you **become** a hiker?
12. We **belong** to a singing club.
13. Rabbits sleep **below** ground.
14. I sat **beside** my friend.
15. We camped **between** trees.

THE SPELLING CONCEPT
- Teach the spelling concept and present the spelling words.

WORD SORT

On the chalkboard, draw the word sort chart. Ask students to sort the spelling words on the chart.

a-		be-
about	agree	become
above	alike	belong
across	alive	below
again	alone	beside
ago	along	between

Have students complete **Spelling Resource Book, page 19.**

SPELLING RESOURCE BOOK p. 19

DAY 2 VOCABULARY PRACTICE

BUILD VOCABULARY: SYNONYMS

- Remind students that synonyms are words that mean the same thing, or almost the same thing. Have students write a spelling word that means "next to." (*beside*) Then have them write spelling words that are synonyms for *similar, past, under.* (*alike, ago, below*)

- Have small groups play a word game by writing synonyms for spelling words on cards and challenging the other students to name the spelling words.

WORD STUDY: PRESENT-TENSE VERBS

- Remind students that a present-tense verb must agree with its subject. In the third person, verbs often end in *-s*. Have students write a sentence using these verbs: *agree, belong, become.*

- Write these sentences:

  1. That book _____ to me.
  2. The caterpillar _____ a butterfly.
  3. She _____ that it's a funny book.

  Ask students to use the verbs from above to fill in the blanks.

Have students complete **Spelling Resource Book, page 20, 21,** or **22.**

SPELLING RESOURCE BOOK pp. 20, 21, 22

DAY 3 WRITE/PROOFREAD

WRITE

- Tell students that they will write and design a travel brochure. Students should use at least two spelling words in their brochures.

- In class, students may brainstorm ideas with partners and list the spelling words they might use. A graphic organizer will help them record ideas.

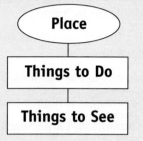

Students may:

- write their travel brochures on a sheet of paper or on a word processor.

- illustrate their brochures and write captions.

PROOFREAD

- Review the proofreading marks, using the class Proofreading Chart for reference.

- Use the following sentence for proofreading practice:

  He always sings beautifully.

Have students complete **Spelling Resource Book, page 23.**

DAY 4 STUDY/REVIEW

ALPHABETIZE

- Remind students that if the first letters of words to be alphabetized are the same, students will need to look at the second letters. If the second letters are the same, students must look at the third letters.

- Write these groups of words on the chalkboard and ask students to alphabetize the words.

beside	*belong*
between	*beside*
belong	*between*

TEST YOURSELF

- Review the Spelling Strategy.

- Ask students to create mnemonic devices to help them remember the spelling of words with *a-* and *be-*. For example, *I see you agree.*

- Students may use the spelling words in sentences and challenge another student to identify and spell the words.

Students may use the **Student Test Form, page 200.**

DAY 5 POSTTEST/SELF-CHECK

ADMINISTER THE POSTTEST

For the Posttest, read aloud the sentences from Day 1. Have students write each spelling word.

Have students:

- self-check.

- record the results of their Posttest on the **Individual Progress Chart.**

- keep a list of their misspelled words in their spelling journals.

ASSESSMENT

Record the results of students' Posttests on the **Class Progress Chart, Spelling Resource Book, page 202.**

See **Handwriting Practice, page 3** for practice writing cursive *e.*

SPELLING RESOURCE BOOK p. 23

SPELLING RESOURCE BOOK p. 200

SPELLING RESOURCE BOOK p. 202

Grammar, Usage, Mechanics

OBJECTIVES

Students will:

- identify common and proper nouns.
- capitalize proper nouns.
- use common and proper nouns in their writing.

RESOURCES

- **Practice Book 1,** p. 37
- **Grammar, Usage, Mechanics, Resource Book,** pp. 12–15

A **common noun** names any person, place, or thing.

A **proper noun** names a particular person, place, or thing. A proper noun begins with a capital letter.

MODIFY Instruction

ESL/ELD

▲ To prepare for classroom work on nouns, ask students to brainstorm their own examples of common nouns. List their ideas on the chalkboard. Do the same for proper nouns. Ask leading questions to elicit these nouns, drawing on familiar vocabulary. **(BRAINSTORM)**

DAY 1 TEACH/MODEL

SELECTION LINK

- On the chalkboard, write the following sentence from *How My Family Lives in America*.

  While we eat our pizza, we play a game to test our wits.

  Ask students to identify the nouns in this sentence. *(pizza, game, wits)* Remind them that a noun names a person, place, or thing. Point out that these are all common nouns. They do not name any particular person, place, or thing.

- Then write the following on the chalkboard:

  My name in America is April.

  Ask students to identify the common noun in this sentence. *(name)* Then ask them to identify the proper nouns. *(America, April)* Point out that a proper noun names a particular person, place, or thing and begins with a capital letter.

- Write the following:

  1. My parents were born in (Taiwan.)
  2. In (July) we will go to (China.)
  3. (Julius) and (April) play (Tangram.)

  Ask students to identify the proper nouns in these sentences. What particular kinds of things do these proper nouns name? Ask volunteers to substitute other proper nouns in each sentence.

As students read:

- have them identify common nouns that name people, places, and things.

- have them list examples of proper nouns that name specific people, places, and things.

DAY 2 PRACTICE

- Review with students that common noun names any person, place or thing. A proper noun names a particular person, place, or thing. Ask students to share some of the common and proper nouns they found in the story.

- Write the following sentences on the chalkboard.

  1. The title of the book is <u>How My Family Lives in</u> (America)
  2. (April's) family celebrates the (Chinese) New Year.
  3. Her family speaks (Chinese.)
  4. On (Saturday,) (April) goes to school.
  5. (Dr. Chang) from (China) teaches at the school.

Ask students to copy each sentence and then circle the proper nouns. Remind them that all proper nouns are capitalized. However, every capitalized word is not necessarily a proper noun. Point out that some titles of people, such as *Dr.* and *Mr.*, are abbreviations. They start with a capital letter and end with a period.

- On the chalkboard, make a list of the proper nouns that students circled. Then ask students to identify the kinds of people, places, or things that the nouns name. Challenge them to add another example of a proper noun for each category.

Proper Noun	What It Names	Another Example
April's	(person)	Beezus
Chinese New Year	(holiday)	Thanksgiving
Chinese	(language)	English
Saturday	(calendar word)	Tuesday
Dr. Chang	(person with title)	Mrs. Lau
China, America	(country)	Brazil

DAY 3 PRACTICE

- Review common and proper nouns with students. Remind them that proper nouns include holidays, languages, calendar words, the titles of people, and countries.
- Write the following sentences on the chalkboard. Ask students to fill in the blanks with proper nouns from *How My Family Lives in America* and "Kids Speak Up to Save Native Languages."

  1. **April speaks _____ .** *(Chinese or Mandarin)*

  2. **David Drake speaks _____ .** *(Hupa)*

  3. **April's story was written by _____ .** *(Susan Kuklin)*

  4. **April's family is from_____.** *(Taiwan)*

  5. **The Navajo reservation is in _____ .** *(Tuba City, Arizona)*

- Explain that there is a comma between the name of a city and a state. Write the following sentences on the chalkboard. Ask students to insert a comma between the city and the state.

  1. **My uncle lives in Dallas, Texas.**

  2. **Do you like to visit Orlando, Florida?**

  3. **I had fun in San Diego, California!**

Have students complete **Practice Book 1, page 37.**

PRACTICE BOOK 1, p. 37

DAY 4 APPLY

WRITING CONNECTION

- Review common and proper nouns with students.
- Write the following categories on the chalkboard: *holidays, important buildings, languages, countries, names and their titles,* and *cities and states.*

  Give students five minutes to write proper nouns under each category. Then create a class chart of proper nouns for each category. Challenge students to write a paragraph that includes at least five proper nouns from the list. Remind them to capitalize the proper nouns and to insert a comma between a city and a state.

REVISE/PROOFREAD

- After students have proofread the factual description that they wrote for the Writing Workshop, have them identify the common and proper nouns they used. Students can list the nouns on a chart such as the one below.

	Common Nouns	Proper Nouns
People		
Places		
Things		

DAY 5 ASSESS

- Ask students to write two sentences about a game that they play with their family. In one sentence they should use only common nouns. In the second sentence they should use at least three proper nouns.
- Write the following sentences on the chalkboard. Have students rewrite them correctly.

> april speaks chinese at school on saturday.
>
> The native languages of north America have been studied by dr. clay slate.

(April speaks Chinese at school on Saturday.)

(The native languages of North America have been studied by Dr. Clay Slate.)

✓ INFORMAL ASSESSMENT
OBSERVATION

Did students:

✔ identify common and proper nouns?

✔ capitalize proper nouns?

✔ use common and proper nouns in their writing?

If students need additonal support, use the **Reteach** lesson on **page R57.**

MATH

A Chinese Puzzle

OBJECTIVE:
Brainstorm multiple approaches.

MATERIALS:
Enlarged copies of tangram below
Scissors

ACTIVITY
Students use tangram pieces to make different shapes.

CONNECT TO THE ANTHOLOGY
Draw students' attention to the description of the tangram on **Anthology page 56.** Point out that a variety of shapes can be made using the tangram pieces.

MAKE NEW DISCOVERIES

• Students carefully cut out the seven tangram pieces from their copies.

• They arrange the pieces to form as many identifiable shapes as they can, then choose their favorites. Point out that all seven pieces must be used for each shape.

• Students share their favorite tangram shapes with the class.

✓ HOW TO ASSESS
Were students able to arrange the tangram pieces to make identifiable images?

SCIENCE

Classify a Chinese Recipe

OBJECTIVE:
Classify information.

MATERIALS:
Paper and pencil
Enlarged copies of food pyramid below

ACTIVITY
Students use the food pyramid to classify the ingredients for the recipe in *How My Family Lives in America.*

CONNECT TO THE ANTHOLOGY
Have students refer to **Anthology page 57** to read the sesame noodles recipe.

MAKE NEW DISCOVERIES

• Partners use copies of the food pyramid.

• They classify each ingredient into a category. If necessary, they can discuss the assignment with other pairs. For example, some students may not know that noodles are made from grains.

• Ask students to use the food pyramid to plan a balanced meal that includes cold sesame noodles.

✓ HOW TO ASSESS
Were students able to classify the recipe ingredients and make a balanced meal?

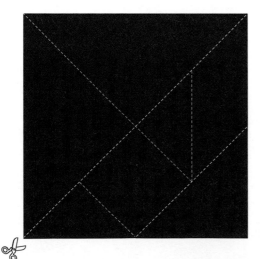

SOCIAL STUDIES

Find a Route to China

OBJECTIVE:
Use charts, graphs, and visual displays.

MATERIALS:
World map
Pencil

ACTIVITY
Students trace the route that Marco Polo took when he traveled to China.

CONNECT TO THE ANTHOLOGY
Tell students that Marco Polo brought back ideas that were new to Europe, such as paper money, burning coal, printing, the postal system, and the magnetic compass.

MAKE NEW DISCOVERIES

• Tell students that Marco Polo started his journey from Venice, Italy. From there he sailed to Israel, then traveled through Iran and Pakistan. He then went to Beijing, China.

• Partners find the locations on the world map, and trace possible routes that Marco Polo might have taken.

✓ HOW TO ASSESS
Did students locate places on the map and trace possible routes connecting the locations?

THE ARTS

Chinese Writing

OBJECTIVE:
Use charts, graphs, and visual displays.

MATERIALS:
Examples of Chinese calligraphy that represent greetings
Paper
Markers

ACTIVITY
Students use calligraphy to make a greeting card for a friend.

CONNECT TO THE ANTHOLOGY
On Saturdays, April goes to Chinese school. One of the skills she learns there is calligraphy.

MAKE NEW DISCOVERIES

• Show students the examples of Chinese calligraphy, and tell them what each character stands for.

• Students choose characters, such as the ones below, to use on the cover of a greeting card.

• They fold a sheet of paper in half, then cut and paste the calligraphy onto the front. Inside the card, they can write a personal message. They may also want to translate the calligraphy.

✓ HOW TO ASSESS
Did students understand the meanings of the characters they chose, and use them in a greeting card?

發財
WEALTH

健康
HEALTH

ASSESSMENT

Select two students in each reading group to observe. Keep anecdotal records on each student's reading performance. Consider the following questions:

✔ **What cues does the student use to figure out words and make meaning while reading?**

✔ **How well does the student retell the story?**

✔ **What sound-spellings or high-frequency words are causing the student difficulty?**

When completed, add the anecdotal records to the student's literacy folder for future use when grading or conferencing.

CONDUCTING GUIDED READING GROUPS

Meet with at least two reading groups each day. Select a book on each group's instructional reading level from the *Scholastic Guided Reading Library* or a book in your classroom library. For more information on conducting guided reading groups, see *Scholastic Guided Reading Library*, Teacher's Guide.

SETTING UP INDEPENDENT CENTERS

While meeting with each reading group, have the rest of the class work in the Independent Centers listed below. Place the appropriate center cards in a pocket chart for student reference. Rotate the cards each day. Students may also use this time to do the following:

• revise or complete writing assignments,

• complete Practice Book pages,

• write in their Journals,

• read independently.

SAMPLE MANAGEMENT PLAN FOR CENTERS

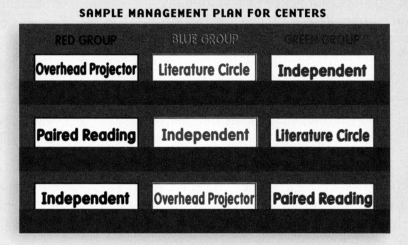

RED GROUP	BLUE GROUP	GREEN GROUP
Overhead Projector	Literature Circle	Independent
Paired Reading	Independent	Literature Circle
Independent	Overhead Projector	Paired Reading

TEACHER TIP

During the guided reading session, have students read softly to themselves. As they read, do the following:

• listen to students.

• pay attention to problem-solving strategies students use to figure out words and make meaning from the text.

• help students with decoding difficulties when necessary.

• jot down notes regarding the strategies each student uses.

Note that guided reading is not "round robin" reading. All students read the entire story.

GAY SU PINNELL

INDEPENDENT CENTERS

Students can work in these centers while you meet with guided reading groups.

LITERATURE CIRCLE

Have three to five students form a discussion group in which they talk about books they have just read independently. Students should have the books with them and be prepared to discuss interesting characters, story lines, and any personal connections they have with the stories. Encourage students to ask questions and to develop their ability to think analytically about literature.

PAIRED READING

Ask pairs of students to choose a book to read together. Suggest that partners take turns reading the book to each other, or they can alternate reading one page at a time. After they finish reading their selection, partners can discuss their favorite parts of the story.

OVERHEAD PROJECTOR

Select several poems and stories, including examples of students' writing, and reproduce them on plastic transparencies. Safely secure the overhead projector in front of a white paper screen, and have a small group of students project and take turns reading the selections aloud.

INDEPENDENT READING

Select several books for each reading group and place them in the appropriate Browsing Box. The books can be ones that the students have read during guided reading, or they might be titles you have identified as suitable for each group's independent reading level. Tell students to pick a book and read or reread it independently. Afterward, students can gather in a small group and talk about the books they read.

Spelling

WEEK 4 RESOURCES Ⓑ

SPELLING RESOURCE BOOK
- **Word Sort,** p. 24
- **Vocabulary Practice,** pp. 25–27
- **Proofread,** p. 28
- **Vocabulary Card,** p. 160
- **Student Test Form,** p. 200
- **Individual Progress Chart,** p. 201
- **Class Progress Chart,** p. 202

ADDITIONAL RESOURCES
- **Spelling Strategy Poster**
- **Proofreading Marks Poster**

THE SPELLING CONCEPT

ng	strong	string
nk	wink	blink

Some consonant sounds are spelled with more than one letter. The last sound in **strong** and **string** is spelled **ng**. The last sound in **wink** and **blink** is spelled **nk**.

SPELLING WORDS

- ring
- rang
- rung
- string
- strong
- long
- spring
- thing
- ★finger
- wink
- drink
- blink
- think
- thank
- bunk

Key: • = core words
★ = exception or difficult word

SELECTION LINK

- Write the following selection words on the chalkboard.

  things   younger   morning

  bring   drank   something

  Have students say aloud each word and listen for /ng/ or /nk/. Then ask students to write a sentence that uses two words from this list.

DAY 1 PRETEST/SELF-CHECK

ADMINISTER THE PRETEST

1. My aunt heard the phone **ring**.
2. The doorbell **rang** loudly.
3. She had **rung** the bell.
4. He tied the box with **string**.
5. The wind was **strong**.
6. I took a **long** walk.
7. My favorite season is **spring**.
8. What is that **thing** over there?
9. Point your **finger** to show me.
10. Learn how to **wink** your eye.
11. I need a **drink** of water.
12. Try not to **blink** your eyes.
13. Can you **think** of an answer?
14. He wanted to **thank** them.
15. Sleep on the top **bunk** bed.

THE SPELLING CONCEPT

- Teach the spelling concept and present the spelling words.

WORD SORT

On the chalkboard, draw the word sort chart. Ask students to sort the spelling words on the chart.

__ng	__ng__	__nk
ring	finger	wink
rang		drink
rung		blink
string		think
strong		thank
long		bunk
spring		
thing		

Have students complete **Spelling Resource Book, page 24.**

DAY 2 VOCABULARY PRACTICE

BUILD VOCABULARY: RHYMES

- Remind students that rhyming words have the same ending sounds. Say *wink* and ask students to identify a spelling word that rhymes with it. *(blink)*

- Have students make a "mini" rhyming dictionary, listing the spelling words that rhyme and adding as many other rhyming words as they can.

WORD STUDY: PLURALS

- Write *thing* and *things* on the chalkboard. Ask students to identify the word that means more than one item. Point out that an *s* added to a noun usually makes the word plural.

- Write on the chalkboard:

  1. I have one _____.

  2. You have two _____.

  Ask students to complete the first sentence using as many spelling words as they can. Then have them write the corresponding plurals in the second sentence.

Have students complete **Spelling Resource Book, page 25, 26,** or **27.**

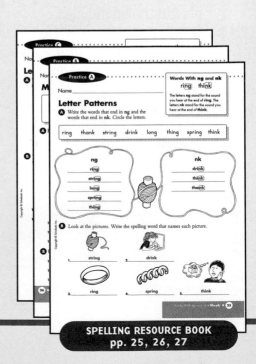

DAY 3 | WRITE/PROOFREAD

WRITE

- Tell students that they will write a conversation between two friends. Students should use at least three spelling words in their conversations.

- In class, students might dramatize their conversations to create dialogue before they begin to write. A graphic organizer will help them record ideas.

Speaker 1	Speaker 2

Students may:

- write their conversations as part of a play on a separate paper or on a word processor.

- add cartoon drawings to the conversations.

PROOFREAD

- Review the proofreading marks, using the class Proofreading Chart for reference.

- Use the following sentence for proofreading practice:

think
Do you ~~thingk~~ you can find the two rings
~~ring~~ ℓ ⑦

Have students complete **Spelling Resource Book, page 28.**

DAY 4 | STUDY/REVIEW

GUIDE WORDS

- Explain that guide words help students find entry words in a dictionary. Guide words appear at the top of each dictionary page with these guide words. The word on the left is the first word on the page and the word on the right is the last word.

- Write this pair of guide words on the chalkboard:

blink   can't

Have students find the spelling word that would appear on the dictionary page with these guide words. *(bunk)* Ask students to do the same for the guide words: **spend•store; lawn•march;** and **rather•rung.** *(spring; long; ring)*

TEST YOURSELF

- Review the Spelling Strategy.

- Students may play a spelling game to practice the spelling words for tomorrow's Posttest. Working in pairs, one student will say the letters *nk* or *ng*. The other student will spell a word with that ending.

- Suggest that students use the words in sentences.

Students may use the **Student Test Form, page 200.**

DAY 5 | POSTTEST/SELF-CHECK

ADMINISTER THE POSTTEST

For the Posttest, read aloud the sentences from Day 1. Have students write each spelling word.

Have students:

- self-check.

- record the results of their Posttest on the **Individual Progress Chart.**

- keep a list of their misspelled words in their spelling journals.

ASSESSMENT

Record the results of students' Posttests on the **Class Progress Chart, Spelling Resource Book, page 202.**

See **Handwriting Practice, page 4** for practice writing cursive *h.*

SPELLING RESOURCE BOOK p. 28

SPELLING RESOURCE BOOK p. 200

SPELLING RESOURCE BOOK p. 202

Grammar, Usage, Mechanics

OBJECTIVES

Students will:
- identify singular and plural nouns.
- form singular and plural nouns.
- use singular and plural nouns in their writing.

RESOURCES
- **Practice Book 1,** p. 49
- **Grammar, Usage, Mechanics, Resource Book,** pp. 16–19

- A **singular noun** names one person, place, or thing.
- A **plural noun** names more than one person, place, or thing. Add -s to form the plural of most nouns.

MODIFY Instruction

ESL/ELD

▲ Make sure English language learners understand the concept of adding **–s** or **–es** to form plurals. Create a chart similar to the one described for Day 1, that consists only of familiar vocabulary. Go over the rule about when to add **–es**, offering a number of examples from daily experience before looking for examples in the story. Guide children to listen for the ending sound of a word and use it as a clue in choosing the correct plural ending. **(AUDITORY CLUES)**

DAY 1 TEACH/MODEL

- On the chalkboard, write this sentence from *On the Pampas*.

  The ranch was called La Carlota, and the gates were made of iron bars from a fort that had been on that very spot a hundred years before.

  Tell students that the sentence contains both singular and plural nouns. A singular noun names one person, place, or thing. A plural noun names more than one person, place, or thing. Have students identify the singular nouns *(ranch, La Carlotta, fort, spot)* and the plural nouns *(gates, bars, years)*.

- Write the following sentence:

  We would brush their coats, trim their hooves, and braid their manes and tails.

  Ask students to name the plural nouns in the sentence. Write them onto a chart such as the one below. Then ask students to fill in the singular form of each plural.

PLURAL	SINGULAR
coats	coat
hooves	hoof
manes	mane
tails	tail

  Ask students to identify which word forms its plural by not simply adding -s. *(hooves)*

  As students read:
- have them identify singular and plural nouns.
- have them list any examples of irregular plurals.

DAY 2 PRACTICE

- Review with students singular and plural nouns. Ask students to share some examples of plurals that they found in the story.
- Write the following sentences on the chalkboard.

  1. Many <u>families</u> came to the <u>parties</u>.
  2. They sat on <u>benches</u> and ate <u>dishes</u> of delicious <u>food</u>.
  3. The <u>girls</u> wore long <u>dresses</u>.
  4. There were <u>boxes</u> filled with sweet <u>treats</u>.
  5. Even the <u>calves</u> joined in when we sang <u>songs</u>.

  Ask volunteers to underline the plural nouns in the sentences.

- Share with students these additional rules for forming plurals.

  Add *-es* to form the plural of nouns that end in *ss, x, ch,* or *sh*.

  If a noun ends in a consonant and *y*, change the *y* to *i* and add *-es* to form the plural.

  If a noun ends in *f*, change the *f* to a *v* and add *-es*.

  Assign students to work with a partner and brainstorm at least ten words that follow the above rules for plurals. Write a class list on the chalkboard. Examples may include: *boxes, branches, bosses, halves, foxes, lunches, classes, hooves, taxes, wishes, glasses, faxes, brushes, guesses.*

  Then have student pairs write two sentences using plurals from the list. Remind them to punctuate their sentences correctly.

DAY 3 PRACTICE

- Review singular and plural nouns with students. Ask how most nouns form their plurals. Then remind them that some plurals follow special rules.
- Write the following riddles on the chalkboard. Ask a volunteer to fill in the correct plural noun.

    1. **We are the tricky animals in many folk tales. We are ____.** *(foxes)*
    2. **We sit on people's arms and tell time. We are ____.** *(watches)*
    3. **Our mothers are cows. We are ____.** *(calves)*
    4. **We can help you to see better. We are ____.** *(glasses)*
    5. **We are small horses. We are ____.** *(ponies)*

- Point out to students that some plural nouns don't follow any rules. They have to be memorized. Examples are *tooth/teeth, mouse/mice, child/children, man/men, foot/feet.*
- Ask students to write riddles for irregular plural nouns, including nouns that change spelling to form the plural.

Have students complete **Practice Book 1, page 49.**

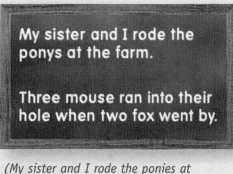

PRACTICE BOOK 1, p. 49

DAY 4 APPLY

WRITING CONNECTION

- Review the different ways plural nouns may be formed. Also review irregular plurals.
- Write the following pairs of words on the chalkboard.

foot	feet
man	men
child	children
mouse	mice
woman	women
goose	geese
tooth	teeth

Ask students to choose one set of words to write about in a short paragraph of three to four sentences. Remind them to use the singular word to name one person, place, or thing and the plural word to name more than one person, place, or thing.

REVISE/PROOFREAD

- After students have proofread the brochures they wrote for the Writing Workshop, have them identify at least three plural nouns that they used. Have them write the plural nouns and their singular forms on a chart such as the one below.

MY BROCHURE	
Singular Nouns	Plural Nouns

DAY 5 ASSESS

- Ask students to write two sentences about what they might see if they visited the pampas. In the first sentence they should use a plural noun that is formed by adding -*s*. In the second sentence they should use an irregular plural noun.
- Write the following sentences on the chalkboard and have students correct the errors.

> My sister and I rode the ponys at the farm.
>
> Three mouse ran into their hole when two fox went by.

(My sister and I rode the ponies at the farm.)

(Three mice ran into their hole when two foxes went by.)

✅ INFORMAL ASSESSMENT
OBSERVATION

Did students:

✔ identify singular and plural nouns?

✔ correctly form singular and plural nouns?

✔ use singular and plural nouns in their writing?

If students need additonal support, use the **Reteach** lesson on **page R57.**

MATH

How Big Is Argentina?

OBJECTIVE:
Make a plan.

MATERIALS:
Western Hemisphere map
Scissors
Ruler
Pencil and paper

ACTIVITY
Students use a map to compare the areas of the United States and Argentina.

CONNECT TO THE ANTHOLOGY
Have students look at the map on **Anthology page 80.** Ask them how much bigger or smaller than the United States they think Argentina might be.

MAKE NEW DISCOVERIES

• Tell partners that they can trace the maps, and use scissors and rulers or other methods to compare the areas of the two countries.

• Have partners compare their answers with those of the rest of the class. (They should find that the United States is about three times larger than Argentina.)

✓ HOW TO ASSESS
Were students able to make plans to compare areas and follow their plans to reach reasonable solutions?

SCIENCE

Stars in Argentina

OBJECTIVE:
Collect data.

MATERIALS:
Constellation maps of the night sky as seen from the Northern and Southern hemispheres
Paper and pencil

ACTIVITY
Students discover the difference in the night sky as seen from the Northern and Southern hemispheres.
(VISUAL LITERACY)

CONNECT TO THE ANTHOLOGY
On **Anthology page 77,** Salguero shows the narrator how to find the Southern Cross. Ask students if they think they could see the Southern Cross from their town.

MAKE NEW DISCOVERIES

• Show students both maps. Tell them that Argentina is in the Southern Hemisphere.

• Have students try to find the Southern Cross. Point out that it's also called *Crux*.

• Ask students to compare the two maps. Do any constellations appear on both?

✓ HOW TO ASSESS
Could students find the Southern Cross, and notice the differences between the two maps?

SOCIAL STUDIES

Find Other Pampas

OBJECTIVE: Interpret information.

MATERIALS: Topographical world map Paper and pencil

ACTIVITY
Students use a topographical world map to find other regions with geography similar to the Argentine pampas.

CONNECT TO THE ANTHOLOGY
Have students look at **Anthology page 66**, and ask them what the main feature of the pampas is.

MAKE NEW DISCOVERIES
- Show students how the colors on the topographical map represent height above sea level. Ask them what it means if there is a large area of a single color.

- Groups look at the map and note areas they think are flat, and whether the areas are higher or lower than the pampas.

- Ask groups which of the areas might be suitable for raising cattle. *(those that aren't too far north or south)*

☑ HOW TO ASSESS
Were students able to interpret the topographical map and find areas that are relatively flat?

THE ARTS

Dance the Zamba

OBJECTIVE: Interpret information.

MATERIALS: Scarves or handkerchiefs Music

ACTIVITY
Students learn the steps to an Argentine dance.

CONNECT TO THE ANTHOLOGY
At the party in *On the Pampas*, everybody danced the *zamba*.

MAKE NEW DISCOVERIES
- Tell students that the *zamba* is danced by couples. The two people don't touch. Each carries a scarf or handkerchief, often stretched between both hands.

- Partners face each other, hold their scarves up in the air, and move slowly in a circle.

- They each make their own circle, move forward toward each other, and then backward away from each other.

- Dancers can embellish the dance with gestures and fancy steps.

☑ HOW TO ASSESS
Were students able to follow the basic steps and add their own touches and interpretations of the dance?

CONDUCTING GUIDED READING GROUPS

Meet with at least two reading groups each day. Select a book on each group's instructional reading level from the *Scholastic Guided Reading Library* or a book in your classroom library. For more information on conducting guided reading groups, see *Scholastic Guided Reading Library*, Teacher's Guide.

SETTING UP INDEPENDENT CENTERS

While meeting with each reading group, have the rest of the class work in the Independent Centers listed below. Place the appropriate center cards in a pocket chart for student reference. Rotate the cards each day. Students may also use this time to do the following:

- revise or complete writing assignments,
- complete Practice Book pages,
- write in their Journals,
- read independently.

ASSESSMENT

Select two students in each reading group to observe. Keep anecdotal records on each student's reading performance. Consider the following questions:

✔ What cues does the student use to figure out words and make meaning while reading?

✔ How well does the student retell the story?

✔ What sound-spellings or high-frequency words are causing the student difficulty?

When completed, add the anecdotal records to the student's literacy folder for future use when grading or conferencing.

SAMPLE MANAGEMENT PLAN FOR CENTERS

RED GROUP	BLUE GROUP	GREEN GROUP
Writing	Poem Box	Independent
Listening	Independent	Poem Box
Independent	Writing	Listening

TEACHER TIP

To evaluate the effectiveness of your guided reading sessions, ask yourself:

- Are my students' learning needs being met?
- Are students using previously taught reading strategies?
- Are students able to read progressively more complex stories?
- Do students enjoy reading?
- Do students have opportunities to problem-solve while reading?
- Do students use what they know to figure out what they don't know when reading?

GAY SU PINNELL

INDEPENDENT CENTERS

Students can work in these centers while you meet with guided reading groups.

INDEPENDENT READING

Place several books for each reading group in the appropriate Browsing Box. The books can be a combination of titles read during guided reading and ones that correspond to each group's independent reading level. Have students choose a book to read or reread independently. Afterward, students can go to the Writing Center and write a brief book report to share with their classmates.

WRITING

Have students spend the activity time in the Writing Center. Ask students to write a short personal narrative about an experience in which they learned an important lesson. Tell students to describe the event and explain how and what they learned. Afterward, volunteers can share their narratives with the class.

POEM BOX

Collect poems for the class poem box. The poems can be ones that you have read together in class or new ones that match the students' reading abilities. You can paste copies of the poems on tagboard. Have students gather in a small group and take turns reading a poem aloud. When they finish reading, they can discuss which poem they like best.

LISTENING

Place three stories on tape in the Listening Center. One of the tapes should be the audiocassette version of *How the World Got Wisdom*. Have students pick one tape and follow along in the book as the story is read aloud on the tape. After listening, students can gather in a group to retell the story in their own words.

Spelling

WEEK 5 RESOURCES

SPELLING RESOURCE BOOK
- **Word Sort,** p. 29
- **Vocabulary Practice,** pp. 30–32
- **Proofread,** p. 33
- **Vocabulary Card,** p. 160
- **Student Test Form,** p. 200
- **Individual Progress Chart,** p. 201
- **Class Progress Chart,** p. 202

ADDITIONAL RESOURCES
- **Spelling Strategy Poster**
- **Proofreading Marks Poster**

THE SPELLING CONCEPT
saw   fault   wash

The letters *aw, au,* and *a* can stand for the vowel sound in **saw**.

SPELLING WORDS

• saw	lawn	haul
paw	yawn	• fault
• draw	crawl	• because
straw	• awful	• water
dawn	★ aunt	• wash

Key: • = core words
★ = exception or difficult word

SELECTION LINK
- Words with *aw, au*:

  saw   because

  Write the above words plus these selection words:

  gauze   always

  tallest   all

  Have students circle the letters that make the vowel sound /ô/. Then have them find a spelling word that has the same pattern.

DAY 1 | PRETEST/SELF-CHECK

ADMINISTER THE PRETEST
1. I **saw** a great movie today.
2. The dog's **paw** was wet.
3. It's fun to **draw** a picture.
4. Sip the soda with a **straw**.
5. I saw the sun rise at **dawn**.
6. They just mowed their **lawn**.
7. When I'm tired, I **yawn**.
8. The baby can **crawl**.
9. Drills make an **awful** noise.
10. Meet my uncle and **aunt**.
11. Use a truck to **haul** trash.
12. It's not my **fault**.
13. He's sad **because** he's sick.
14. The fish need fresh **water**.
15. Please **wash** your clothes.

THE SPELLING CONCEPT
- Teach the spelling concept and present the spelling words.

WORD SORT

On the chalkboard, draw the word sort chart. Ask students to sort the spelling words on the chart.

Dawn's words	Paul's words	Other words
saw, paw draw, straw dawn, lawn yawn, crawl awful	aunt, haul fault because	water, wash

Have students complete **Spelling Resource Book, page 29.**

SPELLING RESOURCE BOOK p. 29

DAY 2 | VOCABULARY PRACTICE

BUILD VOCABULARY: NOUNS AND VERBS
- Review what nouns and verbs are. Tell students that some words can be a noun or a verb depending on how they are used.
- Write on the chalkboard:

  1. Sam cut wood with a <u>saw</u>.

  2. Sam <u>saw</u> a bird in the nest.

  Explain that *saw* is a noun in the first sentence and a verb in the second. Have students write two sentences for each of the following spelling words: *wash, crawl, water.* In one sentence, students should use the word as a noun; in the other sentence, as a verb.

WORD STUDY: WORD MEANING
- Read these clues and have students write the spelling word that goes with each one:
  1. **move very slowly** (*crawl*)
  2. **make a picture** (*draw*)
  3. **a grassy place** (*lawn*)
- Students can work in pairs to write clues for other spelling words on flash cards and identify the word that goes with each clue.

Have students complete **Spelling Resource Book, page 30, 31,** or **32.**

SPELLING RESOURCE BOOK pp. 30, 31, 32

DAY 3 WRITE/PROOFREAD

WRITE

- Tell students that they will write a journal entry about something they have done. Students should use at least three spelling words in their entries.

- In class, students may brainstorm ideas and make a list of spelling words they might use. A graphic organizer will help them record ideas.

What	Who	When

Students may:

- write their journal entry on a separate sheet of paper or on a word processor.

- illustrate their journal entry to highlight an important part of the event.

PROOFREAD

- Review the proofreading marks, using the class Proofreading Chart for reference.

- Use the following sentence for proofreading practice:

 aunt
Today my ~~ant~~ showed me how to
 crawl
swim the ~~crawl~~.

Have students complete **Spelling Resource Book, page 33.**

DAY 4 STUDY/REVIEW

ENTRY WORD

- Remind students that the entry word in a dictionary is the word in dark type before the definition. Discuss the parts of a dictionary entry: the pronunciation, the part of speech, and the definition.

- Write the following entry words on the chalkboard and ask students to identify the parts of each entry. Then have students use the words in sentences and identify the meaning in context.

 lawn (lôn) **noun** A piece of ground planted with grass.

 wash (wôsh) **verb** To clean with water or other liquid. **noun** Things that are being cleaned.

TEST YOURSELF

- Review the Spelling Strategy.

- Students may work in pairs to practice for tomorrow's Posttest. One student provides a meaning and the other student identifies and spells the word, using the spelling word list to check the spelling.

- Students may create sentences and challenge other students to supply the missing spelling word.

Students may use the **Student Test Form, page 200.**

DAY 5 POSTTEST/SELF-CHECK

ADMINISTER THE POSTTEST

For the Posttest, read aloud the sentences from Day 1. Have students write each spelling word.

Have students:

- self-check.

- record the results of their Posttest on the **Individual Progress Chart.**

- keep a list of their misspelled words in their spelling journals.

ASSESSMENT

Record the results of students' Posttests on the **Class Progress Chart, Spelling Resource Book, page 202.**

See **Handwriting Practice, pages 5-6** for practice writing cursive *l, b,* and *p.*

SPELLING RESOURCE BOOK p. 33

SPELLING RESOURCE BOOK p. 200

SPELLING RESOURCE BOOK p. 202

Grammar, Usage, Mechanics

OBJECTIVES

Students will:

- **identify and use singular and plural pronouns.**
- **identify and use subject and object pronouns.**

RESOURCES

- **Practice Book 1,** p. 62
- **Grammar, Usage, Mechanics, Resource Book,** pp. 20–23

A **singular pronoun** takes the place of a noun that names one person, place, or thing.

A **plural pronoun** takes the place of a noun that names more than one person, place, or thing.

ESL/ELD

▲ **Follow up on the Day 3 Practice activity to help English language learners work with singular and plural pronouns. Make up sentence strips for the sentences on the board, along with a set of pronoun cards. Have students read each sentence, choose the pronoun card that replaces the noun or nouns, and place the card over the sentence strip. Create similar sentences based on the characters in this story. (USE SENTENCE STRIPS)**

DAY 1 | TEACH/MODEL

SELECTION LINK

- On the chalkboard, write the following sentence from *How the World Got Wisdom*.

  He put his two top legs around the trunk of the tree as far as they would reach.

  Point out that *he* and *they* are pronouns. Pronouns are words that take the place of nouns. A singular pronoun takes the place of a noun that names one person, place, or thing. A plural pronoun takes the place of a noun that names more than one person, place, or thing.

  Explain that *he* is a singular pronoun taking the place of the word *Spider*. *They* is a plural pronoun taking the place of the word *legs*.

- Write the following sentences:

  1. He picked up the pot of wisdom.
  2. They called out to Spider.

  Explain that *he* and *they* are subject pronouns, which replace nouns in the subject of a sentence.

  The words *I, you, he, she, it, we,* and *they* are subject pronouns. The pronoun *I* is always capitalized.

- Write the following:

  1. Spider had eight legs. (They) were long. *(legs; plural)*

  2. The pot was huge. (It) had a tight lid. *(pot; singular)*

  Have volunteers circle each pronoun and tell which noun it replaces. Ask if the pronoun is singular or plural.

  As students read:

  - have them locate subject pronouns.

  - have them label each subject pronoun as *singular* or *plural*.

DAY 2 | PRACTICE

- Review with students that a subject pronoun takes the place of a noun or nouns as the subject of a sentence. *I, you, she, he,* and *it* are singular subject pronouns. *We, you,* and *they* are plural subject pronouns. The pronoun *I* is always capitalized. Ask students to share some of the subject pronouns they found in the story.

- Write the following sentences on the chalkboard.

  1. Spider took all the wisdom. The wisdom belonged to (him).

  2. The other animals came along. Then the wisdom belonged to (them).

  Point out that pronouns can take the place of words in the predicate of a sentence. These pronouns are called object pronouns. The words *me, you, him, her, it, us,* and *them* are object pronouns. Ask volunteers to circle the object pronouns in the sentences above.

- Write the list of object pronouns on the chalkboard. Then read the following sentence:

  Bibi gave the apples to _____.

  Ask students to take turns completing it with a different pronoun. Discuss how the meaning of the sentence changes each time.

  > Bibi gave the apples to him.

  > Bibi gave the apples to them.

DAY 3 PRACTICE

- Review subject and object pronouns. Explain that, in some cases, one pronoun can take the place of two or more nouns in a sentence.
- Write the following sentences on the chalkboard. Ask students to rewrite each sentence, using a pronoun in the place of the underlined noun or nouns.

  1. <u>Spider</u> fell down. *(He)*
  2. <u>Kuma</u> and <u>Spider</u> were wise. *(They)*
  3. I read about <u>Spider</u> and <u>Kuma</u>. *(them)*
  4. The <u>woman</u> picked up some wisdom. *(She)*
  5. Spider threw the <u>pot</u> on the ground. *(it)*

- Divide the class into two groups: the subject pronouns and the object pronouns. Ask students from each group to work as partners to create sentences together. One will write the subject part of the sentence using a subject pronoun. The other will complete the sentence using an object pronoun in the predicate.

Have students complete **Practice Book 1, page 62.**

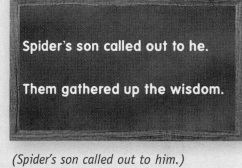

PRACTICE BOOK 1, p. 62

DAY 4 APPLY

WRITING CONNECTION

- Review subject and object pronouns.
- Write the following words on the chalkboard:

he	she	they	I	we	it
him	her	them	me	us	

Ask students to write a paragraph about a spider using four of the pronouns above. They can write about a real spider that they have seen or the character of Spider from the story. Remind students to check that it is clear what noun each pronoun is replacing. Tell them to be sure to capitalize the pronoun *I*.

REVISE/PROOFREAD

- After students have proofread the character sketch that they wrote for the Writing Workshop, have them identify any pronouns they used. Suggest that they list them on a chart such as the one below.

	Singular	Plural
Subject Pronoun		
Object Pronoun		

DAY 5 ASSESS

- Ask students to write two sentences about when they have been wise. The first sentence should contain a subject pronoun. The second sentence should contain an object pronoun.
- Write the sentences on the chalkboard and have students rewrite them correctly.

> Spider's son called out to he.
>
> Them gathered up the wisdom.

(Spider's son called out to him.)
(They gathered up the wisdom.)

⊘ INFORMAL ASSESSMENT
OBSERVATION

Did students:

✔ identify singular and plural pronouns?

✔ identify subject and object pronouns?

✔ correctly use subject and object pronouns in their writing?

✔ capitalize the pronoun *I*?

If students need additonal support, use the **Reteach** lesson on **page R57.**

MATH

Graph Favorite Folk Tales

OBJECTIVE:
Use charts, graphs, and visual displays.

MATERIALS:
Paper and pencil

ACTIVITY
Students graph the results of a survey of classmates' favorite types of folk tales.

CONNECT TO THE ANTHOLOGY
Review with students that *How the World Got Wisdom* is a special kind of folk tale that explains how something came to be. It is also an example of a Spider tale. Remind students that Spider—also called Anansi—is a popular character in West African folk tales.

MAKE NEW DISCOVERIES

• Brainstorm with students the different types of folk tales they have read. List these on the chalkboard as they are offered; for example: Spider tales, "The Three Little Pigs," Cinderella stories, how something came to be.

• Have small groups of students copy the list and survey classmates to determine their favorites. They should make a checkmark next to the type of folk tale for each student who prefers that type.

• Have students make a pictograph of the results of the survey. You may have to give them some assistance.

✅ HOW TO ASSESS
Were students able to show the results of the survey in a pictograph?

SCIENCE

Compare Characters' Characteristics

OBJECTIVE:
Make observations.

MATERIALS:
Encyclopedia
Nature books
Paper and pencil

ACTIVITY
Students compare the qualities of a spider, a hare, and a tortoise.

CONNECT TO THE ANTHOLOGY
Ask students to look at the illustration on **Anthology pages 94-95.** Point out that a tortoise, a hare, and a spider are three very different types of animals.

MAKE NEW DISCOVERIES

• Have students use reference sources to gather information about these three animals—for example, the number of legs each has, body covering, type of animal (reptile, mammal, arachnid), and so on.

• Have students use the information to create charts comparing the three types of animals. They can present their charts and discuss the animals' characteristics.

✅ HOW TO ASSESS
Were students able to articulate differences among the animals?

SOCIAL STUDIES

Jobs That Spread Wisdom

OBJECTIVE: Collect data.

MATERIALS: Paper and pencil

ACTIVITY
Students interview people to gather information about jobs that spread wisdom.

CONNECT TO THE ANTHOLOGY
Point out that in the story, wisdom was spread throughout the world when Spider smashed the pot. Ask students how they think wisdom is really spread throughout the world.

MAKE NEW DISCOVERIES

• Partners or small groups brainstorm a list of people who spread wisdom through their jobs—such as a teacher, writer, or librarian—or who might be a source of information about how wisdom is spread— such as a parent.

• Students list questions they might ask one or more of these people to find out how they or others spread wisdom.

• Students conduct their interviews in school or at home.

• Have students write a brief job description for their interview subjects.

✓ HOW TO ASSESS
Did students' job descriptions include how wisdom is spread?

THE ARTS

Make a Spider Design

OBJECTIVES: Use diagrams and illustrations.

MATERIALS: Paper and markers

ACTIVITY
Students create a design for a T-shirt that incorporates a spider or its web.

CONNECT TO THE ANTHOLOGY
Talk about the illustrations of Spider and the spider and web design on the walking stick. Point out the design on the border of the story. *What other objects have spider decorations?*

MAKE NEW DISCOVERIES

• Have students think about T-shirt designs they can create using a spider or its web.

• Students draw the outline of a T-shirt on a piece of drawing paper. They draw their spider design on the outline.

✓ HOW TO ASSESS
Did students create an original and imaginative design?

Teacher Resources

TEACHER RESOURCES

PHONICS: HOMOPHONES

OBJECTIVE

- Students review their understanding of homophones.

MATERIALS

- Anthology, pp. 12–21

SUGGESTED GROUPING

- Small groups

SKILLS TRACE

Homophones **TESTED**
- Introduce, p. T20
- Practice, pp. T31, T42, T47, T51
- Review, p. R43
- Reteach, p. R52

❶ REVIEW

Review with students that homophones are words that sound the same but are spelled differently and have different meanings. Write *for* and *four* on the chalkboard, and use each in a sentence.

> **When you read, how do you figure out the meaning of a homophone?**

Remind students that good readers use clues from the text as well as clues from pictures and other illustrations to help them understand what a word means.

❷ PRACTICE/APPLY

PUT IT IN CONTEXT Have students work in small groups to look for homophones in *Gila Monsters Meet You at the Airport* and figure out their meaning using context clues. Ask them to use a chart like the one below to record the information. Words they find will include *new, to, here, too, they're, there, you, right, wear, horse, know, be, or, so, wear, flower, brakes, see, hey, our.*

HOMOPHONES	CONTEXT CLUES	MEANING
here	stay	place
brakes	cars, screeching	stops a car
wear	chops, spurs	puts on

❸ ASSESS

DID STUDENTS:

✔ identify words that sound the same but have different meanings and spellings?

✔ use pictures and other text clues to figure out the meanings of homophones?

IF NOT, TRY THIS:

See the **Reteach** lesson on **page R52.**

STUDENT'S SELF-ASSESSMENT:

✔ Can I use story and picture clues to help me figure out the meaning of a word that sounds the same as another word?

PHONICS: VOWEL /ī/ *i, igh, y, i-e, ie*

OBJECTIVE

- Students review their knowledge of vowel /ī/.

MATERIALS

- Anthology, pp. 28–41

SUGGESTED GROUPING

- Whole class

SKILLS TRACE

Vowel /ī/, *i,*   **TESTED**
igh, y, i-e, ie

- Introduce, p. T64
- Practice, pp. T75, T87, T91, T95
- Review, p. T44
- Reteach p. R52

❶ REVIEW

Remind students that several letter combinations can stand for /ī/ as in **nine**. Write **f<u>i</u>nd, l<u>igh</u>t, fl<u>y</u>, n<u>i</u>c<u>e</u>,** and **p<u>ie</u>** on the chalkboard. As you say each word aloud, underline the letters that stand for long *i*.

> **What other words do you know that have the long *i* sound you hear in *find* and *fly*?**

Write the words students name on the chalkboard, grouping them by spelling under the example words.

❷ PRACTICE/APPLY

PUT IT IN CONTEXT Ask students to look back at *Ramona Forever* for words with vowel /ī/ spelled *i, igh, y, i-e*. Help them group the words they find on a chart like the one below.

i (find)	igh (light)	y (fly)	i-e (nice)
climbed	right	cry	time
behind	might	by	like
	nights		white
			insides
			fine
			excitement

Have students brainstorm an additional list of words with vowel /ī/ spelled *ie*. For example: **tie, flies, lie.**

❸ ASSESS

DID STUDENTS:

✔ identify words with long *i*?

✔ connect vowel /ī/ *i* with the letters that stand for this sound, *i, igh, y, i-e, ie*?

IF NOT, TRY THIS:

See the **Reteach** lesson on **page R52.**

STUDENT'S SELF-ASSESSMENT:

✔ Did I identify words with vowel /ī/ and the letters that stand for it?

PHONICS: WORDS WITH /ə/

OBJECTIVE
- Students review their knowledge of schwa /ə/.

MATERIALS
- Anthology, pp. 50–57

SUGGESTED GROUPING
- Whole class

SKILLS TRACE

Words With Schwa /ə/ **TESTED**
- Introduce, p. T114
- Practice, pp. T125, T133, T137, T141
- Review, p. R45
- Reteach, p. R53

① REVIEW

Remind students that schwa /ə/ appears in unstressed syllables. If the unstressed syllable is at the beginning of the word, the word usually begins with the letter a. Write **about, apart,** and **across** on the chalkboard. Say each word. Have students repeat the word and listen for the /ə/ at the beginning of each word.

② PRACTICE/APPLY

PUT IT IN CONTEXT Have students read Anthology page 52. Then write the words *Mandarin, another, parents, different,* and *bottom* on the chalkboard. Read each word emphasizing the schwa /ə/ for *e, a,* and *o.* Then write the words *pencil, dinosaur, protect,* and *circus.* Say each word, and point out the *i, o,* and *u* spellings for schwa /ə/. Help students record all the words on a word map similar to the one below.

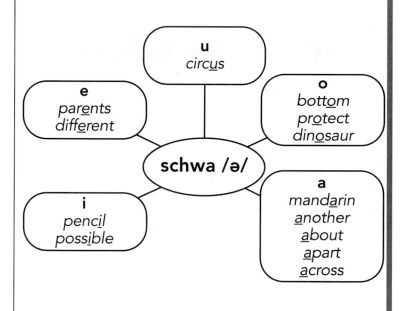

③ ASSESS

DID STUDENTS:
✔ identify words with schwa?

✔ connect schwa /ə/ with the letters that stand for this sound?

IF NOT, TRY THIS:
See the **Reteach** lesson on **page R53.**

STUDENT'S SELF-ASSESSMENT:
✔ Did I identify words with schwa /ə/ and the letters that stand for this sound?

STUDY SKILLS: ALPHABETICAL ORDER

OBJECTIVE

- Students review their knowledge of alphabetical order.

MATERIALS

- Anthology, pp. 50–57
- Telephone directories, yellow pages
- Nonfiction books with indexes

SUGGESTED GROUPING

- Small groups

SKILLS TRACE

Alphabetical Order **TESTED**

- Introduce, p. T138
- Practice, p. T139
- Review, p. R46
- Reteach, p. R53

① REVIEW

Remind students that alphabetical order is ABC order. Explain that knowing and using alphabetical order can help them easily find information in dictionaries and glossaries, encyclopedias, telephone books, and indexes.

Write *noodle, checkers, letter, mark, special, brush, Mandarin, chopsticks* on the chalkboard. Review how to alphabetize words to the third letter. Use *pan, pane, panda, panther, pang, pansy* to review alphabetizing to the fourth letter.

② PRACTICE/APPLY

PUT IT IN CONTEXT Have students use their Anthology, telephone directories, and non-fiction book indexes to locate information. They could look for vocabulary words *orchid, calligraphy, chaps, contagious, chickenpox, stampedes* in their Anthology glossary and names of specific stores and museums under their categories in the yellow pages. Have them locate specific information in the nonfiction books and encyclopedia volumes that you have displayed.

③ ASSESS

DID STUDENTS:

✔ alphabetize words to the third and fourth letters?

✔ use alphabetical order to locate information?

IF NOT, TRY THIS:

See the **Reteach** lesson on **page R53.**

STUDENT'S SELF-ASSESSMENT:

✔ Did I use alphabetical order to organize words in a list and to find information?

SYLLABICATION: ONE-, TWO-, THREE-SYLLABLE WORDS

OBJECTIVE

- Students review their knowledge of syllabication.

MATERIALS

- Anthology, pp. 64–81

SUGGESTED GROUPING

- Partners

SKILLS TRACE

One-, Two-, and Three-Syllable Words **TESTED**

- **Introduce,** p. T154
- **Practice,** pp. T165, T182, T187, T191
- **Review,** p. R47
- **Reteach,** p. R54

① REVIEW

Remind students that every syllable, or word part, has just one vowel sound. Explain that to figure out how many syllables a word has, students should listen to how many vowel sounds they hear. Point out that being able to identify the number of syllables in a word can help them read new words.

Say **my, summer,** and **grandmother** and have students identify the number of syllables in each word. Then write the words on the chalkboard. Ask students to name other words with one, two, and three syllables. Group them with the example words.

② PRACTICE/APPLY

PUT IT IN CONTEXT Have students work in pairs to identify other one-, two-, and three-syllable words from *On the Pampas.* Encourage them to find at least six examples of each and to use a chart like the one below to list the words they find. Suggest that students say the words softly to help identify the number of vowel sounds they hear.

ONE SYLLABLE	TWO SYLLABLES	THREE SYLLABLES
big	country	family
lived	brother	grandfather
ranch	iron	everything
gates	shimmy	thundering

③ ASSESS

DID STUDENTS:

✔ identify the number of vowel sounds they hear in a word?

✔ connect the number of vowel sounds in a word to the number of syllables the word has?

IF NOT, TRY THIS:

See the **Reteach** lesson on **page R54.**

STUDENT'S SELF-ASSESSMENT:

✔ Did I identify the number of vowel sounds in a word to figure out how many syllables the word has?

LITERARY ELEMENT: CHARACTER

OBJECTIVE

- Students apply their knowledge of character to a new text.

MATERIALS

- Anthology, pp. 64–81
- Practice Book 1, p. 45

SUGGESTED GROUPING

- Partners

SKILLS TRACE

Character **TESTED**
- **Introduce**, p. T84
- **Practice**, pp. T69, T86, T94
- **Review**, p. R48
- **Reteach**, p. R54

① REVIEW

Ask students to think about how the narrator of *On the Pampas* acted during her visit to her grandparents' ranch.

> **Were you surprised by the way she behaved when Susanita and the cowhands tried to teach her everything they knew?**

Remind students that characters, like people, have different personality traits, such as being shy, friendly, or adventurous. Have students look for clues to what the narrator in *On the Pampas* is like. To do this, they should think about how she behaved at the ranch and how she responded to experiences that were new for her.

PRACTICE BOOK 1, p. 45

② PRACTICE/APPLY

PUT IT IN CONTEXT Ask students to fill in a character trait chart like the one below about the narrator of *On the Pampas*. Tell them to record three or four traits and give evidence for each one.

NARRATOR OF *ON THE PAMPAS*	
CHARACTER TRAIT	**EVIDENCE**
enthusiastic	wants to learn everything
independent	visits without her family
adventurous	goes swimming in creek; loves galloping and yelling

③ ASSESS

DID STUDENTS:

✔ use what characters say, do, think, or feel to describe them?

✔ draw on personal experience to identify character traits?

IF NOT, TRY THIS:

See the **Reteach** lesson on **page R54.**

STUDENT'S SELF-ASSESSMENT:

✔ Was I able to use story clues to determine the narrator's personality traits?

For additional support, see **Practice Book 1, page 45**

STUDY SKILLS: USING A DICTIONARY

OBJECTIVE

- Students review how to use a dictionary to find and use information.

MATERIALS

- Dictionary

SUGGESTED GROUPING

- Partners

SKILLS TRACE

Using a Dictionary **TESTED**

- Introduce, p. T188
- Practice, p. T189
- Review, p. R49
- Reteach, p. R55

① REVIEW

Have students work with a partner to share a dictionary. Have students turn to a specific page. Point out the alphabetical listing of entry words, their pronunciations, parts of speech, definition, and other information. Ask volunteers to identify the guide words on the page and to locate the pronunciation key.

> **How can the guide words help you find the entry word you want?**

> **How can the pronunciation key help you say the word?**

Then ask students to look at a specific entry and review the pronunciation for the word, its part of speech, and definition.

> **By looking at the entry word, how do you know how many syllables the word has?**

> **How do you know which syllable is stressed?**

② PRACTICE/APPLY

PUT IT IN CONTEXT Ask students to use a dictionary to answer these questions:

> **Look for the word *headline*. Which guide words are on that page?**

> **How many syllables does *headline* have? Which syllable is stressed?**

> **What does *headline* mean? What part of speech is it?**

> **Look up the word *whisk*. What parts of speech can it be used as?**

> **What word in the pronunciation key has the same vowel sound as *whisk*?**

③ ASSESS

DID STUDENTS:

✔ use the guide words to locate an entry word in a dictionary?

✔ know how to identify information presented in each part of an entry?

✔ use the pronunciation key to determine how to pronounce a word?

IF NOT, TRY THIS:

See the **Reteach** lesson on **page R55**.

STUDENT'S SELF-ASSESSMENT:

✔ Did I use guide words to locate an entry word in a dictionary and identify the information given in the entry?

LITERARY ELEMENT: SETTING

OBJECTIVE

- Students review their knowledge of setting and transfer that knowledge to a new text.

MATERIALS

- Anthology, pp. 92–101
- Practice Book 1, p. 59

SUGGESTED GROUPING

- Whole class

SKILLS TRACE

Setting   **TESTED**
- **Introduce,** p. T180
- **Practice,** pp. T159, T182
- **Review,** p. R50
- **Reteach,** p. R55

① REVIEW

Remind students that setting is a story's time and place. Explain that the time can be long ago, in the present, or in the future. It can also be a season or a time of day. Story settings can be anywhere—from a tiny dog house to a huge planet. Explain that to find out the setting, readers ask: *When is this happening? Where is it happening? How do the time and place of the story affect what happens?*

PRACTICE BOOK 1, p. 59

② PRACTICE/APPLY

PUT IT IN CONTEXT Have students turn to *How the World Got Wisdom* and look through the illustrations on pages 92–100. Then have them reread page 92. Tell them to look for clues to the setting in the illustrations and in the story.

> **What do you see in the pictures that tells you about the setting of the story?**

> **What story clue on page 92 tells you when the story takes place?**

Have students skim the story and pictures and record details of the setting in *How the World Got Wisdom* on a chart.

WHERE?	in a forest
WHEN?	long ago
STORY CLUES	"Spider ran through the forest" "tallest tree in the world" "smooth trunk wide enough for Spider's house" "...when the world was young"
PICTURE CLUES	things in a forest: green plants, trees, flowers; Tortoise, Hare, Spider

③ ASSESS

DID STUDENTS:

✔ identify details of time and place?

✔ explain how the setting affects what happens?

IF NOT, TRY THIS:

See the **Reteach** lesson on **page R55.**

STUDENT'S SELF-ASSESSMENT:

✔ When I read, what questions can I ask myself to help me determine the setting of a story?

For additional support, see **Practice Book 1, page 59**

PHONICS: VOWEL /ô/ *a, au, aw*

OBJECTIVE

- Students review the vowel /ô/ (*a, au, aw*).

MATERIALS

- Anthology, pp. 92–101

SUGGESTED GROUPING

- Small groups

SKILLS TRACE

Vowel /ô/, *a, au, aw* **TESTED**

- **Introduce,** p. T210
- **Practice,** p. T221, T228, T229, T233, T237
- **Review,** p. R51
- **Reteach,** p. R56

❶ REVIEW

Remind students that the letters *a, au,* and *aw* can stand for /ô/, as in the words <u>a</u>ll, bec<u>au</u>se, and s<u>aw</u>. Write these words on the chalkboard and ask a volunteer to circle the letters *a, au,* and *aw*. Ask students for other words that have *a, au,* and *aw* that stand for /ô/. Write their examples on the chalkboard.

❷ PRACTICE/APPLY

PUT IT IN CONTEXT Have students work in small groups and turn to page 95 of *How the World Got Wisdom*. Have them read the page aloud quietly and listen for words with the vowel sound they hear in *saw*. *(tallest, gauze)*

Then write the following sentences on the chalkboard. Have students identify the words with the vowel /ô/, and circle *a, au,* or *aw* in each word.

1. Spider t<u>a</u>lks to Tortoise and Hare.
2. He passes sm<u>a</u>ll trees and bushes.
3. He p<u>au</u>ses when he sees a giant tree.
4. Spider and the clay pot f<u>a</u>ll to the ground.
5. It's <u>aw</u>ful; he can't hide the pot.

❸ ASSESS

DID STUDENTS:

✔ identify words with /ô/?

✔ connect /ô/ with the letters *a, au,* and *aw*?

IF NOT, TRY THIS:

See the **Reteach** lesson on **page R56.**

STUDENT'S SELF-ASSESSMENT:

✔ Did I recognize words with /ô/ and identify the letters that stand for /ô/?

HOMOPHONES

❶ CONSTRUCT

Listen carefully to this question: *Can you write the word right?* Which two words in the question sound the same? Do they have the same meaning? How can you use the other words in the sentence to understand the meaning of the words that sound the same?

❷ CONNECT

Look at the words *write* and *right*. You probably figured out that the question asked you to physically *write* the word *right*, as in correctly. You used context clues and what you already know to help you understand the meanings of the words *write* and *right*.

As you read with students, draw their attention to additional homophones. Observe whether students use context clues to figure out their meanings. You may wish to have students challenge each other to find and complete as many homophone pairs as possible.

❸ CONFIRM

How would you explain to a friend how the words *by* and *buy* are alike and how they are different? What clues would you give to help your classmate figure out the meaning of each word?

VOWEL /ī/ *i, igh, y, i-e, ie*

❶ CONSTRUCT

Say the word **high** and tell students it has the long *i* sound. Then write the word **high** on the chalkboard, underlining **igh**. Remind them that these letters stand for /ī/. Explain that the letters *i, y, i-e,* and *ie* also stand for /ī/. Ask students to raise their hands high in the air each time you say a word with the same sound as **high**. Use these words: **fright, little, lie, my, miss, bite, bit**. Write the /ī/ words on the board and have a volunteer underline the letters that stand for /ī/.

❷ CONNECT

Have students cut out the shape of a kite. Help them write the word **kite** on the cutout. As you read the word **riddles**, have students raise the kites high in the air when the answer to the riddle has the sound /ī/.

- This has two wheels and will take you where you want to go. *(bike)*
- You may _____ in this chair. *(sit)*
- When this is turned on, it helps you see _____. *(light)*
- When your shoes do not fit, they feel _____. *(tight)*
- Did you enjoy answering these word _____? *(riddles)*

❸ CONFIRM

Draw on the chalkboard a kite for each spelling of /ī/: *i, igh, y, i-e, ie.* Ask students to write words with /ī/ on each kite, making sure their words include the same spelling for /ī/ that you have written.

WORDS WITH SCHWA /ə/

❶ CONSTRUCT

Say *again, asleep, ago,* emphasizing the unaccented syllable /ə/ in each word. Remind students that words of two or more syllables have one syllable with less stress than the others. Have them say the words aloud and listen for the vowel sound in the unstressed syllable.

Pantomime a conductor of an orchestra and wave a "baton" in the air. Say the word *baton,* emphasizing the /ə/ in the unaccented syllable. Write the following words on the chalkboard one at a time: *lemon, pencil, again, happy, about, spoken, ago, circus, happen.* Have students read each word chorally and wave a "baton" if they hear /ə/ in the unaccented syllable.

❷ CONNECT

When you see a word that you are not sure how to say, try saying it to yourself in different ways to see if it sounds like a word you have heard before. Each time you say it, put the emphasis on a different syllable. Use the schwa vowel sound in an unstressed syllable.

As students read classroom trade books, model for them how to break unfamiliar words into parts and how to practice using /ə/ for vowel letters in unstressed syllables.

❸ CONFIRM

Why is it important to know that the schwa sound is often heard in an unstressed syllable and that different letters can stand for the schwa sound? To answer this question, think about how you can use what you know about the schwa sound to help figure out a word you are not sure you know.

ALPHABETICAL ORDER

❶ CONSTRUCT

For science class, you have to find out what a *locket,* a *loom,* and a *lodge* are. The dictionary is right on your desk. Before you look up the words, you do something that will help you find the words quickly in the dictionary. What do you do? How do you do it?

❷ CONNECT

Since entries in the dictionary are listed in alphabetical order, you know that figuring out the alphabetical order of the words will save time. All the words start with *lo,* so you look at the third letters to see which one comes first in the alphabet. The letter *c* comes before the third letters *d* and *o* in the other words, so you would look up *locket* first. Next, you would look up *lodge,* because *d* comes before *o.* You would look up *loom* last.

Give students another group of words to alphabetize, or have each student write five words on a piece of paper and then trade papers with a partner to alphabetize.

❸ CONFIRM

If a friend had never alphabetized a list of words or names, how would you explain how to do it? To answer the question, think about the sequence of letters in the alphabet. What would you tell your friend to do first?

One-, Two-, Three-Syllable Words

① CONSTRUCT

Remind students that words have parts called syllables and each syllable has only one vowel sound. Say the following words and have students identify the number of syllables in each one: *ranch, brother, animals, drove, adventure, explore, raft, discover.*

② CONNECT

When you read, figuring out the syllables in a word helps you break the word into parts. Then you can try saying different vowel sounds for the vowel letter or letters in each syllable. This can help you figure out how to say the whole word and see if you know it.

Have students determine the number of syllables in the words in a vocabulary list in a social studies or science text and practice saying the vowel in each part in different ways.

③ CONFIRM

How can determining the number of syllables in a word help you figure out how to say the word? To answer the question, think about how breaking a big task into smaller tasks helps get the job done.

Character

① CONSTRUCT

At lunch you notice a group of students arguing. Soon you see the lunch supervisor, a man with a loud voice, walk over to the group. All the students stop yelling. You hear the man ask, "Is there a problem here?" The students start talking all at once. He raises his hand and says, "Everyone will get a chance to talk one at a time so we can listen to each other. Savan, will you begin?" The group quiets down.

How would you describe this supervisor to a friend? On what actions would you base your description?

② CONNECT

When you described the lunch supervisor, you identified his personality, or character, traits. To understand character as you read, follow this same approach: Ask questions such as, "What did she do?" "What did he say?" The answers are clues to a character's personality traits.

This would be a good time to focus on the personality traits of characters in the chapter books and trade books students are reading.

③ CONFIRM

What questions do you ask to understand the characters in a book? How might you use this same approach when meeting a new neighbor or classmate?

USING A DICTIONARY

① CONSTRUCT

Write the word *lynx* on the chalkboard. You're reading a story that takes place in the north woods and the main character sees animal tracks she thinks may be those of the animal whose name is written on the chalkboard. You don't know what the animal is, how to pronounce the word, or how much danger the character may be in because of the animal. What do you do?

② CONNECT

You decide to use a dictionary, which will tell you a little about the animal and how to say its name. You use guide words to help you find the page that *lynx* is on and alphabetical order to find the entry on the page.

After modeling how to find the word, ask a student to read aloud the information in the entry for *lynx*. *How did you know how to say the word? What is a lynx? How does it look and how do you know? What other information is given in the entry?* Write names of other animals on the chalkboard for students to look up: *bison, walrus, panda, jaguar*. Have students share the new words and their meanings with the group.

③ CONFIRM

Why is the dictionary a valuable tool for learning new words? To answer the question, think about what information the dictionary gives about each entry.

SETTING

① CONSTRUCT

This room provides the setting for the people in it. Look around you. What do you see? What do you hear? Feel? Name some activities that people in this room are doing. What objects in the room help them do these activities? Would you expect to find someone riding a horse in this room? Why or why not? How does knowing about this room help you know what the people in this room might be doing?

② CONNECT

In a story, the setting is when and where the action takes place. When you describe this room, you tell about the setting. When you read, use the same approach to identify the setting in a story.

Now would be a good time to choose one of the trade books or another story to read with students. Choose a story that contains rich setting details, and help students focus on story and picture clues to identify the setting.

③ CONFIRM

How does knowing a story's setting help you know how the characters will act? To answer this question, think about how understanding setting helps you to know how to act at the library, the movie theater, or other places you might visit.

Vowel /ô/ *a, au, aw*

❶ CONSTRUCT

Write the recipe *To cook tasty crawfish, add a dash of salt to the sauce.*

You are helping a relative cook dinner, and it is your job to read the recipe. Written on the chalkboard is what the recipe says.

Circle *crawfish, salt,* and *sauce.* Underline *aw* in *crawfish, a* in *salt,* and *au* in *sauce.* Explain that the letters *a, aw,* and *au* can stand for the vowel /ô/ as in *saw.* Have students read the sentence.

❷ CONNECT

You may not have been sure which vowel sound to say for the letters *a, au,* and *aw* in the words I circled. When you are not sure how to pronounce a word, try the different sounds that you know these letters could stand for. Keep trying until the word sounds right in the sentence.

❸ CONFIRM

Why is it important to know that the vowel sound you hear in *saw* can be spelled in different ways? Think about how you can use what you know about this vowel sound to help figure out a word you're not sure you know.

Statements and Questions

RETEACH

A sentence that tells something is a statement. It ends with a period. A sentence that asks something is a question. It ends with a question mark.

PRACTICE
Read the words below. Complete questions with question marks and statements with periods.

1. **Where are we going [?]**
2. **We're going on a surprise adventure [.]**
3. **It's sunny and warm today [.]**
4. **Do you want me to give away the surprise [?]**

Commands and Exclamations

RETEACH

A command gives an order. It ends with a period. An exclamation expresses strong feeling. It ends with an exclamation mark.

PRACTICE
Write the correct punctuation mark at the end of each sentence.

1. **That whale is enormous [!]**
2. **Wait a few minutes [.]**
3. **Watch for its spurt [.]**
4. **There it goes [!]**
5. **Wow, that is amazing [!]**

COMMON AND PROPER NOUNS

A common noun names any person, place, or thing. A proper noun names a particular person, place, or thing. Proper nouns begin with capital letters. For proper nouns of more than one word, begin the first word and all important words with a capital letter.

PRACTICE

Write or say the following sentences and have students identify each common noun.

1. **My brother Bill and I will visit our aunt this summer.**

2. **Aunt Alice lives on a houseboat in Florida.**

3. **We'll stay until September.**

Write or say the following sentences and have students identify each proper noun.

1. **We arrived at Aunt Alice's in June.**

2. **We sailed down the Florida coast.**

3. **We went fishing at Lake Heron.**

SINGULAR AND PLURAL NOUNS

A singular noun names one thing. A plural noun names more than one thing. Add *s* or *es* to form the plural of most nouns. If a noun ends in *f*, change the *f* to *v* and add *es*.

PRACTICE

Write the following sentences on the chalkboard. Have students write each singular underlined noun as a plural.

1. **The <u>dish</u> are on the top shelf. [dishes]**

2. **The <u>glass</u> are there, too. [glasses]**

3. **The top <u>shelf</u> are hard to reach. [shelves]**

4. **Will you help me reach those <u>thing</u>? [things]**

5. **I'll start making two <u>sandwich</u>. [sandwiches]**

SINGULAR AND PLURAL PRONOUNS

A singular pronoun takes the place of a noun that names one thing. A plural pronoun takes the place of two or more nouns.

PRACTICE

Write the following sentences on the chalkboard. Have students write a pronoun for a noun.

1. **<u>Jack and I</u> make lunch. [We]**

2. **<u>Rosa and Todd</u> are coming over. [They]**

3. **<u>The day</u> is bright and cold. [It]**

4. **We have a surprise for <u>Rosa</u>. [Her]**

5. **<u>Jack, Todd and I</u> will sing "Happy Birthday." [We]**

MAIN-IDEA CHART

Selection Title: _____

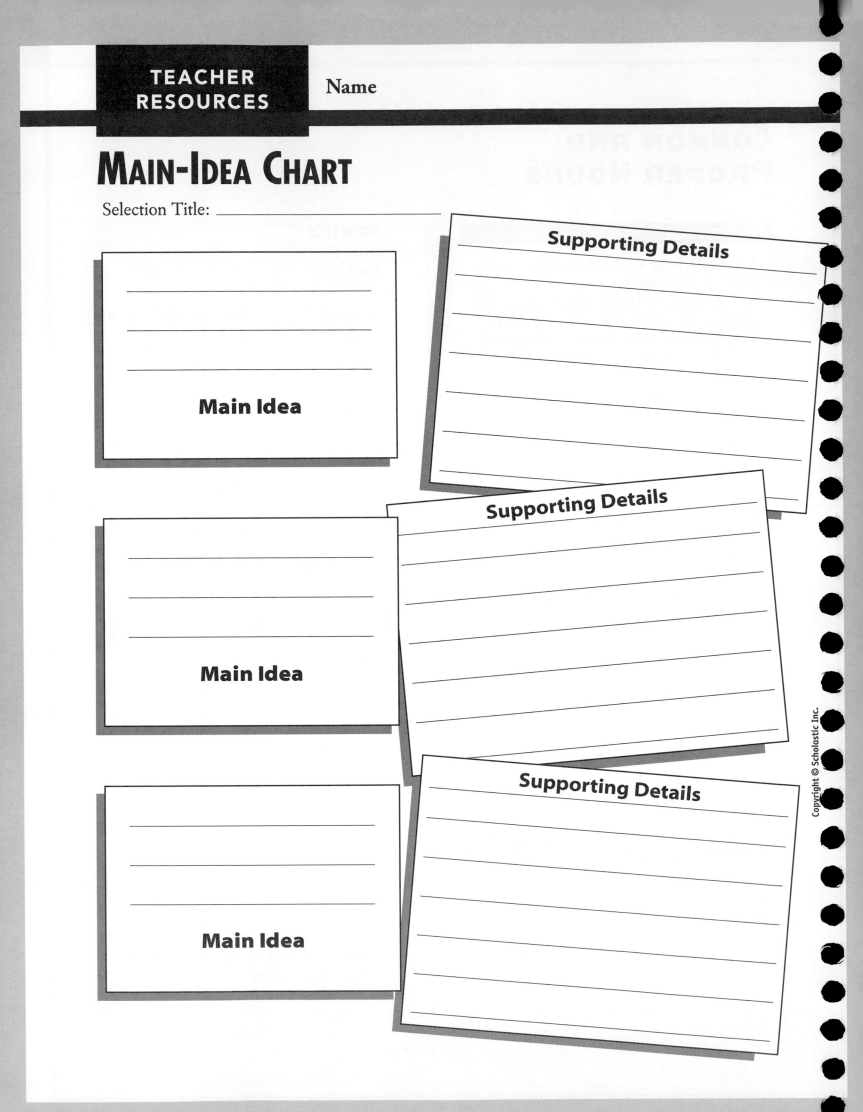

Supporting Details

Main Idea

Supporting Details

Main Idea

Supporting Details

Main Idea

VENN DIAGRAM

Use the diagram to organize your writing.

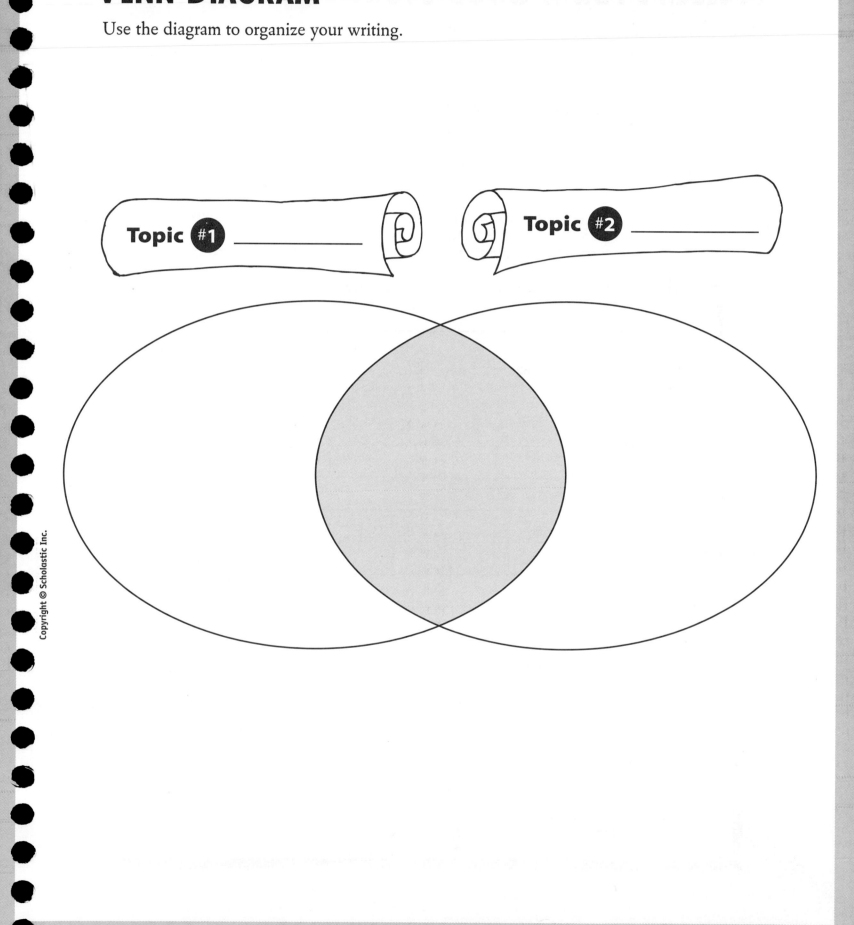

A Recipe for a Good Story

Use the recipe card below to write about the story.

Ingredients:

Plot:	Tell what happens in the story.
Theme:	Tell the message of the story.
Setting:	Tell where the story takes place.
Mood:	Tell if the story is happy, sad, scary, funny, or exciting.
Characters:	Tell the names of the main characters and if they are good, bad, helpful, mean, or funny.

Story Title: _____ **Author:** _____

Here's What's Cooking

Take one plot: _____

_____

_____

Mix in theme: _____

_____

Sprinkle with setting: _____

_____

Fold in the mood gently: _____

_____

_____

What do you get? _____

_____

_____

STORY MAP

As you listen, fill in the story map.

Story Title: _____

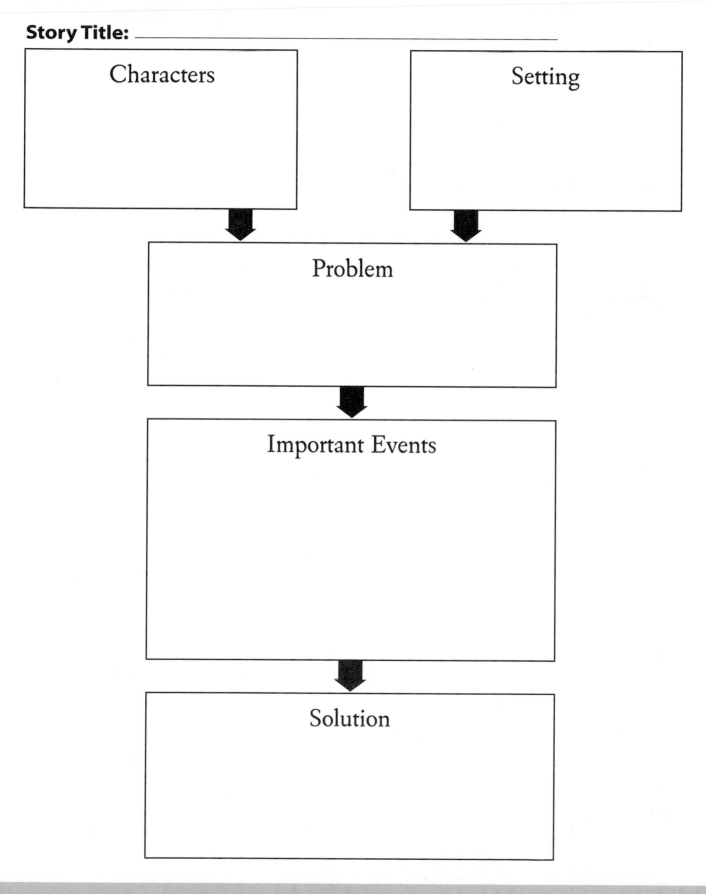

Name

ON THE JOB

As you watch the video, jot down information you learn about the mentor's job.

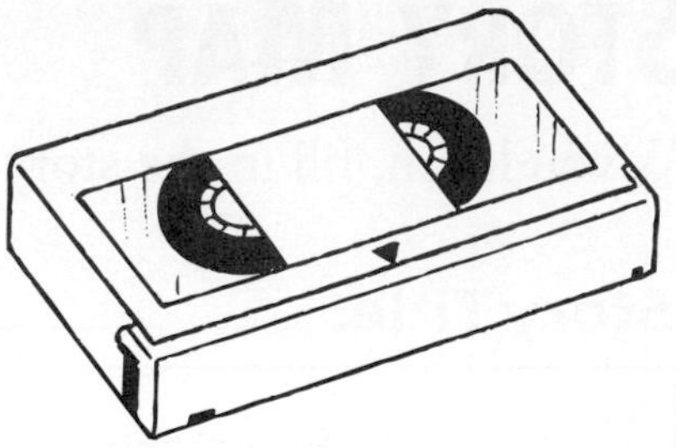

Mentor's Name: _____

Name of Job: _____

Place of Work: _____

On-the-Job Activities

1 _____
_____
_____
_____

2 _____
_____
_____
_____

3 _____
_____
_____
_____

4 _____
_____
_____
_____

PRESENTING/SPEAKING

Every story has a problem and a way of solving it. Think about the story and follow the directions below. Present your story to the class.

1 Tell the main problem in your story.

_____

_____

_____

2 Describe what the characters did to try to solve the problem.

_____

_____

_____

3 Tell how the problem was solved.

_____

_____

_____

4 Think of a different way you might have solved the problem.

_____

_____

5 How would your solution to the problem have changed the story?

_____

_____

_____

Scope and Sequence

READING	GRADE	K	1	2	3	4	5
Print Awareness							
recognize that print messages represent spoken language and convey meaning		●	●				
knows print moves left-right, top-bottom		●	●				
understands that written words are separated by spaces		●	●				
know the difference between individual letters and words		●	●				
know the difference between capital and lowercase letters		●	●				
know the order of the alphabet		●	●				
recognize conventions of capitalization and punctuation		●	●				
understand that spoken words are represented in written language by specific sequences of letters		●	●				
recognize parts of a book		●	●	●	●	●	●
recognize that there are correct spellings		●	●	●	●	●	●
recognize distinguishing features of paragraphs				●	●	●	●
Phonological Awareness							
divide sentences into individual words		●	●	●			
identify, segment, and combine syllables		●	●	●	●		
produce and distinguish rhyming words from non-rhyming		●	●	●	●		
identify and isolate initial and final sounds		●	●	●	●		
blend sounds		●	●	●	●		
segment one-syllable words into individual phonemes clearly producing beginning, medial, and final sounds		●	●	●	●		
Letter–Sound Relationships							
name and identify each letter of the alphabet		●	●				
understand that written words are composed of letters that represent sounds		●	●				
learn and apply letter-sound correspondences of:							
consonants (beginning, middle, end)		●	●	●			
short vowel sounds		●	●	●			
phonograms/word families/patterns		●	●	●			
digraphs			●	●	●	●	●
blends			●	●	●	●	●
long vowel sounds			●	●	●	●	●
diphthongs			●	●	●	●	●
variant vowels			●	●	●	●	●
blend initial letter-sounds with common vowel spelling patterns to read words		●	●	●	●		
decode by using all letter-sound correspondences within regularly spelled words		●	●	●	●	●	●
use letter-sound knowledge to read decodable texts		●	●	●	●		

● = direct instruction   = mastery

Grade	K	1	2	3	4	5
Word Identification						
decode by using all letter-sound correspondences within a word	●	●	●	●	●	●
use common spelling patterns to read words	●	●	●	●	●	●
use structural cues to recognize compounds, base words, and inflectional endings		●	●	●	●	●
use structural cues to recognize prefixes and suffixes			●	●	●	●
use root words and other structural cues to recognize derivational endings			●	●	●	●
identify multisyllabic words by using common syllable patterns			●	●	●	●
recognize high-frequency irregular words	●	●	●	●	●	●
use knowledge or syntax and context to support word identification and confirm meaning	●	●	●	●	●	●
read regular and irregular words automatically		●	●	●	●	●
locate meanings, pronunciations, and derivations of unfamiliar words using dictionaries, glossaries, and other sources		●	●	●	●	●
Fluency						
read regularly in independent-level materials		●	●	●	●	●
read regularly in instructional-level materials		●	●	●	●	●
read orally from familiar texts		●	●	●	●	●
self-select independent-level materials		●	●	●	●	●
read silently for increasing amounts of time		●	●	●	●	●
demonstrate characteristics of fluent and effective reading		●	●	●	●	●
adjust reading rate based on purpose		●	●	●	●	●
read aloud		●	●	●	●	●
Text Structures/Literary Concepts						
distinguish different forms of texts	●	●	●	●	●	●
understand simple story structure	●	●	●	●	●	●
distinguish fiction from nonfiction	●	●	●	●	●	●
distinguish fact from fantasy	●	●	●	●	●	●
distinguish among types of text	●	●	●	●	●	●
distinguish between roles of the author and illustrator	●	●	●	●	●	●
identify text as narrative or expository			●	●	●	●
compare communication in different forms	●	●	●	●	●	●
understand and identify literary terms	●	●	●	●	●	●
analyze characters	●	●	●	●	●	●
identify importance of setting	●	●	●	●	●	●
recognize and analyze story problem/plot and resolution	●	●	●	●	●	●
judge internal consistency or logic of stories and texts		●	●	●	●	●
recognize that authors organize information in specific ways		●	●	●	●	●

Scope and Sequence

	GRADE	K	1	2	3	4	5
identify purposes of different types of texts		●	●	●	●	●	●
recognize the distinguishing features of genres			●	●	●	●	●
describe the author's perspective or point of view				●	●	●	●
Variety of Texts							
read fiction, nonfiction, and poetry for pleasure and information		●	●	●	●	●	●
use graphs, charts, signs, captions and other informational texts to acquire information		●	●	●	●	●	●
read classic and contemporary works		●	●	●	●	●	●
read from print a variety of genres for pleasure and information		●	●	●	●	●	●
read from electronic sources a variety of genres for pleasure and information		●	●	●	●	●	●
read to accomplish various purposes			●	●	●	●	●
select varied sources, i.e., nonfiction, novels, textbooks, newspapers and magazines for information and pleasure			●	●	●	●	●
read for varied purposes, i.e., to be informed, entertained, appreciate writer's craft, and discover models for writing			●	●	●	●	●
Vocabulary Development							
discuss meanings and develop vocabulary through meaningful/concrete experiences		●	●	●	●	●	●
develop vocabulary by listening and discussing selections read aloud		●	●	●	●	●	●
identify words that name persons, places or things, and actions		●	●	●	●	●	●
use dictionaries, glossaries, technology, and context to build word meanings and confirm pronunciation			●	●	●	●	●
demonstrate knowledge of synonyms, antonyms and multiple-meaning words			●	●	●	●	●
draw on experiences to bring meanings to words in context			●	●	●	●	●
use thesaurus, synonym finder, dictionary and software to clarify meanings and usage					●	●	●
determining meanings of derivatives by applying knowledge of root words and affixes				●	●	●	●
use curricular content areas and current events to study words				●	●	●	●
Comprehension							
use prior knowledge and experiences		●	●	●	●	●	●
establish purposes for reading		●	●	●	●	●	●
retell or act out the order of events in stories		●	●	●	●	●	●
monitor own comprehension			●	●	●	●	●
draw, discuss, and describe visual and mental images			●	●	●	●	●
make and explain inferences, i.e., determining important ideas, causes and effects, making predictions, and drawing conclusions			●	●	●	●	●
identify similarities and differences in topics, characters, problems, and themes		●	●	●	●	●	●
produce summaries of text selections			●	●	●	●	●
represent text information through story maps, graphs, charts, outline, time line, or graphic organizer		●	●	●	●	●	●

● = direct instruction   ▓ = mastery

Grade	K	1	2	3	4	5
distinguish fact from opinion			•	•	•	•
practice different kinds of questions and tasks, including test-like questions		•	•	•	•	•
use cause and effect, or chronology to locate and recall information		•	•	•	•	•
determine main idea and supporting details	•	•	•	•	•	•
paraphrase and summarize text	•	•	•	•	•	•
draw inferences and support with text evidence and experience		•	•	•	•	•
find similarities and differences across texts in treatment, scope, organization		•	•	•	•	•
answer different types and levels of questions, i.e., open-ended, literal, and interpretative; multiple-choice, true-false, and short-answer	•	•	•	•	•	•
Literary Response						
listen to stories read aloud	•	•	•	•	•	•
participate actively during a read aloud of predictable and patterned selections	•	•	•	•		
respond through talk, movement, music, art, drama, and writing	•	•	•	•	•	•
describe how illustrations contribute to text	•	•	•	•	•	•
connect, compare, and contrast ideas, themes, and issues across texts	•	•	•	•	•	•
demonstrate understanding of informational texts through writing, illustrating, demonstrations	•	•	•	•	•	•
support interpretations or conclusions with examples from text		•	•	•	•	•
offer observations, make connections, react, speculate, interpret, and raise questions in response to text	•	•	•	•	•	•
interpret texts through journal writing, discussion, enactment, and media	•	•	•	•	•	•
support responses by referring to relevant aspects of the text and own experiences	•	•	•	•	•	•
Inquiry/Research						
identify and form relevant questions for research	•	•	•	•	•	•
use pictures, print, and people to gather and answer questions	•	•	•	•	•	•
draw conclusions from information gathered	•	•	•	•	•	•
locate and use important areas of the library/media center	•	•	•	•	•	•
use alphabetical order to locate information		•	•	•	•	•
recognize and use parts of a book to locate information	•	•	•	•	•	•
use multiple sources to locate information that addresses questions			•	•	•	•
interpret and use graphic sources of information, i.e., charts, graphs, and diagrams	•	•	•	•	•	•
demonstrate learning through productions and displays	•	•	•	•	•	•
organize information in systematic ways		•	•	•	•	•
use compiled information and knowledge to raise additional unanswered questions				•	•	•
use text organizers to locate and organize information			•	•	•	•
summarize and organize information from multiple sources by taking notes, outlining ideas, or making charts			•	•		•

GRADE	K	1	2	3	4	5
Culture						
connect own experiences with life experiences, language, customs, and cultures of others	●	●	●	●	●	●
compare experiences of characters across cultures	●	●	●	●	●	●
compare text events with own and other readers' experiences	●	●	●	●	●	●
determine distinctive and common characteristics of cultures through wide reading	●	●	●	●	●	●
articulate and discuss themes and connections that cross cultures	●	●	●	●	●	●
LISTENING/SPEAKING						
determine purposes	●	●	●	●	●	●
respond to directions and questions	●	●	●	●	●	●
participate in rhymes, songs, conversations and discussions	●	●	●	●	●	●
listen critically to interpret and evaluate	●	●	●	●	●	●
listen to stories and other texts read aloud	●	●	●	●	●	●
identify musical elements of literary language	●	●	●	●	●	●
connect experiences and ideas with those of others	●	●	●	●	●	●
compare language and oral traditions that reflect customs, regions, and cultures	●	●	●	●	●	●
choose appropriate language for audience, purpose, and occasion	●	●	●	●	●	●
use verbal and nonverbal communication when making announcements, directions, introductions	●	●	●	●	●	●
ask and answer relevant questions, and contribute	●	●	●	●	●	●
present dramatics	●	●	●	●	●	
gain control of grammar	●	●	●	●	●	●
learn vocabulary of school	●	●	●	●	▨	▨
use vocabulary to describe ideas, feelings, and experiences	●	●	●	●	●	●
support spoken language using props	●	●	●	●	●	●
retell by summarizing or clarifying	●	●	●	●	●	●
eliminate barriers to effective listening	●	●	●	●	●	●
understand major ideas and supporting evidence	●	●	●	●	●	●
interpret messages, purposes, and perspectives	●	●	●	●	●	●
identify and analyze persuasive techniques			●	●	●	●
distinguish between opinion and fact				●	●	●
monitor own understanding		●	●	●	●	●
listen to proficient models of oral reading	●	●	●	●	●	●
describe how language of literature affects listener	●	●	●	●	●	●
assess language choice and delivery				●	●	●
identify how regional labels/sayings reflect regions and cultures				●	●	●
demonstrate skills that reflect interviewing, reporting, requesting and providing information		●	●	●	●	●

● = direct instruction   ▨ = mastery

	Grade	K	1	2	3	4	5
use effective rate, volume, pitch, tone		•	•	•	•	•	•
give precise directions and instructions in games and tasks		•	•	•	•	•	•
clarify and support with evidence, elaborations and examples			•	•	•	•	•

Writing

Penmanship/Capitalization/Punctuation

		K	1	2	3	4	5
write own name and other important words		•	•				
write each letter of alphabet, capital and lowercase		•	•				
use phonological knowledge to map sounds to letters, in order to write messages		•	•	•	•	•	•
write messages left to right, top to bottom		•	•	•	•		
gain control of pencil grip, paper position, beginning strokes, posture, letter formation, appropriate size, and spacing		•	•				
use word and letter spacing and margins			•	•			
use capitalization and punctuation, i.e., names, first letters in sentences, periods, question marks, exclamation marks, proper nouns, abbreviations, commas, apostrophes, quotation marks, contractions, possessives		•	•	•	•	•	•
write legibly by selecting cursive or manuscript, as appropriate			•	•	•	•	•

Spelling

		K	1	2	3	4	5
write with proficient spelling of: CVC, CVC silent e, one syllable with blends			•	•	•	•	•
inflectional endings: plurals, verb tenses, drop final e when endings are added			•	•	•	•	•
single-syllable words with r-controlled vowels, final consonants			•	•	•	•	•
orthographic patterns, i.e., consonant doubling, dropping e, changing y to i				•	•	•	•
use resources to find correct spellings, synonyms, and replacements				•	•	•	•
use conventional spelling of familiar words in final drafts			•	•	•	•	•
spell multisyllabic words using regularly spelled phonogram patterns				•	•	•	•
write with more proficient spelling of contractions, compounds, and homonyms			•	•	•	•	•
open and closed syllables, consonant before -le, and syllable boundary patterns				•	•	•	•
spell words ending in -tion and -sion					•	•	•
spell accurately in final drafts			•	•	•	•	•

Composition/Process

		K	1	2	3	4	5
dictate messages		•	•	•			
write labels, notes, and captions for illustrations, possessions, charts, and centers		•	•	•	•	•	•
write to record ideas and reflections		•	•	•	•	•	•
generate ideas before writing on self-selected topics		•	•	•	•	•	•
generate ideas before writing on assigned topics		•	•	•	•	•	•
develop drafts			•	•	•	•	•
use available technology to compose text		•	•	•	•	•	•
revise selected drafts for varied purposes			•	•	•	•	•
revise drafts for coherence, progression, and logical support of ideas			•	•	•	•	•

Scope and Sequence

GRADE	K	1	2	3	4	5
edit for appropriate grammar, spelling, punctuation, and features of polished writings		●	●	●	●	●
demonstrate understanding of language use and spelling by bringing pieces to final form and "publishing"		●	●	●	●	●
proofread own writing and that of others		●	●	●	●	●
select and use reference materials and resources for writing		●	●	●	●	●
Purposes						
dictate messages	●	●	●			
write labels, notes, and captions for illustrations, possessions, charts, and centers	●	●	●	●	●	●
write to record ideas and reflections	●	●	●	●	●	●
write to express, discover, record, develop, reflect, and refine ideas, and to problem solve	●	●	●	●	●	●
write to communicate with a variety of audiences	●	●	●	●	●	●
write in different forms for different purposes	●	●	●	●	●	●
write to influence			●	●	●	●
write to inform	●	●	●	●	●	●
write to entertain	●	●	●	●	●	●
exhibit an identifiable voice in personal narratives and stories			●	●	●	●
choose the appropriate form for own purpose for writing				●	●	●
use literary devices, i.e., suspense, dialogue, figurative language			●	●	●	●
Grammar/Usage/Mechanics						
use nouns and verbs in sentences	●	●	●	●	●	●
compose complete sentences and use appropriate punctuation	●	●	●			
use singular and plural forms of regular nouns		●	●	●	●	●
compose sentences with interesting elaborated subjects				●	●	●
edit writing toward standard grammar and usage		●	●	●	●	●
use correct irregular plurals			●	●	●	●
use singular and plural forms of regular nouns, and adjust verbs for agreement		●	●	●	●	●
compose elaborated sentences and use appropriate punctuation				●	●	●
use regular and irregular plurals correctly				●	●	●
write in complete sentences, varying the types				●	●	●
employ standard English usage, subject-verb agreement, pronoun referents, and parts of speech		●	●	●	●	●
use adjectives and adverbs		●	●	●	●	●
use prepositional phrases to elaborate written ideas				●	●	●
use conjunctions to connect ideas				●	●	●
use apostrophes in contractions and possessives		●	●	●	●	●
use objective-case pronouns accurately			●	●	●	●

● = direct instruction   ▓ = mastery

	Grade	K	1	2	3	4	5
Evaluation							
identify the most effective features of a piece by using student and teacher criteria			●	●	●	●	●
respond constructively to others' writing		●	●	●	●	●	●
determine how own writing achieves its purposes			●	●	●	●	●
use published pieces as models		●	●	●	●	●	●
review collection of own work to monitor growth			●	●	●	●	●
apply criteria to evaluate writing			●	●	●	●	●
review a collection of written works to determine its strengths and weaknesses, and to set goals			●	●	●	●	●
Inquiry/Research							
record/dictate questions for investigating		●	●	●	●	●	●
record/dictate own knowledge		●	●	●	●	●	●
take simple notes from sources			●	●	●	●	●
compile notes into outlines, reports, summaries				●	●	●	●
frame questions, to direct research			●	●	●	●	●
organize prior knowledge with graphic organizer		●	●	●	●	●	●
take notes from various sources				●	●	●	●
summarize and organize ideas			●	●	●	●	●
present information in various forms		●	●	●	●	●	●
evaluate own research and raise new questions					●	●	●
Connections							
collaborate with other writers			●	●	●	●	●
correspond with peers or others by e-mail or conventional mail					●	●	●
VIEWING							
Representing/Interpretation							
describe illustrator's choice of style, elements, and media		●	●	●	●	●	●
interpret events and ideas from maps, charts, graphics, video segments, and technology presentations		●	●	●	●	●	●
Representing/Analysis							
interpret and evaluate visual image makers		●	●	●	●	●	●
compare-contrast print, visual, and electronic media		●	●	●	●	●	●
Representing/Production							
select, organize, and produce visuals to complement and extend meanings		●	●	●	●	●	●
produce communications using technology		●	●	●	●	●	●

Index

GRADE 3

This index incorporates references to the Teacher's Edition for all six units in Grade 3 of Literacy Place. For your convenience, the index is divided into three sections, as listed below.

SKILLS AND STRATEGIES

Reading Skills and Strategies*

Comprehension/Thinking Strategies

> **References to the book you're in are in blue.** Each unit in Grade 3 is identified by the initials of its theme.
>
> PV • Personal Voice: What's New?
> PS • Problem Solving: Big Plans
> TW • Teamwork: On the Job
> CE • Creative Expression: Hit Series
> MI • Managing Information: Time Detectives
> CI • Community Involvement: Community Quilt

*Boldface page references indicate full skill lesson.

✳ Index

✴ Index

Writing and Language Arts Skills and Strategies

Grammar, Usage, Mechanics

✱ Index

✴Index

Integrated Curriculum Activities

✳Index

INSTRUCTIONAL ISSUES

CE: T54, T100, T154, T198, T250, T257

MI: T56, T116, T170, T212, T256

CI: T70, T116, T124, T182, T222, T230, T266, T273

Student's Self-Assessment
PV: T93, T104, T200, T235, T253, T255, T258

PS: T61, T116, T222, T275, T293, T295, T298

TW: T114, T212, T271, T273, T276

CE: T97, T108, T206, T265, T267, T270

MI: T53, T124, T220, T271, T273, T276

CI: T124, T179, T230, T281, T283, T286

Intervention and Instructional Alternatives

PV: T15, T42–T43, T86–T87, T132–T133, T228–T229, T246–T247

PS: T15, T54–T55, T98–T99, T156–T157, T204–T205, T268–T269

TW: T15, T48–T49, T96–T97, T148–T149, T194–T195, T246–T247

CE: T15, T41, T43, T44–T45, T52, T61, T89, T90–T91, T98, T113, T143, T144–T145, T151, T161, T177, T188–T189, T196, T211, T240–T241, T248, T249

MI: T15, T46–T47, T106–T107, T160–T161, T202–T203, T246–T247

CI: T15, T60–T61, T106–T107, T172–T173, T212–T213, T256–T257

Portfolio

Literacy Portfolio
PV: T52, T96, T142, T192, T238, T253, T259

PS: T64, T108, T166, T214, T278, T293, T299

TW: T58, T106, T158, T204, T256, T271, T277

CE: T54, T100, T154, T198, T250, T265, T271

MI: T56, T116, T170, T212, T256, T271, T277

CI: T70, T116, T182, T222, T266, T281, T287

Teacher Portfolio

See Teacher Self-Assessment.

QuickCheck

PV: T14, T50, T58, T94, T108, T140, T148, T190, T204, T236

PS: T14, T62, T70, T106, T118, T1654, T172, T212, T224, T276

TW: T14, T56, T62, T104, T118, T156, T164, T196, T216, T224

CE: T14, T40, T52, T60, T88, T98, T112, T142, T152, T160, T186, T196, T210, T238, T248, T263

MI: T14, T54, T62, T114, T128, T168, T176, T210, T224, T254

CI: T14, T68, T74, T114, T128, T180, T188, T220, T234, T264

Reading Assessment

See Formal Assessment: Unit Tests.

References to Assessment Handbook

PV: T14, T51, T58, T95, T108, T141, T148, T191, T204, T237

PS: T14, T63, T70, T107, T118, T165, T172, T213, T224, T277

TW: T14, T57, T62, T105, T118, T157, T164, T197, T216, T225

CE: T14, T53, T60, T99, T112, T153, T160, T197, T210, T249

MI: T14, T55, T62, T115, T128, T169, T176, T211, T224, T255

CI: T14, T69, T74, T115, T128, T181, T188, T221, T234, T265

Teacher Self-Assessment

PV: T259

PS: T299

TW: T277

CE: T271

MI: T277

CI: T287

Tested Skills

Reading Skills and Strategies
PV: T37–T38, T84–T85, T130–T131, T180–T181, T226–T227

PS: T53–T54, T96–T97, T152–T153, T202–T203, T266–T267

TW: T46–T47, T94–T95, T144–T145, T192–T193, T244–T245

CE: T40–T41, T88–T89, T142–T143, T186–T187, T238–T239

MI: T42–T43, T104–T105, T158–T159, T200–T201, T244–T245

CI: T58–T59, T102–T103, T170–T171, T210–T211, T254–T255

Language Arts Skills and Strategies
PV: R6–R7, R14–R15, R22–R23, R30–R31, R38–R39

PS: R6–R7, R14–R15, R22–R23, R30–R31, R38–R39

TW: R6–R7, R14–R15, R22–R23, R30–R31, R38–R39

CE: R6–R7, R14–R15, R22–R23, R30–R31, R38–R39

MI: R6–R7, R14–R15, R22–R23, R30–R31, R38–R39

CI: R6–R7, R14–R15, R22–R23, R30–R31, R38–R39

Think About Reading

PV: T36, T82, T128, T178, T224

PS: T50, T94, T150, T200, T264

TW: T44, T92, T142, T190, T242

CE: T38, T86, T140, T184, T236

MI: T40, T102, T156, T198, T242

CI: T56, T100, T168, T208, T252

Writing Assessment

PV: T52, T96, T142, T192, T238

PS: T64, T108, T166, T214, T278

TW: T58, T106, T158, T204, T256

CE: T54, T100, T154, T198, T250

MI: T56, T116, T170, T212, T256

CI: T70, T116, T182, T222, T266

Index

Cultural Connections

Grouping Strategies

Classroom Management

Cooperative/Small Groups

Individuals

PV: T97, T146, T199, T200, T239, T240, T242

PS: T65, T110, T167, T215, T216

TW: T59, T60, T108, T159, T160, T205, T206, T257, T258

CE: T56, T101, T155, T200, T251, T252, T254–T257

MI: T57, T172, T213, T214

CI: T71, T72, T117, T118, T184, T224

Partners

PV: T20, T21, T39, T42, T43, T47, T49, T53, T64, T80, T85, T86, T99, T131, T132, T137, T138, T143, T169, T177, T178, T179, T191, T210, T227, T228, T232, T236, T237, T240

PS: T20, T32, T52, T53, T54, T55, T59, T98, T140, T168, T181, T190, T209, T275, T280, T281, T282

TW: T21, T30, T48, T53, T92, T94, T95, T96, T101, T105, T120, T124, T137, T147, T153, T157, T160, T161, T193, T194, T199, T203, T240, T246, T251, T258

CE: T20, T44, T80, T95, T101, T102, T140, T144, T145, T149, T156, T184, T188, T222, T234, T240, T245, T251

MI: T20, T34, T38, T43, T44, T45, T46, T50, T55, T57, T58, T68, T99, T102, T103, T105, T106, T107, T115, T156, T159, T160, T171, T172, T173, T186, T196, T214, T230, T246, T254, T258

CI: T20, T41, T54, T60, T68, T72, T90, T94, T102, T103, T106, T136, T144, T150, T153, T170, T177, T181, T183, T184, T217, T246, T254, T255, T261, T265, T261, T268

Whole Class

PV: T187, T194, T240, T242

PS: T65, T109, T168, T216, T280

TW: T206, T224

CE: T193, T245, T252, T257

MI: T51, T58, T111

CI: T72, T111, T117, T118, T183, T223, T224, T268

Modify Instruction

ESL/ELD

PV: T17, T18, T20, T23, T24, T26, T28, T30, T32, T34, T36, T38, T40, T47, T50, T61, T62, T64, T67, T68, T70, T72, T74, T76, T78, T80, T82, T84, T94, T111, T112, T114, T117, T118, T120, T122, T124, T126, T128, T130, T137, T140, T151, T152, T154, T157, T158, T160, T162, T164, T166, T168, T170, T172, T174, T176, T178, T180, T187, T190, T197, T207, T208, T210, T213, T214, T216, T218, T220, T222, T226, T233, T236, T255

PS: T17, T18, T20, T23, T24, T26, T28, T30, T32, T34, T36, T38, T40, T42, T44, T46, T48, T50, T52, T59, T62, T73, T74, T76, T79, T80, T82, T84, T86, T88, T90, T92, T94, T96, T103, T106, T123, T124, T126, T128, T130, T132, T134, T136, T138, T140, T142, T144, T146, T148, T150, T152, T154, T161, T164, T175, T176, T178, T181, T182, T184, T186, T188, T190, T192, T194, T196, T198, T200, T202,

T209, T212, T229, T230, T232, T235, T236, T238, T240, T242, T244, T246, T248, T250, T252, T254, T256, T258, T260, T262, T264, T266, T273, T276, T295

TW: T17, T18, T20, T23, T24, T26, T28, T30, T32, T34, T36, T38, T40, T42, T44, T46, T53, T56, T67, T68, T70, T73, T74, T76, T78, T80, T82, T84, T86, T88, T90, T92, T94, T101, T104, T121, T122, T124, T127, T128, T130, T132, T134, T136, T138, T140, T142, T144, T146, T153, T156, T167, T168, T170, T173, T174, T176, T178, T180, T182, T184, T186, T188, T190, T192, T199, T202, T209, T219, T220, T222, T225, T226, T228, T230, T232, T234, T236, T238, T240, T242, T244, T251, T254, T273

CE: T17, T18, T20, T23, T24, T26, T28, T30, T32, T34, T36, T38, T40, T49, T52, T63, T64, T66, T69, T70, T72, T74, T76, T78, T80, T82, T84, T86, T88, T95, T98, T115, T116, T118, T121, T122, T124, T126, T128, T130, T132, T134, T136, T138, T140, T142, T149, T152, T163, T164, T166, T169, T170, T172, T174, T176, T178, T180, T182, T184, T186, T193, T196, T213, T214, T216, T219, T220, T222, T224, T226, T228, T230, T232, T234, T236, T238, T245, T248, T267

MI: T17, T18, T20, T23, T24, T26, T28, T30, T32, T34, T36, T38, T40, T42, T44, T51, T54, T65, T66, T68, T71, T72, T74, T76, T78, T80, T82, T84, T86, T88, T90, T92, T94, T96, T98, T100, T102, T104, T111, T114, T121, T131, T132, T134, T137, T138, T140, T142, T144, T146, T148, T150, T152, T154, T156, T158, T165, T168, T179, T180, T182, T185, T186, T188, T190, T192, T194, T196, T198, T200, T207, T210, T227, T228, T230, T233, T234, T236, T238, T240, T242, T244, T251, T254, T273

CI: T17, T18, T20, T23, T24, T26, T28, T30, T32, T34, T36, T38, T40, T42, T44, T46, T48, T50, T52, T54, T56, T58, T65, T68, T79, T80, T82, T85, T86, T88, T90, T92, T94, T96, T98, T100, T102, T104, T111, T114, T121, T131, T132, T134, T137, T138, T140, T142, T144, T146, T148, T150, T152, T154, T156, T158, T160, T162, T164, T166, T168, T170, T177, T180, T191, T192, T194, T197, T198, T200, T202, T204, T206, T208, T210, T217, T220, T237, T238, T240, T243, T244, T246, T248, T250, T252, T261, T264, T283

Extra Help

PV: T18, T20, T22, T26, T28, T32, T38, T50, T62, T64, T68, T74, T78, T80, T82, T84, T91, T94, T101, T112, T120, T126, T130, T140, T152, T154, T160, T164, T166, T168, T178, T180, T190, T210, T216, T220, T226, T236, T255

PS: T18, T20, T26, T28, T30, T32, T34, T36, T40, T44, T48, T50, T52, T59, T62, T74, T80, T84, T86, T88, T90, T96, T106, T113, T123, T124, T126, T130, T134, T138, T142, T146, T148, T152, T154, T161, T164, T176, T178, T184, T188, T192, T194, T196, T202, T209, T212, T219, T230, T238, T240, T242, T244, T250, T254, T258, T260, T264, T266, T276, T295

TW: T17, T18, T24, T28, T32, T34, T36, T38, T40, T46, T56, T68, T70, T76, T80, T84, T86, T88, T92, T104, T111, T122, T124, T128, T134, T138, T140, T144, T146, T153, T156, T168, T174, T178, T180, T186, T188, T190, T192, T199, T202, T220, T228, T230, T232, T236, T238, T242, T251, T254, T273

CE: T18, T20, T26, T30, T32, T36, T38, T40, T42, T49, T52, T64, T66, T70, T72, T78, T86, T88, T95, T98, T116, T118, T122, T126, T130, T132, T138, T140, T142, T152, T164, T166, T170, T174, T178, T182, T184, T186, T193, T196, T214, T216, T220, T224, T228, T232, T236, T238, T245, T248, T267

MI: T18, T20, T24, T28, T32, T42, T54, T66, T68, T74, T76, T78, T82, T86, T88, T90, T98, T102, T104, T114, T138, T140, T144, T148, T150, T152, T156, T158, T165, T168, T180, T182, T186, T188, T194, T200, T207, T210, T227, T230, T234, T236, T238, T251, T254, T273

Index

Real-Life Connections

Journal

Mentors

Places

Projects

Strand Connections

Workshops

Technology

Listening Center Audiocassettes

Other Technology

PS: T16, T22, T31, T35, T57, T67, T72, T93, T101, T112, T117, T122, T167, T174, T191, T207, T211, T215, T228, T245, T271, T275, T280, T284, T285, T288, T297

TW: T16, T27, T39, T45, T51, T61, T66, T93, T103, T107, T115, T151, T161, T166, T197, T201, T206, T213, T218, T229, T230, T239, T258, T262, T266

CE: T11, T16, T35, T46, T47, T51, T56, T57, T62, T71, T97, T114, T137, T151, T157, T162, T181, T185, T191, T195, T200, T223, T243, T247, T251, T256, T264

MI: T11, T16, T41, T49, T52, T59, T64, T103, T125, T130, T157, T163, T167, T172, T173, T199, T205, T209. T226, T237, T239, T243, T253, T262, T266, T274

CI: T11, T16, T51, T57, T63, T67, T72, T73, T78, T91, T101, T109, T117, T120, T125, T130, T147, T153, T175, T179, T184, T201, T203, T215, T219, T223, T232, T236, T259, T276, T285

Presentation Tools

PV: T110, T150, T193, T206, T215, T254

PS: T201, T218, T265, T294

TW: T16, T59, T66, T77, T85, T160, T217, T218, T243, T272

CE: T16, T39, T62, T87, T113, T114, T156, T253, T266

MI: T16, T58, T64, T157, T213, T226, T257

CI: T16, T71, T130, T184, T209, T226, T236, T268, T282

Scholastic Network

PV: T11, T60, T71, T110, T196, T201, T206, T219, T244, T257

PS: T11, T16, T51, T61, T66, T109, T122, T135, T183, T228, T297

TW: T11, T66, T77, T166, T177, T218, T229, T275

CE: T16, T27, T62, T62, T75, T109, T162, T175, T191, T228, T237, T269

MI: T16, T25, T64, T73, T130, T145, T226, T237, T274

CI: T16, T33, T78, T85, T130, T145, T236, T251, T253, T272, T285

Smart Place

PV: T16, T31, T37, T49, T60, T83, T93, T100, T110, T125, T129, T145, T150, T161, T193, T206, T215, T235, T256, T257

PS: T35, T72, T74, T83, T95, T105, T122, T149, T169, T174, T201, T211, T215, T223, T228, T245, T265, T296, T297

TW: T16, T66, T77, T85, T93, T110, T120, T129, T137, T143, T155, T181, T191, T205, T208, T218, T243, T257, T275

CE: T39, T62, T87, T113, T114, T127, T135, T207, T227, T237, T252, T253, T266, T267

MI: T16, T31, T58, T63, T64, T93, T103, T104, T130, T178, T197, T203, T213, T226, T236, T257, T259, T274

CI: T16, T51, T71, T78, T113, T130, T169, T185, T190, T207, T223, T224, T236, T247, T268, T285

Videos

PV: T9, T179, T206, T225

PS: T9, T122

TW: T9, T59

CE: T9, T79, T195

MI: T9, T16, T272–T273, T274

CI: T9

Titles, Authors, and Illustrators

✳ Index

Credits and Acknowledgments

TEACHER'S EDITION

Grateful acknowledgment is made to the following sources for permission to reprint from previously published material. The publisher has made diligent efforts to trace the ownership of all copyrighted material in this volume and believes that all necessary permissions have been secured. If any errors or omissions have inadvertently been made, proper corrections will gladly be made in future editions.

Cover: from DOCTOR DE SOTO by William Steig. Copyright © 1982 by William Steig. Reprinted by permission of Farrar, Straus & Giroux, Inc.

Book Cover Credits: Cover from THE CHALK BOX KID by Clyde Robert Bulla, illustrated by Thomas B. Allen. Illustrations copyright © 1987 by Thomas B. Allen. Published by Scholastic Inc., by arrangement with Random House, Inc. Cover from HANNAH by Gloria Whelan, illustrated by Leslie Bowman. Illustrations copyright © 1993 by Leslie Bowman. Published by Scholastic Inc., by arrangement with Alfred A. Knopf, Inc., a division of Random House, Inc. Cover from MUGGIE MAGGIE by Beverly Cleary, illustrated by Kay Life. Illustrations copyright © 1990 by Kay Life. Published by Scholastic Inc., by arrangement with William Morrow & Company, Inc. Cover from UNCLE JED'S BARBER SHOP by Margaree King Mitchell, illustrated by James Ransome. Illustrations copyright © 1993 by James Ransome. Published by Scholastic Inc., by arrangement with Simon & Schuster Books for Young Readers, Simon & Schuster Children's Publishing Division.

Photography and Illustration Credits

Photos: Photo Stylists: Gayna Hoffman, Shawna Johnston. p. T17: Ana Esperanza Nance for Scholastic Inc. p. T40: Ken O'Donoghue for Scholastic Inc. p. T42: Grant Huntington for Scholastic Inc. p. T43: Ken O'Donoghue for Scholastic Inc. p. T45: © Ralph Reinhold/Animals, Animals. p. T54: Grant Huntington for Scholastic Inc. p. T55: Beverly Cleary for Scholastic Inc. p. T86: Grant Huntington for Scholastic Inc. p. T97: Grant Huntington for Scholastic Inc. p. T105: Grant Huntington for Scholastic Inc. p. T115: John Shefelbine for Scholastic Inc. p. T132: Ken O'Donoghue for Scholastic Inc. p. T132: Scott Campbell for Scholastic Inc. p. T138: Ken O'Donoghue for Scholastic Inc. p. T143: Scott Campbell for Scholastic Inc. p. T144: Scott Campbell for Scholastic Inc. p. T159: Grant Huntington for Scholastic Inc. p. T171: © Lisl Steiner/Photo Researchers. p. T182: Grant Huntington for Scholastic Inc. p. T228: Ken O'Donoghue for Scholastic Inc. p. T229: Ken O'Donoghue for Scholastic Inc. p. T239: Scott Campbell for Scholastic Inc. p. T240: Ken O'Donoghue for Scholastic Inc. p. R3: © H. Richard Johnston/FPG International. p. R8: © Henri Georgi/Comstock, Inc. p. R9: Ana Esperanza Nance for Scholastic Inc. p. R9: © Michael Stoklos/FPG International. p. R11: Ken O'Donoghue for Scholastic Inc. p. R17: David Lawrence for Scholastic Inc. p. R19: Grant Huntington for Scholastic Inc. p. R27: Ken O'Donoghue for Scholastic Inc. p. R33: © Lisl Steiner/Photo Researchers. p. R35: Ken O'Donoghue for Scholastic Inc. p. R40: Grant Huntington for Scholastic Inc. p. R41: © C. Allen Morgan/Peter Arnold, Inc.

Upfront pages: All reduced facsimiles of Student Anthologies, Teacher's Editions, ancillary components, and interior pages are credited, if necessary, in their original publication format. p. T6: Rich Miller for Scholastic Inc. p. T7: Eric Burge for Scholastic Inc.

Illustrations: p. T38: Robert Reynolds for Scholastic Inc. p. T47: Deborah Drummond for Scholastic Inc. p. T48: Deborah Drummond for Scholastic Inc. p. T48: Deborah Drummond for Scholastic Inc. p. T84: Garrett Johnson for Scholastic Inc. p. T90: Camille Venti for Scholastic Inc. p. T92: Camille Venti for Scholastic Inc. p. T114: Deborah Drummond for Scholastic Inc. p. T188: Camille Venti for Scholastic Inc. p. T194: Deborah Drummond for Scholastic Inc. p. R27: Deborah Drummond for Scholastic Inc.

Reduced Student Pages

Grateful acknowledgment is made to the following sources for permission to reprint from previously published material. The publisher has made diligent efforts to trace the ownership of all copyrighted material in this volume and believes that all necessary permissions have been secured. If any errors or omissions have inadvertently been made, proper corrections will gladly be made in future editions.

Cover, Unit Opener, and Unit 3 On the Job Table of Contents: from DOCTOR DESOTO by William Steig. Copyright © 1982 by William Steig. Reprinted by permission of Farrar, Straus & Giroux, Inc.

Unit 1 What's New Table of Contents: From RAMONA FOREVER by Beverly Cleary, illustrations by Alan Tiegreen. Copyright © 1984 by Beverly Cleary. Reprinted by permission of Morrow Junior Books, a division of William Morrow & Company, Inc.

Unit 1 What's New: "Gila Monsters Meet You at the Airport" from GILA MONSTERS MEET YOU AT THE AIRPORT. Text copyright © 1980 by Marjorie Weinman Sharmat. Illustrations copyright © 1980 by Byron Barton. Reprinted by permission of Simon & Schuster Books for Young Readers, Simon & Schuster Children's Publishing Division.

"Gila Monster March" and "Alligator Stomp" from THE REPTILE BALL by Jacqueline K. Ogburn. Copyright © 1997 by Jacqueline K. Ogburn. Used by permission of Dial Books for Young Readers, a division of Penguin Putnam Inc.

"Another Big Event" from RAMONA FOREVER by Beverly Cleary. Copyright © 1984 by Beverly Cleary. Reprinted by permission of Morrow Junior Books, a division of William Morrow & Company, Inc.

"I Am" from IT'S RAINING LAUGHTER by Nikki Grimes, photographs by Myles Pinkney. Text copyright © 1997 by Nikki Grimes. Photographs copyright © 1997 by Myles Pinkney. Used by permission of Dial Books for Young Readers, a division of Penguin Putnam Inc.

"How My Family Lives in America" from HOW MY FAMILY LIVES IN AMERICA by Susan Kuklin. Copyright © 1992 by Susan Kuklin. Reprinted with permission of Simon & Schuster Books for Young Readers, Simon & Schuster Children's Publishing Division.

"Kids Speak Up to Save Native Languages" by Sarah Jane Brian from *Scholastic News*, November 12, 1993. Copyright © 1993 by Scholastic Inc. Reprinted by permission.

Credits and Acknowledgments

"On the Pampas" from ON THE PAMPAS by Maria Cristina Brusca. Copyright © 1991 by Maria Cristina Brusca. Reprinted by arrangement with Henry Holt and Co.

"How the World Got Wisdom" from THE ADVENTURES OF SPIDER: WEST AFRICAN FOLK TALES. Text copyright © 1964 by Joyce Cooper Arkhurst. Illustrations copyright © 1964 by Barker/Black Studios Inc. Reprinted by permission of Little, Brown and Company.

"Parent to Child" was originally published as "Black Parent to Child" from ALL BEAUTIFUL THINGS, copyright © 1983 by Naomi F. Faust. Published by Lotus Press, Detroit, Michigan, distributed by Michigan State University Press. Reprinted by permission of the author.

Photos: pp. 10tl, 10ml, 10bl, 49br, 82c, 84bc, 85tc, 91br, 111br, Rich Miller for Scholastic Inc.; pp.10–11bg, 11bl, 82ml, 82bl, 82bc, 84tr, 85mr, Eric Burge for Scholastic Inc.; p. 10tc, © H. Richard Johnston/FPG International; pp. 48bc, 48bl, 48br, 90bl, 107ml, 108bc, 109br, 110c, 166bc, 252bl, 253mr, 350bc, 372bc, 373tl, 374bc, 375tr, 376br, 377bl, Stanley Bach for Scholastic Inc.; pp. 48tl, 48cl, 68, 88bc, 90br, 91bl, 108tl, 108ml, 108bl, 167tr, 214br, 216–217, 250ml, 250bc, 254, 255bl, 255mr, 258bl, 258ml, 258tl, 259bc, 279c, 279tr, 280bl, 281br, 281mr, 308br, 308bl, 308bc, 351br, 373br, 375bc, 375mr, 377bl, John Lei for Scholastic Inc.; p. 63, Courtesy Susan Kuklin; p. 82tc, © Richard Parker/Photo Researchers; p. 84, © Robert A. Isaacs/Photo Researchers, Inc.; p. 101, © The Metropolitan Museum of Art, Gift of The Richard J. Faletti Family, 1986. (1986.475a–c).; p. 103, © Kathleen Atkins Wilson; p. 105, © Myles Pinkney; p. 111, Ana Nance for Scholastic Inc.; pp. 114–115, 167br, 208ml, 208bl, 208tl, 208c, 209mr, 210bl, 210tr, 211mr, 217br, 255br, Steve Leonard for Scholastic Inc.; p. 145, Harper Collins; p. 155, Cordon Art-Baarn, Holland; p. 165, © Steve Solum/ Bruce Coleman Inc.; p. 191, Owl Books; p. 208bg, © Robert Reiff/FPG International; p. 209tr, © Loebl, Schlussman & Hachel; p. 211ml, © Steinkamp/Ballog Chicago; p. 214bc, © Anthony Mercieca/Photo Researchers, Inc.; p. 215, Bryan Hendrix for Scholastic Inc.; pp. 244bg, 245tr, Ana Nance for Scholastic Inc.; pp. 244mr, 247mr, Maura McCasted; p. 250tc, © IFA /Bruce Coleman, Inc.; p. 252bc, © E. Alan McGee/FPG International; pp. 258c, 278ml, 278tl, 278bl, 280mr, Merry Alpern for Scholastic Inc.; pp. 300, 302tl, 302cl, 303br, 303tr, 303, CPD Distribution; p. 302, © Gregory G. Dimijian/ Photo Researchers, Inc.; p. 303, © Peter Essick/Aurora-Quanta Productions; p. 306, Richard Lee for Scholastic Inc.; p. 306br, David S. Waitz for Scholastic Inc.; p. 307, Bie Bostrom for Scholastic Inc.; pp. 310bg, 310tr, 311tc, 313mr, 315, 321br, 326br, © Bob Zellar; pp. 310tc, 317tl, 317br, 320br, 321tr, 323tc, © Larry Mayer; p. 316tr, © James Woodcock; pp. 318, 326br, © Robert Ekey; p. 321bl, © Roosevelt Jet; p. 324c, © National Geographic Society; p. 325, Catherine Baumann for Scholastic Inc.; p. 327, Courtesy Robert Ekey; p. 371, Anne Hall; p. 382bl, © Joseph T. Collins/Photo Researchers, Inc.; p. 383bl, © H.A. Thornhill, ASPA/ Photo Researchers, Inc.; p. 384bl, © Richard T. Nowitz/ Photo Researchers, Inc.; p. 385bl, © Pascal Baudry/GLMR/Liaison International; p. 386bl, © Georg Gerster/Photo Researchers, Inc.; p. 388bl, © USDA/ Science Source/ Photo Researchers, Inc.; p. 388bc, © Stuart Cohen/ Comstock, Inc.; p. 389bl, © Aaron Haupt/Photo Researchers, Inc.

Illustrations: pp. 2–3,28–29,44–45: Alan Tiegreen for Scholastic Inc. p. 215: Bryan Hendrix for Scholastic Inc. pp. 312, 322–323: Karen Minot for Scholastic Inc. pp. 218–243: Doug Geiger b/g for Scholastic Inc.

Illustrated Author Photos: pp. 27, 45, 63, 87, 105, 347: Gabriel DiFiore for Scholastic Inc. pp. 145, 163, 191, 213, 249, 283, 305, 327, 371: David Franck for Scholastic Inc.